REVIEW
OF
RESEARCH

CONTRIBUTORS

DAVID COOPER
DONNA DEYHLE
LISA FRANKES
JEFFREY E. MIREL
SUSAN NOFFKE
JOHN L. RURY
KAREN SWISHER
WILLIAM F. TATE IV
LINDA VALLI
GEOFF WHITTY

IN EDUCATION

22   1997

MICHAEL W. APPLE
EDITOR
UNIVERSITY OF WISCONSIN, MADISON

PUBLISHED BY THE
AMERICAN EDUCATIONAL RESEARCH ASSOCIATION
1230 Seventeenth Street, NW
Washington, DC 20036-3078

Contents

Introduction

Getting a coherent sense of the state of educational research is not an easy task. The reasons for this are varied. First, surveying a field is itself an act of cultural production (Noblit & Pink, 1995, p. 8). Like social and cultural activity in general, any field encompasses multiple dynamics, multiple and partly overlapping histories, and is in constant motion. Second, and equally important, what actually *counts* as educational research is a construction. Academic boundaries are themselves culturally produced and are often the results of complex "policing" actions on the part of those who have the power to enforce them. This "policing" action involves the power to declare what is or is not the subject of "legitimate" inquiry or what is or is not a "legitimate" approach to understand it (Apple, 1996b). Yet, as the French sociologist Pierre Bourdieu reminds us, it is the ability to "trespass" that may lead to major gains in our understanding (Bourdieu, 1990).

Furthermore, developments in any field are not necessarily linear. Rather, fields often are untidy and uneven. What may be important in the development of a field—especially one as diverse as education—are the breaks from the past in which previous traditions are disrupted, displaced, and regrouped under new problematics. These breaks tend to transform the questions being asked and the manner in which they are answered.

One of the strengths of the growth of multiple traditions of "critical" educational research—the traditions that have guided Volumes 21 and 22 of the *Review of Research in Education*—can be found by contemplating the very word *multiple*. There is no single axis and no single theory around which they turn. This very multiplicity demonstrates the complexity of the issues focused on in these volumes; but it also creates some dilemmas for editors and editorial boards. How does one choose? Which tendencies, in which areas, should be represented? These are not easy questions, and neither the editor nor the editorial board of these two volumes want to suggest that we have answered them in a totally satisfactory way.

For example, even a simple listing of some of the various critically oriented approaches now being employed in educational research shows the theoretical and empirical diversity embodied in the field: structurally oriented analyses based in political economy; postmodern and poststructural investigations; critical discourse analysis; critical pragmatism; multiple feminisms; research organized around issues of "voice" such as those drawing on narratives, testimonies, and life histories; critical ethnographies; critically oriented action research; critical race theory; and the list goes on. Yet, even this list is deceptive, because within each of these tendencies there are conceptual and methodological—as well as valuative—debates. Although trying to capture the vitality of a number of these multiple approaches and portray how they are now being applied to issues of educational research on theory, policy, and practice were part of the agenda of these two volumes, we do not want to give the impression that these approaches are untried and totally "new." Exactly the opposite is the case, for there can be no doubt that the concepts, methods, and values represented here are increasingly influential within the educational research community and are connected to a long history of these concerns in educational research.

There currently are very real tensions within the multiple traditions of educational research, in part because of what has been called the "academic/ scientific project." The attempt to gain recognition as a "science" has meant that until rather recently quantitative, "value neutral" orientations have dominated the field. For some interpreters, this had a chilling effect on those educational researchers whose major interest was not a generalizable understanding of educational policies and practices, but instead the development of either thick descriptions of particularities or the disclosure of hidden power relations that created these supposedly stable regularities (Noblit & Pink, 1995, p. 27).

The trajectory of this project has had other effects as well, some of which continue to be constitutive tensions in the field. Thus, as Noblit and Pink (1995) state,

the academic/scientific project also generated a tension between knowledge production—the legitimated activity of the professorate in academe—and knowledge use as exemplified by social intervention to change and improve educational practice. . . . These tensions are at the very heart of the remaking of [educational research. Furthermore,] questions of how best to understand how education works for different people in various settings, how best to evaluate educational outcomes, and how best to restructure schools to maximize the educational benefits for all students, must now begin with discussions concerning (a) whose knowledge is privileged most . . . and on what basis these competing knowledge bases are constructed . . . and (b) which role (observer or [active] participant) is most appropriate for the [researcher] to adopt. (p. 27)

There are dangers in stereotyping any "scientific" concerns, of course. Too often any quantitative work is given the label of "positivist." This not only is an unfortunate stereotype, but it also creates a "deskilled" field (see Apple, 1995; Apple, 1996b) in which important forms of research and argument are made unavailable.

There are, however, attempts to deal with these tensions in quite disciplined ways. Thus, a number of ways of combining methodological rigor with principled sociocultural criticism are now available (see, e.g., Carspecken, 1996). Examples of overcoming the often tense relationships caused by the differing methodological, conceptual, and political emphases within the critical research communities in education are also beginning to be more highly visible. Thus, for instance, there are concrete attempts to combine critical structural analyses with those of postmodern and poststructural analyses—two communities that have approached each other all too warily over the past decade (see, e.g., Apple, 1996a; Curtis, 1992).

We take these as positive signs, because it is clear that there is a growing recognition both of the dangers of stereotyping any approach and that the complexity of educational phenomena cannot be understood through any single lens in isolation from others.

This is the second of two volumes of the *Review of Research in Education* that I agreed to edit. The editorial board of these two volumes and I had a number of specific interests in organizing these books. These included issues of methodology, theory, politics, and values and how these should be thought about in educational research and policy.

In the previous volume (Apple, 1996c), I noted that the editorial board had a number of things it wanted to do. It wanted to give a greater voice to "newer" forms of research methodologies and theories, such as critical discourse analysis; action research; research on the relationship among the "state," economy, and education; and on race, gender, and class relations. It was interested as well in showing how these kinds of approaches might inform our analyses of politically difficult policy areas. In doing this, the board wanted to center on more engaged models of research and policy that would provide examples of how social values could inform research in more reflexive ways. Further, we all had serious questions about what might be called the "distanced observer" model of doing reviews of "what we know" about all of this.

The editorial board also agreed to continue to structure a volume that was more flexible in terms of chapter length, in this way giving authors more space to develop arguments, to portray complexity, and to provide readers with a greater sense of the underlying values, nuances, complexities, and implications of the areas they were discussing. This seemed quite important to us because we felt that, even though there is burgeoning interest in more critical forms of educational research, many of our readers might not be familiar with these areas.

These two volumes—21 and 22—are guided by a *relational* understanding of education. They see educational research, policy, and practice as connected in crucial ways to the patterns of economic, political, and cultural power in the larger society. They review areas of research that hold education up to critical scrutiny along three dynamics—gender, race, and class. These, of course, are not the only dynamics that need to be dealt with. Nor are these dynamics always easily separable, as if there weren't complex interactions among and within them (Apple, 1996a). However, they provide a starting point to understanding the ways in which education participates in, mediates, and affects power relations.

Volume 21 reviewed a number of methodological, empirical, and political issues associated with these multiple critical traditions. These included reviews of critical discourse analysis; of the role of gender both in the construction of teaching and professionalism and in the construction of teenage pregnancy as a social problem; and synthetic analyses both of the methodological, theoretical, and political status of narrative approaches in educational research and of the more structural accounts of the connections between education and the state. Volume 22 continues the focus on critical investigations. The contributions include critical reviews and appraisals of research on urban education and school choice programs; action research; equity issues in teacher education, and selected aspects of racial dynamics in education. Although the specific topics are diverse, the guiding theme throughout each of these contributions is socially critical. Each wants to examine the possibly differential outcomes—outcomes that are visibly patterned in specific ways—that occur from the ways our research is carried out, from the ways we think about social problems, from the organization of education now, and from "reforms" that are now being carried out.

In a number of nations throughout the world, educational policy is experiencing profound changes. There is considerable pressure to move toward marketized solutions. "Public" is now seen as inefficient, bureaucratic, and wasteful; "private" is seen as more efficient, less wasteful, and more cost-effective. Marketization, it is claimed, will provide solutions to educational and larger social problems.

These changes have been accompanied by transformations in the basic conceptual and political frameworks we employ to understand education and its social and individual roles. The turn to marketized policies in education has required that the very meaning of democracy be altered. Rather than democracy being a political concept, it becomes an economic one. The "citizen" becomes the "consumer," an individual who is guided by "rational economic choices" in a market. It has been claimed that one of the effects of this transformation is the deracing, declassing, and degendering of people and that such policies can and do have hidden negative effects (Apple, 1996a). Although I personally have very serious reservations about marketized "solutions" to deep-seated educational problems, the empirical question of whether such solutions are successful, in what ways, on whose terms, is of great importance. Geoff Whitty takes this as the fundamental set of questions in his analysis of a number of the "reforms" now being proposed in the organization and control of schooling such as voucher and privatized school choice programs. Whitty's conclusion is of considerable moment to the debates about school choice in this regard. As he puts it, "far from being the best hope for the poor, . . . the creation of quasi-markets is likely to exacerbate existing inequalities."

Earlier critical models of explanation of the supposed failures of the reform of educational policies and practices often stressed the determining nature of the economy. Perhaps the most well known was Bowles and Gintis (1976). For them, there was a structurally determined correspondence between what happened in schools and the need for differentially trained labor in the economy. Within the community(ies) of critically oriented educational researchers, there were many criticisms of this kind of approach, especially in terms of its reductive and essentializing tendencies, its historical and empirical overstatements, and its neglect of the complex and contradictory happenings of daily life inside schools (See, for example, Apple, 1995; Cole, 1988). Less economistic and more subtle and dynamic—though equally socially critical—perspectives have been developed over the past 2 decades. At the same time, the rise of postmodern and poststructural perspectives among some researchers in education has led to a move away from issues involving political economy and structural forces for a number of these researchers. This has had a salutary effect in many ways. However, it has also led to a number of dangers. Among these dangers is the neglect of what might best be called the "gritty materiality" of the structures that surround us all. There is a world of difference between reducing everything in schools down to economic causes and recognizing that structures cannot simply be wished away.

Because of this and because of the increasing power of neoliberal and neoconservative discourse in education—including the aforementioned focus on the market as the solution to educational problems—there has been a rebirth of structural arguments within critical educational research. The reemergence of research in political economy is a sign of this tendency. This has been accomplished through the incorporation of some of the best of the newer material on critical urban studies and on the social organization of race and class. Thus, in this book, the chapter by Rury and Mirel provides an insightful discussion of the political economy of urban education. Rury and Mirel demonstrate how many of the previous traditions that have attempted to analyze urban contexts are weakened by their inability to situate the transformations of cities and their educational institutions back into the histories of race and class dynamics and structures.

One of the aims that we set ourselves for Volume 21 and Volume 22 was, in commonsense terms, to "get ahead of the curve." That is, in addition to providing coherent and synthetic analyses of an important constellation of issues that have well developed critical traditions of research, we wanted to illuminate a number of areas where we felt impressive gains would come in the near future. For instance, critical discourse analysis was among the areas we highlighted in the previous volume. The analysis of classroom discourse, of course, has a long history. But its recent impulses are even more theoretically, empirically, and politically nuanced, and its ability to critically document how power works in schools is becoming even more evident (see Luke, 1996).

Another area that has shown considerable promise is "critical race theory." This area, originally developed within legal scholarship, has the potential to fundamentally challenge the ways we think about core concepts that underpin many goals of educational research and reform—equality, equality of opportunity, equity, and so on. It can give us a number significant conceptual tools that might enable us—in the words of William Tate, the author of the chapter on critical race theory included here—to "provide a more cogent analysis of 'raced' people and to move discussions of race and racism from the margins of scholarly activity to the fore of educational discourse." Thus, much as Maxine Greene did in an impressive essay on new epistemologies in an earlier *Review of Research in Education* (Greene, 1994), we want to argue that one of the areas that will show the clearest gains in our understanding of some of the most powerful dynamics in education will center around race and how we think about racial structures, identities, and policies.

Let me say more about this issue. It would be hard to overstate the constitutive role played by overt and covert racial dynamics historically and currently in the construction of "official knowledge," teaching, evaluation, public policies, popular culture, identities, economic divisions, and the state itself in the United States and many other nations. An understanding of education that does not recognize this lives in a world divorced from reality, for race is not an "add-on." The realities and predicaments of people of color are neither additions to nor defections from American life. Rather, they are among the *defining* elements of that life (Ladson-Billings & Tate, 1995; West, 1993). In the words of one of the most impressive analyses of race and government in the United States, "Concepts of race structure both state and civil society. Race continues to shape both identities and institutions in significant ways" (Omi & Winant, 1995, p.vii).

Race is not a stable category. What it means, how it is used, by whom, how it is mobilized in public discourse, and its role in educational and more general social policy—all of this is contingent and historical. Of course, it is misleading to talk of race as an "it." "It" is not a thing, a reified object that can be tracked and measured as if it were a simple biological entity. Race is a set a fully social relationships. This unfortunately does not stop people from talking about race in simplistic ways that ignore the realities of differential power and history, which is all the more reason to listen carefully to more complex accounts. And it does require that we pay considerably more attention to the educational situations of people of color in our nations that have arisen because of this history.

The effects of this history—and the continuing struggles to deal with the conditions that are not simply in the past, but are structurally built into the very core institutions of this society today—are made very visible in Deyhle and Swisher's analysis of the education of Native Americans. The situation of the education of Native Americans reveals much about the commitments that underpin educational and larger social structures. Deyhle and Swisher conclude with a call for collaborative research that recognizes the complexity and importance of the cultural capital within Native American and Alaska Native communities. In essence, while not denying the importance of basic research, one of their messages is that we need more research "with" not "on" these communities and nations.

Tate's discussion of critical race theory—of its historical genesis, its modes of analysis, and its implications for educational theory and policy—provides us with a powerful lens for examining not only our educational institutions but also all of the dominant institutions in this and many other societies. The approaches taken by critical race theorists may be relatively unfamiliar to many educational researchers, but they too have a considerable history. Although they do have parallels to other critical structural analyses in education and to other approaches to the issue of identity, as Tate shows, critical race theory enables connections to be made between education and other spheres of society that place racial dynamics at the very center of our analyses.

We fully realize that these chapters do not deal with the full range of issues or people who are "raced" in this society. Too often discussions of race in education take the experiences of one specific group as a paradigm case for the experiences of all other groups. This is unfortunate. While being seen as "the other" in this society does mean that there are powerful similarities in the historical and current experiences of people in and out of schools, there are also important historical and current differences. Although this volume cannot speak to all of the multiple histories and experiences, Deyhle and Swisher's clear synthesis of the research on Native American education and Tate's critical overview of the increasingly important area of critical race theory do point to the importance of thinking both about the specifics of one situation as well as recognizing the parallels that cut across the ways this society constructs "race."

One other thing needs to be stated here. Although most of the theory and research reviewed here in Deyhle and Swisher and in Tate justifiably places its emphasis on the experiences of people of color, it is important that we not limit the discussion of racial dynamics in education to people of color. For instance, an assumption that has underpinned much of the research on race and racial identity renders "Whiteness" invisible or transparent. Thus, being White becomes the unarticulated normative structure. It becomes so naturalized that "European-Americans" do not even have to think about "being White." In the language of critical cultural theory, it becomes an absent presence, the "there that is not there." In this way, race becomes a "reified synonym" that is applied only to racially subordinate groups (Roman, 1993, p. 72). This more complicated understanding of race is crucial and suggests an important path to take in the future in research both on the politics of educational policy and on the dynamics of racial identity.

Behind the issues raised by Whitty, by Rury and Mirel, by Tate, and by Deyhle and Swisher is a concern with one simple question—Who benefits? This question asks us to pay attention to the patterns of differential benefits that may arise from educational activity. Even our best efforts at "reforming" education need to be scrutinized with this issue in mind. This is exactly what Valli, Cooper, and Frankes focus on in their review of the research on professional development schools and equity. Many people are deeply concerned with issues of teacher preparation. Major efforts have been devoted to recreate the connections between teacher education programs and the "realities" of schools. Among the most visible efforts here have been the development of professional development schools. These institutions have been subject to a good deal of research about their effectiveness. Yet, equally important is the question of "Effectiveness for whom?" This is where Valli and her co-authors enter. Among the major questions underpinning their analysis of professional development schools are "What are the equity implications of change efforts?" and "Does the new organizational structure of the PDS promote equity?" They conclude that most PDS have either not attempted to deal with these broader issues of equity or are floundering in their efforts.

Among the methodological approaches that aim to reconnect research to the daily lives of schools is action research. It, too, is concerned with power relations. One of its aims has been to reduce the hierarchical structuring of who does research, how research is used, and who benefits from it; yet action research has a complex history and has a complex politics attached to it. Susan Noffke's chapter provides a synthetic reading of this history and of the political/ethical orientations embodied within action research. Her reading is largely grounded in a critical and feminist position. She too has concerns about the social commitments embodied in the ways such research is carried out and in whether larger issues of social justice and caring are taken as seriously as they deserve.

Some Lessons We Have Learned

Volumes that are part of a continuing series, such as the *Review of Research in Education*, are often produced and read in particular ways. The fact that both editors and editorial boards change every 2 or 3 years provides an opportunity for different emphases and different areas to be made visible to the larger research community in education. Given the diversity of AERA's membership, this allows for greater responsiveness to the various constituencies held together under the broad umbrella of the Association. It also enables a greater number of these diverse groups to become knowledgeable both about areas of research and policy they might not otherwise know and about methodological, empirical, theoretical, and political debates and tensions that might otherwise be less visible. All of these characteristics are good for the field.

Yet, in part because editors and boards change relatively rapidly, there is sometimes a loss of collective memory of what was tried and what was learned from trying. Thus, I would like to briefly describe a few parts of what the editorial board and I have learned.

One of the clear lessons was the impact of *intensification* on authorship. Although I and other board members have written about the ways in which the intensification of educators' lives (so much more to do, with less time and fewer resources to actually accomplish all of it; see, e.g., Apple, 1988, Apple. 1993, Gitlin & Margonis, 1995), the effects of this on our own lives as teachers, researchers, and writers were more than a little visible during the period these books were being organized and written. The growing pressures at and on universities, the decline of resources and support staff, the increasing work load of and bureaucratic requirements on people who work at institutions of higher education and other educational agencies, and so much more, made it ever more difficult for authors to meet deadlines and required the constant rethinking of schedules.

These issues surrounding intensification are not inconsequential. They mean that our own lives, the quality of the entire research enterprise, and our ability to say important and at times critical things about the processes and effects of education are increasingly subject to difficult conditions. In essence, it embodies a condition that has been called "management by stress" (Whitty, Edwards, & Gewirtz, 1993).

Furthermore, as we have found, the lives of many new researchers who have very important things to tell us about crucial developments in debates over research on educational theory, methodology, politics, policy, and practice are often even more intense. Research demands for tenure are escalating at many institutions. Although this is certanly not a new issue, quantity too often serves as a proxy for quality, and the newer research forms researchers are attempting to build and use sometimes are looked upon with unease and even outright hostility. Those relatively young scholars who are deeply committed to integrating their political/ethical and research lives—for example, many researchers who are African American, Native American, Chicano/a, Latino/a, and others—have even more emotional and intellectual demands placed on them.

Since the editorial board that helped sheperd Volumes 21 and 22 was very interested in providing a forum for some of these "newer" and more engaged models of research and wanted to find voices that could bring them to a larger audience, all of these pressures and transformations in the daily lives of researchers had an impact on our ability to bring volumes out on time.

The preceeding paragraphs focused on some of the negative things we learned. Other lessons were more positive. The importance of providing a more international perspective also became clear. Thus, for example, the fact that a number of the authors and contributing editors of the chapters included in both volumes are from outside the borders of the United States has enabled the integration of a considerably wider set of perspectives on pressing research and policy issues. Not only does this make our research "wiser," but it also enables us to see relations that might have otherwise been hidden. For example, a number of the chapters included in these two volumes demonstrate that theoretical and empirical work of major importance has been and is currently being done in Latin America, Europe, Australia, and elsewhere. Too often, there has been an unstated assumption in the United States that research in other countries is but a reflection of what is happening here. Not only is this inaccurate—certainly for critical social research in education—but it also tacitly reproduces "center/periphery" ideological impulses. If the research enterprise is to be a truly collective and collaborative one, such assumptions need to be questioned.

One of the things that we instituted, and about whose worthiness we have become even more convinced, was to commission synthetic essays that review research on overlapping areas. These reviews were done by individuals who had somewhat different perspectives on the material. Thus, in Volume 21, each of the chapters on discourse analysis offered a different take on what was important, on what it meant, and on its connections to the micro and macro relations of power and authority in classrooms. Our decision to do so was grounded in our understanding of the complexity of the act of synthesis. Synthesis is not a "pristine" act, cut off from the person and her or his commitments. The net that an author drops down to understand and organize an area is woven out of the questions one asks, the valuative commitments that underlie these questions, the political and epistemological assumptions surrounding what counts as research and warranted knowledge, and so on. These assumptions and commitments may be overt or they may be hidden; but they are there.

We believe that this policy of having scholars with different commitments review overlapping areas to tell us what (they think) "the research says" is of considerable importance and should continue. It could enhance our understanding of the very real complexities of educational phenomena and of the relationship between ourselves as social actors and the areas we study.

ACKNOWLEDGMENTS

The editorial board and I would like to thank a number of people for their "hidden" labor on this volume. Susan Wantland and Tom Campbell at AERA provided considerable assistance and demonstrated immense patience in the face of unavoidable delays. Christopher Zenk served as the Assistant to the Editor on these volumes.

August 15, 1996
University of Wisconsin, Madison

Michael W. Apple
Editor

REFERENCES

Apple, M.W. (1988). *Teachers and texts*. New York: Routledge.
Apple, M.W. (1993). *Official knowledge*. New York: Routledge.
Apple, M.W. (1995). *Education and power* (2nd ed.). New York: Routledge.
Apple, M.W. (1996a). *Cultural politics and education*. New York: Teachers College Press.
Apple, M.W. (1996b). Power, meaning, and identity. *British Journal of Sociology of Education, 17*, 125–144.
Apple, M.W. (Ed.). (1996c). *Review of research in education* (Vol. 21). Washington, DC: American Educational Research Association.
Bourdieu, P. (1990). *In other words*. Stanford: Stanford University Press.
Bowles, S., & Gintis, H. (1996). *Schooling in capitalist America*. New York: Basic Books.
Carspecken, P. (1995). *Critical ethnography in educational research*. New York: Routledge.
Cole, M. (Ed.). (1988). *Bowles and Gintis Revisited*. Philadelphia: Falmer Press.
Curtis, B. (1992). *True government by choice men?* Toronto: University of Toronto press.
Gitlin, A., & Margonis, F. (1995). The political aspect of reform. *American Journal of Education, 103*, 377–405.
Greene, M. (1994). Epistemology and educational research. In L. Darling-Hammond (Ed.), *Review of research in education* (Vol. 20, pp. 423–464). Washington, DC: American Educational Research Association.

Ladson-Billings, G., & Tate, W. (1995). Towards a critical race theory of education. *Teachers College Record, 97*, 47–68.

Luke, A. (1996). Text and discourse in education. In M.W. Apple (Ed.), *Review of research in education* (Vol. 21, pp. 3–48). Washington, DC: American Educational Research Association.

Noblit, G., & Pink, W. (1995). Mapping the alternative paths of the sociology of education. In W. Pink & G. Noblit (Eds.), *Continuities and Contradictions: The Futures of the Sociology of Education* (pp. 1–29). Cresskill: Hampton Press.

Omi, M., & Winant, H. (1994). *Racial formation in the United States* (2nd ed.). New York: Routledge.

Roman, L. (1993). White is a color! In C. McCarthy & W. Crichlow (Eds.), *Race, identity, and representation in education* (pp. 71–88). New York: Routledge.

West, C. (1993). *Race matters.* New York: Vintage Books.

Whitty, G., Edwards, T., & Gewirtz, S. (1993). *Specialization and choice in urban education.* New York: Routledge.

I.
POLITICS AND POLICY

Chapter 1

Creating Quasi-Markets in Education: A Review of Recent Research on Parental Choice and School Autonomy in Three Countries

GEOFF WHITTY
Institute of Education, University of London

INTRODUCTION

This chapter will review recent research literature concerning the progress and effects of the currently fashionable "parental choice" and "school autonomy" agendas in contemporary education policy. In discussing *parental choice,* the chapter will be particularly concerned with those policies that claim to enhance opportunities for choice among public schools[1] and those that use public funds to extend choice into the private sector. *School autonomy,* as used here, refers to moves to devolve various aspects of decision making from regional and district offices to individual public schools, whether to site-based professionals, community-based councils, or a combination of both. Advocates of both sets of policies argue that they will enhance the efficiency, effectiveness, and responsiveness of the education system as a whole.

The rationale for considering these two agendas together may need some explanation, especially in the United States, where the provenance of the two reforms is quite different and where, in some respects, they are competing strategies. Thus, for example, Moe (1994) suggests that school-based management is a self-serving reform favored by professional educators and designed to resist demands for the radical alternative of choice, which puts power in the hands of consumers. Yet, while he is critical of site-based management as it is generally practiced in

This paper draws on research carried out with support from the Economic and Social Research Council and the Institute of Education, University of London. I am also grateful to the University of Canterbury, Christchurch, New Zealand and the University of Wisconsin-Madison for visiting fellowships that enabled me to review relevant research in New Zealand and the United States respectively. The paper has benefited from visits to institutions and conversations with many individuals in all three countries. Particular thanks are due to Tony Bryk, John Chubb, Bruce Cooper, Fred Hess, Allan Odden, Kent Peterson, Penny Sebring, Amy Stuart Wells and John Witte in the United States; to Liz Gordon and Cathy Wylie in New Zealand; and members of the Parental Choice and Market Forces seminar at King's College London. I am grateful to Michael Apple, Marianne Bloch, Bill Boyd, Jim Cibulka, and Hugh Lauder for their helpful comments on an earlier version of the paper. None of those named should be held responsible for the ways in which I have interpreted their comments.

the United States and of some of the versions of devolution practiced elsewhere, he actually wants schools to have much greater autonomy from public authorities. Schools of choice, argue Chubb and Moe (1992), "are entirely autonomous, and they run their affairs as they see fit" (p. 12). This is what is beginning to happen in two other national contexts in which reforms that foster choice and school self-management are even more in evidence than in the United States: England and New Zealand. In those contexts, the interaction of parental choice and school autonomy within public education systems is beginning to create "quasi-markets" in education.

This review will concentrate on the ways in which these two reforms are contributing to the creation of such quasi-markets and on the implications of such a development. Levacic (1995) suggests that the distinguishing characteristics of a quasi-market for a public service are "the separation of purchaser from provider and an element of user choice between providers" (p. 167). She notes that there usually remains a high degree of government regulation, arguably considerably more than would be favored by Chubb and Moe (1992, p. 13). Most commentators see quasi-markets in education as involving a combination of parental choice and school autonomy, together with a greater or lesser degree of public accountability and government regulation. Partly because all of these elements are not always present in existing reforms, reviewing the research evidence is not a straightforward task.

Nor, indeed, is research evidence necessarily the key issue in debates about school reform. Cookson (1994) has characterized the debate about choice as a "struggle for the soul of American education," indicating quite clearly that the struggle is a highly political one involving conflicting values and interests. Similarly, Henig (1994) comments that "the story of choice-in-practice . . . reminds us that the conflicts that are most compelling and difficult to resolve revolve around questions about the kind of society we wish to become" (p. 116). Thus, terms such as choice and autonomy are used and contested in debates that are about much more than technical issues concerning school effectiveness and systemic efficiency.

Nevertheless, research evidence has itself become an important discursive resource in those debates. Furthermore, evidence from one national context is increasingly being mobilized and recontextualized in another. On the basis of a brief visit to Britain sponsored by *The Sunday Times,* Chubb and Moe (1992) declared the British reforms a qualified success and lamented the way in which the complexities of the American constitution had so far prevented similarly root-and-branch reforms in the United States. Moe (1994) argued that while "it's really quite remarkable how similar the [reform] movements have been in the two countries . . . the difference is, [Britain] actually followed through" (p. 24).

Conversely, a British proponent of increased parental choice (Pollard, 1995a, 1995b) recently gained considerable media attention with the claim that, where choice programs have been introduced in the United States, "they are popular, successful and demanded elsewhere" (Pollard, 1995a, p. 4). He suggested that "many ethnic minority and 'poverty lobby' groups are among the leading advocates of choice, seeing it as a way to escape from inner-city sink schools and the culture of low expectations" (Pollard, 1995a, p. 4). Meanwhile, Sexton (1991), a leading advocate of the market-oriented approach in Britain, has tried to use the smaller New Zealand "system"[2] as a laboratory for his ideas. Reports of the "progress" of reform in one context have thus become resources in the struggle for reform in another. Much the same is true of the use of evidence relating to the problems of reform. For example, Carnoy (1995) has recently cited research on choice in Europe (Ambler 1994) to support arguments against vouchers in the United States.

In view of this, it is as well to state at the outset the particular concerns that I bring to my task. Not only do I write from the perspective of an English commentator, as a sociologist of education I have a particular interest in the relationship between education and social inequality, and this is likely to have influenced the way in which I look at the evidence. It will become clear that, while not denying that parental choice and school autonomy can bring benefits to individual schools and students and even have their progressive moments, my conclusion from the evidence we have to date is that, far from being the best hope for the poor, as Moe (1994) suggests, the creation of quasi-markets is likely to exacerbate existing inequalities, especially in instances in which the broader political climate and the prevailing approach to government regulation are geared to other priorities. This is particularly relevant to the cases on which I focus here, England, New Zealand and the United States, where the debate about these reforms has often become linked to a broader conservative agenda.[3]

As we shall see, it is also possible for similar reforms to be related to rather different political agendas. The different political meanings given to reform are important in judging its significance and assessing its effects. Even in the three countries being considered here, the reforms are being implemented in significantly different social and cultural contexts. Education systems have particular structures and embody particular assumptions that are deeply embedded in their time and place. Halpin and Troyna (1994) argue that "fine-grain detail of their implementation" is necessary before reforms in one context can be used as models for policy-making in another, and much the same might be said about the lessons that can be learned from them (p. 1). As Seddon, Angus, and Poole (1991) point out in an Australian contribution to the literature on school-based management, "decisions at proximal [or school] level are circumscribed by decisions at higher levels" and these higher level frames are likely to differ from context to context (p. 32).

I should also preface my comments with a mention of three more specific limitations of any review of the efficacy of parental choice and school autonomy policies undertaken at this time. First, in all three countries, other, sometimes conflicting reforms are being introduced at the same time. In England, for example, the recent extension of parental choice and school autonomy came in at the same time as a controversial national curriculum and system of national testing at ages 7, 11, 14, and 16. It is therefore virtually impossible to separate out the specific effects of any one of these policies. Second, many of the most ardent neo-liberal advocates of school autonomy and parental choice, such as Sexton in Britain (and, indeed, Chubb and Moe in the United States), argue that the reforms are inadequate because the reformers have so far been too cautious. They suggest that the reforms would have worked better if taken to their logical conclusion: ultimately, perhaps, a fully privatized system with vouchers. Finally, it is actually somewhat early to reach a conclusive judgment about these reforms. Indeed, in Britain, the left has often attacked the right for declaring comprehensive education a failure before it had a chance to get established, but that is now what the left often does in attacking the right's reforms. The right not unreasonably replies that one cannot effect a culture shift overnight and that schools and their communities will really reap the benefits only once they have escaped from the welfare state dependency culture and appreciate that they now have real choices.

Nevertheless, given that most advocates of these reforms tend, with missionary zeal, to herald them as a success and that many conservative politicians are seeking to extend them even before they have been properly evaluated, it is important to consider what can be gleaned from the early research, what sorts of claims it can reasonably be used to uphold, and what lessons might inform future reform efforts. In what follows, I first attempt to contextualize and characterize the nature of the reforms in the three countries. I go on to review research on the effects of school choice in each country and then do the same with research on the effects of school autonomy. In the final section of the chapter, I suggest that there is nothing in the research evidence to support the extravagant claims of the reform advocates but that it is nevertheless likely that some variant of these reforms will continue for the foreseeable future. Yet, in the absence of substantial safeguards, reforms that trade on the "market metaphor" are likely to increase rather than reduce inequalities in education in the circumstances currently prevailing in these three countries. I suggest that there is therefore a need to reassert the role of citizen rights in relation to consumer rights and thus to redress a balance that is veering dangerously toward treating education as merely a private consumption good.

PARENTAL CHOICE AND SCHOOL AUTONOMY
IN THREE COUNTRIES

Two of the countries addressed here, England and New Zealand, have national systems of public education, while compulsory education in the United States is primarily the responsibility of individual states. It is also important to bear in mind that the total population of New Zealand is 3.5 million and that of England and Wales[4] is about 50 million, as compared with the population of more than 200 million in the United States. This means that it is easier, though not necessarily easy, to generalize about education policy in the first two of the countries under consideration here. On the other hand, those advocates of choice who argue that it will lead to greater diversity of provision tend to suggest that, prior to the recent reforms, the "one best system" in the United States had produced an unusual degree of uniformity and mediocrity in the public school system as a whole (Chubb & Moe, 1990); however, this has been challenged by Witte (1990).

In England, prior to the 1980s, the vast majority of children were educated in public schools maintained by democratically elected local education authorities (LEAs) that exercised political and bureaucratic control over their schools but also often provided them with considerable professional support. Also within the public school system were most church schools, which received funding from and were accorded varying degrees of autonomy by these LEAs. During the 1970s, the media had begun to focus attention on the supposed failings and "excesses" of schools and teachers, particularly in inner city LEAs controlled by left-wing Labour administrations committed to fostering equal opportunities. After the Conservative "revolution" of 1979, the Thatcher and Major governments set about trying to break the LEA monopoly on public schooling through the provisions of a series of education acts passed in the 1980s and early 1990s. Alongside a national curriculum, designed to impose more central government control over what was taught and to increase public accountability through a national system of testing, other policies sought to enhance parental choice and transfer responsibilities from LEAs to individual schools.

The early legislation of the Thatcher government made only tentative inroads into the powers of LEAs. The 1980 Education Act introduced a number of measures to enhance parental choice among public schools and an assisted places scheme that provided government funding to enable academically able children from poor homes to attend some of the country's elite private schools (see Edwards, Fitz, & Whitty, 1989). In the 1986 act, the individual governing bodies (which all public schools are required to have) were reformed by removing the inbuilt majority of allegedly self-serving local politicians and increasing the representation of parents and local business interests.

In the latter part of the 1980s, the government sought to create new forms of public school entirely outside the influence of LEAs. City technology colleges (CTCs), announced in 1986, were intended to be new secondary schools for the inner city. CTCs, with a curriculum emphasis on science and technology, were run by independent trusts with business sponsors. The latter were expected to provide much of the capital funding but with recurrent funding coming from the central government, although the reluctance of business to fund this experiment meant that the government eventually had to meet most of the capital costs as well (Whitty, Edwards, & Gewirtz, 1993). Subsequently, a clause in the 1988 Education Reform Act offered many existing public schools the opportunity to "opt out" of their LEAs after a parental ballot and run themselves as grant-maintained schools with direct funding from central government. Margaret Thatcher expressed the hope that most schools would eventually take this route.

Meanwhile, local management of schools, another aspect of the 1988 act, gave many of those schools that remained with their LEAs more control over their own budgets and day to day management, receiving funds according to a formula that ensured that at least 85% of the LEA's budget was handed down to schools and that 80% of each school's budget was determined directly by the number and ages of its pupils. This severely limited the extent to which the LEA could provide ear-marked funding to counter disadvantage. The funding formula included teachers' salaries, and teachers became *de facto* employees of the governing body, even though most remained *de jure* employees of the LEA.

Open enrolment, which was also part of the 1988 act, went much further than the limited enhancement of parental choice introduced in the 1980 Education Act. It allowed popular public schools to attract as many students as possible, at least up to their physical capacity, instead of being kept to lower limits or strict catch-ment areas (zoning) in order that other schools could remain open. This was seen as the necessary corollary of per capita funding in creating a quasi-market in edu-cation. In some respects, it was a "virtual voucher" system (Sexton, 1987), that was expected to make all schools more responsive to their clients and either become more effective or go to the wall. However, existing rules on admission, based on sibling enrollment, proximity, and so forth, were retained once schools were full, although these rules were more flexible in some areas than others and parents were given enhanced opportunities to appeal.

Although elements of the reforms have been concerned with enhancing both parental "voice" and parental "choice," the emphasis has been firmly on the latter. The 1993 Education Act extended the principles of diversity, choice, and institu-tional autonomy throughout the school system. It extended local management of schools and the right to opt out to virtually all schools, permitted schools to apply to change their character by varying their enrollment schemes, sought to encour-age new types of specialist schools, and made it possible for some private schools to opt in to grant maintained status. While the rhetoric has been largely about devolving power to schools, parents, and communities, the act also created a potentially powerful national funding agency for schools that has taken over the planning function from LEAs where grant-maintained schools are in the majority (Department for Education, 1992).

These measures were widely expected to reduce the role of LEAs to a marginal and residual one over the succeeding few years. However, schools have so far been much more reluctant to opt out of their LEAs than the government antici-pated, so the Major government has recently advanced the idea of introducing leg-islation to make all schools grant maintained. While claiming to have already increased diversity and choice, the prime minister looks forward to the day "when all publicly funded schools will be run as free self-governing schools." He believes in "trusting headmasters (*sic*), teachers and governing bodies to run their schools and in trusting parents to make the right choice for their children" (Anderson, 1995). Comprehensive schools are also to be permitted to introduce selection for up to 15% of their intake without having to apply to change their character.

By contrast with England, New Zealand in the 1980s was a somewhat surprising context for a radical experiment in school reform, let alone one associated with the conservative agenda. Unlike in England and the United States, there was no widespread disquiet about educational standards in the public school system nor were there the vast discrepancies in school performance that contributed to a "moral panic" about urban education in those two countries. The initial reforms were introduced by a Labour government, albeit one that had enthusiastically embraced monetarism and "new public management" techniques in the mid-1980s (Wylie, 1995). The education reforms, which were introduced in October 1989, were based on the Picot Report (Picot, 1988) and the government's response, *Tomorrow's Schools* (Minister of Education, 1988). They led to a shift in the responsibility for budget allocation, staff employment, and educational outcomes from central government and regional educational boards to individual schools. Schools were given boards of trustees, originally composed of parents (but extended in 1991 to encourage the inclusion of businesspeople) who had to negotiate goals with the local community and agree on a charter with the central government.

Because boards of trustees have effective control over establishing their own enrollment schemes when a school is oversubscribed, the New Zealand reforms have ushered in a much more thoroughgoing experiment in free parental choice in the public sector than was introduced in England. Extending choice into the private sector has been slower, but a 3-year pilot study of a targeted individual entitlement scheme, the New Zealand equivalent of the British assisted places scheme, has recently been announced. This has led to claims that "it marks the start of a move towards a voucher system in which schools compete for parents' education dollar" (Wellington *Evening Post,* 9/28/95).

However, Wylie (1994) argues that other aspects of the New Zealand reforms "offer a model of school self-management which is more balanced than the English experience [because they put] a great emphasis on equity . . . on community involvement . . . on parental involvement [and on] partnership: between parents and professionals" (p. xv). Furthermore, neither the costs of teacher salaries nor the costs of some central support services were devolved to individual school budgets, although there have subsequently been moves in this direction since the election of a conservative administration in 1990. Currently, only 3% of New Zealand schools are involved in a pilot scheme for "bulk funding" (or devolution of 100% of their funding, including teachers' salaries), but a "direct funding" option is to be opened up to all schools in 1996 for a trial period of 3 years. Unlike the English funding formulas, according to which schools are funded on the basis of average teacher salaries, the New Zealand scheme will be based on actual teacher salaries and a given teacher-student ratio. Alongside these reforms, national curriculum guidelines were introduced, but these guidelines were far less

detailed and prescriptive than the English model and paid more attention to
minority Maori interests. On the other hand, an outcome-based approach to
national assessment is being phased in, and this could provide central government
and employers with a highly controversial alternative mode of accountability
and control.

In the United States, Newmann (1993) includes parental choice, greater school
autonomy, and shared decision making as among the 11 most popular restructuring reforms. However, given the limited role of the federal government in relation
to education, it is much harder to generalize about the nature and provenance of
such attempts to enhance parental choice and devolve decision making to schools.
Even in the context of America 2000 and Goals 2000, which exhibit something of
the same tension between centralizing and decentralizing measures found in
England and New Zealand, the role of the federal Department of Education had to
be largely one of exhortation. Cookson (1995) suggests that, during the 1980s,
President Reagan used it as "a 'bully pulpit' for espousing his beliefs in school
choice and local educational autonomy," while George Bush "went further . . . in
attempting to reorganize the public school system according to what he believed
were sound market principles" (p. 409). This included support for parental choice,
self-governing charter schools, and the New American Schools program, which,
in the original Bush version, displayed some parallels with the English CTC initiative. Although neither Congress nor the states collectively endorsed this overall approach, the National Governors' Association was an early advocate of
choice, and the national educational goals did receive bipartisan support and a
modest amount of federal funding.

In Goals 2000, the Clinton administration has taken work on voluntary standards and accountability measures much further in the context of what Cookson
(1995) describes as the "new federalism" and "a firm but cautious belief in the
efficacy of public institutions" (p. 412). Title III of the Goals 2000: Educate
America Act provides support for state and local educational improvement efforts
designed to help all students attain high academic standards. Site-based management continues to be seen as one way of contributing to this aim, as does parental
and community involvement. Choice, though, has been much less in evidence in
the federal rhetoric under the Clinton administration.

Meanwhile, the more significant decisions continue to be made at state and district levels, even if, as Cookson (1995) claims, the authors of Goals 2000 saw the
federal government as "crafting, shaping and, to some degree, controlling education throughout the fifty states" (p. 414). While a few states, such as Minnesota,
have statewide choice plans, many initiatives have been more local. Wells
(1993b) demonstrates the huge variety in origins and probable effects of the various choice plans that have been mooted or implemented in the United States over
the past few years. Similarly, Raywid (1994) includes among the specialist
or "focus" schools (Hill, Foster, & Gendler, 1990) that she advocates a whole
variety of schools with very different origins and purposes. These include long-

standing specialty schools, such as Boston Latin School and New York's highly academic Stuyvesant High School; magnet schools associated with desegregation plans; alternative schools, sometimes based on progressive pedagogic principles; and private Catholic schools. The nature and provenance of charter schools and that of site-based management within school districts also vary considerably (Murphy & Beck, 1995; Wohlstetter, Wenning, & Briggs, 1995).

However, despite the variety of different reforms in the United States, there are a number of distinctive styles of reform. Some, such as the Coalition of Essential Schools, have been based on particular educational philosophies, while others have been linked to broader political programs. While desegregation was an early impetus for reform, the impact of the broader ideological context and the changed political context since the 1994 congressional elections may now be rather more important than the "new federalism" of the Clinton administration in determining the current direction of policy. This, together with the particular circumstances of individual states and districts, has ensured that much of the neoliberal and neo-conservative momentum of the Reagan and Bush administrations has continued to be reflected in local reform efforts.

Even so, it is often claimed that devolution and choice in the United States continue to enlist significant support from more progressive forces, particularly among those representing people of color. Insofar as such claims are true, this may be partly because the initial criticisms of large urban school bureaucracies in general, and of zoning in particular, were often associated with moves to foster desegregation. Yet, far from reflecting the free play of market forces, initiatives such as magnet schools were as much examples of state intervention as the segregated systems they replaced. And, whatever the fiction of particular court challenges, such initiatives were also as much the product of popular political struggles as of individual market choices.

Nevertheless, the rather mixed evidence on the efficacy and effects of desegregation and magnet schools in the 1980s (Blank, 1990; Moore & Davenport, 1990) has sometimes led to the conclusion that enhanced parental voice and choice, rather than more concerted political intervention, will provide the best chance of educational salvation for minority parents and their children. Moe (1994) goes so far as to claim that the best hope for the poor to gain the right "to leave bad schools and seek out good ones" is through an "unorthodox alliance [with] Republicans and business . . . who are the only powerful groups willing to transform the system" (p 33). For this reason, some aspects of the current reform agenda have developed a populist appeal well beyond the coteries of conservative politicians or even the White populations to which they usually appeal, although some of the more extreme voucher-style proposals, such as that included on the ballot in California in 1994, have been rejected at the polls.

Key icons of the school choice movement, such as controlled choice in Cambridge, Massachusetts and Montclair, New Jersey; the East Harlem "choice" experiment in New York; and the Milwaukee private school "voucher" experiment have certainly had active support among the mainly minority populations of these inner-city school districts. The same is true of some of the better known examples of specialist schools, site-based management and shared decision-making in Miami (Dade County) and New York City and of the establishment of local school councils in Chicago. Whether the research evidence actually justifies such support even in some of these cases, let alone the more ambitious plans of market advocates, is more questionable. It is certainly doubtful whether these policies have brought benefits for minority groups as a whole, even in instances in which they have brought particular benefits for specific communities. To explore these issues further, I now consider the limited evidence that is available on the effects of recent policies to encourage parental choice and school self-management.

RESEARCH ON CHOICE

It is clear that *parental choice* is a term that covers a wide range of different policies, even though there are some strong parallels between developments in New Zealand, England, and the United States. There are also particular concerns within the histories of the three countries that influence the terms in which policies are framed. Thus, as we have seen, race has been a much more influential issue in the United States and New Zealand than it has in England, where a government minister was prepared to dismiss concerns about the potential of choice to produce racial segregation with the statement that her government did not wish "to circumscribe [parental] choice in any way" (in Blackburne, 1988, p. A6). On the other hand, concerns about providing opportunities for the single-sex education of girls have been more prominent in England and New Zealand than in the United States, although David (1993) points out that gender perspectives are "curiously absent" in most of the research on school choice. Also, the controversy about choice in England and New Zealand has focused mainly on transfer between primary and secondary schools, whereas much of the American debate has been concerned with elementary as well as middle and high school choice.[5] Not surprisingly, these different concerns have also influenced the focus of evaluations of the reforms in the three countries. Furthermore, the styles of research adopted have been rather different. Paradoxically, given what I have stated earlier about the scope of the reforms in the different countries, the emphasis in the United States is often on the analysis and reanalysis of large data sets and that in England on in-depth ethnographic research in particular communities. The major New Zealand studies tend to combine quantitative and qualitative methods. Even so, research findings on the effects of choice in the three countries display more similarities than differences.

In England, there has been a considerable amount of research looking both at the "marketization" of public services in general and the impact of policies designed to enhance parental choice in education in particular. These latter studies have focused on the effects of open enrollment and the provision of opportunities for parents to choose from a greater variety of types of schools, particularly at the secondary level, including schools outside of LEA control. While some studies have examined the impact of the choice agenda as a whole (Bowe, Ball, & Gold, 1992; Gewirtz, Ball, & Bowe, 1995; Glatter, Woods, & Bagley, 1995), others, such as those on the assisted places scheme (Edwards et al., 1989), CTCs (Whitty et al., 1993) or grant-maintained schools (Fitz, Halpin, & Power, 1993), have concentrated on the impact of the new choices that have been made available.

In a substantial study of quasi-markets in British social policy, Le Grand and Bartlett (1993) argue that the reforms in education and housing have been rather more successful than those in health and social care. In a local case study of education, Bartlett (1993) found that the reforms had been welcomed by many headteachers (school principals) but less so by other teachers. However, he pointed out that, although parental choice has been increased by open enrollment "the door is firmly closed once a school [is full]. And by encouraging an increasingly selective admissions policy in [oversubscribed] schools open enrolment may be having the effect of bringing about increased opportunity for cream-skimming and hence increased inequality" (Bartlett, 1993, p. 150). Furthermore, he found that "those schools which faced financial losses under the formula funding system tended to be schools which drew the greatest proportion of pupils from the most disadvantaged section of the community" (p. 149). Thus, whatever gains may have emerged from the reforms in terms of efficiency and responsiveness to some clients, there were serious concerns about their implications for equity.

Le Grand and Bartlett (1993) take the view that "cream-skimming" poses the biggest threat to equity in the sorts of quasi markets created by the Thatcher government. This danger is clearly demonstrated in an important series of studies by Ball and his colleagues on the operation of quasi-markets in London. In an early study, Bowe et al. (1992) concluded that schools were competing to attract greater cultural capital and thus higher yielding returns. Subsequently, Gewirtz and Ball (1995; Gewirtz et al., 1995) have shown schools seeking students who are "able," "gifted," "motivated and committed," and middle class, with girls and children from South Asian backgrounds being seen as particular assets in terms of their potential to enhance test scores.[6] The least desirable clientele include those who are "less able" and those who have special educational needs (especially emotional and behavioral difficulties), as well as children from working-class backgrounds and boys, unless they also have some of the more desirable attributes.

In these circumstances, popular schools are tempted to become increasingly selective, both academically and socially, through overt as well as covert methods of selection. Particularly if there is no chance of expanding, they try to capitalize on and enhance the scarcity value of their product. Elite private schools in England did not choose to expand during the 1980s despite the demand for their product by the *nouveau riche* of the Thatcherite era. Although the government has provided the possibility of expansion for successful and popular public schools, some have already indicated that they are not interested in this option because it would threaten the ethos they have developed.

Most studies of education markets confirm that cream skimming is a major issue, although the composition of the cream takes a particular form in English education. Bartlett and Le Grand (1993) suggest that cream skimming involves favoring those clients who will bring the greatest return for the least investment, thus leading to discrimination by providers against the more expensive users. It is sometimes argued that, in education, this would involve going for the middle of the market; the gifted and those defined as having special educational needs will cost more to process. There is certainly evidence of discrimination against children with special educational needs. Bartlett (1993) argues that such discrimination will not occur only if the market price varies with the needs of the client. In other words, funding formulas need to be weighted to give schools an incentive to take more "expensive" children. The current premium paid for children with special educational needs may not be enough if it makes the school less popular with clients who, although bringing in less money, bring in other desirable attributes. Bowe et al. (1992) and Vincent, Evans, Lunt, and Young (1995) give examples of schools making just this sort of calculation. However, the academically able are the "cream" that most schools do seek to attract. Such students stay in the system longer and thus bring in more money, as well as making the school appear successful in terms of its test scores and hence attractive to other desirable clients.

Le Grand and Bartlett (1993) found lack of information a major limitation within quasi-markets as they currently operate in England. Glennerster (1991) suggests that, given the opportunity, most schools will want to become more selective because taking children who will bring scores down will affect their overall market position. This is especially so when there is imperfect information about school effectiveness and when only "raw" test scores are made available, as they currently are in England.[7] Schools with the highest scores appear best even if other schools enhance achievement more.[8]

As long as schools tend to be judged on a unidimensional scale of academic excellence, many commentators have predicted that choice, rather than leading to more diverse and responsive forms of provision as claimed by many of its advocates, will reinforce the existing hierarchy of schools based on academic test results and social class. Walford and Miller (1991) suggest that this will run from elite private schools through CTCs, grant-maintained schools, voluntary aided (church) schools, and a rump of LEA schools providing mainly for children with special educational needs: the ultimate residualized or safety-net provision.

My own research (Edwards et al., 1989; Whitty et al., 1993) suggests that, within English culture, schools judged to be good and hence over-subscribed are most likely to be academically selective schools or formerly selective schools with a persisting academic reputation. They are also likely to have socially advantaged intakes. Although parents may choose new types of schools because they are different from the standard local comprehensive school, that does not seem to lead in England to a truly diversified system.[9] Instead, those parents who are in a position to choose are choosing those schools that are closest to the traditional academic model of education that used to be associated with selective grammar schools. Even new types of schools tend to be judged in these terms. Our research showed that many parents chose CTCs not so much for their hi-tech image but because they were perceived as the next best thing to grammar schools or even elite private schools (Whitty et al., 1993).

In this situation, those *schools* that are in a position to choose often seek to identify their success with an emphasis on traditional academic virtues and thus attract those students most likely to display them. Fitz et al. (1993) have shown that many of the first schools to opt out and become grant maintained were selective, single-sex schools with traditional sixth forms, and this gave the sector an aura of elite status. The Grant Maintained Schools Centre has claimed that the sector's test results demonstrate its academic superiority, even though those results are almost certainly determined by the nature of the intakes of the early grant-maintained schools. Some grant-maintained comprehensive schools have reverted to being overtly academically selective, and only those that have clearly failed on traditional academic criteria are likely to risk deviating significantly from the dominant definition of excellence in their curriculum offering. Power, Halpin, and Fitz (1994) found "no indications of any changes relating to the curriculum or pedagogy" and a renewed emphasis on traditional imagery in the way grant maintained schools presented themselves (p. 29). Furthermore, Bush, Coleman, and Glover (1993) suggested that 30% of the grant-maintained "comprehensive" schools they studied were using covert selection, which is also likely to increase their appearance of academic superiority. In addition, grant-maintained schools have been identified as among those with the highest rates of exclusion of their existing pupils and among the least willing to cater for pupils with special educational needs (Feintuck, 1994).

A recent Australian review of such evidence suggested that "paradoxically, the market exacerbates differences between schools on the basis of class, race, and ethnicity, but does not encourage diversity in image, clientele, organisation, curriculum or pedagogy" (Blackmore, 1995, p. 53). Regardless of the rhetoric of restructuring that stresses diversity, "market status is maintained by conforming to the dominant image of a good school as being well uniformed, well-disciplined and academically successful" (Blackmore, 1995, p. 48). Gewirtz et al. (1995) suggest that one effect of the development of an education market in England has been a narrowing of the "scope" of education, in that "almost exclusive emphasis [has been placed] on instrumental, academic and cognitive goals" (p. 174).

According to Walford and Miller (1991), even some of those intended beacons of an entirely *new* form of excellence, CTCs, may be abandoning that distinctiveness in favor of traditional academic excellence. More generally, in a major empirical study of school parental choice and school response, Glatter et al. (1995) conclude that there is no evidence to date of choice producing greater diversity in the school system and some evidence of a tendency toward greater uniformity, except where there has been additional government funding to foster the development of specialist technology schools. In other words, government intervention, rather than parental choice, has brought innovation on the supply side. With regard to hierarchy, Glatter et al. have found no dramatic movement to date but certainly no evidence that it has been reduced by the reforms.

Thus, in England, the entrenched prestige of traditionally academic education has produced a persistent devaluing of alternatives. The government's claim (Department for Education, 1992) that it is policy neither to encourage nor discourage schools from becoming selective ignores the reality of what is happening, both overtly and covertly, when schools are oversubscribed. If different versions of schooling have very different exchange values in competition for entry to higher education and to privileged occupations, then the high value placed on traditional academic success makes access to it a positional good and therefore one in short supply. Schools seeming to offer the best chance of academic success are likely to be considerably overchosen. In instances in which they are, the producer is empowered, and the consumer must establish fitness for the school's purposes.

As long as the notion of fitness remains a narrow one, it is unlikely that those groups that have traditionally performed poorly within the education system will benefit. Behind the superficially appealing rhetoric of choice and diversity, the reforms are resulting in a reduction in choice for many parents rather than the comprehensive empowerment of consumers that markets are presumed by their advocates to produce. While they may be enhancing the educational performance of some children, and certainly that of those schools in which the more advantaged children are concentrated, they seem to be further disadvantaging many of those very groups that were disadvantaged by the previous system. Our own figures (Edwards et al., 1989) on the failure of assisted places schemes to reach the intended clientele of disadvantaged inner-city families are likely to be repeated in the case of other schools of choice with a strong market appeal, as advantaged parents and advantaged schools search each other out in a progressive segmentation of the market (Ranson, 1993).

Walford (1992a) argues that, while choice will lead to better quality schooling for some children, the evidence so far suggests that it will "discriminate in particular against working class children and children of Afro-Caribbean descent" (p. 137). T. Smith and Noble (1995) also conclude, from the evidence, that English choice policies are further disadvantaging already disadvantaged groups. Although schools have always been socially and racially segregated to the extent that residential segregation exists, Gewirtz et al. (1995) suggest that choice may well exacerbate this segregation by extending it into previously integrated schools serving mixed localities. Their research indicates that working-class children and, particularly, children with special educational needs are likely to be increasingly "ghettoized" in poorly resourced schools.

Such trends are particularly evident in inner London, where admissions policies have been relaxed. The former Inner London Education Authority used to operate a "banding" system that sought to ensure that all schools had a reasonable balance of levels of academic ability among their intakes. A recent study (Pennell & West 1995) has suggested that, in light of the abandonment of this system in many parts of London and an increasing number of autonomous schools operating their own admissions policies, there is a danger of growing polarization between schools. They argue that the new system is serving to reinforce the privilege of "those parents who are able and prepared to negotiate the complexities [of the system] compared with those who are less willing or less able to do so" (p. 14).

The Smithfield Project, a major study of the impact of choice policies in New Zealand, suggests that much the same sort of social polarization is taking place there (Lauder et al., 1994; Waslander & Thrupp, 1995). In another New Zealand study (Fowler 1993), schools located in areas of low socioeconomic were found to be judged negatively because of factors over which they had no influence, such as type of intake, location and problems perceived by parents as linked to these factors. Wylie (1994) too has noted that schools in low income areas there are more likely to be losing students to other schools. If we could be sure that their poor reputation was deserved, this might be taken as evidence that the market was working well with effective schools reaping their just rewards. But, as in England, judgments of schools tend to be made on social grounds or narrow academic criteria and with little reference to their overall performance or even their academic effectiveness on value-added measures. Gordon (1994a) points out that

schools with a mainly middle class and Pakeha (or, increasingly, Asian) population, tend to achieve better on national examinations because of the high level of "readiness" and motivation of the pupils, and relatively low levels of social problems that impinge on educational processes. (p. 19)

Furthermore, advantaged schools are able to introduce enrollment schemes that "have a tendency to reinforce their social exclusivity" (p. 18). Yet schools perceived to be poor are not actually closing but rather remaining open with reduced rolls, declining funding, and low morale, thus producing a self-fulfilling prophecy.

The current funding regime in New Zealand makes it extremely difficult for schools in disadvantaged areas to break out of the cycle of decline. Yet research studies suggest that many of the differences between schools result from factors largely beyond the control of parents and schools, except the power of advantaged parents and advantaged schools to further enhance their advantage and thus increase educational inequalities and social polarization. Lauder et al. (1995) show that, when schools can choose the students they admit, socioeconomic status and ethnic factors "appear to influence school selection, even when prior achievement has been taken into account" (p. 53). This is not necessarily an argument against choice, but it is clear that procedures for selection to oversubscribed schools need reconsideration. Significantly, the Smithfield Project also found that social polarization between popular and unpopular schools decreased only in the single year in which allocations to oversubscribed schools were based on "balloting" (or drawing lots).

Wylie (1994, 1995) reports that the combination of choice and accountability measures has led to schools paying more attention to the attractiveness of physical plant and public image than to changes to teaching and learning other than the spread of computers. It has also led to increased attention to the information about school programs and children's progress that reaches parents, changes that "are clearly not without value in themselves" (p. 163). But she also notes that "they do not seem able to counter or outweigh factors affecting school rolls which lie beyond school power, such as local demographics affected by employment, ethnicity, and class" (Wylie, 1995, p. 163, citing Gordon, 1994b, Waslander & Thrupp 1995).

In the United States, the early association of public school choice with racial desegregation may have ensured that equity considerations continue to play a greater part in education reform than in England or even New Zealand. Nevertheless, there are considerable concerns about the equity effects of more recent attempts to enhance choice, especially because there is no clear evidence to date of a positive impact on student achievement. Indeed, the claim by Witte (1990) that there were few, if any, acceptable studies of the effects of choice on student achievement remains largely true today, notwithstanding his own pioneering studies in Milwaukee. In what follows, I concentrate largely on research or reanalyses of the effects of choice that have been published since Clune and Witte's (1990a, 1990b) two volume collection.[10]

What evidence there is about the effects of choice policies on student achievement and equity continues to be, at best, inconclusive (Plank, Schiller, Schneider, & Coleman, 1993), despite claims by choice advocates that "the best available evidence" indicates that parental choice can and does work to improve the education of all children, especially low income and minority students" (Domanico, 1990, p. 15). Even some of the more positive evidence from controlled choice districts, such as Cambridge, Massachussetts (Rossell & Glenn, 1988; Tan, 1990) and Montclair, New Jersey (Clewell & Joy, 1990), which seemed to show gradual overall achievement gains, is now regarded by Henig (1994) as methodologically flawed, making it difficult to attribute improvements to choice *per se.* Furthermore, although choice has not always led to resegregation, as its critics feared, improvements in the racial balance of Montclair and Cambridge schools were most noticeable during periods of strong government intervention. Henig goes on to argue that the much vaunted East Harlem "miracle" (Bolick, 1990; Fliegel, 1990) has "escaped any serious effort at controlled analysis" even though it has had a special role "in countering charges that the benefits of choice programs will not accrue to minorities and the poor" (p. 142). Not only have the apparently impressive gains in achievement now leveled off or even been reversed, it is impossible to be sure that the earlier figures were not merely the effect of schools being able to choose students from higher socioeconomic groups outside the area or, alternatively, the empowerment of teachers. Overall, both Henig (1994) and Wells (1993b) conclude from exhaustive reviews that the stronger claims of choice advocates cannot be upheld and that choice needs to be carefully regulated if it is not to have damaging equity effects. It is probably too early to assess how the newest forms of choice, such as those involving charter schools, perform in this respect. However, while Medler and Nathan (1995) suggest that charter schools recruit a high proportion of "at-risk" students, both Becker, Nakagawa, and Corwin (1995) and Grutzik, Bernal, Hirschberg, and Wells (1995) argue that some of the features of these schools, such as the emphasis on parental involvement, may have the effect of excluding students from certain disadvantaged groups.[11]

The evidence with regard to private school choice is also contentious but relevant to the present concerns in view of current demands for an extension of the use of public funds to permit students to attend private schools. Much of the controversy centers around the various interpretations of the data from Coleman's high school studies (Coleman, Hoffer, & Kilgore, 1982) and, in particular, the work of Chubb and Moe (1990). While the data show a consistent but relatively small performance advantage for private schools once background variables have been controlled, some argue that it is a product of their methodology and that any advantage would disappear with the use of more subtle measures of the cultural differences between low-income families using private and public schools (Henig, 1994, p. 144). Lee and Bryk (1993) accuse Chubb and Moe of a circularity in their argument in support of school choice and suggest that their conclusions concerning the power of choice and school autonomy are not supported by the evidence as presented. Nevertheless, Bryk, Lee, and Holland (1993) claim on the basis of their own work that Catholic schools do have positive impact on the performance of low-income families; however, they attribute this at least as much to an ethos of strong community values antithetical to the marketplace as to the espousal of market forces. Critics argue that the socioeconomic status of the clientele of Catholic schools is generally above the average and that the figures are affected by leakage into the public sector in the higher grades (K. B. Smith & Meier, 1995; Witte, Thorn, & Pritchard, 1995).

Witte's evaluation of the controversial Milwaukee private school choice experiment, which enables children from poor families to attend private schools at public expense, concludes in its fourth-year report that "in terms of achievement test scores . . . students perform approximately the same as [Milwaukee Public School] students" (p. 28). However, attendance rates for choice children are slightly higher, and parental satisfaction has been high. For the schools, "the program has generally been positive, has allowed several to survive, several to expand, and contributed to the building of a new school" (Witte, Thorn, Pritchard, & Claibourn 1994, p. 28). Yet some of the stronger claims made both for and against this type of program cannot be sustained by the evidence; the Milwaukee program is small and narrowly targeted and is certainly not a basis on which to judge the probable effects of a more thoroughgoing voucher initiative. Its planned extension to include religious schools is, at the time of writing, the subject of a court challenge.

The Milwaukee program overall has not hitherto been oversubscribed and, although students are self-selected, the schools involved have not been in a position to exercise choice. Elsewhere, the combination of oversubscription and self-selection in explaining apparent performance gains through private school choice suggests that cream skimming is a major issue, as in England and New Zealand. K. B. Smith and Meier (1995) use existing data to test the school choice hypothesis and conclude that "competition between public and private schools appears to result in a cream-skimming effect" (p. 61). They also argue that there is no reason to expect that such effects will disappear in greater competition among public schools, especially because some schools would begin with competitive advantages, an issue they regard as seriously underplayed by Chubb and Moe and other advocates of choice. Indeed, they predict that choice could lead to a "two tier system" (p. 61), similar to that which is developing in England and New Zealand.

There is little in this recent evidence to counter the conclusions of Carnoy (1993) in an overview of historical data about choice in the United States. He argues that choice plans that place an undue emphasis on parental choice will benefit the performance only of high-demand, low-middle-income families and that a large fraction of students, particularly those from low-demand families, are likely to be worse off. This will merely increase the variance in student achievement, with some students decidedly worse off, rather than bringing about the overall improvement envisaged by the exponents of choice.

Wells (1993a) points out that the economic metaphor that schools will improve once they behave more like private, profit-driven corporations and respond to the demands of consumers "ignores critical sociological issues that make the school consumption process extremely complex." Some of those issues are explored further in an important contribution to the sociology of school choice by Wells and Crain (1992). That paper and Wells's own research suggest that many choice plans are based on false assumptions about how families behave in the educational marketplace. This means that competition will certainly not lead to school improvement "in those schools where students end up because they did not choose to attend a 'better' school." Escape from poor schools will not necessarily emerge from choice plans because "the lack of power that some families experience is embedded in their social and economic lives" (Wells, 1993a, p. 48). Anyon (1995) concludes from a study of the difficulty of reform in an urban ghetto school that "the only solution to educational resignation and failure in the inner city is the ultimate elimination of poverty and racial degradation" (p. 89). There is no convincing evidence to date that the provision of notional choices of other schools is a realistic alternative solution for most families.

Adler (1993) has suggested some revisions to current British policies that would take choice seriously but avoid the most unacceptable consequences of recent legislation. His particular proposals include retaining LEAs with a responsibility for formulating admissions policies for all local schools, encouraging schools to develop distinctive characteristics, requiring positive choices on behalf of all children and not only the children of "active choosers," involving teachers and older pupils in making decisions that are not necessarily tied to parental preferences, and giving priority in oversubscribed schools to the applicants who are most strongly supported. However, Walford (1992b) advocates that entry to oversubscribed schools should be based on random selection, an approach that is still used in some schools in New Zealand. In the United States, Wells (1990) argues that equitable choice schemes require clear goal statements; outreach work; information and counseling for parents; a fair, unrestrictive, non-competitive, and equitable admissions procedure; and provision of adequate transportation for students.

Similar safeguards were recommended in an international study of choice policies in England, Australia, the Netherlands, New Zealand, Sweden and the United States. This study concluded that in instances in which there is a dominant model of schooling, choice is as likely to reinforce hierarchies as it is to improve educational opportunities and the overall quality of schooling. It was also argued that demand pressures are rarely sufficient to produce real diversity of provision and that positive supply side initiatives are necessary to create real choice. To avoid reinforcing tendencies toward academic and social selection, popular schools may need positive incentives to expand and disadvantaged groups need better information, better transport, and perhaps even privileged access to certain schools (Organization for Economic Cooperation and Development, 1994). Lauder et al. (1995) point out that the enhanced information and travel funds alone may have little effect on the deep-rooted tendency of families of low socioeconomic status not to seek entry to high-status schools.

RESEARCH ON SCHOOL AUTONOMY

If choice policies without appropriate safeguards tend to empower advantaged parents, and perhaps even more so advantaged schools, what has been the impact of moves toward greater *school autonomy*? In origin, reforms that emphasize school autonomy are less clearly associated with the conservative agenda than parental choice. Yet, although Moe (1994) suggests that choice is a far more potent reform measure than school self-management, school autonomy is necessary to free schools to respond positively to market forces. Similarly, while Domanico (1990) states that "public school choice is not an alternative to school-based management; it is the most effective way of instituting school-based management" (p. 1), he also regards school-based management as "the most promising supply-side educational reform" (p. 2).

As I noted earlier, the extent of school autonomy and school self-management varies not only among the three countries but also within them. In general terms, New Zealand schools have the most autonomy and those in the United States the least. Within England, CTCs and grant-maintained schools have the most autonomy, but even LEA schools, which virtually all now have local management, have considerably more autonomy than U.S. schools with site-based management, including many charter schools (Wohlstetter et al., 1995). In terms of financial management, English schools operating under local management currently have more resources under their direct control than New Zealand schools, apart from those of the latter participating in the "direct funding" trials. Whatever the degree of autonomy, few school principals and teachers would wish to revert to a system of detailed day-to-day control of individual schools by local authorities, regional offices, or school districts. On that measure, the reforms could be (and often have been) judged a success. However, a closer look at the details of the relevant research suggests that there have also been some disturbing consequences of the more extreme forms of devolution found in England and New Zealand.

The major national study of the impact of local management of schools in England and Wales was conducted at Birmingham University, over a period of 3 years, with funding from the National Association of Head Teachers. It was largely based on surveys of headteachers' views, followed by visits to a subsample of schools to interview staff. The study was broadly positive but conceded that direct evidence of the influence of self-management on learning was "elusive." The team's initial survey (Arnott, Bullock, & Thomas, 1992) showed that the vast majority of school principals agreed with the statement that "local management allows schools to make more effective use of their resources." However, a majority also believed that, as a result of local management, meetings were being taken up by administrative issues, which lessened attention to students' learning. They were thoroughly divided on the question of whether children's learning is benefiting from local management. Thus, it was rather unclear as to what their concept of greater effectiveness actually related to.

In the final report of the study (Bullock & Thomas, 1994), the proportion of headteachers making a positive assessment concerning improvements in pupil learning had increased over the previous 3 years; significantly however, this assessment came mainly from those schools that had experienced an increase in funding as a result of self-management. A recent book that draws on a number of different research studies also concludes that, although local management enhances cost-efficiency, there is "a lack of strong theoretical argument and empirical evidence" to show that it improves the quality of teaching and learning, as claimed by the government (Levacic, 1995, p. xi).

The limited evidence there is of improvement at this level seems to be associated with increased funding rather than self-management *per se*. These findings might be expected on the basis of work carried out by Cooper (1994) in the United States suggesting that, as more money is passed down to the instructional context, including paying for better qualified or experienced teachers, there are tangible benefits for pupil performance. However, funding of teachers' salaries in England is done on the basis of average rather than actual salaries and schools whose budgets have been squeezed by the effect of this can therefore expect negative consequences. Furthermore, Cooper's research also suggests that if the funding that is, in fact, passed down to schools does not reach the instructional context (i.e., teachers and classrooms), then its benefits will be more questionable. In England, the linking of self-management with parental choice in the creation of quasi-markets has sometimes meant that resources are diverted into marketing rather than instruction and, indeed, successful marketing becomes essential to protect budgets in future years. Some headteachers may divert funds from the classroom on the basis of a judgment that it is in the best long-term interests of the school; however, there is little evidence of immediate benefits as far as teachers and pupils are concerned.

While the Birmingham team concluded that self-management was broadly a successful reform, they conceded that, before a more definitive conclusion could be drawn, more evidence was needed, particularly on the relationship between resourcing levels and learning outcomes. If that link is a close one, as Cooper suggests, then it argues against the current English funding formula that can reward or punish a school with sharp year-to-year changes in resourcing as a result of changes in school rolls. Indeed, it almost argues for a retreat from an extreme form of pupil-based funding either to funding based on average rolls over a number of years (as the research team suggests) or a return to curriculum led staffing with additional resources for disadvantaged schools. This is particularly important in that the schools most affected by budgetary difficulties—and therefore least likely to report a positive impact on pupils' learning—were often found to be those with pupils from disadvantaged communities. This reinforces the concerns of Le Grand and Bartlett (1993) reported earlier.

Wylie's (1994) study of the fifth year of self-managing schools in New Zealand also identified schools in low-income areas, as well as schools with high Maori enrollments, as experiencing greater resource problems than others. She did not find that this correlated with perceptions of the success of the reforms or with evaluations of the influence of the reforms on pupil learning, and she admits to being puzzled by this. However, apart from in a few pilot schools, New Zealand did not yet have direct funding of teacher salaries, and there remained more opportunities to apply for equity funding, so it may be that the funding differences there are less severe in their impact than those in England.

The English results cited here came mainly from headteacher respondents (i.e., from those responsible for the efficient management of the delegated budget and whose authority has been significantly enhanced by the self-management reform). There is, as yet, no similar study of classroom teachers or pupils. But it may be significant that the relatively few classroom teachers who were interviewed by the Birmingham research team were far more cautious than their headteachers about the benefits of self-management for pupil learning and overall standards. This takes on even more significance when one considers a recent report from school inspectors indicating that 70% of primary headteachers are failing to monitor how well their pupils are being taught. According to this report, "most attempts by heads to evaluate their staff's performance centred on what lessons covered rather than their quality or the standards of children's learning" (Office for Standards in Education, 1994). One has then to be somewhat skeptical about the value of claims by these same headteachers that self-management has improved pupil learning.

A local study by Marren and Levacic (1994; Levacic, 1995), independently funded by the Economic and Social Research Council, also found classroom teachers less positive about self-management than either school governors or headteachers. In this study, headteachers generally welcomed self-management even where their school had lost resources as a result of it, while classroom teachers were far more skeptical about its benefits even in schools that had gained in terms of resources. In New Zealand, Wylie (1994) reports that 41% of teachers, as compared with 46% of principals, believed that the quality of children's learning had improved since the shift to school-based management.

As indicated earlier, one of the difficulties in making sense of the British evidence of decentralization is that budgetary autonomy and school-based management were implemented at the same time as a highly centralizing measure, the National Curriculum and national testing. It is therefore difficult to separate their different effects on teachers' work and pupil learning. Interestingly, however, a recent survey conducted by Warwick University (Campbell & Neill, 1994) on the effects of the National Curriculum on primary school teachers, this time funded by a teachers' rather than a headteachers' union, concludes that there has been no overall improvement in standards but that teachers have been driven to burnout. They found that a 54-hour week was now the norm for teachers of children 4–7 years old, with 1 in 10 working more than 60 hours, and respondents spoke of tiredness, irritability and depression, sleeping badly, increased drinking, occasional crying in the staffroom, and a sense of guilt that they were neglecting their own families. While this has to be seen as coming from a particular pressure group, the research was actually sponsored by one of the least militant unions and one broadly in favor of the reforms.[12]

Studies in New Zealand (Bridges, 1993; Livingstone, 1994; Wylie 1994), where the National Curriculum workload is a less significant factor, have produced similar figures. As a result, New Zealand teachers have reported high levels of stress, declining job satisfaction, and a desire to leave the profession, even in cases in which they believed that the reforms had brought some benefits. Wylie (1994) concluded that New Zealand school communities had probably reached the limit of what they could provide to support the reforms in terms of money and time. Her various surveys for the New Zealand Council for Educational Research show a steady decline in teacher morale since the introduction of the reforms and also "quite a high turnover rate for principals (42% in all the schools in the sample between 1991 and 1993)" (Wylie, 1995, p. 163). New Zealand teachers varied considerably in their views about the influence of the reforms on relationships within the school, but Wylie (1994) herself alerts us to the fact that a significant proportion of them reported some deterioration in their relationship with their principal attributable to the reforms. The growing gap between principals' and teachers' perceptions of the effects of reform found in Wylie's 1993 (Wylie, 1994) survey was even more pronounced in a recent evaluation of the bulk funding trial for teachers' salaries. While principals still saw themselves as curriculum leaders, teachers stressed "the current role as being more of a business manager" (Hawk & Hill, 1994, p. 97). Wylie concludes her own most recent assessment with "the troubling thought" that the reforms "may produce only a small gain for the substantial cost of foregone attention to teaching and learning, within positive, supportive relationships" (Wylie, 1995, p. 163).

Some of the small-scale ethnographic evidence from Britain and New Zealand chronicles in more detail the effects of the intensification of teachers' work and its consequences for industrial relations in schools. One of the ironies in England is that, seemingly, both the devolution of self-management and the centralization of the National Curriculum are having detrimental effects on teacher morale and workload. Bowe et al. (1992) point to real problems with both self-management and the National Curriculum in secondary schools and see these problems as contributing to a growing gulf between senior managers and teachers and a clash between managerial and educational values. Broadbent, Laughlin, Shearn, and Dandy (1993), however, report evidence from other schools that the demands of local management were (initially at any rate) absorbed by a core "coping group" of senior managers whose efforts resulted in the core educational values of the school being relatively unscathed. However, some recent work from New Zealand (Murfitt, 1995) seems to suggest that it is middle managers in secondary schools who experience the greatest pressures, from both above and below.

Marren and Levacic (1994) are not sure whether their own evidence that classroom teachers are more critical of self-management than are senior managers is necessarily evidence of a cleavage in values between teachers and managers. They argue that greater class teacher involvement in financial decision making may be needed if self-management is to result in significant improvements in teaching and learning, but they recognize that there is a contrary view that financial management is a specialized task and that senior management needs to become better at it rather than to share it. Hargreaves (1994) goes further and argues for a formal separation between nonteacher chief executives and headteachers as leading professionals, making an analogy with the health service.[13]

Nevertheless, a key issue arising from the research is to what extent it is possible to give classroom teachers a sufficient sense of involvement in resource management decisions to empower them without diverting them from student-related activities in the same way as had happened to headteachers on the evidence of the Birmingham study. Thus, all of these studies raise some serious questions about the effects of self-management on the nature of the school community. While headteachers themselves often claim that local management has increased the involvement of teaching staff in decision making, a study of the effects of self-management on industrial relations in schools, by Sinclair, Ironside, and Siefert (1993) at Keele University, suggests that the very logic of the reforms is that

headteachers are no longer partners in the process of educating pupils—they become allocators of resources within the school, managers who are driven to ensure that the activities of employees are appropriate to the needs of the business, and givers of rewards to those whose contribution to the business is most highly regarded.

This claim is more consistent with the conclusions of Bowe et al. (1992) than with those of Marren and Levacic (1994) or even Broadbent et al. (1993).[14]

When schools were managed from a more distant bureaucracy, there was often a sense of headteacher and teachers being the professionals fighting a common cause against the distant bureaucracy. With self-management, there has sometimes been a much sharper sense that the school governors and the senior management team are "management" and the teachers and other staff are the "workers." Halpin, Power, and Fitz (1993) suggest that, in the case of grant-maintained schools, the very process of running a self-managing unit can result in an increase in the distance of headteachers from classroom teachers. In some cases, headteachers themselves are coming under pressure from governing bodies acting like Boards of Directors and one dispute of this nature is before the High Court at the time of this writing.

At the same time, many teachers in self-managing schools are feeling the loss of some of the more positive aspects of being part of a larger concern. In the past, LEA support networks fulfilled an important function in Britain. With the devolution of most funds to individual schools, local teachers' centers and other forms of support have often been removed or reduced in scope, even for teachers in LEA schools operating under local management. This problem can be even more acute in the case of grant maintained schools and CTCs, whose staff can easily become isolated from the broader professional community.

Glatter (1993) argues that the quasi-market model does not preclude partnerships between autonomous schools but that "the environment of heightened competition is now framing all such relationships" (p. 8). He also questions whether, without some kind of semi-permanent infrastructure to promote and facilitate collaboration, the start-up and maintenance costs of partnership may be too great for most schools to contemplate. Citing Fullan (1991) and Louis and Miles (1992), he suggests that the erosion of customary networks and support structures could have very serious consequences, because "as we should know well by now, effective change in schools depends as much on providing support as it does on applying pressure" (Glatter, 1993, p. 9). Levacic (1995, pp. 183–185) gives some examples of the continuation and development of cooperative networks among self-managing schools in particular circumstances. However, the possibilities for this depended on trust, which, in turn, could be influenced by the extent of local competition. Significantly, vertical collaboration between primary and secondary schools seemed more in evidence than horizontal networks among schools serving the same phase.

One source of support for teachers has traditionally been their trade unions. As a result of the reforms, teachers face increased workloads, attempts to use them more flexibly to counter the effects of budget restrictions, divisive approaches to performance-related pay, and the substitution of full-time, permanent, qualified, and experienced staff by part-time, temporary, less qualified less experienced, and, therefore, less expensive alternatives. A recent report by the National Foundation for Educational Research confirms that many of these trends have accelerated since the introduction of local management, particularly in those schools adversely affected by the use of average staffing costs in funding formulas (Maychell, 1994). This, of course, has potential implications not only for teachers' conditions of service but also the quality of education. It also poses new challenges for the teacher unions. The research carried out by Sinclair et al. (1993) suggests that the atomization associated with self-management has not yet entirely succeeded in breaking down the traditional power of teacher unions within the state education system. In this respect at least, many of the district-wide networks are still in place, and legal confusion about who is technically the employer in LEA schools operating under local management means that there are a number of issues that still have to be tested in the courts. However, in some grant-maintained schools and CTCs, where the legal issues are more clear cut, unions are being forced to strengthen their plant bargaining capacity or are being marginalized by management. Only one grant-maintained school has so far derecognized teacher unions and withdrawn from national pay agreements, but some CTCs that operate outside both national and local agreements have established in-house staff associations within individual schools or offered the less militant unions "no-strike" agreements in return for recognition.

There have been suggestions, for example by Kerchner and Mitchell (1988) in the United States and Barber (1992) in the United Kingdom, that the teaching unions need to develop a new mode of operation, sometimes termed *third generation* or *professional* unionism, in which they negotiate educational as well as industrial issues and potentially become partners with management in educational decision making to serve the best interests of learners. Self-management has been seen to pose a threat to traditional styles of trade unionism, but to provide real opportunities for this new version. It could also be a way of giving classroom teachers a voice in management without diverting them from their primary role.

Barber, Rowe and Whitty (1995) mounted a small research project, with funding from a national teachers union, to determine to what extent union representatives in England were actually involved in school-based decision making on the ground. During the 1992–1993 school year, we conducted a survey among a sample of school-based union representatives to discover the extent to which they were involved in decision making about budgets, curriculum, and school development planning. Only about 15% of school union representatives had ever been consulted about the budget, the curriculum, or the school development plan. Our subsequent fieldwork suggested that even these figures exaggerated the extent of genuine consultation, let alone formal involvement of unions in school management.

Given the broader political and industrial context in which the British reforms have been introduced, this is hardly surprising. Nor is it surprising that both unions and management were skeptical about whether greater union involvement in management was feasible in the prevailing circumstances. As in the United States, the labor process more generally has been subject to processes of deskilling, reskilling, intensification, and substitution of labor, the relevance of which to our understanding of education has been clearly demonstrated by Apple (1986, 1993, 1995). In this context, we found little evidence of union representatives participating in issues other than those associated with "second generation unionism," that is, giving advice to members, negotiating with management over grievances, and campaigning on issues related to pay and conditions of work.

Some headteachers stated that playing down their members' interests was a prerequisite to the unions becoming more involved in school development planning, but school representatives pointed to the danger of their unique critical perspective thereby disappearing to the detriment of all concerned. With the potential breakdown of national or even LEA-level bargaining on certain issues, leaving these issues to be resolved at the site level, it is likely to become increasingly important for school representatives to be able to explore the relationship among resources, conditions of service, and educational outcomes at the institutional level. Yet both headteachers and union representatives believed that a central concern with the needs of learners might involve union representatives abandoning their more traditional concerns.

There is a fine line to be drawn between third-generation trade unionism and the sort of collaboration that makes it difficult for unions to bargain for their members' interests. In some CTCs, trade unions were not recognized for bargaining purposes and staff associations lacked any teeth. These CTCs are run by trusts dominated by business sponsors, and they have sometimes been seen as the model for the future: post-Fordist schools for a postmodern society. While pay in these schools was usually at a higher level than other local schools, however, conditions of service were also very different. It is a moot point whether free private health insurance is adequate compensation for longer working hours, fixed-term contracts, performance-related pay, and so forth. Flexibility and claims of enhanced professionalism can sometimes become a cover for exploitation of teachers and worsening conditions of service. And, as Blackmore (1995) points out, the self-managing school often retains "strong modernist tendencies for a top-down, executive mode of decision-making . . . [alongside its] 'weaker' post-modern claims to decentralise and encourage diversity, community ownership, local discretion, professional autonomy and flexible decision-making" (p. 45).

Nevertheless, in New Zealand, a report for one of the teachers' unions has emphasized the considerable potential of shared decision making for enhancing the efficiency and effectiveness of self-managing schools (R. Hill, 1992). As a result, action research on the value of various models of shared decision making is currently being undertaken (Capper 1994). Yet, unless they are handled very carefully, any positive moves in this direction are likely to be stymied by already excessive workloads and the growing tensions between teachers and school principals referred to earlier (Livingstone, 1994; Murfitt, 1995; Wylie, 1995). Indeed, Sullivan (1994) has suggested that lack of consultation with teachers over the reforms may create a low-trust hierarchical system rather than a high-trust collegial one.

In the United States, site-based management within school districts has not generally gone as far as it has in either England or New Zealand, certainly in terms of the bulk funding of teachers' salaries and resources for professional development. It is difficult to generalize about the degree of autonomy in site-based management schools (Ogawa & White, 1994) or even charter schools (Wohlstetter et al., 1995). In many cases, the only significant discretionary funds to be disbursed at the site level come from federal and state funding for disadvantaged students. In some states, even charter schools have to negotiate with local school districts for their resources. In that respect, little of the American experience of site-based management is directly relevant to the claims made by advocates of more radical supply side reforms, and, unfortunately, there is little detailed research yet available on the situation in charter schools.[15] In discussing the available research on site-based management, I shall again concentrate on items that have appeared since the publication of Clune and Witte's (1990a, 1990b) work and the rather pessimistic conclusions of Malen, Ogawa, and Kranz (1990) in that collection.

The rhetoric of reform in the United States has often made far more reference to school-based shared decision making as a way of enhancing teacher professionalism than has hitherto been the case in England, where the reforms have been accompanied by attacks on the integrity of the teaching profession in general and teachers' unions in particular. Yet, although much of the rhetoric of the American reform movement has emphasized the importance of empowering teachers, this has often not come about in practice. In reviewing the failure of many American site-based management initiatives to bring about the expected improvement in school performance, Wohlstetter and Odden (1992) have pointed to a lack of employee involvement in many schemes. Rather than merely devolving budgetary, personnel and curriculum decision making to the school level, they argue for regarding site-based management as a comprehensive governance reform that will involve teachers actively in making changes to curriculum and instruction. Other studies show considerable variations in the extent to which schools have changed in practice (Cawelti 1994) and identify important differences in the meanings given to site-based management by some of the key actors involved (Gibbs 1991). Often, site-based management has been treated as merely "an experiment in governance" shifting power from the central office to the school, while "the consequences of decentralization on student achievement remain unknown" (Carlos & Amsler, 1993).

Few programs have been evaluated in terms of performance, and few evaluations have shown clear achievement gains. Although some studies do show gains, the overall impact has so far been disappointing (Ogawa & White, 1994). Wohlstetter and her colleagues (Mohrman, Wohlstetter, & Associates, 1994; Odden & Wohlstetter, 1995; Wohlstetter & Mohrman, 1993; Wohlstetter & Odden, 1992; Wohlstetter, Smyer, & Mohrman, 1994) have suggested that site-based management will have a positive effect only if it is implemented in accordance with what, drawing on the literature of private sector management, they term the "high-involvement model." This requires teacher involvement in decision making, good information, knowledge and skills, power, and rewards, and Wohlstetter et al. suggest that this last condition has too rarely been met. Robertson, Wohlstetter, and Mohrman (1995) argue that, if such conditions are in place, innovations in curriculum and instruction do take place. Wohlstetter (1995) also suggests that site-based management must be augmented by a range of school-, district-, and state-level strategies that facilitate interactions involving various stakeholders and provide a direction for those interactions.

It seems clear that teacher participation in decision making does not necessarily, of itself, improve outcomes for teachers and students (Taylor & Bogotch, 1994). Marks and Louis (1995) argue that teacher empowerment is a necessary rather than a sufficient condition of instructional improvement and that different modes of empowerment can have different effects. Murphy (1994) suggests that one of the reasons why very few studies have shown clear gains in student achievement is that some of the key conditions for success have not been met and that the effect of site-based management (as in the case of the more radical reforms in England and New Zealand) has too often merely been to place additional administrative burdens on teachers. Even the more participatory forms of teacher involvement in decision-making can have unintended consequences. In Minnesota charter schools, for example, "as much as teachers appreciated being board members and making administrative decisions, wearing two hats required a great deal of time and effort" from which they would eventually require some relief (Urahn & Stewart 1994, p. 51). Even in this context, it may therefore be important to take seriously the political insights of those teachers who resist attempts to engage them in management without addressing the broader meaning and consequences of the reforms (Gitlin & Margonis, 1995).

Some of the contributors to Hannaway and Carnoy's (1993) publication argue that the historical record shows that changes in governance, by themselves, are unlikely to produce major changes in the classroom (Elmore, 1993; Tyack, 1993). Discussing the evidence on shared decision making in the context of employee participation in business corporations, Brown (1993) concludes that participation in decision making "cannot be expected to overcome serious shortcomings [in an organization]. Once schools are at a functional baseline, however, innovative [employee involvement] can be a powerful tool for making continual improvements and maintaining high performance" (p. 229).

Critics of site-based management as currently practiced have usually argued for self-management to be taken further. Some have then argued the need to focus on professional improvement in the instructional context (Guskey & Peterson, in press), while others have called for greater empowerment of local communities. These are not always seen as conflicting strategies, although Raywid (1994) advocates "focus" schools, partly because they do not generally seek to engage the community or parents directly in school governance. This, she suggests, would simply shift the interest group politics of the school district down to the site level, presumably with deadening consequences attributed by Chubb and Moe (1990) to political control of schooling. In some respects, the conclusion of Murphy and Beck (1995) that the "structural focus" of site-based management pulls stakeholders toward issues of governance and organization seems to confirm this fear, although their proposed refocusing on issues of teaching and learning still requires the "deep involvement" of teachers and parents. For Raywid, though, the effectiveness of focus schools derives from the very fact that they are "built around specific educational and ethical principles, not around accommodating the interests of all parties" (P. T. Hill et al., 1990). The site policymakers are the principal and teachers. In Raywid's model, even parents are not really regarded as partners in the educational process, since their empowerment should derive from choice rather than voice in a quasi-market.

By contrast, the recent reforms in Chicago are probably the farthest toward the community empowerment end of the continuum. Elmore (1991) argues that "while the Chicago reform has elements of both regulatory and professional control, it is mainly based on a theory of democratic control." It has seemed to move beyond the notion of school and system improvement through professional empowerment to a model placing far more emphasis on parental and community empowerment in achieving this end. The local school councils in Chicago are the nearest equivalent in the United States to governing bodies in England or boards of trustees in New Zealand. Like the latter, they have a majority of parents and responsibility for a similar proportion of the school budget. Although it was initially suggested that local school councils might hire and fire principals at will, the councils have generally concentrated on buildings and health and safety issues; however, they have sometimes also taken a key role in relation to equal opportunities. The advocacy group Designs for Change (1991) claims that the Chicago reforms "nearly doubled the number of African Americans and Hispanics making educational policy decisions in the United States" (p. 1). However, in a major study of community involvement in American school governance, Lewis and Nakagawa (1995) concluded that most parents in Chicago have assumed supportive "enablement" roles rather than being genuinely empowered by involvement with the local school councils. And, ironically, the few parents on the local school councils who seemed to adopt an "empowerment" stance were White, middle-class men.[16]

A recent report (Sebring, Bryk, & Easton, 1995) suggests that the reforms have brought better ties to the community in a number of Chicago schools without threatening principal and teacher responsibility for professional matters. More than 40% of teachers believed that the reforms had had a positive impact on relations with the community, and this seems to have been the single most significant outcome. About a third reported other changes in practice that might be expected to bring eventual benefits in learning outcomes, but these were concentrated in about a third of elementary schools; the impact of the reforms on high schools has remained hard to discern. Only a quarter of teachers reported that the reforms had so far enhanced the quality of student academic performance, and rather more reported a negative effect on student behavior than a positive one. Although data on students' actual achievement have yet to be made available, and there are considerable technical difficulties in making comparisons (Bryk, Easton, Luppescu, & Thum, 1994), there is likely to be little overall improvement on prereform figures.

Thus, as with other forms of site-based management, the Chicago version seems so far to have changed the form of governance without having the widespread impact on outcomes predicted by its advocates. The ambitious goal of bringing student achievement in Chicago up to national norms within 5 years seems to have been quietly forgotten. Lewis and Nakagawa (1995) suggest that the reform has come "to stand for process rather than outcome" and that "even if reformers alter the indicia of success to equal simply community participation, the Chicago school reform falls short—because participation alone has not led to empowerment in any real terms" (p. 168). They regard it as having had more to do with the politics of racial inclusion and the defusing of conflict and argue that, whatever the intention, "the very participation of the parents legitimizes the professionals' grip on policy making and school operations" (p. 149).

This study seems to lend support to those contributors to Hannaway and Carnoy's (1993) publication who argue that governance reforms in education have more to do with external political conditions than with what happens in schools. For such commentators, "centralization-decentralization debates reflect inevitable, cyclical, unresolvable tensions and contradictions in society and . . . the connection between these tensions and school performance is weak at best" (Hannaway & Carnoy, 1993, p. xii). Furthermore, there seems to be an accumulation of evidence that school autonomy, especially when combined with school choice, is as likely to exacerbate differences between schools as it is to lead to school improvement across the system as a whole. While enabling a few schools to take advantage of their new-found freedom, there is little evidence that schoolbased initiatives alone can overcome systemwide sociological influences on schooling.

There is also a danger that too much emphasis on the power of individual school faculty members to seek their own salvation will, in some contexts, result only in further damage to the morale of an increasingly exploited work force. Even community empowerment has its limitations in this respect, since communities are far from equally endowed with the material and cultural resources for self-management of their schools, as Gordon (1993, 1995) has demonstrated in the case of New Zealand. Lewis and Nakagawa's (1995) conclusions are even more pessimistic: "even if the model is implemented well, a tall order in and of itself, the exogenous factors that lead to the failure of the minority poor in school . . . would seem to require more than a change in school governance can deliver" (p. 172). Certainly, such a strategy is unlikely to succeed in the absence of other changes.

CONSUMER RIGHTS AND CITIZEN RIGHTS
IN PUBLIC EDUCATION

It is clear that the significance of reforms such as those involving parental choice and school autonomy can be properly evaluated only in a broader political context. Pointing to the damaging consequences of particular policies is not necessarily to question the motives of those proposing the reform agenda.[17] Many advocates of choice and school autonomy base their support on claims that competition will enhance the efficiency and responsiveness of schools and thus increase their effectiveness. Many hoped that market forces would overcome a leveling-down tendency that they ascribed to bureaucratic systems of mass education, while others saw them as a way of giving disadvantaged children the sorts of opportunities hitherto available only to those who could afford to buy them through private schooling or their position in the housing market. Yet these hopes are not being realized and are unlikely to be realized in the context of broader policies that do nothing to challenge deeper social and cultural inequalities. Atomized decision making in a highly stratified society may appear to give everyone equal opportunities, but transferring responsibility for decision making from the public to the private sphere can actually reduce the scope for collective action to improve the quality of education for all.

Even so, some aspects of the parental choice and school autonomy agendas are almost certain to outlive current conservative administrations. In some other countries, similar reforms are being advocated and implemented by parties and administrations associated with the political left.[18] In some senses, then, the current interest in devolution and choice may be indicative of tendencies of global proportions perhaps associated with post-Fordism or postmodernity.[19] Such a shift in the nature of education policy and administration reflects a more general repositioning of education in relation to the state and civil society (Whitty, in press). Thus, alongside—and potentially in place of—collective provision by public bodies with a responsibility to cater for the needs of the whole population, there are likely to be increasing numbers of quasi-autonomous schools with devolved budgets competing for individual clients in the marketplace.

However, the effects of such policies will be highly dependent on the broader context in which they are introduced. Although the concept of quasi-market always involves some degree of government regulation, there is disagreement about its nature and extent. In the three countries discussed here, conservative commentators wish to move further toward marketized and even privatized forms of education provision. Indeed, as I indicated earlier, some advocates of devolution and choice have argued that the indifferent performance of the reforms so far is merely evidence that they have not gone far enough.[20] For example, a government Minister responsible for the introduction of the assisted places scheme in England used our research showing that the scheme had failed to attract its target group (Edwards et al., 1989) as a basis for arguing in favor of a full-fledged voucher scheme (Boyson, 1990). Similarly, Chubb and Moe's (1992) major criticism of the British reforms was that the government had "created an open enrollment system in which there is very little to choose from, because the supply of schools is controlled by the LEAs" (Moe, 1994, p. 27). Their solution was that all schools should become autonomous.

Empirical research does not, indeed in principle could not, show that such reforms can never have beneficial effects. Yet, the studies reported here suggest that going further in the direction of marketization would be unlikely to yield major overall improvements in the quality of education and would almost certainly have damaging equity effects. The broad conclusion of these studies seems to be that, although the rhetoric of reform often suggests that the hidden hand of the market will produce the best possible outcome, the reality suggests that this is unlikely to be the case. Nor, apparently, has decentralization to schools and local communities done much to correct inequities in the system. In current circumstances in England, New Zealand, and the United States, not only have the positive benefits claimed for the reforms yet to be forthcoming, research suggests that, far from breaking the links between educational and social inequality, reforms may even intensify these links unless appropriate safeguards are put in place.

Tooley (1995), an articulate British advocate of choice, has argued that the potential of markets in education cannot be properly assessed by looking at the effects of quasi-markets or what he prefers to term "so-called" markets. There is an obvious sense in which this is true, and, to that extent, it is a valid criticism of the conclusions drawn from some of the studies reported here. However, insofar as attempts are being made to justify further moves toward the marketization of education, it is becoming increasingly important to try to model the effects of increasing choice options. Thus, for example, Witte, Thorn, and Pritchard (1995) have undertaken an analysis of the current social composition of private and public schools in Wisconsin and concluded that "an open-ended voucher scheme would clearly benefit households that are more affluent than the average household in Wisconsin." They went on to say that, although some might believe that making vouchers available to everyone would open up private schools to the poor, the opposite argument seems equally plausible. With more money available, private schools that cannot afford to select (e.g., some of the inner city private schools in the Milwaukee choice experiment) could become more selective. The already highly selective schools could then maintain their advantage by demanding add-on payments in addition to vouchers.

Thus, in an inegalitarian society, it seems highly improbable that the sort of "bottom-up" accountability associated with markets, and favored by Chubb and Moe (1992, p. 13), can replace the need for democratic accountability if equity is to remain an important consideration. A telling Carnegie report on school choice (Boyer, 1992) provided a reminder that although the school choice debate was, quite correctly, giving much attention to helping individual families, "American education has, throughout its history, focused not just on the empowerment of individuals but also on the building of community" (p. xviii). If devolution and choice are to produce positive effects throughout the school system and benefit all students, there is an urgent need to provide a counter-balance to the overemphasis on self-interest that is currently fostered by the reforms. Henig (1994) suggests that "the logical coherence, academic legitimacy, and conservative appeal of conventional economic theory results in the market rationale dominating the choice movement in public," but he also observes that "non market rationales account for most of the enthusiasm and support" (p. 194). Furthermore, he claims that "where school choice has appeared most successful—as in some of the many experiments with magnets, magnetized districts, and statewide open enrollment—it has been at the instigation and under the direction of strong and affirmative government action" (p. 193). Cookson (1994) too makes a distinction between market-driven and democratic-driven choice policies.

In their critique of Chubb and Moe (1990), K. B. Smith and Meier (1995) suggest that neither the abolition of democratic control nor the abolition of union power is a prerequisite for tackling the problems of bureaucracy, which are at the heart of many critiques of conventional mass education systems. More specifically, they claim to demonstrate that neither democratic control nor strong teachers' unions correlate positively with the size of bureaucracies in U.S. school districts. Smith and Meier also argue that bureaucracy *per se* may not be the problem institutional theorists claim. Rather, they suggest, it may be poverty that leads to enlarged bureaucracies and to depressed educational performance. Their own book is an argument for extending rather than reducing democratic control of education, although on a rather centralized model.

Carnoy (1993) argues that school site measures are likely to contribute to school improvement only in combination with higher performance demands from central authorities, while Gintis (1995) suggests that government regulation and the market should not necessarily be seen as in opposition. He argues that the choice of educational goals can still be debated in the educational arena and the results implemented through the proper choice of policy tools, which might include devolution and choice with appropriate rules for funding and accrediting schools. Thus, "the use of the market is in this sense an *instrument of* rather than an *alternative to* democratic policymaking" (Carnoy, 1993, p. 510).

All of this means that, whatever gains are to be had from handing decision making to parents and teachers (and they seem to be far fewer than the advocates claim), key decisions about goals and frameworks still need to be made in the broader political arena. The reality is that devolution and choice are occurring as part of a broader political strategy. Certainly, the recent education reforms in Britain have as much to do with transferring power to central government as with giving autonomy to parents and schools, even though the rhetoric accompanying reform often seeks to suggest that education has been taken out of politics as normally understood (Chubb & Moe, 1992). McKenzie (1993) has argued that "British governments have actually increased their claims to knowledge and authority over the education system whilst promoting a theoretical and superficial movement towards consumer sovereignty" and Harris (1993) suggests that this is more generally the case. Thus, the key issues remain political ones that need to be pursued at a political level and that cannot be avoided by technical and administrative solutions.

Even Chubb and Moe (1990), who argue that equality is better "protected" by markets than by political institutions, have to concede that choice of school cannot be unlimited and should not be entirely unregulated. In England and New Zealand, far too much is being left to the market, to be determined by the self-interest of some consumers and the competitive advantages of some schools. Yet, even though much of the American research suggests that the most equitable choice schemes are those that retain considerable degrees of regulation, Chubb and Moe (1992) argue that the British approach is a "lesson in school reform" that the United States should follow. My own view is that, in all three countries, much more attention needs to be given both to mechanisms of regulation and to the most appropriate ways of deciding on them. In Britain, devolution and choice have been accompanied by imposed and draconian accountability measures that mitigate against both professional collegiality and a concern with meeting the needs of disadvantaged students. In New Zealand, the adoption of a new public management accountability framework has had similar, although more muted, effects (Wylie, 1995). While similar developments are in evidence in parts of the United States, the more complex constitutional arrangements derided by Chubb and Moe (1992) have hitherto preserved more opportunities for professional and local democratic input in some areas.

Regulating choice and pursuing equity necessitate the existence of contexts for determining rules and processes for adjudicating between different claims and priorities. This entails the revival or creation of democratic contexts within which such issues can be determined. Unfortunately, however, those public institutions that might act on behalf of the broader interests of the community have been progressively dismantled by new right governments, which means that creating a new public sphere in which educational matters can even be debated—let alone determined—poses considerable challenges. According to Foucault, new forms of association, such as trade unions and political parties, arose in the 19th century as a counterbalance to the prerogative of the state and acted as the seedbed of new ideas (Kritzman 1988). Modern versions of these collectivist forms of association may now need to emerge to counterbalance not only the prerogative of the state, as currently exercised in forms of accountability associated with the new public management, but also the prerogative of the market.

Part of the challenge must be to move away from atomized decision making to the reassertion of collective responsibility without re-creating the very bureaucratic systems whose shortcomings have helped to legitimate the current tendency to treat education as a private good rather than a public responsibility. While choice policies are part of a social text that helps to create new subject positions that undermine traditional forms of collectivism, those forms of collectivism themselves failed to empower many members of society, including women and people of color. Margonis and Parker (1995) point out that the "communitarian metaphors" that are often used to oppose the "laissez-faire metaphors" of the choice proponents fail to take account of institutional racism and the deep structural inequalities in American society that indicate that public education has itself never fostered inclusive communities. Unfortunately, however, they give little indication of what a progressive alternative might look like.

We need to ask how we can use the positive aspects of choice and autonomy to facilitate the development of new forms of community empowerment rather than exacerbating social differentiation. So far, in England, the Labour Party has adopted many rightist policies, while the left has done little yet to develop a concept of public education that looks significantly different from the state education that some of us spent our earlier political and academic careers critiquing for its role in reproducing and legitimating social inequalities (Young & Whitty, 1977). Even if the social democratic era looks better in retrospect, and in comparison with current policies, than it did at the time, that does not remove the need to rethink what might be progressive policies for the next century. As Henig (1994) says of the United States, "the sad irony of the current education-reform movement is that, through overidentification with school-choice proposals rooted in market-based ideas, the healthy impulse to consider radical reforms to address social problems may be channeled into initiatives that further erode the potential for collective deliberation and collective response" (p. 222). In New Zealand, Gordon (1994a) argues for "a policy approach that combines the older social democratic goal of educational comparability across class and ethnic boundaries, with real choice for families" (p. 21).

It is surely necessary to think through alternatives as a matter of urgency since the rhetoric—although not the reality—of some of the recent reforms *has* probably been more responsive than critics sometimes recognize to those limited, but nonetheless tangible, social and cultural shifts that have been taking place in modern societies. A straightforward return to the old order of things would be neither feasible nor sensible. Those approaches to education that continue to favor the idea of a common public school are still faced with the need to respond to increasing specialization and social diversity. Connell (1993) reminds us that

justice cannot be achieved by distributing the same amount of a standard good to children of all social classes. . . . That "good" means different things to ruling class and working class children, and will do different things for them (or to them).

As Mouffe (1989, 1992) has argued, we need to develop a conception of citizenship, and by implication an education system, that involves creating unity without denying specificity.

In this context, it is possible to see that there may well be progressive moments within policies that foster devolution and choice. Apple (1995) has indicated that, in different political circumstances, education vouchers could be used to radical ends, while Atkinson (1994) sees self-managing schools as a basis for rebuilding communities in blighted inner city areas. This potential was recognized in some of the early moves toward devolution in New Zealand, but the recent evidence from New Zealand, as well as England, suggests that other considerations are currently more dominant. Nevertheless, Wylie (1995) argues that, in New Zealand, new forms of accountability and managerialism may still have "more form than substance" and that other practices and values "can be, and often are, given priority at the 'chalkface' " (p. 163).

Yet it is certainly proving increasingly difficult to realize progressive moments at the school site level in a situation of diminishing resources and when the broader political climate is pointing firmly in the opposite direction. Similarly, in the United States, where it is arguable that equity considerations have continued to mitigate the more extreme forms of marketization in education, "the difficult problem of protecting the conditions that make choice work from erosion due to fiscal and political pressures" (Henig, 1994, p. 169) will undoubtedly pose a considerable challenge to progressive forces within education for the foreseeable future. To that extent, while some forms of devolution and choice may warrant further exploration as ways of realizing the legitimate aspirations of disadvantaged groups, they should not be seen as a panacea for the ills of society or as an alternative to broader struggles for social justice.

NOTES

[1] In this review, I use the term *public school* in the North American sense of publicly funded and publicly provided schools, rather than the English sense of elite private schools.

[2] Hirsch (1995) claims that school autonomy has gone so far in New Zealand that the notion of a public education "system" is fast becoming an oxymoron.

[3] Elsewhere (Whitty, 1989), I have characterized this as a new right agenda that combines a neoliberal commitment to market forces with a neoconservative reassertion of "traditional" values. The balance between these aspects of contemporary conservatism varies among (and indeed within) the three countries under consideration here.

[4] Different education legislation applies to Scotland and Northern Ireland. There are also some minor differences between England and Wales. This review focuses on developments in England, although some of the studies cited also include Wales.

[5] One of the few studies of primary school choice in England is reported in Hughes, Wikeley, and Nash (1990). This study concluded that the majority of parents were not exercising a wide range of choice at that level (see also Hughes, Wikeley, and Nash, 1994).

[6] The growth of the "girl-friendliness" of coeducational schools was one of the unanticipated findings of this research. The research team has also explored the role of single-sex girls' schools in the education market for girls (Ball & Gewirtz, in press).

[7] Although scores on National Curriculum tests are only just becoming available, and their publication has been the subject of a dispute with teacher unions, schools in receipt of public funds were required by the 1980 Education Act to make public the results of school leaving examinations at 16+ and 18+ years. In recent years, these results for all schools have been published in the national press.

[8] It remains to be seen whether the British government's recent and reluctant acceptance that "value-added" measures could be helpful will change that situation. Value-added measures of school effectiveness seek to determine how well a school has performed relative to what might be expected in light of the nature of its clientele, either in terms of prior test scores or socioeconomic status or a combination of such indices.

[9] Although the failure of the reforms to promote more genuine diversity has been exacerbated in the English case by a restrictive national curriculum embodying a particularly narrow and nationalistic notion of British culture (Whitty, 1992), much of the evidence also implicates the way choice operates in a highly stratified society.

[10] Unfortunately, I have not had access to a new collection of studies of choice which is to appear in 1996 (Fuller, Elmore, & Orfield, in press).

[11] This would certainly be consistent with British research (Whitty et al., 1993) suggesting that the definitions of "merit" adopted by CTCs can favor members of some minority ethnic groups over others.

[12] The School Teachers' Pay Review Body reported similar or even higher workloads for headteachers but gave slightly lower figures for classroom teachers (Rafferty, 1994a). The publication of these figures coincided with evidence of a steep rise in the numbers of heads and deputies retiring early (Rafferty, 1994b).

[13] The evidence of recent disputes in the health service suggests that few doctors in National Health Service Trust hospitals in Britain or Crown Health Enterprises in New Zealand would argue that this separation has enhanced their professionality or made it easier for them to make clinical decisions independently of financial considerations.

[14] A new study of local management of schools and its equivalent in Scotland is exploring, among other things, the range of variation in management styles and strategies under devolved management.

[15] But see some preliminary work in Bauman, Banks, Murphy, and Kuczwara (1994); Becker et al. (1995); Datnow, Hirschberg, and Wells (1994); Grutzik et al. (1995); Urahn and Stewart (1994); Medler and Nathan (1995); and Wohlstetter et al. (1995). A major evaluation of charter schools is planned by the federal Department of Education, and the Pew Charitable Trusts are funding a study by Chester Finn and Louann Bierlein at the Hudson Institute.

[16] Blackmore (1995) cites English and New Zealand research by Deem (1990) and Middleton (1992) to make a more general claim that "local school boards in newly devolved systems are generally dominated or chaired by white, professional males, who are positioned to claim to represent the universal interests of a homogeneous parent constituency, the clients and 'the school' " (p. 52; see also Deem, Brehony, & Heath, 1995).

[17] However, the devolution of decision making can serve to divert responsibility for cuts in education expenditures from government to parents and schools (Weiss, 1993), and it can thus have considerable political utility in crisis contexts (Malen, 1994).

[18] In Victoria, Australia in the early 1980s, moves toward devolution were being talked of in terms of progressive ideals of community empowerment, although more recent policies there have been associated with the new right. This was also the case with the multi-accented Picot reforms in New Zealand in the 1980s (Gordon, 1992; Grace, 1991). Similarly, the reforms in Chicago were supported by groups of varying political persuasions (Hess, 1990).

[19] Although these reforms are currently most in evidence in the Anglophone world, interest in such measures is spreading to other parts of the world. Even some of the most

successful education systems of the Pacific Rim and continental Europe are now considering pursuing similar policies, although Green (1994) suggests that this trend is far from
universal.
[20] Lauder et al. (1995) suggest that, even if this is the case, the disenchantment of
working-class parents with the "false promise" of choice in the current reforms will enter
the "wisdom of the working class" and thus inhibit any likelihood that they will become the
active choosers envisaged by market advocates even in the future (p. 49).

REFERENCES

Adler, M. (1993). *An alternative approach to parental choice* (National Commission on
   Education Briefing Paper 13). London: National Commission on Education.
Ambler, J. (1994). Who benefits from educational choice? Some evidence from Europe.
   Journal of Policy Analysis and Management, 13 (3).
Anderson, B. (1995, August 24). Major urges nation to seize opportunity. *The Times,* 5.
Anyon, J. (1995). Race, social class, and educational reform in an inner-city school.
   Teachers College Record, 97 (1), 69–94.
Apple, M.W. (1986). *Teachers and texts.* New York: Routledge.
Apple, M.W. (1993). *Official knowledge.* New York: Routledge.
Apple, M.W. (1995). *Education and power* (2nd ed.). New York: Routledge.
Arnott, M., Bullock, A., & Thomas, H. (1992, February). Consequences of local manage-
   ment: An assessment by head teachers. Paper presented at the Education Reform Act
   Research Network, University of Warwick.
Atkinson, D. (1994). *Radical urban solutions.* London: Cassell.
Ball, S. J., & Gewirtz, S. (in press). Girls in the education market: Choice, competition and
   complexity. *Gender and Education.*
Barber, M. (1992). *Education and the teacher unions.* London: Cassell.
Barber, M., Rowe, G., & Whitty, G. (1995). School development planning: Towards a new
   role for teaching unions? Mimeograph.
Bartlett, W. (1993). Quasi-markets and educational reforms. In J. Le Grand & W. Bartlett
   (Eds.), *Quasi-Markets and Social Policy* (pp. 125–153). London: Macmillan.
Bartlett, W., & LeGrand, J. (1993). The theory of quasi-markets. In J. LeGrand & W.
   Bartlett (Eds.), *Quasi-markets and social policy* (pp. 13–34). London: Macmillian.
Bauman, P., Banks, D., Murphy, M., & Kuczwara, H. (1994, April). *The charter school
   movement: Preliminary findings from the first three states.* Paper presented at the annual
   meeting of the American Educational Research Association, New Orleans, LA.
Becker, H. J., Nakagawa, K., & Corwin, R.G. (1995, April). *Parental involvement con-
   tracts in California's charter schools.* Paper presented at the annual meeting of the
   American Educational Research Association, San Francisco, CA.
Blackburne, L. (1988, May 13). Peers back policy on open enrolment. *The Times
   Educational Supplement,* A6.
Blackmore, J. (1995). Breaking out from a masculinist politics of education. In
   B. Limerick & B. Lingard (Eds.), *Gender and Changing Education Management.*
   Rydalmere, New South Wales, Australia: Hodder Education.
Blank, R. (1990). Educational effects of magnet high schools. In W. H. Clune & J. F. Witte
   (Eds.), *Choice and Control in American Education* (Vol. 2, 77–109). New York: Falmer
   Press.
Bolick, C. (1990). *A primer on choice in education: Part 1—How choice works.*
   Washington, DC: Heritage Foundation.
Bowe, R., Ball, S., with Gold, A. (1992). *Reforming education and changing schools.*
   London: Routledge.
Boyer, E. L. (1992). *School choice: A special report.* Princeton, NJ: Carnegie Foundation.

Boyson, R. (1990, May). Review of *The state and private education. Times Higher Education Supplement*, 18.

Bridges, S. (1992). *Working in tomorrow's schools: Effects on primary teachers.* Christchurch, New Zealand: University of Canterbury.

Broadbent, J., Laughlin, R., Shearn, D., & Dandy, N. (1993). Implementing local management of schools: A theoretical and empirical analysis. *Research Papers in Education, 8* (2), 149–176.

Brown, C. (1993). Employee involvement in industrial decision making: Lessons for public schools. In J. Hannaway & M. Carnoy (Eds.), *Decentralization and school improvement: Can we fulfill the promise?* (pp. 202–231). San Francisco: Jossey-Bass.

Bryk, A.S., Easton, J.Q., Luppescu, S., & Thum, Y.M. (1994). Measuring achievement gains in the Chicago public schools. *Education and Urban Society, 26,* 306–319.

Bryk, A.S., Lee, V.E., & Holland, P.B. (1993). *Catholic schools and the common good.* Cambridge, MA: Harvard University Press.

Bullock, A., & Thomas, H. (1994). *The impact of local management of schools: Final report.* Birmingham, England: University of Birmingham.

Bush, T., Coleman, M., & Glover, D. (1993). *Managing autonomous schools.* London: Paul Chapman.

Campbell, J., & Neill, S. (1994). *Curriculum at key stage 1: Teacher commitment and policy failure.* Harlow, England: Longman.

Capper, P. (1994). *Participation and partnership: Exploring shared decision-making in twelve New Zealand secondary schools.* Wellington, New Zealand: Post Primary Teachers' Association.

Carlos, J., & Amsler, M. (1993). *Site-based management: An experiment in governance* (Policy Briefs 20). San Francisco: Far West Laboratory for Educational Research and Development.

Carnoy, M. (1993). School Improvement: Is Privatization the Answer? In J. Hannaway & M. Carnoy (Eds.), *Decentralization and school improvement: Can we fulfill the promise?* (pp. 163–201). San Francisco: Jossey-Bass.

Carnoy, M. (1995, July 12). Is school privatization the answer? Data from the experience of other countries suggest not. *Education Week,* 29–33.

Cawelti, G. (1994). *High school restructuring: A national study.* Arlington: Educational Research Service.

Chubb, J., & Moe, T. (1990). *Politics, Markets and America's Schools.* Washington, DC: Brookings Institution.

Chubb, J., & Moe, T. (1992). *A lesson in school reform from Great Britain.* Washington, DC: Brookings Institution.

Clewell, B.C., & Joy, M.F. (1990). *Choice in Montclair, New Jersey.* Princeton, NJ: Educational Testing Service.

Clune, W.H., & Witte, J.F. (Eds.). (1990a). *Choice and Control in American Education* (Vol. 1). New York: Falmer Press.

Clune, W.H., & Witte, J.F. (Eds.) (1990b). *Choice and Control in American Education* (Vol. 2). New York: Falmer Press.

Coleman, J.S., Hoffer, T., & Kilgore, S. (1982). *High school achievement: Public, Catholic and private schools.* New York: Basic Books.

Connell, R.W. (1993). *Schools and social justice.* Toronto: Our Schools/Our Selves Education Foundation.

Cookson, P.W. (1994). *School choice: The struggle for the soul of American education.* New Haven, CT: Yale University Press.

Cookson, P.W. (1995). Goals 2000: Framework for the new educational federalism. *Teachers College Record, 96* (3) , pp 405–417.

Cooper, B. (1994, April). *Administrative and economic efficiency in education: Using school-site ratio analysis.* Paper presented at the annual meeting of the American Educational Research Association, New Orleans, LA.

Datnow, A., Hirschberg, D., & Wells, A.S. (1994, April). *Charter schools: Teacher professionalism and decentralisation.* Paper presented at the annual meeting of the American Educational Research Association, New Orleans, LA.

David, M.E. (1993). *Parents, gender, and education reform.* Cambridge, England: Polity Press.

Deem, R. (1990). Governing by gender—The new school governing bodies. In P. Abbott & C. Wallace (Eds.), *Gender, power, and sexuality* (pp. 58–76). London: Macmillan.

Deem, R., Brehony, K., & Heath, S. (1995). *Active citizenship and the governing of schools.* Buckingham, England: Open University Press.

Department for Education. (1992). *Choice and diversity.* London: Her Majesty's Stationery Office.

Designs for Change. (1991). *Chicago School Reform, 1,* 1–5.

Domanico, R.J. (1990). *Restructuring New York City's public schools: The case for public school choice* (Education Policy Paper 3). New York: Manhattan Institute for Policy Research.

Edwards, T., Fitz, J., & Whitty, G. (1989). *The state and private education: An evaluation of the assisted places scheme.* London: Falmer Press.

Elmore, R.F. (1991). Foreword. In G.A. Hess (Ed.), *School restructuring Chicago style.* Newbury Park, CA: Corwin.

Elmore, R.F. (1993). School Decentralization: Who Gains? Who Loses? In J. Hannaway & M. Carnoy (Eds.), *Decentralization and school improvement: Can we fulfill the promise?* (pp. 33–54). San Francisco: Jossey-Bass.

Feintuck, M. (1994). *Accountability and choice in schooling.* Buckingham, England: Open University Press.

Fitz, J., Halpin, D., & Power, S. (1993). *Grant maintained schools: Education in the marketplace.* London: Kogan Page.

Fliegel, S., with Macguire, J. (1990). *Miracle in East Harlem: The fight for choice in public education.* New York: Random House.

Fowler, M. (1993). *Factors influencing choice of secondary schools.* Christchurch, New Zealand: University of Canterbury.

Fullan, M. (1991). *The new meaning of educational change.* London: Cassell.

Fuller, B., Elmore, R., & Orfield, G. (Eds.). (in press). *School choice: The cultural logic of families, the political rationality of schools.* New York: Teachers College Press.

Gewirtz, S., & Ball, S.J. (1995, April). *Schools, signs and values: The impact of market forces on education provision in England.* Paper presented at the annual meeting of the American Educational Research Association, San Francisco, CA.

Gewirtz, S., Ball, S.J., & Bowe, R. (1995). *Markets, choice and equity.* Buckingham, England: Open University Press.

Gibbs, G.J. (1991). School-based management: Are we ready? *Intercultural Development Research Association Newsletter, 18* (4).

Gintis, H. (1995). The political economy of school choice. *Teachers College Record, 96,* 493–511.

Gitlin, A., & Margonis, F. (1995). The political aspect of reform: Teacher resistance as good sense. *American Journal of Education, 103,* 377–405.

Glatter, R. (1993, September). *Partnership in the market model: Is it dying?* Paper presented at the annual conference of the British Educational Management and Administration Society, Edinburgh, Scotland.

Glatter, R., Woods, P., & Bagley, C. (1995, June). *Diversity, differentiation, and hierarchy: School choice and parental preference.* Paper presented at the ESRC/CEPAM

Invitation Seminar on Research on Parental Choice and School Response, Milton Keynes, England.

Glennerster, H. (1991). Quasi-markets for education? *Economic Journal, 101,* 1268–1276.

Gordon, L. (1992, April). *The New Zealand state and education reforms: "Competing" interests.* Paper presented at the annual meeting of the American Educational Research Association, San Francisco, CA.

Gordon, L. (1993). *A study of boards of trustees in Canterbury schools.* Christchurch, New Zealand: University of Canterbury.

Gordon, L. (1994a) Is school choice a sustainable policy for New Zealand? A review of recent research findings and a look to the future. *New Zealand Annual Review of Education, 4,* 9–24.

Gordon, L. (1994b). "Rich" and "Poor" Schools in Aotearoa. *New Zealand Journal of Educational Studies, 29,* 113–125.

Gordon, L. (1995). Controlling education: Agency theory and the reformation of New Zealand schools. *Educational Policy, 9,* 55–74.

Grace, G. (1991). Welfare labourism versus the new right. *International Studies in the Sociology of Education, 1,* 37–48.

Green, A. (1994). Postmodernism and state education. *Journal of Education Policy, 9,* 67–84.

Grutzik, C., Bernal, D., Hirschberg, D., & Wells, A.S. (1995, April). *Resources and access in California charter schools.* Paper presented at the annual meeting of the American Educational Research Association, San Francisco, CA.

Guskey, T. R., & Peterson, K.D. (in press). School based shared decision making: The road to the classroom. *Educational Leadership.*

Halpin, D., Power, S., & Fitz, J. (1993). Opting into state control? Headteachers and the paradoxes of grant-maintained status. *International Studies in the Sociology of Education, 3,* 3–23.

Halpin, D., & Troyna, B. (1994, April). *Lessons in school reform from Great Britain.* Paper presented at the annual meeting of the American Educational Research Association, New Orleans, LA.

Hannaway, J., & Carnoy, M. (Eds.). (1993). *Decentralization and school improvement: Can we fulfill the promise?* San Francisco: Jossey-Bass.

Hargreaves, D. (1994). *The mosaic of learning: Schools and teachers for the next century.* London: Demos.

Harris, K. (1993). Power to the people? Local management of schools. *Education Links, 45,* 4–8.

Hawk, K., & Hill, J. (1994). *Evaluation of teacher salaries grant scheme trial: The third year.* Palmerston North, New Zealand: Massey University.

Henig, J.R. (1994). *Rethinking school choice: Limits of the market metaphor.* Princeton, NJ: Princeton University Press.

Hess, G.A. (1990). *Chicago school reform: How it is and how it came to be.* Chicago: Chicago Panel on Public School Policy and Finance.

Hill, R. (1992). *Managing today's schools: The case for shared decision-making.* Wellington, New Zealand: Institute for Social Research and Development.

Hill, P.T., Foster G.E., & Gendler, T. (1990). *High schools with character.* Santa Monica, CA: RAND.

Hirsch, D. (1995, May). The other school choice—how should over-subscribed schools select their pupils? Open lecture presented at the Institute of Education, University of London.

Hughes, M., Wikeley, F., & Nash, T. (1990). *Parents and the national curriculum: An interim report.* Exeter, England: University of Exeter.

Hughes, M., Wikeley, F., & Nash, T. (1994). *Parents and their children's schools.* Oxford: Blackwell.

Kerchner, C., & Mitchell, D. (1988). *The changing idea of a teachers' union.* London: Falmer Press.

Kritzman, L. D. (Ed.). (1988). *Foucault: Politics/philosophy/culture.* New York: Routledge.

Lauder, H., Hughes, D., Waslander, S., Thrupp, M., McGlinn, J., Newton, S., & Dupuis, A. (1994). *The creation of market competition for education in New Zealand.* Wellington, New Zealand: Victoria University of Wellington.

Lauder, H., Hughes, D., Watson, S., Simiyu, I., Strathdee, R., & Waslander, S. (1995). *Trading in futures: The nature of choice in educational markets in New Zealand.* Wellington, New Zealand: Ministry of Education.

Lee, V. E., & Bryk, A. S. (1993). Science or Policy Argument? In E. Rasell & R. Rothstein (Eds.), *School choice: Examining the evidence.* Washington, DC: Economic Policy Institute.

Le Grand, J., & Bartlett, W. (Eds.). (1993). *Quasi-markets and social policy.* London: Macmillan.

Levacic, R. (1995). *Local management of schools: Analysis and practice.* Buckingham, England: Open University Press.

Lewis, D. A., & Nakagawa, K. (1995). *Race and educational reform in the American metropolis: A study of school decentralization.* Albany: SUNY Press.

Livingstone, I. (1994). *The workloads of primary school teachers—A Wellington region survey.* Wellington, New Zealand: Chartwell Consultants.

Louis, K. S., & Miles, M. B. (1992). *Improving the urban high school: What works and why.* London: Cassell.

Malen, B. (1994). Enacting site-based management: A political utilities analysis. *Educational Evaluation and Policy Analysis, 16* (3), 249–267.

Malen, B., Ogawa, R. T., & Kranz, J. (1990). What do we know about school-based management? A case-study of the literature—a call for research. In W. H. Clune & J. F. Witte (Eds.), *Choice and Control in American Education: Volume 2* (pp. 289–342). New York: Falmer Press.

Margonis, F., & Parker, L. (1995). Choice, privatization, and unspoken strategies of containment. *Educational Policy, 9* (4), 375–403.

Marks, H. M., & Louis, K. S. (1995). *Does teacher empowerment affect the classroom? The implications of teacher empowerment for teachers' instructional practice and student academic performance.* Madison: Center on Organization and Restructuring of Schools, University of Wisconsin.

Marren, E., & Levacic, R. (1994). Senior management, classroom teacher and governor responses to local management of schools. *Educational Management and Administration, 22* (1), 39–53.

Maychell, K. (1994). *Counting the cost: The impact of LMS on schools' patterns of spending.* Slough, England: National Foundation for Educational Research.

McKenzie, J. (1993, January). Education as a Private Problem or a Public Issue? The Process of Excluding "Education" from the "Public Sphere." Paper presented at the International Conference on the Public Sphere, Manchester, England.

Medler, A., & Nathan, J. (1995). *Charter schools: What are they up to?* Denver, CO: Education Commission of the States.

Middleton, S. (1992). Gender equity and school charters: Theoretical and political questions for the 1990s. In S. Middleton & A. Jones (Eds.), *Women and education in Aotearoa 2* (pp. 1–17). Wellington, New Zealand: Bridget Williams Books.

Minister of Education. (1988). *Tomorrow's schools: The reform of education administration in New Zealand.* Wellington, New Zealand: Government Printer.

Moe, T. (1994). The British battle for choice. In K. L. Billingsley (Ed.), *Voices on choice: The education reform debate* (pp. 23–33). San Francisco: Pacific Institute for Public Policy.

Mohrman, S. A., Wohlstetter, P., & Associates. (1994). *School-based management: Organizing for high performance.* San Francisco: Jossey-Bass.

Moore, D., & Davenport, S. (1990). School choice: The new improved sorting machine. In W. Boyd & H. Walberg (Eds.), *Choice in education* (pp. 187–223). Berkeley, CA: McCutchan.

Mouffe, C. (1989). Toward a radical democratic citizenship. *Democratic Left, 17,* 6–7.

Mouffe, C. (Ed.). (1992). *Dimensions of radical democracy: Pluralism, citizenship, democracy.* London: Verso.

Murfitt, D. (1995). *The implementation of new right reform in education: Teachers and the intensification of work.* Unpublished Masters Thesis, Education Department, University of Canterbury, Christchurch, New Zealand.

Murphy, J. (1994). *Principles of school-based management.* Chapel Hill: North Carolina Educational Policy Research Center.

Murphy, J., & Beck, L. G. (1995). *School-based management as school reform: Taking stock.* Thousand Oaks. CA: Corwin Press.

Newmann, F. (1993). Beyond common sense in educational restructuring: The issues of content and leadership. *Educational Researcher, 22* (2), 4–13.

Odden, E. R., & Wohlstetter, P. (1995). Making School-Based Management Work. *Educational Leadership, 52* (5), 32–36.

Office for Standards in Education. (1994). *Primary matters: A discussion of teaching and learning in primary schools.* London: Author.

Ogawa, R. T., & White, P. A. (1994). School-based management: An overview. In S. A. Mohrman, P. Wohlstetter, and Associates (Eds.), *School-based management: Organizing for high performance* (pp. 53–80). San Francisco: Jossey-Bass.

Organization for Economic Cooperation and Development. (1994). *School: A matter of choice.* Paris: OECD/CERI.

Pennell, H., & West, A. (1995). *Changing schools: Secondary schools' admissions policies in inner London in 1995* (Clare Market Paper 9). London: London School of Economics and Political Science.

Picot, B. (1988). *Administering for excellence.* Wellington, New Zealand: Government Printer.

Plank, S., Schiller, K. S., Schneider, B., & Coleman, J. S. (1993). Effects of choice in education. In E. Rasell & R. Rothstein (Eds.), *School choice: Examining the evidence.* Washington, DC: Economic Policy Institute.

Pollard, S. (1995a, October 22). Labour's slow learners. *Observer Review,* p. 4.

Pollard, S. (1995b). *Schools, selection and the left.* London: Social Market Foundation.

Power, S., Halpin, D., & Fitz, J. (1994). Underpinning choice and diversity? The grant maintained schools policy in context. In S. Tomlinson (Ed.), *Educational reform and its consequences* (pp. 26–40). London: IPPR/Rivers Oram Press.

Rafferty, F. (1994a, August 5). Alarm at growth of 60-hour week. *Times Educational Supplement,* p. 1.

Rafferty, F. (1994b, September 2). Many more heads leave jobs. *Times Educational Supplement,* p. 9.

Ranson, S. (1993, March). *Renewing education for democracy.* Paper presented at the Institute of Public Policy Research Seminar on Alternative Education Policies, London, England.

Raywid, M. A. (1994). *Focus schools: A genre to consider* (Urban Diversity Series 106). New York: Columbia University, ERIC Clearinghouse on Urban Education.

Robertson, P. J., Wohlstetter, P., & Mohrman, S. A. (1995). Generating curriculum and instructional innovations through school-based management. *Educational Administration Quarterly, 31* (3), 375–404.

Rossell, C. H., & Glenn, C. L. (1988). The Cambridge controlled choice plan. *Urban Review, 20* (2), 75–94.

Sebring, P. B., Bryk, A. S., & Easton, J. Q. (1995). *Charting reform: Chicago teachers take stock.* Chicago: Consortium on Chicago School Research.

Seddon, T., Angus, L., & Poole, M. (1991). Pressures on the move to school-based decision-making and management. In J. Chapman (Ed.), *School-based decision-making and management* (pp. 29–54). London: Falmer Press.

Sexton, S. (1987). *Our schools—A radical policy.* Warlingham, England: Institute of Economic Affairs, Education Unit.

Sexton, S. (1991). *New Zealand schools.* Wellington, New Zealand: Business Round Table.

Sinclair, J., Ironside, M., & Seifert, R. (1993, April). *Classroom struggle? Market oriented education reforms and their impact on teachers' professional autonomy, labour intensification and resistance.* Paper presented at the International Labour Process Conference.

Smith, K. B., & Meier, K. J. (1995). *The case against school choice: Politics, markets and fools.* Armonk, NY: M. E. Sharpe.

Smith, T., & Noble, M. (1995). *Education divides: Poverty and schooling in the 1990s.* London: Child Poverty Action Group.

Sullivan, K. (1994). The impact of education reform on teachers' professional ideologies. *New Zealand Journal of Educational Studies, 29* (1), 3–20.

Tan, N. (1990). *The Cambridge controlled choice program: Improving educational equity and integration* (Education Policy Paper 4). New York: Manhattan Institute for Policy Research.

Taylor, D. L., & Bogotch, I. E. (1994). School-level effects of teachers' participation in decision making. *Educational Evaluation and Policy Analysis, 16* (3), 302–319.

Tooley, J. (1995). Markets or democracy? A reply to Stewart Ranson. *British Journal of Educational Studies, 43* (1), 21–34.

Tyack, D. (1993). School governance in the United States: Historical puzzles and anomalies. In J. Hannaway & M. Carnoy (Eds.), *Decentralization and school improvement: Can we fulfill the promise?* (pp. 1–32). San Francisco: Jossey-Bass.

Urahn, S., & Stewart, D. (1994). *Minnesota charter schools: A research report.* St Paul, MN: Research Department, Minnesota House of Representatives.

Vincent, C., Evans, J., Lunt, I., & Young, P. (1995). Policy and practice: The changing nature of special educational provision in schools. *British Journal of Special Education, 22* (1), 4–11.

Walford, G. (1992a). Educational choice and equity in Great Britain. *Educational Policy, 6* (2), 123–138.

Walford, G. (1992b). *Selection for secondary schooling* (National Commission on Education Briefing Paper 7). London: National Commission on Education.

Walford, G., & Miller, H. (1991). *City technology college.* Milton Keynes, England: Open University Press.

Waslander, S., & Thrupp, M. (1995). Choice, competition and segregation: An empirical analysis of a New Zealand secondary school market 1990–1993. *Journal of Education Policy, 10,* 1–26.

Weiss, M. (1993). New guiding principles in educational policy: The case of Germany. *Journal of Education Policy, 8,* 307–320.

Wells, A. S. (1990). *Public school choice: Issues and concerns for urban educators* (ERIC/CUE Digest 63). New York: ERIC Clearinghouse on Urban Education.

Wells, A. S. (1993a). The sociology of school choice: Why some win and others lose in the educational marketplace. In E. Rasell & R. Rothstein (Eds.), *School choice: Examining the evidence.* Washington, DC: Economic Policy Institute.

Wells, A.S. (1993b). *Time to choose: America at the crossroads of school choice policy.* New York: Hill and Wang.

Wells, A.S., & Crain, R.L. (1992). Do parents choose school quality or school status? A sociological theory of free market education. In P.W. Cookson (Ed.), *The choice controversy* (pp. 65–82). Newbury Park, CA: Corwin Press.

Whitty, G. (1989). The new right and the national curriculum: State control or market forces? *Journal of Education Policy, 4,* 329–341.

Whitty, G. (1992). Education, economy and national culture. In R. Bocock & K. Thompson (Eds.), *Social and cultural forms of modernity* (pp. 267–320). Cambridge, England: Polity Press.

Whitty, G. (in press). Citizens or consumers? Continuity and change in contemporary education policy. In D. Carlson & M. Apple (Eds.), *Critical Educational theory in unsettling times.* Boulder, CO: Westview Press.

Whitty, G., Edwards, T., & Gewirtz, S. (1993). *Specialisation and choice in urban education: The city technology college experiment.* London: Routledge.

Witte, J.F. (1990). Choice and control: An analytical overview. In W.H. Clune & J.F. Witte (Eds.), *Choice and control in American education* (Vol. 1, 11–46). New York: Falmer Press.

Witte, J.F., Thorn, C.A., & Pritchard, K.A. (1995). *Private and public education in Wisconsin: Implications for the choice debate.* Madison: University of Wisconsin.

Witte, J.F., Thorn, C.A., Pritchard, K.M., & Claibourn, M. (1994). *Fourth year report: Milwaukee parental choice program.* Madison: Department of Public Instruction.

Wohlstetter, P. (1995). Getting school-based management right: What works and what doesn't. *Phi Delta Kappan, 77* (1), 22–26.

Wohlstetter, P., & Mohrman, S.A. (1993). *School-based management: Strategies for success.* New Brunswick, NJ: Consortium for Policy Research in Education.

Wohlstetter, P., & Odden, A. (1992). Rethinking school-based management policy and research. *Educational Administration Quarterly, 28,* 529–549.

Wohlstetter, P., Smyer, R., & Mohrman, S.A. (1994). New boundaries for school-based management: The high involvement model. *Educational Evaluation and Policy Analysis, 16* (3), pp 268–286.

Wohlstetter, P., Wenning, R., & Briggs, K. L. (1995). Charter schools in the United States: The question of autonomy. *Educational Policy, 9,* 331–358.

Wylie, C. (1994). *Self managing schools in New Zealand: The Fifth year.* Wellington: New Zealand Council for Educational Research.

Wylie, C. (1995). Contrary currents: The application of the public sector reform framework in education. *New Zealand Journal of Educational Studies, 30,* 149–164.

Young, M., & Whitty, G. (Eds.). (1977). *Society, State and Schooling.* Lewes, England: Falmer Press.

Manuscript received January 15, 1996
Accepted March 15, 1996

Chapter 2

The Political Economy of Urban Education

JOHN L. RURY
DePaul University

JEFFREY E. MIREL
Northern Illinois University

With his best-selling book, *Savage Inequalities* (1991), Jonathan Kozol brought to the nation's attention the shocking disparities in educational resources that distinguish schools in central cities and suburbs. This is not a new issue, of course; James Bryant Conant (1961) made a similar point some 30 years earlier. Indeed, one could argue that little had changed since Conant's time, except perhaps as a matter of degree. Schools in cities have long been poor, populated by students from racial and ethnic minority groups, and saddled with a reputation for inadequate performance (Rury, 1993; Tyack, 1974). What Kozol and Conant and dozens of other observers have wrestled with over the past several decades is addressing the question of why this is so. The answer, we would suggest, lies in the political economy of urban education.

In this chapter, we consider the political and economic forces that have shaped urban schools, drawing upon the extant research literature on urban education and related social science disciplines to identify and discuss them. It is from this that we derive the term *political economy* . The intention is to be inclusive of factors in the larger social context of schools that affect schools' performance. Our choice of the term stems from its use in both classical (or market) and Marxist economic analysis and is meant to convey our recognition that large-scale social phenomena cannot be easily analyzed within a single disciplinary tradition. Put another way, we think that it is naive to suggest that economic and social or cultural relationships are not closely related to the distribution of political power in society. Consequently, both political and economic dimensions of critical social problems must be considered simultaneously if one is to understand how these dilemmas have evolved.

We would like to thank Michael Apple, Larry Bennett, David Tyack, and Kenneth Wong for their helpful comments on earlier versions of this essay. Jeffrey E. Mirel would also like to thank the Social Science Research Institute, Northern Illinois University, which provided support for his work on the essay.

In considering educational research, for example, this means combining the strengths of the functional analysis that has defined so much of the past inquiry about urban schooling and the insights gained from the more recent political studies of education. Thus, in this essay, we examine a variety of research traditions ranging from the ecological model that has dominated the field of urban studies for more than a half century to the "new" political perspective which has informed much educational and sociological research in recent decades. As such, the discussion provides a historical overview of much research on urban schooling, revealing the evolution of ideas and debates that have informed the development of a broad field of inquiry.

Perhaps the best way to start a consideration of urban education is to consider the term *urban* itself, a step rarely taken in the literature on education. *Urban* has come to denote many different things, of course, but we suggest that at its most essential level it is a measure of space (Gottdiener, 1985). This, after all, is the dimension of social life implicitly featured by Kozol, Conant, and the many other commentators who have chosen to feature contrasts between schools in different locales. At their most basic level, cities are defined by spatial relationships: Population density, the geographic arrangement of districts with different functional activities, and residential status hierarchies are simply a few of the more obvious sociospatial dimensions of city life. And because schools are so often defined by their immediate social environment, the social geography of cities and their larger metropolitan regions exerts a telling effect on education. Kozol and others have dramatically documented the results of this process, but few studies have addressed the more challenging question of why these spatial patterns of organization have come to exist.

Our focus is defined at the level of what might best be described as large-scale policy studies. For the most part, we consider factors that affect school systems rather than individual schools or students. Consequently, for example, we will not engage the growing literature on school-level organization questions; nor will we address such urban curricular issues as bilingual education or dropout prevention programs. Rather, our purpose is to consider factors shaping the larger social and political environment of urban schools, conditions that account for many of the differences noted by observers over the years. We are concerned with the forces of historical change that have affected city schools and ways in which the research community has thought about them.

The goal of this exercise, however, is not simply one of historical exposition and reflection. Defining a political economy of urban education entails considering the dynamics of power and wealth and the manner in which they function in contemporary urban settings (Feagin, 1980). Considering the political economy of urban education means addressing the spatial relationships that have shaped the existing conceptions of city schools. It necessitates analysis of the larger urban social and economic context and consideration of the historical forces that have brought the schools to their present state. Only when each of these factors has been properly appraised will we appreciate just how the current crisis in urban education developed and how we can begin to identify ways in which it might be resolved.

THE UNDERLYING PROBLEM: A DEEPENING CRISIS IN URBAN EDUCATION

While the issues addressed in the works of Conant (1961) and Kozol (1991) may have been similar, the problems of urban education have grown more severe in the intervening three decades. It would be wrong, in that case, to conclude that little had changed in city schools since the 1960s. The populations served by big-city school systems have shifted dramatically, just as the cities themselves have changed demographically and economically. And these developments have signaled a host of new challenges to the schools.

Of course, in urban school systems themselves much has transpired in the years between the early 1960s and the 1990s. City schools in all parts of the country have been subjected to desegregation plans, as the civil rights revolution of the 1960s and 1970s made racial isolation in the schools a major public issue (Armor, 1995; Orfield, 1983). Urban school systems have struggled with major organizational reform movements, many of them designed to decentralize power and authority. The politics of education often became volatile, as previously disenfranchised groups sought a voice in school governance and administration (Cibulka & Olson, 1993; Mirel 1993a). Unlike earlier periods in the history of urban education, in that case, the years following 1961 were a time of considerable instability in the institutional life of big city schools. But these were hardly the most important developments in urban education. Other, more telling changes altered the day-to-day life of city schools profoundly.

Perhaps the most striking developments concerned the racial and ethnic composition of the urban student population. When Conant wrote his book, the number of Black students in major urban school systems was historically large—and rising—but had not yet surpassed the number of White children anywhere outside of the South. Indeed, in 1960 the proportional size of big-city Black populations was smaller in the North than in most large southern cities (Havighurst, 1966). This had changed 30 years later. Today the largest concentrations of African Americans are in large northern cities, although several southern metropolitan areas continue to have high numbers as well (Massey & Denton, 1993). The effects of these population changes on schools have been manifold. By the 1980s Whites were a shrinking minority in virtually all of the nation's largest city systems and in a growing number of smaller ones as well (Kantor & Brenzel, 1993). By the early 1990s the numbers of White students had become very small. In Chicago, Whites constituted barely 10% of the public school student population in 1990, while the numbers in other cities rarely exceeded 25% (Levine and Zipp, 1993; Mirel, 1993b). As several observers have noted, changes such as these have made it extremely difficult to address questions of racial isolation within big-city schools systems, regardless of their size (Rury, 1993). In the very largest cities, consequently, desegregation virtually has become a moot point. If anything, the problems that Conant and others associated with racial segregation in urban schools have grown worse in the past 10 to 15 years.

Similar trends can be noted for the numbers of children from low income or poverty households and those from families with one parent. During the late 1960s, urban poverty levels were estimated at about 15%, with perhaps as many as one in four black families classified as below the poverty line (Hummel & Nagle, 1973). As William Julius Wilson (1987) and others have demonstrated, the concentration of poverty in central cities, particularly among African Americans, has increased sharply since then. By the early 1990s, the poverty rate in central cities across the country was nearly 20% for all groups and 33% for African Americans (Goldman & Blakely, 1992). Much of this is due to changes in the largest northern metropolitan areas, where a very large proportion of the nation's urban poor reside. And in these settings the numbers are considerably worse (Wilson, 1987).

Here, too, the statistics from Chicago are instructive. Among the city's Black population, the proportion of children living in low-income and single-parent families had reached more than half by the early 1990s (Chicago Department of Planning and Development, 1992). By 1990, children from low-income backgrounds also constituted a large majority of the public schools' Black student population. Similar trends have affected the Hispanic population, which has grown rapidly in the past several decades. Altogether, by 1993 about three quarters of the students in Chicago's public schools were from low-income households (Chicago Panel on School Policy, 1995). Historically, we believe that this is an unprecedented set of circumstances for Chicago and other big-city school systems.

The implications of these trends are clear. The relationships among racial isolation, poverty, and school achievement are well established, even if continually subject to respecification (Crane, 1991; Natriello, McDill, & Pallas, 1990). Given the large concentrations of children from poor neighborhoods and family backgrounds they are required to serve, it is little wonder that big-city schools exhibit low levels of achievement, high dropout rates, and a host of other problems (Rury, 1993). In diverse cities such as Chicago, children from more affluent neighborhoods perform better in school, and this relationship has been demonstrated consistently for several decades. (Kantor & Brenzel, 1993). It follows that as the numbers of students from such backgrounds increase rapidly, schools will face enormous problems. In the case of Chicago, even if the schools were remarkably well organized and staffed by exceptional educators, they would be hard pressed to contend with changes such as these. Schools in other large central cities have faced similar challenges during the past 2 decades (Borman & Spring, 1985).

Context, in that case, matters a great deal. In fact, many of the biggest problems facing urban education today may lie outside of the schools themselves. There is a growing body of research, moreover, suggesting that contextual factors such as neighborhood and student population characteristics affect school policy and organization (M. Fine, 1991; Oakes, 1985). Other studies have pointed to ways in which demographic and economic changes have affected school politics, contributing to the atmosphere of instability and crisis that has come to characterize urban education in the past several decades (Mirel 1993a, 1993b).

Cities have changed a great deal since Conant wrote *Slums and Suburbs*, and the problems of city schools have grown correspondingly more difficult. To comprehend the changes in urban education, one must look outside of the schools and beyond the usual definitions of educational research. In approaching the question of urban education from the standpoint of context, we hope to define a political economy of urban education. We believe that this is indispensable in identifying ways to improve research on the deepening crisis in city schools.

COMPREHENDING THE URBAN CONTEXT: CHANGING CONCEPTIONS OF CITY DEVELOPMENT

As suggested earlier, we submit that the first step in understanding urban education is to consider the social, political, and economic forces that shape cities themselves. Much of the crisis that has gripped city schools for the past several decades, after all, has paralleled a larger set of developments in many dimensions of urban life. It is an old but accurate commonplace that schooling is simply one of the myriad institutional activities that have been affected by the deterioration of central cities (Levine & Zipp, 1993). Put simply, many of the problems that plague big-city schools today stem from the predicament of the cities themselves.

But just how are we to interpret the problems of the city and its larger metropolitan context? Another reason for considering the larger urban scene concerns theory and research. The study of urban education has been influenced by analytical models drawn from the related fields of urban sociology, political science, and economics. Indeed, we suggest that identifying key trends in these fields is essential to understanding recent developments in the study of urban education policy. Just as it is important to consider the larger urban context in order to understand schools, it is also imperative to examine the literature on urban development to comprehend changes in educational research focused on city schools.

In the discussion that follows, we consider the major traditions that have guided inquiry and theory building in the urban disciplines over the past 70 years. There has been a good deal of change in the way scholars have pondered the city, and we believe this—in turn—has important implications for the course of educational research.

The Ecological Tradition

The dominant mode of research and deliberation about cities has been described as "ecological." The term was derived from biology, but long before its more contemporary use in conveying a concern for the natural environment. When used in connection with urban studies, the expression is intended to focus attention on ways in which the physical and social environments interact to produce certain types of behavior and to affect the growth of urban communities (Blau, 1977; Forrester, 1969; Sjoberg, 1965). Elements in the physical environment can include such obvious geographical attributes as lakes, rivers, and mountains as well as other natural resources that can aid the development of a community. Factors in the social environment consist of community characteristics such as population size, demographic composition, and institutional (organizational) development. And, of course, the advancement of productive (economic) activities is critical to community change and growth as well (Hauser, 1965).

In 1961, Otis Dudley Duncan gave specific shape to the ecological conception of urban development by identifying four primary dimensions of a city's "ecosystem": population (size and composition), organization (institution and status systems), environment (natural setting and resources), and technology (advances in productive activity). In analyzing the interaction of these elements, expressed with the acronym POET, Dudley proposed that social scientists could identify essential processes of urban development (Duncan, 1961).

The biological analogy in Duncan's scheme is quite characteristic of the ecological tradition in urban studies (Gettys, 1961). By postulating that features of environment (social as well as natural) shape human conduct, the ecological tradition opened a wide field for investigation (Schnore, 1961). At its base is a sweeping theory of social development. It employs a logic that is virtually Darwinian in its orientation and aspirations. The parallels with the logic of natural selection are clear. Certain behaviors are rational, after all, only in particular settings. And in this regard, given social and physical environments can be seen as acting, for practical purposes, to designate a certain range of outcomes. From the beginning, in that case, ecological thinking about cities has been marked by a potent variety of functional determinism. In its most extreme forms, this view holds that the existing array of social and economic structures makes given forms of conduct virtually inevitable. For individuals and social groups to behave otherwise would be tantamount to defying a law of nature (Thomlinson, 1969).

Perhaps the earliest and most influential proponents of the ecological perspective were the famous "Chicago School" sociologists, Robert E. Park, Ernest W. Burgess, Louis Wirth and their associates. Working in the 1920s and 1930s, these men and their students examined the ways in which competition and industrialization produced certain forms of behavior in cities and specific patterns of spatial organization (Gottdeiner, 1985; Sjoberg, 1965). Using central place theory and the idea of functional differentiation, constructs integral to the ecological framework, Burgess formulated his widely known zonal model of city growth and development. Neighborhood formation was subject to clearly defined patterns of urban expansion (Burgess, 1928). In the industrial cities of the early 20th century, transportation technology (railroads) dictated that productive activities be located in or near central locations, which meant that working-class districts lay near the center of the city (Schnore, 1965). More desirable residential areas lay on the out-skirts, a dramatic change from the "walking city" of the preindustrial era (Sjoberg, 1960). While alternative models of urban development existed (Harris & Ullman, 1945; Hoyt, 1939), Burgess's conception of the spatial organization of city life has exerted a profound influence.

The industrial city that the Chicago sociologists postulated was marked by a highly developed division of labor and a corresponding specialization in the spa-tial distribution of social activities (Schnore, 1965; Thompson, 1965). Vast areas of the city were dominated by particular social groups (this was the era of early ghettos described by Jacob Riis and other reformers), with profound cultural and political ramifications (Wirth, 1928; Zorbaugh, 1929). The resulting model of urban development is a familiar one to those accustomed to the large, diversified cities of the industrial Northeast and Upper Midwest. It is another question, how-ever, whether Burgess and his compatriots had discovered incontrovertible rules of urban growth (Alihan, 1938; London & Flanagan, 1979).

While Burgess was mapping the spatial organization of the city, Park and Wirth were busy cataloguing its sociocultural dimensions. In his famous essay, "Urbanism as a Way of Life," Wirth (1938) submitted that cities induce the break-down of traditional institutions and beliefs, substituting functional (or "sec-ondary") relationships for those of kinship and locale. These changes, Wirth argued, were the result of an extensive and complex division of labor and the rapid pace of change that characterized large scale urban development. Employing the logic of ecological reasoning, Wirth maintained that these changes were a function of city size; larger places inevitably manifested a higher degree of differentiation than smaller ones. In short, the larger the city, the greater the ero-sion of traditional conventions and the corresponding potential for social disloca-tion (Hauser, 1965). Urbanization, with its inevitably corrosive effect on familiar patterns of social behavior, lay at the root of a host of societal problems. Presented as a set of theorems for the new social science of human ecology, this was a per-spective that would have a telling influence on both research and public policy in decades to come (Thomlinson, 1969).

In the period following World War II the human ecology framework continued to dominate academic thinking about urban issues. Amos Hawley's seminal text, *Human Ecology: A Theory of Community Structure* (1950), expanded upon the ideas of the Chicago sociologists to articulate a comprehensive explanation of urban development premised on central place theory and the logic of differentia-tion and specialization endemic to labor processes under capitalism. A large body of empirical work emerged as a fresh generation of scholars examined the new urban forms of the post war United States. Using comprehensive, large scale data sets and statistical techniques unavailable to their predecessors, this enterprising group of ecologically minded researchers examined urban hierarchies, patterns of suburbanization and central city decline, and problems of racial change and inequality (Catanese, 1972; Forrester, 1969; Hauser, 1965; Taeuber and Taeuber,

1965; Thomlinson, 1969). Drawing upon a complex of related disciples in the social sciences, scholars such as Philip Hauser (1965), Leo Schnore (1965, 1972), Brian Berry (1965), and Duncan employed the functionalist logic of human ecology to explain the development of the urban crisis that burst into public view in the 1960s. While competing theories of spatial evolution were offered and anomalistic findings were often reported, the general thrust of this research continued to support a conception of urban development first articulated in the 1920s (Sjoberg, 1965).

The functionalist explanation of metropolitan development held that changes in transportation technology and the social division of labor were primary contributing factors to suburbanization and changing standards of living in central cities. The logic of these changes, however, extended directly from the scheme of spatial differentiation in Burgess's zonal hypothesis. Key productive activities clustered at central locations surrounded by service and working class residential districts, while higher status residential areas extended outward. As population density declined and transportation costs increased with distance from the center, social status rose (Jackson, 1975, 1985; Thompson, 1965). But it was in the city center, where densities were greatest and status differences were most extreme, that the effects of urban development were most telling (Bowden, 1975; Mayer 1965).

Following the tradition of observational and case study methodologies used by Park and his students, a host of studies examined the problems of inner-city communities. New theoretical perspectives were offered to account for the escalation of social problems in these areas and their seeming intractability. Perhaps the best known of these was Oscar Lewis's "culture of poverty" (Lewis, 1965, 1968), but a number of other explanatory frameworks were also proposed. In one of the most controversial works of the period, Edward Banfield (1968) presented a sweeping characterization of poor inner-city residents that highlighted the destructive, alienating, and dysfunctional sides of life in these areas. While Banfield's depiction was criticized as being excessively bleak, even callous, it was quite consistent with many of the elements of Wirth's characterization of the effects of urbanism nearly three decades earlier and with the culture of poverty perspective (Katz, 1993). At the center of the city, where the forces of concentration, differentiation, and contention exhibit their greatest weight, one could expect to find the most extreme distortions of traditional social behavior.

The structural, functionalist logic of the ecological tradition shaped most of the research on urban problems—including education—through most of the 1970s. Much of this work focused on the central city, and growing disparities in metropolitan regions, although there were studies of suburban communities as well (Farley, Schuman, Bianchi, Colasanto, & Hatchet, 1978; Frey, 1978; Guest, 1978; Guest & Zuiches, 1971; Hauser, 1977; Hawley & Zimmer, 1970; Popenoe, 1977; Taeuber, 1975). To one degree or another, research conducted in this tradition depicted central city problems as a natural consequence of the forces of urban development, which dictated that the poor and low status social groups would be clustered in central locations. To the extent that the process of urbanization resulted in even higher degrees of functional differentiation and specialization, with corresponding residential isolation, the problems they experienced appeared unavoidable. In one way or another, the people who lived in these areas were simply victims of seemingly inexorable laws of metropolitan growth (Berry, 1973; Hauser, 1965).

The "New" Urban Sociology

Over the past 2 decades, an alternative perspective has emerged in research and debate on urban development. Although it is difficult to characterize this body of work, its proponents have all started from the premise that the ecological model does not provide a complete explanation of the dynamics of city growth and change (Feagin & Parker, 1983; Gottdiener, 1985; Gottdiener & Feagin, 1988; Katznelson, 1992; Saunders, 1981; Walton, 1979, 1981). For many of these scholars, the missing element is politics, or the role of conflict between groups competing for power and prestige in the emerging urban social-spatial structure. In the ecological framework, this dimension of city life would be subsumed under Duncan's term "organization" (the "O" in POET), but critics of the ecological tradition hold that the question of power and influence is central to the entire process of urbanization (Feagin & Smith, 1987). Where ecologists see factors such as population size and technology creating firm structural parameters within which cities must develop, the new urban sociology suggests that economic and political relationships are even more important to determining the particular form of the urban system and the quality of life in its constituent parts (Feagin, 1988).

This distinctive view of urban development has exerted less influence on educational research than the ecological tradition. There are a variety of reasons for this. First, it does not represent a fully articulated theoretical position about cities and their growth (Gottdiener, 1985; Gottdiener & Feagin, 1988). Rather, it is the product of a series of important studies that have challenged the premises of ecological reasoning. As such, it represents a critique and an emerging research agenda rather than a mature explanatory framework for spatial and social organization. Second, unlike the ecological model, it has had the benefit of relatively little empirical elaboration. Only a few studies have explored themes suggested by the new urban sociology (see later discussion). And, finally, this alternative way of thinking about cities has emerged at a time when there has been less public and academic interest in cities and their problems. This has confined the debate over theoretical models to explain city growth to a relatively small group of scholars working in the various urban disciplines. Had the debate been somewhat wider, it is conceivable that the influence of this perspective could have been greater (Katznelson, 1992).

Two works stand as particularly important in specifying the break with human ecology that has defined the new urban sociology. Both represent a Marxist viewpoint, although they differ in the way in which this task is approached. The first was David Harvey's *Social Justice and the City* (1973), which argued that the question of spatial relationships must be considered in light of power and justice and not mechanical laws of development. Ultimately, Harvey maintains that cities have historically developed according to a capitalist logic, wherein the process of growth is dictated by the logic of capital investment and accumulation, particularly in real estate. In studying Baltimore and other cities, Harvey has suggested that patterns of urban development represent clear patterns of capital investment or "circulation" rather than benign laws of urban development. With this, the spatial organization of the city takes on an implicitly political character, representing the interests of different groups of capitalists. Harvey has further articulated this perspective in subsequent work (Harvey, 1989).

The second work, Manuel Castells's *The Urban Question: A Marxist Approach* (1977) was even more ambitious in scope. Noting that the spatial models developed by Burgess and other Americans fit only a limited range of settings, Castells recommended a different model of urban development based on cycles in the circulation of capital and labor power, basic categories of Marxist economic analysis. Although he addressed political dimensions of the process, Castells's early work represented a structuralist tradition in Marxist scholarship. In many respects, Castells simply recast the logic of ecological reasoning to capture a different set of economic laws shaping city growth. Like Harvey, however, he also pointed to the importance of examining basic class relations in assessing how cities evolve. In this respect, the influence of the Marxist position has been to suggest specific sets of political interests that historically have wielded influence over the spatial development of urban areas. This offered a new way of thinking about a host of questions.

Since the publication of these books, there has been a flurry of new works elaborating on the positions Harvey and Castells articulated, including new books of their own. Two sweeping syntheses of this literature have been provided by Mark Gottdiener (1985) and Ira Katznelson (1992). Although he is quite critical of both the ecological tradition and much of the new Marxist urban scholarship, Gottdiener calls for a theory of space that takes into view both the structural requirements of capitalism and the political questions of power and status that invest spatial relationships with social significance. Building on the work of other new urban scholars, Gottdiener expels central place theory and differentiation from their positions at the center of urban theory, and begins to explicate a new interpretation of urban growth premised on the idea that space is used to create authority and social standing (Gottdiener, 1985).

For his part, Katznelson (1992) is critical of this perspective but acknowledges the departure that such a politically conscious representation of spatial relationships signifies. Given the contributions of the new urban sociology, which have only been touched upon herein, it is no longer possible to view the spatial arrangement of urban structure as the result of impersonal "laws" of social development.

For better or worse, it seems, the urban is now political as well as economic. In an article published in 1988, Gottdiener and Feagin describe the new urban sociology as a "new paradigm" for understanding urban development, one that places the question of power and influence at the center of the research agenda. While Katznelson and other critics of the ecological perspective may not agree entirely with this characterization, there is a growing consensus on the need to give more attention to political dimensions of urban development. But this perspective is only beginning to be evident in research on urban education.

A few recent studies have explored the question of how power and influence affect the spatial organization of cities. Gottdiener (1977), Davita Glasberg (1989), and Edward Soja (1987) have each conducted studies of how real estate interests and banks actively intervene to shape the form of particular metropolitan areas. A path-breaking historical study by Arnold Hirsch (1983) examined ways in which real estate interests and local business and governmental elites conspired to affect the development of Chicago's Black community in the years following World War II. In more theoretically explicit works, Logan and Molotch (1987) and Feagin and Parker (1990) suggest that local real estate and investment capital interests dictate urban "growth" policies that are often contrary to the interests of local residents. Each of these studies is a valuable guide to determining new ways of exploring the political economy of cities and, with it, the political and economic forces that shape educational activities.

The new urban sociology represents a dramatic break with the ecological model that has dominated research and dialogue on cities for nearly 70 years. While it hardly repudiates all of the insights occasioned by the ecological framework—and these have been considerable—it does represent a rather distinctive outlook on the process of urban development. What binds this group of studies together most clearly is an interest in power and the ways in which it shapes urban development. Interestingly, the new urban sociologists have not devoted much attention to conventional political processes and, with a few exceptions, generally do not assign the state a major role in urban development (Logan & Molotch, 1987). These questions remain the province of political scientists. But the new urban sociology is beginning to change essential ideas about cities and their development that have influenced a variety of disciplinary traditions. In the discussion to follow, we turn to considering how these old and new conceptions of cities and their evolution have shaped research on urban schooling.

Understanding Urban Education: The Ecological Tradition

Given the importance of the ecological perspective in scholarship on city growth and development, it is little wonder that much of the research on urban education has been shaped by its cardinal propositions. For several decades, a good deal of educational research simply picked up where urban sociology and economics left off: with metropolitan systems that have been spatially structured by a logic of differentiation and outward expansion from a central core. Certain features of urban educational systems flow organically from these conditions, and they have been the topics of a great deal of inquiry: the deteriorating quality of inner city schools (and the superior state of suburban schools), the changing tax base of urban school districts, problems of racial or ethnic isolation in inner city schools, questions of teacher recruitment and retention, and behavioral matters such as student subcultures and related issues of violence and crime.

To the extent that the urban environments that engendered these aspects of city schools are seen as naturally occurring phenomena, the ecological tradition in urban education offers a useful analysis of essential problems in city schools. As long as schools are shaped by their immediate social context and laws of metropolitan development dictate deep, spatially defined inequalities, schools in central cities face immense disadvantages in the competition for status and resources (Havighurst, 1966).

The ecological perspective has appeared in relatively few historical studies of urban education. Kaestle and Vinovskis (1979) and Field (1976) have debated the impact of urbanization on schooling practices in 19th-century Massachusetts. Rury (1984, 1989, 1991) has examined interurban differences in school participation and curricular development, employing such basic ecological concepts as city function and regional differentiation to explain the development of certain features of American city schools in the 20th century. As Vinovskis (1985) has noted, even studies of school attendance in the past have been insensitive to spatial dimensions of urban development. In this regard, the history of urban schooling has not achieved the theoretical sophistication of Olivier Zunz's pioneering work on Detroit (1983), which meticulously examined the manner in which social classes were distributed across the city's physical space. Angus (1992) has provided an excellent summary of the ecological model and the influence it has exerted on educational historians.

The ecological tradition, with its emphasis on spatial organization, was probably most influential in sociological studies of education. Much of this research, after all, has been concerned with identifying and assessing inequality. And few features of the modern urban landscape are more evident than the territorial distribution of wealth. As noted earlier, the ecological model of urban development holds that socioeconomic status is directly related to spatial proximity to the city center. With the exception of the immediate center and certain affluent inner city enclaves, status generally rises with distance to the metropolitan periphery (Schnore, 1965). The inequities that result may be aggravated by racial discrimination, but they are rooted in the more basic economic relationships.

The implications of these patterns of metropolitan development have been a theme in educational research since James Bryant Conant's *Slums and Suburbs* (1961). Even as he lamented the sharp differences in educational funding between inner-city and suburban communities, Conant argued that schools in these areas should prepare students for different occupational roles. Accepting the apparent division of labor between these areas, he proposed development of vocational education in the central city and college prepatory curricula in the affluent suburbs.

Other scholars were less prescriptive. Robert Havighurst led the way in documenting differences in educational resources and outcomes across metropolitan areas in a number of studies (Burkhead, 1967; Goldberg, 1963; Havighurst, 1961; D. Levine & Havighurst 1968). While favoring measures to ameliorate the most dramatic differences in educational provision, Havighurst (1971) and other ecologically minded investigators (A. K. Campbell & Meranto, 1967; Cohen, 1968; Derr, 1967; Glatt & Roaden, 1967) did not challenge the underlying premise that much of the observed inequality in schooling was an outgrowth of a naturally occurring process of urbanization. If some measure of inequality was inevitable, after all, it was logical to expect it to conform to well established patterns of spatial differentiation (Havighurst, 1966).

The implications of this assessment extend to the analysis of behavior in central city schools. If the schoolchildren of the city are problematic, it is because they exhibit the behavioral characteristics that Louis Wirth and other ecologically minded students of the urban scene had identified earlier (Riessman, 1962). In his influential book, Conant (1961) introduced the ecological concept of "social cohesion," arguing that schools in big cities exhibit fewer shared values and social norms than those in smaller communities. The effect of this on education, Conant suggested, was profound, because it shaped both the attitudes of the community toward schooling and the ways schools were viewed by families and students. Such observations echoed Wirth's contention that large cities contributed to the breakdown of traditional social mores and contributed to the development of highly rationalistic or even pathological patterns of behavior. After quoting Wirth at length, one textbook survey of urban education issues in the early 1970s (Hummel & Nagle, 1973) characterized poor inner city schoolchildren in terms that reflected this perspective, quoting the words of a "big-city school superintendent."

A victim of his environment, the ghetto child begins his school career psychologically, socially, and physically disadvantaged. He is oriented to the present rather than the future, to immediate needs rather than delayed gratification, to the concrete rather than the abstract. He is often handicapped by limited verbal skills, low self-esteem, and a stunted drive toward achievement; by sight, hearing and dental deficiencies, by hernias, malnutrition and anemia. (p. 116)

The ecological reasoning in the foregoing is apparent in the opening phrase, which declares that inner city children are victims of their setting (and, by implication, not the political or economic interests that may have shaped it). The attributes that follow, seemingly derived from Wirth, Banfield, and other commentators in the ecological tradition, correspond to the frenetic, unstable, highly competitive and conflict-ridden environment of the densely populated and economically insulated central city. Children raised in these surroundings were labeled "deprived" or "disadvantaged," not because of a personal or moral fault but because of their circumstances (Goldberg, 1963; Shepard, 1969). Having the misfortune to live in the wrong spatial zone of the metropolitan system, these children were depicted as requiring special educational interventions (Passow, 1963; Reismann, 1962).

There is more to school problems, of course, than the characteristics of students. An important theme in the ecological discourse on urban education has been the dilemma of resource inequality, a matter closely related to the spatial distribution of poverty. This was a key point in Conant's study (1961), and other accounts expanded upon his insights. By the end of the 1960s it was commonplace to observe that central city schools were poorly funded in comparison with their suburban counterparts (even if big-city schools did compare favorably with national standards in support for public education) (Campbell, 1969; Sacks, 1972; Wise, 1968).

The reasons for this were manifold, but all were related to the spatial dynamics of urban growth. The most basic factors could be described as structural, because they stemmed from essential demographic and economic characteristics of the metropolitan system. Because of the higher density and incidence of indigence and crime in central city communities, for instance, demands for a variety of public services were greater. This led to higher rates of taxation but a lower level of support for public education, the schools being forced to compete with other agencies for public support. Thus, even though taxes were lower in the suburbs, larger amounts could be lavished on the schools there (Cohen, 1969).

The second set of factors was historical and tied to the outward progression of urban expansion. As the central cities stopped growing, construction of new homes and businesses shifted to the suburbs. This meant that assessed values dropped in the cities, and other sources of revenue, such as business and sales taxes, also leveled off or even dropped in relative terms. Thus, precisely at the point at which additional funding was needed to expand programs to stay abreast of educational advances elsewhere, big-city schools were losing ground to the suburbs (Hummel & Nagle, 1973, Ch. 7). As the process of urbanization drew middle class residents out of the city, the tax base eroded further.

These inequities were observed to have contributed to the inability of large urban school districts to improve their aging physical plants (Campbell, 1969; Cohen, 1968) and to higher student-teacher ratios in city schools (Usdan, 1967), among other difficulties. The dilemma, however, lay in the fact that these problems were often presented as being the by-product of the process of city growth itself. To a very large extent, in that case, they were quite natural—or at least blameless—and were often depicted as virtually intractable. The ecologically minded research of the time held out few prospects for change. Indeed, many commentators predicted that the logic of metropolitan development dictated even bigger problems in decades to come (Hummel & Nagle, 1973).

When change in urban education did become an object of discussion, it was often the focal point of a carefully proposed policy intervention. David K. Cohen (1968), for instance, weighed the advantages of integration and compensatory education strategies for inner city schools, favoring the former as likely to produce the best long-term outcomes (but admitting that such a solution seemed unlikely). In a book-length treatment, Martin Katzman (1971) considered a variety of factors in what was, for the time, a sophisticated analysis of educational performance in inner-city schools, and he made specific recommendations for improving the quality of instruction in such settings. Other researchers proposed a variety of interventions, such as "educational parks" (to protect the school from the urban environment) and special programs to boost Black achievement (U.S. Civil Rights Commission, 1967, Appendixes D 2.3 and D 2.4). Havighurst (1961) suggested that better metropolitan planning techniques could lead to higher degrees of educational equity.

These proposals, and the analyses that spawned them, often seemed to reduce the problems of inner-city children and their local institutions to technical issues in school organization or instructional delivery. Such approaches were, in part, a corollary of the ecological framework, which postulates that the structure of an urban system is subject to technical intervention. Taken to an extreme, education could be seen as simply one additional element of the urban environment that could be remedied with the appropriate policies and technical instrumentalities, however limited they may be (Cohen, 1968).

Also related to the ecological tradition in urban educational research were studies that treated urban schools as native sites for observation of the condition of inner-city children, a tradition that extends back to the discovery and detailed description of largely Black inner-city schools in the 1960s. Employing methods similar to those of Park and Wirth, most of the earliest such studies treated these settings and the behavior that occurred in them as a spontaneous, natural phenomenon, a product of the social forces at play in the central city. These books were animated by a thinly veiled sense of moral indignation at the conditions in these schools, placing much of the blame on educational bureaucracies, but they also depicted the children as victims of the larger urban environment. New York City was a center for such research, and studies of ghetto life by Sexton (1965) and Greene and Ryan (1965) were quite influential.

Other studies focused on the schools, documenting their failure to address the problems of inner-city children. Peter Schrag's 1967 study of the Boston schools was an influential example of this approach; even though Schrag tried to emphasize political questions, the thrust of the book is one of contrasting conditions in schools located in different types of neighborhoods. It was Kozol's 1967 account of his experiences as a teacher in the Boston schools, however, that popularized this type of research and associated perceptions of inner-city communities and their schools. In addition to Kozol, other generally descriptive studies appeared, taking stock of the central city and its schools as a distinctive but nonetheless natural environment for observation and reflection (Kohl, 1967).

The ecological interpretation of problems in urban education has contributed a great deal to our understanding of city schools. It accepted, however, the prevailing spatial structure of inequality in metropolitan areas as a natural product of urbanization, and it adopted many of the assumptions of earlier researchers about the behavior of inner city residents. What research in this tradition tended to overlook or to slight, on the other hand, were the political relationships that have helped to fashion the existing spatial structure of urban education and to enforce its boundaries. Before moving on to more recent studies that have examined the political and economic dimensions of urban education together, it is necessary to consider the question of the politics of urban education.

THE POLITICS OF EDUCATION: HISTORICAL AND CONTEMPORARY PERSPECTIVES

The politics of education is a relatively new field of study. Traditionally, it has been linked to studies of school organization and the functional workings of bureaucratic organizations (Wong, 1991). As we will discuss in greater detail later, for much of the 20th century school systems have been considered to be relatively autonomous political entities, sheltered from partisan politics by professionally defined administrative prerogatives. Furthermore, they also have been viewed as agencies with relatively few mechanisms for political power to be exerted from outside of the organization (Peterson, 1974; Wong, 1993). In effect, they were the political equivalent of largely autonomous nation-states, entities with sovereign power to determine their own destiny. Consequently, much research in this area dealt with questions of resource allocation within and between districts, but without carefully focusing on political interests that may have affected their behavior as a key point of analysis. Peterson's 1976 study of school politics in Chicago represented a turning point in this respect. Its publication exemplified a wave of new studies examining ways in which interest groups shaped school policies and practices or, as Peterson put it, "policy outputs" (Boyd, 1975; Peterson, 1974, p. 348; Wong, 1990). Not all of this work has had an explicitly urban framework, and relatively little research has been conceived to address spatial dimensions of urban organization. But recent work in the politics of education is a critical element in comprehending the political economy of city schools.

Another group of scholars who have examined the politics of education, of course, is the historians. Even though the history of education is rarely considered a branch of political history, a significant number of educational historians have focused on explicitly political questions in their work. Indeed, Wong (1992) and others have indicated that historical studies of education have shaped much of the current field of political studies in education. A logical place to begin a review of the politics of education, in that case, is with the field of educational history.

Historians, Cities and the Politics of Schooling

Educational historians have been among the most enthusiastic researchers of the politics of urban education. Since at least the early 1960s, numerous historians have tried to shed light on contemporary problems afflicting urban schools by examining important political events, trends, and controversies in the past (e.g., see Callahan, 1962; Cremin, 1961; Katz, 1968; Tyack, 1974). This relentless search for what one group of historians has called "the roots of crisis" has produced a remarkably rich body of literature, inspired lively historiographic debates, and influenced the way scholars in such fields as economics, sociology and political science view urban public education (Karier, Violas, & Spring, 1973). This scholarly tradition has been particularly effective in identifying the development and clash of interest groups, tracing the formation and fragmentation of coalitions, and assessing the apparent consequences of specific victories and defeats on educational policy and practice.

However, educational historians and the many scholars in the other fields who draw on historical studies have generally paid scant attention to several elements vital to a fuller understanding of urban educational politics both in the past and present. First, most of these scholars focus almost exclusively on the actions of elites and their effect on state entities, particularly school districts. Popular behavior, when it is recognized at all, usually appears only in occasional analyses of elections. The responses of parents and students to political changes wrought by elites are almost always assumed rather than demonstrated. Second, most of these scholars use the term *politics* in a broad, general fashion, usually referring to the actions of such interest groups as business or union leaders and their effect on state-determined school policies. Rarely do they define or even consider educational politics defined more traditionally, for example, as influenced by partisan (party-based) politics, which often have involved the mobilization of large popular constituencies (Kleppner, 1985). Third, and perhaps most important from the standpoint of comprehending urban education, most of these studies ignore the spatial dimension of urban politics and the ways in which competing interest groups are tied to specific structural aspects of city life.

These three tendencies have given studies of urban educational politics an existence separate from larger questions of context, one that enables them to accommodate various theoretical perspectives but weakens their explanatory power when applied to actual urban situations, especially current situations. Nevertheless, in recent years, some historians and political scientists have tried to broaden their perspective and weave into their studies other factors—such as popular movements, partisan politics, and spatial relations—in order to provide a more comprehensive vision of the development of urban educational politics and urban education.

Educational Historians and Urban Politics: Where the Elites Meet

In one of the most widely quoted statements from his classic work *The Transformation of the School*, Lawrence Cremin (1961) declared that "progressive education began as part of a vast humanitarian effort to apply the promise of American life—the ideal of government by, of, and for the people. . . .

[Progressive education was] the educational phase of American progressivism writ large" (p. viii). Cremin thus linked political and educational reform more explicitly than had any previous historian. Moreover, he presented a compelling argument that, at the turn of the century, political and social reformers joined with educators to change the course of both American life and education. Because political and educational progressivism were primarily urban phenomena, Cremin's work also implicitly encouraged scholars to examine city schools at precisely the time when the nation was awakening to a host of serious and complex urban problems. Demanding that scholars expand their research beyond schools to a host of other social institutions and forces in explaining the evolution of these problems, Cremin set educational researchers on a fruitful, new course (see also Cremin, 1965, 1988).

While Cremin, who was primarily interested in the intellectual underpinnings of political and educational movements, realized only part of his quest for a more expansive understanding of American education, his work inspired a new generation of scholars to explore the relationship between politics and educational reform in American cities. In the process, however, many of these scholars, challenged Cremin's broad-based view of educational reform. In a series of influential works, they focused on formal control of schools through the authority of the state. For scholars focusing on the 19th century, this entailed consideration of a wide assortment of issues, ranging from the development of bureaucratic instrumentalities of control to mechanisms for exerting influence over school policies. (Kaestle, 1973; Lazerson, 1970; Schultz, 1973) Others examined how social and business elites joined together in political campaigns to take control of urban school systems during the 19th and early 20th centuries. Influenced by Marxist and anarchist writings, these scholars maintained that school reformers were not motivated by "humanitarian" sentiments. Rather, they argued that these elite reformers sought control of state institutions in order to link public education more directly to the shifting needs of American capitalism (Karier et al., 1973; Katz, 1968, 1972; Spring, 1972; Violas, 1978).

In many respects this shift in emphasis reflected a debates along a similar dimension of political analysis in the study of urban government. In the 1940s and 1950s Hunter (1953) and others suggested that elite organizations exercised considerable autonomy in exerting control over local state institutions. This view was challenged by Dahl (1961) and his students, who argued that political conflict in cities was pluralistic in quality. Cremin's early pluralistic orientation notwithstanding, scholarship in the history of urban education appears to have followed somewhat the same trajectory. The earliest studies of urban schooling focused on the behavior and influence of social and economic elites and their organizations.

Perhaps the clearest example of this interpretation can be found in the work of Bowles and Gintis, two economists who drew heavily on studies by educational historians in fashioning a comprehensive critique of American public schools (Bowles & Gintis, 1976). Noting that the most important periods of educational reform coincided with periods of dramatic change in the development of capitalism, Bowles and Gintis saw educational politics primarily as an arena in which social and economic elites use the power of the state to shape schools to meet the demands of the changing American economy. Thus, they depicted campaigns for progressive educational reform in major cities merely as elite-inspired political movements to bring schools into line with the growing needs of corporate capitalism.

Bowles and Gintis argued that the first step in transforming the schools along these lines was for the reformers to take control of urban school boards, instruments of state authority in determining school policy. Thus, Bowles and Gintis saw Progressive Era political campaigns "to take schools out of politics" and end corruption largely as ploys by elite reformers to break the power of ethnic and working-class communities that controlled urban boards in the early 20th century and take over urban school systems themselves. By shifting the basis of school board elections from wards to the city at large and by drastically reducing the size of the boards (key mechanisms, according to reformers, for reducing corruption and political manipulation), these reformers ushered in a massive governance change in urban education. By 1920, practically every major American city had implemented these types of changes, which virtually ensured that people sharing the points of views of the reformers would win school board elections. In 1916, according to Scott Nearing, these political reforms had been so successful that nearly 45% of the members of a sample of 104 urban school boards were businessmen, 34% were professionals, and only 9% were workers. Once in power, these elite-dominated boards then centralized school systems and introduced a series of programmatic and curricular reforms (ranging from the introduction of IQ tests to the expansion of vocational education) whose ultimate effect, Bowles and Gintis argue, was to make schools adjuncts of the capitalist system and agencies for the reproduction of social and economic inequality (Bowles & Gintis, 1976, pp. 187–200).

In order to solidify these curricular and programmatic changes, the new boards and their educational allies (what David Tyack has termed "the interlocking directorate of urban elites") strengthened the power of educational professionals and the bureaucracies they controlled (Tyack, 1974, p. 7). As Tyack notes, these new school organizations succeeded in taking schools out of conventional partisan politics to such an extent that they became almost as impervious to public demands as the large corporations on which they were modeled. There can be little doubt that the highly centralized, state-sponsored, and authoritative school system that came to exist in most of the nation's largest systems represented a distinctive era in the history of urban education (Mirel, 1990, Rury, 1993). To the extent that elites came to dominate these forms of school organization, the decisions of historians to focus so closely on them may have been justified. But even at the height of elite power in the history of urban schools, the politics of education entailed more than simple control from above.

These initial studies of urban educational politics had a profound impact on how scholars, policy analysts, and policymakers viewed the problems of urban education and their potential solutions. Indeed, many of the current reform efforts, ranging from the creation of elected local school councils (something of a return to ward-based control of schools), to the slashing of central school bureaucracies (to break the power of entrenched educational professionals), to campaigns for educational vouchers and choice (to extend power to parents over professional educators) often rest their claims on the studies cited earlier (e.g., see Chubb & Moe, 1990; Katz 1992).

Yet some critics found major problems with these influential studies and focused new attention on aspects of urban education that went unacknowledged in their treatment of educational politics (Ravitch, 1978). These lacunae were due in part to the fact that most of these studies concentrated almost exclusively on the activities of elites. In addition, much of this research seemed to rely on a form of economic determinism that saw the development of American capitalism as closely linked to the state and used overt political control to determine the direction of educational change. As a consequence, such studies often overlooked the dynamic and dialectical nature of educational politics, neglected the role of political partisanship in shaping educational controversies or issues, and assumed that success in the political struggles for control of state institutions was automatically and precisely translated into policy and practice (Peterson, 1985). In addition, they ignored spatial dimensions of urban educational politics, writing as if schools were abstract institutions existing in an immaterial world (Angus, 1992).

In her 1974 study of the New York City schools, Diane Ravitch presented a somewhat less deterministic view of educational politics, one in which diverse groups played leading roles. While she devoted considerable attention to the actions of elite New Yorkers, her work also explored how major immigrant and minority groups (primarily the Irish, Jews, African Americans, and Puerto Ricans) resisted and reshaped educational initiatives that they believed were contrary to their interests. Rather than seeing the politics of urban education as a record of elite imposition through the state, Ravitch described the development of the New York schools as a series of compromises between opposing interest groups. Consequently, Ravitch argued, public schools historically have provided an effective vehicle for entry into American society and participation in governance for numerous groups (Ravitch, 1974).

In the mid-1980s, historically minded social scientists added credence to this perspective in two studies of educational politics in Atlanta, Chicago, and San Francisco (Katznelson & Weir, 1985; Peterson, 1985; Wrigley, 1982). Katznelson and Weir specifically chastise previous researchers in the history and politics of urban education for their narrow focus on elite action. "We take issue," they write, "with the disappearance of the working class from educational analyses and the glib dismissals of education from the agendas of democratic and egalitarian movements and aspirations" (p. 14). Peterson and his collaborators viewed the process of educational change in even more dynamic terms, with competing status groups vying for power over educational policy in these cities. While both of these works came under criticism from historians for matters of evidence and interpretation, they represented a sharp break with the perspective of earlier studies.

Although Peterson and Katznelson and Weir do differ over conclusions, they nevertheless present a strikingly similar picture of the politics of state authority in urban education as contested terrain in which neither elite interest groups nor the working class organizations that challenged them continuously had the upper hand. Other researchers have added to this perspective by identifying a variety of other interest groups including women's organizations, left-wing political groups, ethnic associations, and civil rights organizations that have had an important impact on urban educational politics and policy (Anderson & Pickering, 1986; Hogan, 1985; Raftery, 1992; Reese, 1986) From this perspective, schools are not simply state-sponsored mechanisms of elite domination. Rather, they represent an institutional arena in which various interests compete for power and influence.

Katznelson and Weir go further than any of these scholars in seeking the underlying political causes of current urban educational problems. They maintain that, in the 1930s, the working class organizations (specifically organized labor) that had been the major champion of equal educational opportunity began to withdraw from partisan educational politics, thus allowing educational professionals and their elite allies to complete the takeover of state-run urban education that began in the Progressive Era. In essence, Katznelson and Weir shift the timing from the 1920s to 1940s or 1950s for when Tyack's "interlocking directorate of urban elites" really assumed power through the state over these systems. Only after that takeover was complete could professional educators and their allies pursue with impunity the policies that may have contributed to the conflicts in urban education during the 1960s and after.

It is worth noting, however, that neither Tyack, Lowe, and Hansot's (1984) study of education in the 1930s nor Mirel's (1993a) examination of educational politics in Detroit (one that devotes considerable attention to the role of organized labor in the Depression, war, and postwar years) found substantial evidence of the trends that Katznelson and Weir posit. Moreover, other scholars such as economists Carnoy and Levin speculate that, during the 1930s and 1940s, organized labor became increasingly involved in partisan educational politics and used its newfound power to enhance educational opportunities for disadvantaged students (Carnoy & Levin, 1985).

Despite such criticism, these studies have unquestionably provided a much fuller picture of the politics of state authority in urban education than previous works. However, many of them rest on two questionable assumptions about the nature of this dimension of educational politics in big cities. First, all of them seem to assume that issues defined by national and regional political organizations, formal parties, and related organizations had little or no bearing on the politics of urban education. This is particularly surprising because some of the most important recent work on the history and politics of urban education has been done by political scientists, scholars who ought to be particularly sensitive to such influences (Katznelson & Weir, 1985; Peterson, 1985). For instance, the relationship between city schools and state governments, which generated fierce partisan controversies as far back as the 1930s and 1940s, has rarely been explored (Mirel, 1993a).

One reason for this assumption of political autonomy is that many of these historical studies focused on cities during the pre–World War II years when strong local economies ensured that cities did not need to confront state government over such issues as state school aid. However, since the 1950s, state aid and state politics have become increasingly important to the fiscal health of urban public schools. Another reason, certainly, for this neglect of the larger context of partisan politics is the fact that much of this research has been done on such one-party towns as Atlanta, New York, and Chicago, where battles between the major political parties for control of state agencies such as schools were often inconsequential (Katnelson & Weir, 1985; Peterson, 1985).

In the end, many of these scholars seem to believe that progressive reformers actually succeeded in "taking the schools out of politics," at least eventually. They accept the idea of school contests without opposing political parties at face value without recognizing that even such nonpartisan contests can provide vehicles for the clash of ideas often linked to larger partisan agendas on the federal or state level of government. Such assumptions, of course, make it very difficult to recognize the importance of geography in political struggles for state control of city schools or, more precisely, the social production of urban space, both within cities and within states (Gottdiener, 1985). Indeed, only a few scholars have even addressed the topic of geography, and then in just a few select instances (Angus, 1992).

Place and Race in Urban Educational Politics

Unlike the larger field of urban studies, ecological interpretations of educational politics have been rare. Moreover, even when education scholars take spatial considerations into account, they are rarely guided explicitly by theory; rather, they more often use an ecological framework to address questions of location. Educational historians are fairly typical in this regard. Certainly the most widely known historical discussion of the importance of geography (or space) as a variable in educational politics focuses on an election in Beverly, Massachusetts, in 1861 and the intense interpretive debate about the meaning of that election (Katz & Vinovskis, 1987). Katz (1968) saw the outcome of that election in which working-class voters rejected an elite-sponsored proposal to maintain a high school, as a rebellion against educational "reform by imposition." In his analysis, Katz explicitly rejected a geographic interpretation of the electoral results, arguing instead that class conflict linked to tensions over industrialization and urbanization led to the rejection of Beverly High School by most voters (p. 79). This analysis became one of the leading sources of evidence for the left-wing critique of American education cited earlier. However, in his reinterpretation of the Beverly election using more sophisticated statistical techniques, Vinovskis (1985) argued that geography played a larger role than class in explaining the outcome, with voters indicating their disapproval of the educational priorities of high school promoters and their fears about the consolidation and centralization of school power (pp. 104–105).

Despite the obvious importance of geography to many highly charged issues in educational politics (including consolidating school districts, locating new schools, and changing attendance boundaries), few educational researchers have systematically explored this variable. Vinovskis continued to examine geography and region in work on Essex County in the 19th century, but few others have followed his lead (1995). One of the few studies that examined the spatial dimension of 20th century urban education politics was David Angus's study of progressive reform in Grand Rapids, Michigan (1982). Angus analyzed a series of elite led campaigns to approve bonds to build a vocational high school in the city. All of these efforts failed at the ballot box, with clear opposition coming from working-class wards. However, Angus found that in the working-class ward in which the high school was to be located and in the working-class wards on the streetcar lines that would have made the proposed school easily accessible to students, geography rather than class was the best predictor of the electoral outcomes, with some working-class voters seeming to support the high school on the belief that it would be useful for their children. In other words, by considering geography, Angus was able to provide a more complex analysis that includes a glimpse into family strategies for coping with changing economic and educational conditions (see also Angus, 1992).

The one area in which analyses of educational politics and geography readily can be found is in studies of segregation and its effects on education. Although we deal with desegregation research in greater detail later, questions of race have figured prominently in scholarship on the politics of education in recent years. Many of these works focus on Chicago, whose White political leaders (at times in league with Black politicians) have supported a policy of racial segregation in housing and schools for most of this century (Grimshaw, 1992; Lemann 1991; Rivlin 1992). Michael Homel (1984) has demonstrated how, by the 1930s, Chicago's political and educational elite had deliberately transformed a fairly integrated school system into one that blatantly segregated students by race. Paul Peterson (1976) specifically focused on how the Chicago Board of Education maintained that segregated system and thus perpetuated residential segregation throughout the city.

Other studies focused on political conflict and partisan politics around questions of race and education. Anderson and Pickering (1986) examine the efforts by civil rights organizations in the 1950s and 1960s to gain both open housing and school integration in Chicago and the means used by such political leaders as Mayor Richard J. Daley to effectively thwart those efforts. By the mid-1970s, the system of racial segregation in both housing and schools had become vital to maintaining the power of the Democratic machine in the city, and consequently these issues became flashpoints for intensifying political conflicts well into the 1980s (Kleppner, 1985). Such analyses are common in other cities as well and at times have played a significant role in desegregation cases (Armor, 1995; Orfield, 1978).

By far the most important recent development linking race, politics, and geography is the relationship between predominantly Black cities and predominantly White suburbs. Again, we also examine this question in connection with desegregation issues, but here we consider its political implications, which are significant indeed. Since the 1960s, middle-class Whites have been leaving major cities in large numbers, and by 1990 more Americans lived in suburbs than in central cities (Edsall and Edsall, 1991; Massey & Denton, 1993). The relationship between cities and suburbs brings together a number of previously neglected topics in education literature, namely spatial relations and partisan politics.

In the 1970s and 1980s, some political scientists interested in education believed that cities were entering a new era with declining middle-class populations and increasing numbers of poor and minority residents. As early as 1976, for example, Peterson noted the looming educational problems that were facing cities that "have lost . . . their virtual monopolistic control over land use in the surrounding region," a development that had severe consequences for urban school funding (p. 250). Declining tax revenues and the increasing demand for city service that these developments engender have forced cities to repeatedly turn to state governments for aid at precisely the time when shrinking urban populations translates into less political power on the state level. Katznelson and Weir (1985) described a situation of increasingly political, social, and economic isolation for cities that was making the goal of equal educational opportunity for urban students an elusive one.

During the 1980s, these developments were compounded by three other trends. First, state budgets were becoming tighter as the federal government shifted larger and larger shares of Medicaid and welfare burdens to the states. Schools that had often occupied a prominent (if not favored) position in state budget deliberations suddenly found themselves competing bitterly with other institutions such as homes for the aged, hospitals, and prisons for scarce resources (Timar, 1992). Second, the demographic trends that created majority White suburbs and predominantly minority cities were increasingly translating not only into racial and economic segregation but into partisan political divisions as well (Edsall & Edsall, 1991). As a result of a variety of developments, including reapportionment and redistricting, cities became bastions of Democratic power, and suburbs became the main source of strength for the Republicans. In that situation, as populations shifted in favor of suburbs, power and influence also began to flow from

Democrats to Republicans in many state governments. Consequently, cities faced increasingly difficult battles for additional state funding and support for dealing with their spiraling social and economic problems (Edsall & Edsall, 1991). Since the mid-1970s, educational politics have been in transition from a long period in which politicians from both parties often agreed in principle on educational issues (although still fighting intensely over means and other questions) to a situation in which issues are dividing people clearly along partisan lines. By the late 1980s, school choice, school prayer, state aid, property tax relief, state-mandated standards, school accountability, and bilingual education were just some of the issues that had become sources of fierce partisan conflict in many states. City schools were deeply involved in all of these controversies, usually on the opposite side of politicians from suburban and rural legislative districts (Mirel, 1993a, 1993b).

In all, the national mood of distrust of larger government, opposition to increased taxes (especially redistributive taxes on the federal and state levels), and the growing political power of suburbs could not have come at a worse time for urban public education. Faced with increasing social and educational problems and decreased political power and resources, city schools appear to be entering one of the most crisis filled periods in their long, tumultuous history. Making this situation even more complicated is the fact that race and related issues are at the heart of many of these developments.

RACE AND EDUCATION: ELEMENTS OF A POLITICAL ECONOMY

As suggestive earlier, race has become a major factor in virtually all areas of American life (Omi & Winant, 1994). For better or worse, however, the question of race has become incontrovertibly tied to urban education. As big city school districts have lost White students and the majority of those who remain are Black, Hispanic, or members of other ethnic minority groups, issues in urban education have increasingly revolved around matters of race and ethnicity. As we have seen, these issues have loomed large in the politics of urban education. And they have been important topics in the ecological tradition of educational research as well.

Perhaps because it provides researchers with a discrete and conspicuous focal point, or because the associated patterns of inequality are so dramatic and the related conflicts so important, the question of race has been a topic of great interest to educational researchers. What is more, however, much of the very best research in recent years has examined problems related to race and associated inequalities. It is within this research tradition that we can begin to identify a number of models for a political economy of urban education.

Historians, Race, and the City

There is a small but important body of historical research on the question of race in urban education. Unlike other studies of urban educational history, these works feature a strong spatial element. One of the central themes in the history of African Americans in cities, after all, is geographic segregation. This invariably becomes a major question in historical studies of Black education. As with studies of particular urban Black communities (Grossman, 1989; Kusmer, 1976; Osofsky, 1963; Spear, 1967), most research on the historical development of Black education in cities has taken the form of case studies, although there are exceptions (Tyack, 1974). Working in this vein, Franklin (1979) has examined the evolution of Black education in Philadelphia and Mohraz (1979) has compared its development in Memphis, San Francisco and Chicago. As noted earlier, Homel (1984) has also examined Chicago.

These studies point to a common pattern that began to emerge in the middle of the 20th century in the large industrial cities of the Northeast and Midwest. Regardless of the history of formal segregation in a particular school district, residential segregation becomes more pronounced as the city's Black population grows and segregated schools become the norm. Homel's study of Chicago (1984) is the clearest in this regard. Homel documented the declining quality of education for the city's African American population in the period between the First and Second World Wars. As Black schools became progressively more isolated, socially and geographically, such tangible indices of quality as books, student-teacher ratios, and building maintenance deteriorated dramatically. Other studies document similar changes elsewhere (Franklin, 1979).

Because African Americans represent a clear political interest group, historians have been able to examine questions of political influence on Black education as well. African American leaders campaigned tirelessly for more resources for schools, only to have their ambitions for equity thwarted by local school officials (Homel, 1984; Mohraz, 1979). Again, this was a common pattern in American cities prior to the Second World War (and the civil rights movement that followed it). There were important regional variations on this, of course, with Blacks in Southern cities being required to lobby for change in somewhat different ways (Homel, 1990). In all cases, however, African American communities found themselves pitted against predominantly White school authorities who resisted efforts to make urban public schooling equitable.

Historical studies of African American education have been able to combine the study of social-spatial dimensions of urban life with consideration of the political environment. As noted earlier, this is considerably more manageable when dealing with a particular group, especially one as conspicuously segregated as American Blacks. Still, this body of research provides a rich example of what is possible in attempting a comprehensive study of urban education.

Desegregation Research: Debates Over Causes and Consequences

There can be little doubt that the topic connected to urban education that has received the most attention over the past several decades has been school desegregation. In many respects, the question of desegregation embraces all of the elements of a political economy of urban schooling, including the spatial dynamics of community development and related matters in education. Research on desegregation has been so problem focused, however, and associated with the litigation of a wide array of federal antidiscrimination cases that it has become somewhat insulated from mainstream scholarship in education (Hawley, Rossell, & Crain, 1983; Prager, Longshore, & Seeman, 1986). Here, too, the focus in much research has been restricted to questions of the state intervention, usually expressed by federal courts. Consequently, desegregation has become something of a self-contained world of scholars pursuing similar problems in different settings and debating a rather limited range of technical questions of state authority (Armor, 1995). In the discussion that follows, we examine the history of this line of research to determine its relationship to the various research traditions identified earlier. Desegregation research holds great implications for a political economy of urban education, but relatively few of its practitioners seem to have been concerned with theorizing about the larger question of city schools and their future (Ogbu, 1986; Prager, 1986).

The earliest research on desegregation was concerned with identifying the extent of the problem posed by the segregation of urban Black neighborhoods, perhaps the most perceptible and politically volatile feature of the spatial differentiation of modern metropolitan systems (Havighurst, 1963). Interestingly, the highly influential study issued by the U.S. Civil Rights Commission in 1967, *Racial Isolation in the Public Schools*, touched on the role of real estate interests and local government in fostering racial segregation across urbanized areas. A certain degree of culpability was required, of course, as legal grounds for federal intervention into this question. As de facto school desegregation became an issue both for the civil rights movement of the 1960s and 1970s and for the federal courts, the matter of distinguishing between segregation that occurred "naturally" as a result of metropolitan development and that which could be linked to some type of governmental action became critical (Armor, 1995; Wilkerson, 1979). Indeed, the debate over causes of racial segregation in metropolitan public schools became a major point of legal contention as federal courts in the latter 1960s and early 1970s weighed evidence and heard much expert testimony on the question (Orfield, 1978; Wolf, 1981).

Desegregation scholars agree that it was the Keyes decision in 1973 that established the point that any degree of governmental involvement in school segregation (even to the point of acquiescence) represented grounds for legal challenge (Armor, 1995; Orfield, 1978; Stolee, 1993). Since that time, there has been considerable controversy over whether governmental influences were a necessary cause and whether court action has brought meaningful change in the spatial differentiation of school populations. Much of the desegregation literature has focused on assessing evidence to determine whether certain legal requirements have been met in one instance or another or whether technical solutions have been achieved (Armor, 1995; Fife 1992; Fiss, 1971; Foster, 1973; Harding, 1983; Hawley, Crain, & Rossel, 1983; Read, 1975; Rossell, 1987; Sedler, 1975). For our purposes, however, the research on school desegregation provides a unique perspective on the spatial organization of educational systems in urbanized areas. In many respects, even though it is hardly their purpose, school desegregation studies come very close to defining the elements of a political economy of urban education.

Not surprisingly, the desegregation literature can be divided into two broad groups: studies suggesting that interest group politics are important in determining the success and failure of antisegregation measures (and by implication, in segregation itself), and those which suggest that politics—at least as conventionally defined—is largely irrelevant, or certainly unimportant, in determining the course of such efforts.

Important early studies of desegregation emphasized the political dimensions of the process, and it remained an important theme in major analyses through the 1980s. In one of the first important national studies, Crain (1968) analyzed desegregation cases as partially an outgrowth of the civil rights movement, a function of a political challenge to segregation from Black communities. He also described resistance on the part of school boards and other state or governmental agencies. The cases Crain and his associates examined, of course, preceded major interventions by federal courts, at least in northern and western cities. In another national study published 10 years later, Gary Orfield (1978) again emphasized that political processes were critical to achieving successful desegregation. Noting that court orders to integrate public school systems would work only if supported by local political leaders, Orfield decried the failure of elected officials to champion desegregation as a basic principle of liberal democracy. In yet another national study, Jennifer Hochschild (1984) argued that desegregation clearly was most successful in settings where political elites had been clear and unwavering in their support for integration (we discuss this perspective in greater detail later).

A host of additional works have examined political issues in the desegregation controversies that came to preoccupy city school districts across the country (Kirp, 1982; Rossell, 1977; Rubin, 1972). Case studies of particular cities considered the dynamics of local civil rights activists positioning themselves to challenge school authorities, often resuming conflicts that had occurred earlier but with broader public support and recourse to federal courts. (Anderson & Pickering, 1986; Dentler & Scott, 1981; Fine, 1986; Mirel, 1993a). There were important differences in these struggles from one part of the country to another. Struggles in the South occurred in the wake of the larger civil rights movement. These conflicts often featured dramatic confrontations with local public officials; education was only one of several issues in contention—and often it was not the most immediate or important (Chafe, 1981; Orfield, 1969). In northern cities, on the other hand, school equity issues became a major rallying point for civil rights activists, and conflicts over education were more difficult to resolve (Formasano, 1991; Hochschild, 1984; Orfield, 1978). In many ways, resistance to desegregation was more prolonged and bitter in the North, where school boards and other governmental authorities often came to resent the suggestion that there was an element of culpability in existing patterns of racial isolation (Fine 1986; Kirp, 1981; Stolee, 1993). Taken together, this body of work on the local politics of education during the era of desegregation represents a rich vein of scholarship on social and political forces shaping the development of urban education at a particular point in time (Rossell, 1983b).

A second line of research on desegregation has focused on outcomes of the process, with particular attention to the question of educational benefits and costs (Armor, 1995; Rossell, 1990; Rossell & Hawley, 1983). Unlike the political studies, this body of work has been rather practical in orientation and has been especially concerned with establishing clear legal evidence of the success or failure of school desegregation (Fife, 1992; Hawley, Crain, & Rossell, 1983; Welch, Light, Dong, & Ross, 1987). Recent efforts to summarize findings about the educational benefits of desegregation have been inconclusive, largely because the many studies conducted for particular cases have such different designs and are difficult to compare (Armor, 1995). Even if the educational benefits are questionable, however, there remains the matter of social relations and the effect that segregation has on deeply rooted perceptions of social status. The research on these matters is quite thin (Hochschild, 1984; Massey & Denton, 1993).

A related set of issues concerns the viability of various approaches to desegregation, particularly the technical question of designing plans to meet legal definitions of integrated schools. Here the role of the state is often presented as a matter of meeting formal legal requirements, and there is little suggestion that political interests have a bearing on policies or the outcome of particular desegregation plans (Armor, 1995). Given the enormous investment of public interest and local school resources in these issues, it is little wonder that a virtual cottage industry of research on these points has developed over the past two decades, much of it conducted by scholars retained by litigants in desegregation cases (C. Campbell & Brandsetter, 1977; Foster, 1973; Henig, 1989; Rossell, 1979, 1983a, 1985, 1987, 1988). How is a successful school integration plan designed? What are the best implementation strategies? These have been critical legal issues in dozens of suits over the question of desegregation in particular localities (Armor, 1995; Fife, 1992; Hochschild, 1984; Rossell, 1990).

Debates on these matters have been sharp, and, unlike many other academic issues, the stakes have been high. Much of the research generated in this area has been derived from evidence gathered for court proceedings on specific desegregation plans (Armor, 1995; Hochschild, 1984). Consequently, it has examined certain points in great detail while giving others considerably less attention. One of the most critical debates has revolved around the question of "White flight," the tendency of Whites to flee central cities as a consequence of desegregation. In one of the early statements on this point, Coleman (1975) declared that evidence from national studies showed desegregation fostering the loss of White residents from affected neighborhoods. Coleman's assertions were challenged in a number of studies (Rossell, 1975; Wegmann, 1977), but, beginning in the 1980s, there was a growing consensus that the loss of White residents from central cities was a major mitigating factor in desegregation plans (Armor, 1980, 1995). As Christine Rossell and David Armor report in separate national works, recent court decisions have considered the likelihood of White population loss as a factor in determining the merits of particular desegregation approaches (Armor, 1995; Rossell, 1990).

In many respects, the question of White flight is central one to the political economy of urban education. If the development of court-mandated, state enforced school desegregation plans was a result of political conflict over equity, White flight represents yet another dimension of the political process. The compelling question is how one interprets it. One set of studies portrays the loss of central city White residents as a natural consequence of discriminatory tastes and the proclivity of people with resources to prefer the newer, capacious housing stock and stable real estate values of suburban communities (Armor, 1995; Rossell, 1990). In this regard, White flight can be viewed as simply just another demographic shift in a continuing pattern of metropolitan expansion, albeit with the added feature of racial selectivity. Writing in the ecological tradition, Amos Hawley emphasized that most suburban development—population movement out of the city to adjacent communities—cannot be explained by group conflict or prejudice (Hawley & Zimmer, 1970). Hoyt (1939) and other students of urban growth had noted clear patterns of ethnic differentiation in earlier eras, so even the fact of persistent racial partitioning hardly can be depicted as a historically novel attribute of metropolitan development.

Studies that rely on census data from large numbers of cities and examine racial patterns of population change typically use this variant of ecological reasoning as an explanatory framework (Farley, Richards, & Wurdock, 1980; Farley et al., 1978; Farley, et. al., 1980; Frey, 1979; Welch et al., 1987). David Armor (1995) has provided perhaps the most recent example. Invoking the oft-noted finding from survey data that Blacks and Whites differ in preferred integration scenarios (Blacks prefer a higher Black-White ratio than most Whites will accept), he maintains that desegregation is inherently a question of competing tastes. With this, Armor reduces the question of racial change to a set of technical issues in policy development, arguing that certain desegregation approaches are more likely to produce White flight than others. Prejudicial tastes are taken as a natural condition in this line of reasoning, as are the responses of local political systems. The results of Armor's analysis may be correct in a predictive sense of the term; however, the analysis does little to advance our understanding of the processes by which such tastes are sustained and reproduced in metropolitan populations and how they might be confronted effectively. Reducing the problem of urban school desegregation to an ecological model of social forces that affect population movement simply does not take us very far toward grasping the historical significance that spatial organization has acquired in the political economy of urban schooling.

A major point of debate in desegregation studies has been the question of whether mandatory or voluntary desegregation plans work best to achieve lasting racial integration. One school of thought maintains that voluntary programs, featuring magnet schools and other educational enticements to keep White families in city school districts, are more effective than mandatory plans which frighten them away (Armor, 1995; Rossell, 1990). Another maintains that mandatory (or "command and control") plans are required to overcome deep-seated White resistance to integration and that such coercive tactics are more effective than those that permit Whites to "choose" desegregation (Fife, 1992; Hochschild, 1984). The evidence is contradictory, with studies supporting both positions, but even Armor—a strong supporter of the voluntary position—allows that voluntary plans eventually result in patterns of White population loss similar to those seen in mandatory plans (1995, p. 210). Despite the substantial amount of research that has been conducted on this question, we still know relatively little about why Whites leave cities undergoing school desegregation.

Another way to view patterns of White flight, of course, is as a political response to a given environment. As noted earlier, political scientists who study desegregation consider the political context of key decisions and the ways in which important elites (or groups and organizations) respond to them. Orfield, for instance, has emphasized the ways in which government policy fosters certain types of behavior in housing, which has direct implications for schooling. In this analysis, White flight is less a matter of "tastes" than it is a set of behaviors augmented—or even induced—by relevant policy decisions at various levels of government.

The phenomenon described as white flight by those studying school desegregation is often seen from another angle as a true triumph of the basic tools of U.S. housing policy during the post-World War II period. Facilitating White suburbanization has been a basic goal—explicit at first and implicit still. Federal policies have helped shape the environment in which every family makes its choice about where to live, and those policies have skewed the choice heavily in favor of the suburbs. When these policies are superimposed on a dual housing market where blacks are excluded from most new suburban housing, the policies clearly foster white flight. (Orfield, 1977, p. 81).

Yet another aspect of the political environment, of course, is the roles played by political leaders. Hochschild has argued that political elites can have a decisive impact on the course of desegregation plans. Looking at cases featuring mandatory plans in all parts of the country, she argued that the disposition of community leaders, and school leaders in particular, often played a critical role in determining success or stalemate. While Hochschild did not have data for long-term assessments of the effectiveness of such leadership roles, she maintained that the short-term effects were telling (Hochschild, 1984). Other studies have corroborated this argument to some extent (Fife, 1992). Case studies conducted by yet other scholars support the view that the political climate within which desegregation is conducted can have a considerable effect on its immediate success or failure (Kirp, 1982; Rubin, 1972). Leaders who are supportive of change and who work systematically to allay public fears have proven capable of lessening opposition to integration, at least in the early phases of desegregation plans.

Some political scientists have argued that much of the opposition to busing and other aspects of desegregation springs from "symbolic" racism, or the perception that Blacks and other minority groups represent a threat to basic social norms and values (Sears, Hensler, & Speer, 1979). Insofar as opposition is engendered by attitudes and judgments affected by symbols and their manipulation in the political arena, the stance taken by particular leaders—and the public response to them—would seem to be critical. Regardless of White and Black "tastes" for integration or their attitudes about desegregation, this line of research and theory construction suggests that there is considerable variability in civil reaction to school integration depending on the local political environment (Sears, 1988). This alone would suggest that an ecological approach to comprehending the desegregation question, regardless of how many cities constitute the data set, is hardly sufficient.

The conflicting social and political forces that precede and follow any school desegregation decision are quite intricate and difficult to assess even with carefully conducted case studies (Kirp, 1982). In the end, a broad range of methodologies and a good deal more debate and discussion will be necessary to resolve the question of why school integration efforts may have succeeded or failed. But the broad contours of the process are now evident.

As mentioned earlier, the desegregation controversy began as a political strategy during the civil rights movement to highlight and put an end to inequalities predicated on race. Education was a focal point because of its ubiquitous quality and the rhetoric of universal access associated with public schooling in this country. The White response was multifarious, but in the end it seems incontrovertible that large numbers of Whites left the central cities as a consequence. This too can be viewed as a political act, no less strategic than the decision to initiate legal actions against local school authorities. The interesting questions—ones that have not been explored by many researchers—concern the processes by which these decisions are made (Feagin, 1980). If White city residents voted with their feet, after all, who or what provided them with the relevant ballot? How did the question of White response to desegregation get framed? Why did some communities react in one fashion while others responded in another? These questions and a host of others will have to be addressed in greater detail before the larger meaning of the desegregation problem becomes clear. It may be the case—as David Armor (1995) and others have recently suggested—that the nation is finally putting the divisive question of desegregation behind it, but it will take a great deal of additional study to fathom the larger meaning of desegregation for the social and political life of the nation's metropolitan areas.

What does the desegregation research tell us about the underlying social and political forces that have shaped urban education? The answer seems to be a great deal about some aspects and rather little about others. Given the great volume of research on this topic, there can be little doubt about the assertion that race has become a preoccupation of scholars investigating urban education. Race has long posed a dilemma for American society, of course, and the clash over equity in school matters has been only the most dramatic episode in a lengthy history of conflict over equal rights. This alone may account for the large number of school desegregation studies and the wide array of disciplines and perspectives represented within this topical area. Race has also proven to be something of a special case in examining the development of urban education, and this too may account for the attention it—and desegregation—has received (Kirp, 1982). While—as we noted earlier—many studies have documented conflict over ethnicity in education, and urban differentiation along ethnic lines is hardly new, the persistence of racial segregation and the magnitude of conflict it has engendered make it unique.

As Jennifer Hochschild (1984) and others have noted, the question of compulsory integration of public schools poses something of a "new" dilemma for Americans. The problem is that an element of coercion has historically been required to achieve this social and political goal. This, of course, unleashes a wide array of political and social responses that are complex and often difficult to comprehend. This, too, has made the desegregation controversy very attractive to scholars from several disciplines in the social sciences but particularly political scientists.

In the end, of course, desegregation is about the social and political construction of space. This facet of the controversy, however, has received considerably less attention than those mentioned earlier. But at the very center of contention is the matter of location: where people from different socially constructed groups will live and attend school. From the vantage point of urban history, this is a most unusual set of issues. This is not to say that the spatial organization of schooling has not been important in the past (it most certainly has; as we have noted, however, this issue remains largely unexamined). Rather, what is striking is its new significance in the late 20th century. Put simply, it seems that space has become, if anything, increasingly more important with time, particularly as issues of race have assumed a larger role in metropolitan differentiation. The question of desegregation was undoubtedly a part of this historic process, one that is still only dimly understood. But it is today a widely recognized fact that questions of race and the spatial organization of metropolitan areas have become matters of critical importance in local politics also (Mirel, 1993b). And this takes us into the current period and the efforts of scholars today to understand the shifting political economy of cities, as well as the place of education in the changing urban scene.

RESEARCH ON CITIES AND URBAN EDUCATION POLICY FOR THE 1990S

There can be little doubt today that the urban "crisis" observed in the 1960s and 1970s has worsened considerably. As noted at the outset of this chapter, historians and other social scientists have documented the rise of long-term unemployment and welfare dependency in large central cities in this period (M. Levine & Zipp, 1993; Sugrue, 1993). Meanwhile, large numbers of middle-class city residents have left for the suburbs or for smaller metropolitan areas elsewhere (Farley et. al., 1994; Frey & Speare, 1988). The related questions of race and the spatial organization of metropolitan areas have not been resolved since the onset of the desegregation movement. The degree of racial segregation in the nation's principal urban areas has not appreciably lessened (Massey & Denton, 1993).

At the same time, a widely acknowledged crisis has unfolded in the public schools of large central cities (Peterson, 1988; Rury, 1993). As noted earlier, when conditions deteriorated in central cities, their schools served larger populations of poor and minority children, straining already limited resources (Orfield, 1983). In 1987, Secretary of Education William Bennett visited Chicago and declared its schools "the worst in the nation" (Mirel, 1993b). His comment can be taken less as a judgment about the policies of the Chicago public schools, however, than an observation of problems in most big city schools. As bad as they were, the public schools of Chicago exhibited problems similar to urban schools in other large cities. Dropout rates soared in city school districts, and a host of new disciplinary and supervisory questions emerged. Test scores and other forms of standardized assessment in these districts were consistently below national standards (Kantor & Brenzel, 1993).

How did this situation develop in the nation's largest cities? What accounts for the deepening of the "urban crisis" identified some 30 years earlier in the 1960s. What was the impact of the desegregation movement, if any, and how are educators and urban policymakers supposed to respond to these conditions? These are only a few of the questions facing urban public education as the 20th century draws to a close.

Neo-Ecologists and the Current Crisis of the Cities

In 1991, a leader of the National League of Cities declared that "cities are caught in a death spiral" (Mirel, 1993, p. 406). While such rumors about the imminent demise of America's great cities may be greatly exaggerated, there is no doubt that a series of complex, interrelated problems have created monumental challenges for urban institutions, particularly public schools. These problems include chronic unemployment, poverty, and welfare dependency; an ongoing nightmare of gang violence and homicide (with young Black men being the most common victimizers and victims); an epidemic of drug use and criminal behavior associated with the drug trade; soaring rates of teenage pregnancy and female-headed single-parent families (Peterson, 1991; Wilson, 1987). Indeed, the situation in America's largest cities has deteriorated so badly in the past quarter century that the 1960s, which spawned terrible series of riots, now appear as almost a halcyon era. In assessing the conditions that led to the 1967 Detroit riot, at the time the worst race riot in American history, historian Sidney Fine remarked

Were the Detroit of the late 1980s to return to the conditions prevailing in the city in 1967 with regard to the state of the economy, the level of unemployment, the percentage of inhabitants living in poverty and on the welfare roles, the quality of the public schools and of housing, the degree of violent crime, and the general quality of life, it would undoubtedly be hailed as a remarkable and happy achievement. (1989, p. 461)

The same could be said of many of America's major urban centers.

In the late 1980s, a number of social scientists addressed the question of change in the nation's largest cities by looking specifically at the urban "underclass," a term coined to describe the group most deeply affected by and implicated in the problems cited earlier. These scholars have continued to emphasize structural factors of urban development—the elements of Duncan's ecological complex—and in this respect their work is clearly rooted in the ecological tradition of urban sociology. Unlike earlier ecologists, however, they recognize that the problems they have identified require solutions that can be accomplished only within the political system.

Perhaps the most widely discussed study in this effort is William Julius Wilson's *The Truly Disadvantaged* (1987), which presented a complex argument explaining why the situation of the urban poor is so significantly worse now than it was two decades ago. This influential yet controversial study maintains that race has less to do with the creation and growth of Black poverty than does "a complex web of other factors, such as the changes in the urban economy, which have produced extraordinary rates of Black joblessness that exacerbate other social problems in the ghetto, and the class transformation of the inner city" (p. ix). Wilson's argument rests on the fact that minorities, particularly African Americans, are especially vulnerable to changes in the economy (Omi & Winant, 1994). As the national economy shifted from a manufacturing to an information and service base, and as major industries either shut down entirely or left central cities, Blacks suffered an acute loss of jobs that provided enough income to sustain families (Bluestone & Harrison, 1982). The loss of these jobs, the subsequent rise of unemployment and welfare dependency, and the increasing levels of poverty among working-class Blacks occurred at almost the same time that the successes of the civil rights movement made it possible for middle-class Blacks to leave the ghetto for more prosperous parts of metropolitan areas. These simultaneous developments led to increased social isolation and dislocation for the poor and the decline of such institutions as churches, stores, and recreational facilities that had provided some stability and order in the ghetto in the past.

As joblessness persisted and with these institutions unable or unavailable to fulfil their stabilizing role, ghetto life began to rapidly deteriorate. Wilson notes, for example, that with increased unemployment of Black men, Black marriage rates declined and the rate of single-parent female-headed families increased. In short, Wilson argues that we are facing an unprecedented crisis with the "underclass" but that this crisis can be ameliorated by targeting the root cause of poverty and instability in the ghetto, namely the lack of decent jobs and the attendant social isolation that comes with high rates of unemployment.

Several years after *The Truly Disadvantaged* appeared, Massey and Denton (1993) challenged and refined Wilson's argument. They questioned his assertion that current racist attitudes (as opposed to historic discrimination, which Wilson did acknowledge) did not play a prominent role in the creation and maintenance of urban poverty. Specifically, they argued that past and present racist behavior

reflected in residential segregation are at the heart of many of the problems identified with the underclass. They took issue with scholars such as Wilson who have
failed to systematically "consider the important role that segregation has played in
mediating, exacerbating, ultimately amplifying the harmful social and economic
process they treat" (p. 7).

Massey and Denton argue that the historic and current residential segregation
of Black Americans is unlike the experience of any other group in this nation's
history. No immigrant or ethnic group, even those living in what appear to be
thoroughly homogeneous neighborhoods, has ever been as so closely and uni-
formly concentrated as have Blacks. That phenomenon alone, Massey and Denton
believe, helps account for many of the problems currently associated with
extreme poverty and furthermore helps explain a number of aspects of Wilson's
theory that his study fails to consider. For example, Massey and Denton argue that
the reason unemployment has had such an enormous impact on inner city Blacks
is that the intense concentration of poor Black residents in socially isolated communities had a "multiplier" effect on such negative developments as unemployment. In more racially and economically heterogeneous neighborhoods,
unemployment and its attendant ills affect only a small minority of residents and
do not threaten social stability. In communities suffering high degrees of racial
and economic segregation, however, even a modest downturn in the economy can
have a devastating impact as large numbers of residents find themselves out of
work and unable to maintain their families. Moreover, such segregated and isolated communities have few strong social institutions able to cope with the growing social problems. Consequently, these neighborhoods deteriorate quickly into
violent urban wastelands. Massey and Denton argue that only through a national
commitment to open housing and residential integration can the problems of the
urban poor be effectively challenged and eliminated.

While Wilson and Massey and Denton still disagree about a number of points,
it is also clear that their arguments complement one another quite well. Indeed,
Wilson has incorporated the idea of concentrations of poverty into his argument
and now replaces the term "underclass" with "ghetto poor," a phrase that captures
more of a sense of residential segregation (Wilson, 1991). Perhaps more important, the policy recommendations of Wilson and Massey and Denton lead almost
inexorably back to the political arena. Massey and Denton are somewhat clearer
in this regard, declaring that

for the walls of the ghetto to be breached at this point will require an unprecedented commitment by
the public and a fundamental change in leadership at the highest levels. Residential segregation will
only be eliminated from American society when federal authorities, backed by the American people,
become directly involved in guaranteeing open housing markets and eliminating discrimination from
public life. Rather than relying on private individuals to identify and prosecute those who break the
law, the U.S. Department of Housing and Urban Development and the Office of the Attorney General
must throw their full institutional weight into locating instances of housing discrimination and bringing those who violate the Fair Housing Act to justice; they must vigorously prosecute White racists
who harass and intimidate Blacks seeking to exercise their rights of residential freedom; and they must

establish new bureaucratic mechanisms to counterbalance the forces that continue to sustain the residential color line (1993, pp. 217–218)

However, Massey and Denton, Wilson, and many other commentators on the plight of the urban poor (Peterson, 1991; Katz, 1993) have not looked comprehensively at the political dimensions of these problems. As Massey and Denton indicate so clearly, historically worsening patterns of poverty concentration in cities cannot be resolved without radical intervention initiated and sustained at the national level. As the new political urban sociologists have asserted, this is because the problems big cities face today are the result of economic, social, and political developments affecting the entire country, not simply the cities themselves (Feagin, 1988). The recent body of ecological research on central cities and urban poverty points to these processes but does not examine them. As such, they raise a host of questions for additional research and deliberation. Specifically, how have political decisions and actions contributed to residential segregation, the concentration of poverty, deindustrialization, the exodus of middle-class residents and jobs from cities, and associated matters? Whose interests have been represented by these decisions and actions, and how have they been legitimated? As it stands, there is precious little research on these questions. But they are the matters that must be addressed if effective public policies are to be enacted and sustained.

There is also relatively little research on urban schooling that can be linked to the most recent group of ecological studies of cities (Mark & Anderson, 1984). Clearly the work of Wilson, Massey and Denton, and other scholars working in this area has profound implications for comprehending the problems of urban schools. Yet educational researchers too often accept the urban environment as a given natural setting, rather than one that has itself been determined by larger economic and political processes (Apple, 1991; Bettis, 1994). Consequently, at the same time that there is no national policy initiative to effectively address urban problems, there is scant attention among educational researchers to political processes at the national level that affect urban schools. A number of commentators have noted that schools would undoubtedly have a prominent role to play in any constructive effort to aid the cities. But educational researchers have given little thought to the obstacles to such initiatives or to what types of educational interventions would be best suited to such a broad set of policy objectives.

The Politics of Education With an Ecological Perspective

During much the same time that sociologists have become more concerned about political factors affecting urban development (and, by implication, city schools), political scientists have become sensitive to ecological components (economic and demographic) of the urban environment that help to shape policy alternatives. As in earlier studies, much of this work focuses on the role of the state and forces that influence the employment of state power and resources. But these more recent studies employ sophisticated analytical models to consider these questions in the light of changing spatial relationships in the nation's large urban areas. They also consider such contextual factors as the development of federal policies that affect local state agencies—and urban schools in particular— and the shape of larger regional and national economies. The result has been a promising new direction in research on the politics of urban education.

A ground-breaking work in this regard was Paul E. Peterson's *City Limits* (1981). Peterson argued that the abilities of city governments to effect changes in their environment were delimited by demographic and economic forces affecting city growth and material development. Much of his analysis followed a long tradition in the study of urban politics, focusing on competition among interest groups (Banfield & Wilson, 1963; Dahl, 1961; Long, 1972). But pursuing the logic of classical ecological analysis, Peterson maintained that cities were constrained by their economic functions (specific economic activities they performed in the national and international division of labor) and such demographic variables as the size and composition of the local population. Reflecting the influence of analysts such as Tiebout (1956) and Oates (1969), he maintained that these characteristics represented clear policy alternatives to local leaders. If city governments and other institutions are to succeed, he argued, they must maximize the potential of these elements for growth and political stability. Indeed, Peterson suggested that growth (or development) and stability are often conflicting objectives in urban politics, making questions of organization (or the balancing of political interests) critical within the limits set by economic and demographic structure.

This view of city politics is clearly quite different from that suggested by the "new" urban sociologists. In specifying clear policy alternatives for cities, Peterson suggests a rational choice model of urban politics that is linked to a long tradition in studies of political behavior (Oates, 1969; Peterson, 1976). For their part, urban sociologists have been quite critical of Peterson, even while acknowledging the importance of his contribution (Logan & Molotch, 1987; Logan & Swanstrom, 1990). By and large, Peterson accepts the logic of ecological explanations of urban development, and augments it by identifying patterns of political behavior that contribute to city growth or decline.

In discussing specific policy arenas, Peterson distinguishes between political forces representing "development" (or growth) and "redistributive" interests, those advocating compensatory programs of various sorts. Because of their size and diversity, large cities find it difficult to maintain stability between these elements. Smaller communities, on the other hand, often feature one or the other, but usually developmental interests predominate. When redistributive policies begin to outweigh developmental activities, according to the logic of this model, an urban system can begin to change dramatically. For instance, developmental interests (both organizations and the social groups associated with them) will leave the central city at a faster pace (and will be replaced by fewer such elements). This, of course, can be seen as an important dimension of what has happened with the process of suburbanization.

For city school systems, the implications of this model are clear, and Peterson spells them out in his analysis. As resources are spread across a large and diverse district, wealthier households will see the cost of necessary redistributive policies as a significant burden of membership in the community. As the number of poor children increases, these costs escalate, and wealthier families leave for districts with a better array of developmental activities. This process results in a malignant downward spiral that is very difficult for city school systems and urban political leaders to reverse. And efforts to create programs to attract or hold the children of wealthier parents almost inevitably lead to political conflict. This is a framework that can account for the flow of population groups and resources from one community to another, and thus it is well suited to interpreting the changing spatial arrangements in large metropolitan areas.

Peterson's model provides a vehicle for considering the ways in which organizational (or political) factors interact with the mix of ecological factors to determine certain policy outcomes. Kenneth Wong has used the logic of Peterson's analysis to examine policy determination around school and housing issues in Milwaukee and Baltimore (1990). Comparing political choices made within economic constraints, Wong identifies the elements of coalition building and leadership that contributed to success and failure in each setting. To the extent that the framework that Peterson has provided allows scholars to identify an ecology of factors that contribute to policy development in this fashion, it represents a significant advance over earlier treatments of urban politics, which have focused on the actions of elites or discrete interest groups. In proposing a way to think about space as a dimension of political analysis, Peterson has helped to define a line of inquiry that is distinctively urban, even if his reasoning accepts the underlying logic of the ecological tradition in urban studies.

There are other factors that shape urban development, of course. One of the most important is the various forms of federal assistance to cities and urban institutions, which can promote either redistributive or developmental ends. In a volume published 5 years after *City Limits*, Peterson, Rabe, and Wong (1986) examined the impact of federal assistance programs in a number of urban settings. By and large, they found that federal aid to improve housing, extend health care services, and support public education often succeeded in accomplishing the redistributive ends for which it was designed. In some instances, such programs encountered resistance from local political elites, particularly when they were perceived to be in conflict with particular developmental strategies. In the highly charged political environment of some cities, Peterson and his collaborators found that several federal programs were seen as favoring certain social groups over others and thereby fostering dissention and conflict. These were themes that Wong (1990) identified in his more detailed study of Baltimore and Milwaukee as well. But Peterson et al. concluded that federal programs of assistance to urban institutions were quite successful in instances in which local political leaders worked to use these resources effectively. Indeed, they were quite critical of

Reagan administration efforts at the time to limit the federal role in providing redistributive resources to cities. On balance, Peterson et al. argued that major programs of federal assistance to cities—and to urban schools in particular—represented an effective strategy to ameliorate the problems wrought by urban development and suburbanization.

In many respects, the conclusions reached by Peterson et al. (1986) flow naturally from Peterson's analysis in *City Limits.* If big cities cannot control the forces of differentiation that lead to urban decline, after all, it is necessary for an external authority such as the federal government to supply them with the resources to stem such developments. In a more recent study, Gary Orfield and Carol Ashkinaze (1993) have identified social and political factors contributing to growing inequalities in metropolitan Atlanta, and they too have given special attention to the role of federal policies in urban development. In examining a single large urban area, including both the central city and suburbs, they implicitly use many of the principles Peterson identified in *City Limits,* and focus on ways in which metropolitan growth patterns contribute to the processes identified in recent ecological studies. But their perspective also is different from that of Peterson and his collaborators. Insofar as it documents patterns of historical development in one major metropolitan area, Orfield and Ashkinaze are able to address the question of spatial relationships and their change over time quite explicitly. Beyond this, they note the critical role of changes in federal policy in the course of these processes and point to important connections between the historic shift in national urban policy experienced during the 1980s and the changes evident in greater Atlanta. While their study is hardly an exhaustive treatment of the ways in which local political responses to race and inequality are shaped by national political events, it clearly points to patterns of change that deserve more comprehensive and detailed study.

Orfield and Ashkinaze use a number of important recent studies of urban development and public policy as reference points in their argument. Specifically, they suggest that Atlanta provides a good case to test Wilson's (1987) proposition that economic growth is more important to the amelioration of urban inequality than race-specific policies and programs promulgated at the national or state level. Orfield and Ashkinaze found significant evidence of growing inequality in the greater Atlanta area, despite tight labor markets during much of the period they examined. Their findings corroborate those of Massey and Denton (1993) in that they found persistent patterns of racial isolation, even as large numbers of African Americans left the central city. They also documented growing inequality in educational attainment, with Black-White differences again being most striking. They maintained that this evidence indicates market forces are not sufficient in themselves to reverse historically grounded patterns of racial inequality in large metropolitan areas. Indeed, Orfield and Ashkinaze suggested that conditions for African Americans as a group have worsened significantly in Atlanta as a result of rapid economic development. Orfield and Ashkinaze devoted less attention to explicitly political factors and the role of the state in the development of Atlanta in this period than Peterson and his associates did in the cities they examined. But they clearly identified the impact of diminished federal support in areas of housing and education on overall patterns of inequality. In this regard, they have answered critics of federal support for urban residents and institutions (Murray, 1984), who suggested that such programs actually contributed to inequality. Instead, Orfield and Ashkinaze found that the relaxation of federally enforced mandates for racial equality led to widening differences along a number of dimensions. Like the work of Peterson et al. (1986), in that case, Orfield and Ashkinaze's study underscores the importance of federal intervention in urban development to promote policies of redistribution.

As evident in two recent review articles by Kenneth Wong (1991, 1993), there is a paucity of research on the politics of education that can be labeled distinctively urban. While there is a growing body of work on the federal role in education, much of it has not focused on the implications of national and state-level political events for city schools and their immediate urban settings. Given the importance that ecological scholars have come to assign these questions, this is no small oversight. Paul Peterson, Gary Orfield, Kenneth Wong, and a number of the other scholars cited earlier have pointed to fruitful lines of investigation. There are yet other questions to pursue, of course, suggested by the new urban sociologists, particularly the roles played by local real estate and urban development interests. The effects of political factors such as these on educational inequality would seem to be an especially critical area for research in the future.

Decentralization and Choice: Current Policy Initiatives and Research on Urban Schooling

In the last 15 years, most of the research and policy initiatives in urban education have gone in a very different direction than the ones we have described here. In those years, scholars, activists, and political leaders have pushed primarily for various forms of school decentralization in urban districts, a process that involves shifting power and/or resources from centralized educational bureaucracies to local schools or parents. These efforts fall into three broad categories: experiments with school-based management in which greater power and authority are placed in the hands of teachers, the creation of local school governance councils controlled by parents and community members, and "school choice" or voucher initiatives that give parents the possibility of sending their children to schools other than the one located in their immediate neighborhood. While these efforts differ greatly in many of their key provisions, all share several assumptions about the problems of urban education and about some of the solutions to those problems. These include: (a) bureaucratic control of urban public schools has been one of the main causes of the deterioration of education in these schools; (b) people closest to the educational process (building administrators, teachers, or parents) should have the greatest amount of control over school policy and practice; and

(c) shifting control of education from centralized bureaucracies to schools or parents will lead to improved educational outcomes for students.

Wisely implemented, we believe, all of these initiatives may have a positive impact on urban education, but they are hardly sufficient for dealing with the massive problems facing big city school districts in this country. In considering the basis of all of these decentralization initiatives, we are struck by their seeming neglect of the role that political economy has played in shaping these problems and in considerations of efforts to solve them. Each of these endeavors rests on the belief that basic governance changes in individual schools will have a positive effect on educational outcomes. The social, economic, and spatial issues that we have previously described play almost no part in these analyses or policies. This section traces the development of these decentralization efforts and assesses why urban educational researchers and political leaders have chosen this direction for reform rather than more expansive efforts.

Decentralizing power within urban school districts is, of course, not a new phenomenon. In fact, the current campaigns to shift the locus of power had important antecedents in the 1960s when critics began targeting the highly centralized organizations of these systems as the root of many educational problems. In 1968, for example, sociologist David Rogers described the New York City Public Schools as a "sick" bureaucracy, an institution "whose traditions, structure and operations subvert their stated missions and prevent any flexible accommodation to changing client demands" (p. 267). For Rogers, the New York schools were a "model of bureaucratic pathology" (1968, p. 267). In the past quarter century, there have been two major campaigns to decentralize urban schools. Both have focused on governance and structural change for public schools, but they have sought somewhat distinct goals and have had different outcomes.

The initial campaigns to decentralize urban schools were largely products of the political upheavals of the 1960s. As suggested earlier, these struggles over the spatial distribution of resources and power were linked to larger battles over civil rights and status for ethnic and racial minority groups (Anderson & Pickering, 1986). These campaigns transformed the governance structures of the public schools in New York City and Detroit (Mirel, 1993a; Ravitch, 1974). The second series of decentralization campaigns, currently under way in, among other areas, Dade County (Florida), Rochester, and Chicago, owes it origins to research on effective schools and the current trends in corporate restructuring (Hess, 1990). Both campaigns were premised on the conviction that educational bureaucracies impeded the improvement of urban schools, and the underlying ideas of both campaigns are similar to and at times have been strongly influenced by many of the historical and political studies that we considered earlier.

As we have noted, educational bureaucracies in urban schools developed in the latter part of the 19th and early part of the 20th century. Largely implemented by elite, business-oriented reform groups, these structures were touted as mechanisms that would free the schools from the political manipulation, graft, and corruption associated with the decentralized ward-based governance system of the past. Progressive Era reformers successfully transformed school boards into policy making rather than overly political bodies, and these boards placed educational professionals in charge of the day-to-day operation of schools (Katz, 1972; Tyack, 1974).

These educational structures, which had long been resistant to demands for improved education in minority communities, quickly became prime targets for both mainstream civil rights groups and later militant Black power organizations (Anderson & Pickering, 1986; Mirel, 1993a; Stolee, 1993). Hoping to bring "power to the people," these groups sought to smash the reigning educational power structures through decentralization. In the late 1960s and early 1970s, advocates of decentralization succeeded in getting the governance system of two of the largest school systems in the nation, New York City and Detroit, divided into regions (32 in New York, 8 in Detroit) with regional boards of education elected by the communities to oversee operations, hiring, and curriculum. Both of these early experiments with decentralization produced bitter conflicts between minority activists seeking community control and predominantly White teachers unions seeking to protect contracts and job security. Neither initiative produced significant educational gains for students and, in 1981, Detroit voters approved the recentralization of the system. In New York, many of the decentralized regions became far better known for their corruption and patronage than for their educational progress (Lewis 1989; D. A. Lewis & Nakagawa, 1995; Mirel 1993a; Ravitch 1974).

The failure of these early efforts in decentralization was a serious setback in the effort to restructure the governance of urban districts. Nevertheless, the idea that a change in school governance and organization would lead to a change in school outcomes persisted. But the idea also underwent some important changes. By the mid-1980s, the focus of decentralization efforts had shifted from an emphasis on simply redistributing political power within the system to redistributing both power and educational authority between the system and individual schools (Hess, 1990).

A key element in this change was a shift in attitude regarding educational professionals. The decentralization campaigns in both New York and Detroit were predicated to a large extent on the belief that urban schools were failing because many school administrators and teachers were, at worst, racist or, at best, out of touch with the community (Mirel, 1993a; Ravitch, 1974). By the 1980s, however, such ideas had far less currency, probably because of the increasing number of minority teachers and administrators in urban districts. Thus, rather than viewing educational professionals as an important part of the problem, leaders of this second wave of decentralization were considerably more willing than earlier decentralizers to view educational professionals as vital elements of the solution. (Mirel, 1993b). Three other important developments explain that change in perspective: (a) the dissemination of "effective schools" research, (b) the structural revolution in American corporate organization, and (c) the changing demographics of urban public school populations.

The effective schools research was a very specific response to the questions raised by the 1966 Coleman Report. If increased funding, improved facilities, and tougher credentialing standards for teachers did not raise educational outcomes, as the Coleman report argued, what did? Effective schools researchers sought an answer to that question by looking at schools in which children demonstrated high achievement, schools with poor and minority children whose family backgrounds, according to Coleman's research, should have predicted failure. After a series of case studies, these researchers identified one variable that seemed to make a difference: school organization. Effective schools, they argued, shared a number of important characteristics such as strong leadership by their principals; clear goals for the school; high academic standards and high expectations from the teachers that students could meet these standards; considerable involvement by teachers in decision making, order and discipline within the school; a commitment to homework; and extensive cooperation between the school and home (Comer 1988; Edmonds 1979; Purkey & Smith, 1983, U.S. Department of Education, 1986). Ironically, in 1982, these ideas were strongly endorsed by James S. Coleman himself on the basis of his subsequent research that found students from similar background performing better in private schools than in public schools. School organization, Coleman and his colleagues maintained, was the key variable that explained these differences (Coleman, Hoffer, & Kilgore, 1982).

This new interest in school organization occurred concurrently with the implementation of a similar set of ideas in leading American corporations. Tracing their source to W. Edwards Deming, the theorist often associated with the resurgence of Japanese industry, these ideas sought to revamp corporate organization by drastically reducing corporate hierarchies, redistributing authority to front-line managers, setting clear goals for quality products and excellent service, involving workers in decision making, and putting the needs and demands of customers and clients first. Throughout the late 1970s and early 1980s, many of what Tom Peters and Robert Waterman, Jr., described in *In Search of Excellence* (1982) as "Americas best run companies" were applying these ideas and transforming American industry. These trends, as Peters (1987) later noted, involved "decentralizing, information, authority, and strategic planning" (p. 505). In its most simple terms, Peters declared, this corporate revolution demanded that individuals become "emotional, vociferous, repetitive, public hater[s] of bureaucracy" (1987, 505, p. 459).

There is also evidence that political elites and the leaders of such national educational organizations as the major teacher unions and influential foundations played an important role in defining this line of research and policy development. In a comprehensive survey, Rodney Ogawa (1994) has determined that actors such as these at the national level established an agenda for urban school reform that preceded local initiatives. School or "site-based management" reform strategies, which became popular in the late 1980s, emerged from this domain, providing further legitimation to the general theme of decentralization in educational leadership.

Already sensitive to these kinds of ideas from the effective schools research, educational activists in some major cities began a second campaign to break the grip of central bureaucracies by establishing site-based management at individual schools (David, 1989; Hills, Wise, & Shapiro, 1989; McPike, 1987). As one educational leader noted

The principles that underlie [these developments] find strong support in both the literature describing the characteristics of effective schools . . . and in theories of modern management that emphasize the importance of decentralization, employee involvement in the decisions that affect their work, and the development of a feeling of "ownership" of those decisions (McPike, 1987, p. 10)

These developments occurred during a fortuitous period for this model of urban educational reform. Not only were large numbers of activists, politicians, and scholars denouncing urban schools as top-heavy organizational bureaucracies that produced large numbers of poorly educated students, but a third factor in the form of a major demographic shift in urban public school enrollments was occurring that also helped encourage decentralization efforts. Prior to the 1980s, calls for shifting greater power and authority to local schools surely would have foundered on the issue of racial integration. During the great battles over integration and busing in the 1960s and 1970s, "defending the neighborhood school" became the rallying cry of opponents of desegregation (Anderson & Pickering 1986; Lukas 1986; Peterson 1976). From that perspective, any effort to strengthen or further "legitimize" neighborhood schools at that time would have been seen as an attempt to advance the interests of those opposition groups. In such situations, civil rights organizations undoubtedly would have filed suit against the reform efforts.

However, as a consequence of the continuing exodus of White students from urban districts, as noted earlier, enrollments in most urban schools in the nation became overwhelmingly minority. With so few Whites left in these systems, and federal courts rejecting the extension of desegregation plans to suburban school districts after the 1974 *Milliken v. Bradley* decision, desegregation efforts lost much of their momentum and—eventually—much of their controversy. (Armor, 1995; Wolf, 1981). In this new historical context, strengthening and improving neighborhood schools suddenly became a viable policy option. Major decentralization efforts probably would not have been launched had large numbers of White students remained in these systems and had busing remained the main thrust of urban school desegregation policy.

As suggested earlier, this new interest in decentralization has taken a number of forms. One of the most important has been described as school-based management. Since 1987, the Dade County, Florida, and Rochester, New York, public schools have led the nation in experimenting with "school-based management" and "shared decision making." In both cases, the reform efforts were spearheaded by union leaders and teachers who worked with school administrators to set up the "site-based" management programs at the participating schools. In Dade County, the union leaders and administrators agreed to form school improvement councils that would determine policy and practice within their buildings. Parents and community leaders were invited to join these groups, but control of the councils was strongly in the hands of the educational professionals (Bradley, 1990; Fiske 1988, 1989; D. A. Lewis & Nakagawa, 1995).

In Rochester, the decentralization experiment began with teachers who agreed to accept greater accountability for student performance in exchange for greater control over their schools and for higher salaries. School leaders also agreed to reduce the size of the central bureaucracy. As a result of these agreements, each school in the system is run by a planning team chaired by the principal and composed primarily of teachers. Some parents are involved in the teams, but, as in Dade County, professional educators run the schools. The teams draft improvement plans for all of the schools in the district and set performance goals to assess progress within each building. In addition, lead teachers are chosen to act as mentors and change agents within each school. Leaders from major businesses have lent their support to specific schools (Bradley, 1989; Chira, 1991; Gutis, 1988; Urbanski, 1991).

In both Rochester and Dade County, the councils have considerable power to reshape the educational environment of the schools. In Dade County, they can, for example, change class sizes, alter the length of the school day and the class periods, and create new instructional programs. As these changes in local schools have been implemented, school officials in the central administration have been reducing the central bureaucracy and assessing the progress of the reforms by issuing annual school "report cards" to each school. In neither case, however, have the reforms had a dramatic impact on educational outcomes (Bradley, 1989; Chira, 1991).

By far the most sweeping American attempt to shift power from the central bureaucracy to local schools is currently under way in Chicago. Here the emphasis was less on management issues than the creation of agencies for political control of individual schools through local school councils. Unlike the Dade County or Rochester experiments, school reform in Chicago came about through the efforts of local activist groups, business leaders, and politicians. The Chicago Teachers Union played virtually no part in developing the reforms. The key elements of school reform in Chicago involve drastically reducing the size and power of the central bureaucracy, shifting power to the schools through the creation of elected councils dominated by parents, and seriously limiting the control educational professionals have over school policy while expanding their control over how policies can be carried out (Carl, 1995; Hess, 1990: Mirel, 1993b; Vander Weele, 1994).

The most striking aspect of the Chicago experiment is its attempt to markedly reduce the size, power, and resources of the central bureaucracy and to move much of educational decision making down to the school level. Since reform was implemented, the central bureaucracy has been substantially reduced. Moreover, power, authority, and funds have flowed to local schools. Every school in the city is now run by a local school council that has the power to hire and fire school principals, determine the school budget (including how to spend fairly large amounts of state Chapter 1 funds), and determine curriculum. The principals, in turn, have greater authority in deciding on which teachers to hire, in filling nonprofessional positions within the school, and in allocating funds (Carl, 1995; Ford & Bennett 1994; Hess 1990; Wong & Sunderman 1994).

Chicago school reform has been in place for 7 years. During that time, the school system clearly has undergone major organizational changes. As noted earlier, the reduction of the central bureaucracy has proceeded apace. Moreover, recent studies conducted by the Consortium for Chicago School Research at the University of Chicago found that between one quarter and one third of the elementary schools in the district had "strong democracy" in their new governance system, that school administrators were generally pleased with the reforms, and that the process had initiated restructuring activities in a number of schools (Hess, 1994). However, in terms of improving student achievement the results have been disappointing. Studies of student achievement found little change in the academic performance of Chicago students (as measured by standardized tests) in the previous 3 years, a period in which the reforms were firmly in place (Bryk, Deabster, Easton, & Thum, 1994; Downes & Horowitz 1994).

The theoretical roots of the previous two reform efforts lay to some degree in the work of historians, political scientists, and sociologists who came to celebrate the concept of community control of local schools during the tumultuous period of the late 1960s and early 1970s (e.g., see Katz, 1972, 1992). Yet another set of reform proposals has sprung from an altogether different source: what has become known as "school choice," or the idea that public support for schools should be based on the numbers of families that choose to send their children to them (Raywid, 1992). The ideas behind choice and voucher initiatives also have roots in the 1960s, in that they are most closely identified with the writings of Milton Friedman and other market theorists (Henig, 1994). The most fully developed argument on choice has appeared relatively recently in Chubb and Moe's *Politics, Markets, and America's Schools* (1990). Chubb and Moe argue that many of the ills of urban schools also arise from excessive bureaucracy control, but they trace the problem to a more fundamental source: direct democratic control. They write:

> The real cause [of the problems of urban education] is the public education system as a whole. Its institutions of democratic control are inherently destructive of school autonomy and inherently conducive to bureaucracy. This happens because of the way all the major participants—politicians, interest groups, bureaucrats—are motivated and empowered by their institutional setting to play the game of structural politics. Whatever the technological and intellectual arguments against bureaucracy may be, and however frustrated people from all walks of life may be with the unworkable constraints under which schools are forced to operate, virtually all are driven to pursue their own goals by adding to the bureaucracy problem. (Chubb & Moe, 1990, p.47)

In short, Chubb and Moe argue that the winners of democratic political contests for control of school governance institutionalize their victories by adding layers to the school bureaucracy and thus breed further ossification of the systems. This process, they believe, will eventually undo all efforts at decentralization and reform. They claim that true educational reform will occur only if parents gain the right to choose the schools their children attend. If parents receive vouchers that can be used at any school, the competition between schools (the force of the market) will stimulate improvement in urban education. The Chubb and Moe argument has been subjected to intense criticism on both conceptual and empirical grounds (Lee & Bryk, 1993; Sukstorf, Wells, & Crain, 1993; Wells, 1993b; Wells & Crain, 1992). Making some form of choice a centerpiece of reform, however, has become a fashionable idea among certain groups of educators and policymakers. (Cookson, 1994; Wells, 1993b)

Although less far reaching than what Chubb and Moe propose, some cities are experimenting with choice and voucher programs. The most ambitious of these is occurring in Milwaukee, where a small number of nonreligious private schools have accepted state support for students who had previously attended the Milwaukee Public Schools (Bennett, 1990; Carl, 1995). The program has come under legal challenges, but hundreds of students have participated over the past several years. The achievement results have been largely inconclusive, although it has not been possible to conduct an evaluation of long-term effects (Peterson, 1993; Witte & Thorn, 1994). Other programs that feature state-sponsored "choice" opportunities enable inner-city students to attend suburban schools, with the largest being in Milwaukee and St. Louis. However, these programs have not attracted large numbers of students. (Stolee, 1993; Wells, 1993a). Despite the enthusiastic support for school choice as a remedy for the problems of big-city school systems in some quarters (Peterson, 1993), the results of these experiments have not been exceptional (Cookson, 1994; Witte & Thorn, 1994).

In recent years the term *choice* has come to assume additional meanings and has been used to describe programs that feature competition among public schools within a single district for students and resources. Perhaps the best-known public school choice program of this sort has been established in New York City's East Harlem, where a number of public schools operate independently of district guidelines about whom they must accept and how they conduct educational programs (Fliegel, 1989). Additional large-scale public school choice programs have been established in Buffalo, New York; Montclair, New Jersey; Cambridge, Massachusetts; and a number of other cities, usually in conjunction with a magnet school strategy to achieving desegregation (Alves & Willie, 1987; Clewell & Joy, 1990; Rossell, 1987; Rossell & Glenn, 1988). While the East Harlem experiment has been described as a "miracle" and has received much attention in the media (Fliegel, 1993), more sober assessments hold that the achievement results of these reforms—where subject to evaluation—have been positive but open to question on methodological grounds (Blank, 1990; Henig, 1994).

There are yet more wrinkles to the "choice" model of school improvement that have emerged in the past few years, with perhaps the most important being the charter school movement. This movement proposes creating special schools exempt from bureaucratic rules that can serve as models or sources of productive competition for other public schools (M. Fine, 1993, 1994).

The idea that binds all of these proposals together, however, is that the problems of city schools stem from the organization of schooling and its governance. As suggested earlier, few of these reform impulses consider the profound effect of the transformation of urban life that has occurred in the last several decades. Given this, we wonder whether they are adequate to the task of reversing the long term decline of urban schools. It is not surprising, for instance, that choice plans that cross city-suburban school district lines are not very popular; there is a long history of hostility to inner-city residents in suburban communities (Massey & Denton, 1993). Problems such as these highlight the difficult spatial dimension facing most choice programs, an issue that lies at the very heart of the current crisis in urban education. For choice to operate effectively in any guise, there must be freedom of movement; space must be overcome. Even supporters of various choice plans recognize this problem. (Moe, 1994) And yet, as we have seen above, urban space has become more exacting and stratified in the past several decades.

Choice programs that exist in big cities, such as the East Harlem initiative, have been accused of accepting only the best students, leaving the others for the ordinary public schools. (Elmore, 1991; Kirp, 1992). While this may make the experiment appear to be a success, it cannot be considered a formula for raising educational performance across the district as a whole. Indeed, programs that select on the basis of academic ability may aggravate existing patterns of social and economic segregation in large cities (Lee, Croninger, & Smith, 1994). This can hardly be seen as a long-term solution to the larger problem of urban education in the late 20th century.

Most choice proposals have focused on the question of simply improving the performance of city schools. There is another issue, however, in the social justice of gross educational inequality. This, of course, was a major theme in Kozol's *Savage Inequalities* (1991), but a number of observers have argued that choice programs of one sort or another ought to be designed to extend opportunities on grounds of equity and fairness. (Henig, 1994; Ravitch, 1994). While this does not make the issue any less politically difficult, we believe it is a dimension of the choice debate that deserves more attention.

In the end, focusing on questions of school organization and competitive mechanisms for allocating resources within urban school systems probably will not resolve the problems of big city schools. If indeed the crisis in urban education is largely a product of the general crisis of the cities themselves, the solution to the crisis probably lies outside of the schools altogether. In saying this, we do not intend to denigrate the work of contemporary school reformers. Their efforts, however, are not likely to produce the dramatic results that the public often has been led to expect from these reforms. While the current urban reform movement, extending from school based management to local school councils to the various configurations of choice, may improve education for some students in the cities, it probably will not have such an effect for the majority. Indeed, even a massive new investment of resources to expand educational programs on a scale sufficient to address the needs of inner-city school populations (a development we would welcome) may not be adequate to answer the problems that such scholars as Wilson (1987), Massey and Denton (1993), Orfield and Ashkinaze (1993) and others have identified. The real problem in urban education, we propose, is less a matter of bureaucracy and the organization of governance than it is one of the political economy of urban development and change.

TOWARD A CONCLUSION

What, then, are the elements of a political economy of urban education? First, it would seem, are the essential social and economic dimensions of the city itself, the fundamental processes that contribute to the peculiar spatial configuration of people and relationships that we know as cities and their environs. This, of course, has been the domain of the ecological school, and through their work we have learned much about both cities and urban schooling over the past half century. But this is not enough. As the new urban sociology suggests, space is profoundly political, and there is considerable evidence that it has become more politically potent with time. The implications for education in this formulation are clear. As cities are shaped, after all, so are their schools. And there is little evidence to suggest that schooling is in any important way independent of political forces at work in the larger urban setting, despite the arguments of administrative progressives and professional educators to the contrary.

A central task of a political economy of urban education, in that case, is one of addressing the ways in which identifiable social and economic interests employ the political domain to define the spatial distribution of educational activities. As Peterson (1981) reminds us, this must be done with due appreciation of the economic constraints present in any particular urban setting. Duncan's well known elements of the urban environment are hardly irrelevant, after all. But once these dimensions are clear, politics becomes critical. And it is important to examine ways in which local political processes are shaped by events at the national and state levels as well. As Massey and Denton (1993) demonstrate, ultimately individual cities do not determine their own fate; they are each caught within a larger web of social, economic, and political forces. The same, of course, is true of urban schools. They are likely to prove highly resistant to change until the deteriorating and often oppressive quality of their urban environment is altered in fundamental ways.

Does this mean that it is futile to attempt educational reform in the nation's big cities? We think not. As indicated earlier, there have been many valuable and important reform efforts over the past two decades. Urban schools certainly can benefit from attention to organizational problems, improved governance structures, and a measure of independence from bureaucratic authority. But changes such as these cannot address the underlying problems of political and social isolation that make the future of big-city schools appear so bleak. As long as the city limits that Peterson (1981) and other observers have identified remain such a barrier to the sharing of resources and experience, the condition of urban education will remain problematic. The politics of improving urban schooling, in that case, must tackle the difficult question of linking schools in central cities and the surrounding suburbs. The central issue remains one of geography, and finding ways to study—and eventually to overcome—the difficult politics of space is perhaps the key to resolving the ongoing crisis of urban education.

REFERENCES

Alihan, M.A. (1938) *Social ecology.* New York: Columbia University Press.

Alves, M.J., & Willie, C. (1987). Controlled choice assignments: A new and more effective approach to school desegregation. *Urban Review, 19* (2), pp. 67–88.

Anderson, A.B., & Pickering, G.W. (1986). *Confronting the color line: The broken promise of the civil rights movement in Chicago.* Athens: University of Georgia Press.

Angus, D.L. (1982). The politics of progressive school reform, 1900–1910. *Michigan Academician 14,* 239–258.

Angus, D.L. (1992). The uses and abuses of comparison in urban educational history. In R. K. Goodenow & W.E. Marsden (Eds.), *The city and education in four nations* (pp. 221–242). New York: Cambridge University Press.

Apple, M. (1991). Conservative agendas and progressive possibilities: Understanding the wider politics of curriculum and teaching. *Education and Urban Society 23* (3), 279–291.

Armor, D.J. (1980). White flight and the future of school desegregation. In W. G. Stephan & J. R. Feagin (Eds.), *School desegregation: Past, present and future* (pp. 187–225). New York: Plenum Press.

Armor, D.J. (1995) *Forced justice: School desegregation and the law.* New York: Oxford University Press.

Banfield, E.C. (1968). *The unheavenly city: The nature and the future of our urban crisis.* Boston: Little, Brown.

Banfield, E.C., & Wilson, J.Q. (1963). *City politics.* Cambridge: Harvard University Press.

Bennett, D. (1990). Choice and desegregation. In W. Clune & J. Witte (Eds.), *Choice and control in American education.* New York: Falmer Press

Berry, B.J.L. (1965). Research frontiers in urban geography. In P. M. Hauser & L. Schnore (Eds.), *The study of urbanization* (pp. 403–430). New York: John Wiley.

Berry, B.J.L. (1973). *The human consequences of urbanization.* New York: St. Martins Press.

Bettis, P.J. (1994). Deindustrialization and urban schools: Some theoretical considerations. *Urban Review 26* (2), 75–94.

Blank, R.K. (1990). Educational effect of magnet high schools. In W. Clune & J. Witte (Eds.), *Choice and control in American education. Volume 2: The practice of choice, decentralization, and school restructuring* (pp. 77–110). New York: Falmer Press.

Blau, P.M. (1977). *Inequality and heterogeneity: A primitive theory of social structure.* New York: The Free Press.

Bluestone, B., & Harrison, B. (1982). *The deindustrialization of America.* New York: Basic Books.

Borman, K.M., & Spring, J.H. (1984). *Schools in central cities: Structure and process.* New York: Longman.

Bowden, M.J. (1975). Growth of the central districts in large cities. In L.F. Schnore (Ed.), *The new urban history: Quantitative explorations by American historians* (pp. 75–109). Princeton, NJ: Princeton University Press.

Bowles, S., & Gintis, H. (1976). *Schooling in capitalist America: Education reform and the contradictions of economic life.* New York: Basic Books.

Boyd, W.L. (1975). *Community and status group conflict in suburban school politics.* Beverley Hills, CA: Sage

Bradley, A. (1989, December). "This is damned hard." *Teacher Magazine,* pp. 12–13.

Bradley, A. (1990, June 6). In Dade County, company gears up to help district run a public school. *Education Week.*

Bryk, A.S., Deabster, P.E., Easton, J.Q.,Luppescu, S., & Thum, Y.M. (1994). Measuring achievement gains in the Chicago public schools. *Education and Urban Society, 26,* 306–319.

Burgess, E.W. (1928). Residential segregation in American cities. *Annals of the American Academy of Political and Social Science, 140,* 105–110.

Burkhead, J. (1967). *Input and output in large city high schools.* Syracuse, NY: Syracuse University Press.

Callahan, R.E. (1962). *Education and the cult of efficiency: A study of the social forces that have shaped the administration of the public schools.* Chicago: University of Chicago Press.

Campbell, A.K. (1969, January 11). Inequities of school finance. *Saturday Review,* 46.

Campbell, A.K., & Meranto, P. (1967). The metropolitan educational dilemma. In M. Gittell (Ed.), *Educating and urban population.* Beverly Hills, CA: Sage Publications.

Campbell, C., & Brandsetter, J. (1977). The magnet school plan in Houston. In D.U. Levine & R.J. Havighurst (Eds.), *The future of big-city schools: Desegregation policies and magnet alternatives* (pp. 124–138). Berkeley: McCutchen Publishing.

Carl, J.C. (1995). The politics of education in a new key: The 1988 Chicago school reform act and the 1990 Milwaukee parental choice program. Unpublished doctoral dissertation, University of Wisconsin.

Carnoy, M., & Levin, H.M. (1985). *Schooling and work in the democratic state.* Stanford, CA: Stanford University Press.

Castells, M. (1977). *The urban question: A Marxist approach.* Cambridge: MIT Press.

Catanese, A.J. (1972). *Scientific methods of urban analysis.* Urbana: University of Illinois Press.

Chafe, W. (1981). *Civil rights and civilities.* New York: Oxford University Press.

Chicago Department of Planning and Development. (1992). *Social and economic characteristics of Chicago's population.* Chicago: Author.

Chira, S. (1991, April 10). Rochester: An uneasy symbol of school reform. *New York Times,* A22.

Chubb, J.E., & Moe, T.M. (1990). *Politics, markets, and America's schools.* Washington, DC: The Brookings Institution.

Cibulka, J.G., & Olson, F.I. (1993). The organization and politics of the Milwaukee public school system, 1920–1986. In J. L. Rury & F. A. Cassell (Eds.), *Seeds of crisis: Public schooling in Milwaukee since 1920* (pp. 73–109). Madison: University of Wisconsin Press.

Clewell, B.C., & Joy, M.F. (1990). *Choice in Montclair, New Jersey.* Princeton, NJ: Educational Testing Service.

Cohen, D.K. (1968, Winter). Policy for the public schools: Compensation and integration. *Harvard Educational Review,* 114–137.

Cohen, D.K. (1969, April 19). The economics of inequality. *Saturday Review,* 64.

Coleman, J.S. (1975). Recent trends in school integration. *Educational Researcher, 4* (7), 3–12.

Coleman, J.S., Hoffer, T., & Kilgore, S. (1982). *High school achievement: Public, Catholic, and private schools compared.* New York: Basic Books.

Comer, J.P. (1988). Educating poor minority children. *Scientific American, 259,* 58–59.

Conant, J.B. (1961). Slums and suburbs: A commentary on schools in metropolitan areas. New York: McGraw Hill.

Cookson, P. (1994). *School choice: The struggle for the soul of American education.* New Haven: Yale University Press.

Crain, R.L. (1968). *The politics of school desegregation: Comparative case studies of community structure and policy making.* Chicago: Aldine Publishing Company.

Crane, J. (1991). Effects of neighborhoods on dropping out of school and teenage child-bearing. In C. Jencks & P.E. Peterson (Eds.), *The urban underclass* (pp. 299–320). Washington, DC: The Brookings Institution.

Cremin, L.A. (1961). *The transformation of the school: Progressivism in American education, 1876–1957.* New York: Alfred A. Knopf.

Cremin, L.A. (1965). *The wonderful world of Ellwood Patterson Cubberly.* New York: Teachers College Press.

Cremin, L.A. (1988). *American education: The metropolitan experience, 1876–1980.* New York: Harper & Row.

Dahl, R. (1961). *Who governs? Democracy and power in an American city.* New Haven, CT: Yale University Press.

David, J.L. (1989). Synthesis of research on school-based management. *Educational Leadership, 46,* 45–47, 50–53.

Dentler, R.A., & Scott, M.B. (1981). *Schools on trial: An inside account of the Boston Desegregation case.* Cambridge, MA: Abt Books.

Derr, R.L. (1967). Urban educational problems: Models and strategies. In M. Gittell (Ed.), *Educating an urban population* (pp. 273–283). Beverly Hills: Sage Publications.

Downes, T.A., & Horowitz, J.L. (1994). An analysis of the effect of Chicago school reform on student performance. In T.A. Downes & W.A. Testa (Eds.) *Midwest approaches to school reform* (pp. 192–221). Chicago: Federal Reserve Bank of Chicago.

Duncan, O.D. (1961). From social system to ecosystem. *Sociological Inquiry, 31,* 140–149.

Edmonds, R. (1979). Effective schools for the urban poor. *Educational Leadership, 37,* pp. 15–23.

Edsall, T.B., & Edsall, M.D. (1991). *Chain reaction: The impact of race, rights, and taxes on American politics.* New York: Norton.

Elmore, R. (1991). Public school choice as a policy issue. In W.T. Gormley (Ed.), *Privatization and its alternatives.* Madison: University of Wisconsin Press, 55–78.

Farley, R., & Frey, W. (1994). Changes in the segregation of Whites from Blacks during the 1980s: Small steps toward a more integrated society. *American Sociological Review, 59* (1), 23–45.

Farley, R., Richards, T., & Wurdock, C. (1980). School desegregation and White flight: An investigation of competing models and their discrepent findings. *Sociology of Education, 53,* 123–139.

Farley, R., Schuman, H., Bianchi, S., Colasanto, D., & Hatchet, S. (1978). Chocolate cities and vanilla suburbs: Will the trend toward racially separate communities continue? *Social Science Research, 7,* 319–344.

Feagin, J.R. (1980). School desgregation: A political-economic perspective. In W.G. Stephan & J.R. Feagin (Eds.), *School desegregation: Past, present and future* (pp. 25–50). New York: Plenum Press.

Feagin, J.R. (1988). *The free enterprise city: Houston in politcal economic perspective.* New Brunswick, NJ: Rutgers University Press.

Feagin, J.R., & Parker, R. (1990). *Building American cities: The urban real estate game.* Englewood Cliffs: Prentice Hall.

Feagin, J., & Smith, M. (1987). Cities and the new international division of labor. In M. Smith & J. Feagin (Eds.), *The capitalist city: Global restructuring and community politics* (pp. 3–34). New York: Basil Blackwell

Field, A.J. (1976). Educational expansion in mid-nineteenth century Massachusetts: Human capital formation or structural reinforcement. *Harvard Educational Review, 46,* 521–552.

Fine, D.R. (1986). *When leadership fails: Desgregation and demoralization in the San Fransisco Schools.* New Brunswick, NJ: Transaction Books.

Fine, M. (1991). *Framing dropouts: Notes on the politics of an urban public high school.* Albany: SUNY Press.

Fine, M. (1993). Democratizing choice: Reinventing, not retreating from, public education. In E. Rasell & R. Rothstein (Eds.), *School choice: Examining the evidence* (pp. 269–300). Washington, DC: Economic Policy Institute.

Fine, M. (1994). Chartering urban school reform. In M. Fine (Ed.), *Chartering urban school reform: Reflections on public high schools in the midst of change* (pp. 5–30). New York: Teachers College Press.

Fine, S. (1989). *Violence in the model city: The Cavanagh administration, race relations, and the Detroit riot of 1967.* Ann Arbor: University of Michigan Press.

Fife, B.L. (1992). *Desegregation in American schools: Comparative intervention strategies.* New York: Praeger Publishers.

Fiske, E.B. (1988, October 1). Miami schools: Laboratory for major changes. *New York Times.*

Fiske, E.B. (1989, May 17). An odd couple reorders Miami's school establishment. *New York Times.*

Fiss, O.M. (1971). The Charlotte-Mecklenberg case—Its significance for northern school desgregation. *University of Chicago Law Review, 38,* 319–344.

Fliegel, S. (1989). Parental choice in East Harlem schools. In J. Nathan (Ed.), *Public schools by choice: Expanding opportunities for parents, students and teachers.* Bloomington, IN: Meyer-Stone Books.

Fliegel, S. (1993). *Miracle in East Harlem: The fight for choice in public education.* New York: Times Books.

Ford, D., & Bennett, A. (1994). The changing principalship in Chicago. *Education and Urban Society, 26,* 238–247.

Formasano, R.P. (1991). *Boston against bussing: Race, class and ethnicity in the 1960s and 1970s* Chapel Hill: University of North Carolina Press.

Forrester, J. (1969). *Urban dynamics.* Cambridge, MA: MIT Press.

Foster, G. (1973). Desegregating urban schools: A review of techniques. *Harvard Educational Review, 43,* 5–36.

Franklin, V. (1979). *The education of Black Philadelphia: The social and educational history of a minority community.* Philadelphia: University of Pennsylvania Press.

Frey, W.H. (1979). Central city White flight: Racial and non-racial causes. *American Sociological Review, 44,* 425–448

Frey, W.H., & Speare, A. Jr. (1988). *Regional metropolitan growth and decline in the United States.* New York: Russell Sage Foundation.

Gettys, W.E. (1961). Human ecology and social theory. In G.A. Theodorson (Ed.), *Studies in Human Ecology* (pp. 98–103). New York: Harper & Row.

Glassberg, D. (1989). *The power of collective purse strings: The effects of bank hegemony on corporations and the state.* Berkeley: University of California Press.

Glatt, C.A., & Roaden, A.L. (1967). Demographic analysis as a tool for educational planning. In M. Gittell (Ed.), *Educating an urban population* (pp. 117–134). Beverly Hills, CA: Sage.

Goldberg, M. (1963). Factors affecting educational attainment in depressed urban areas. In A. H. Passow (Ed.), *Education in depressed areas* (pp. 68–100). New York: Teachers College Press.

Goldman, W. W., & Blakely, E. J. (1992). *Separate societies: Poverty and inequality in U.S. Cities.* Philadelphia: Temple University Press.

Gottdiener, M. (1977). *Planned sprawl: Private and public interests in suburbia.* Beverly Hills, CA: Sage Publications.

Gottdiener, M. (1985). *The social production of urban space.* Austin: University of Texas Press.

Gottdiener, M. & Feagin, J. R. (1988). The paradigm shift in urban sociology. *Urban Affairs Quarterly, 24,* 163–187.

Greene, M. F., & Ryan, O. (1965). *The school children growing up in the slums.* New York: Pantheon Books.

Grimshaw, W. A. (1992). *Bitter fruit: Black politics and the Chicago machine, 1931–1991.* Chicago: University of Chicago Press.

Grossman, J. R. (1989). *Land of hope: Chicago, Black southerners and the great migration* Chicago: University of Chicago Press.

Guest, A. (1978). Suburban social status: Persistence or evolution. *American Sociological Review, 43,* 251–264.

Guest, A., & Zuiches, J. J. (1971). Another look at residential turnover in urban neighborhoods. *American Journal of Sociology, 77,* 457–467.

Gutis, P. S. (1988, February 18). Rochester asks teachers for "extra mile." *New York Times,* Sec. 2, 1–2.

Harding, R. R. (1983). Housing discrimination as a basis for interdistrict school desegregation measures. *Yale Law Journal, 93,* 340–361

Harris, C., & Ullman, E. (1945). The nature of cities. *The Annals of the American Academy of Political and Social Science, 252,* 1–17.

Harvey, D. (1973). *Social justice and the city.* London: Edward Arnold.

Harvey, D. (1989). *The urban experience.* Baltimore: Johns Hopkins University Press.

Hauser, P. M. (1965). Urbanization: An overview. In P. M. Hauser & L. Schnore (Eds.), *The study of urbanization* (pp. 1–47). New York: John Wiley.

Hauser, P. M. (1977). Chicago—urban crisis exemplar. In J. J. Palen (Ed.), *City scenes* (pp. 15–25). Boston: Little Brown.

Havighurst, R. J. (1961). Metropolitan development and the educational system. *The School Review, 69,* 251–269.

Havighurst, R. J. (1963). Urban development and the educational system. In A. H. Passow (Ed.), *Education in depressed areas* (pp. 34–36).

Havighurst, R. J. (1966). *Education in metropolitan areas.* Boston: Allyn & Bacon.

Havighurst, R. J. (1971). The reorganization of education in metropolitan areas. *Phi Delta Kappan, 52,* 354–358.

Hawley, A. H. (1950). *Human ecology: A theory of community structure.* New York: Ronald Press.

Hawley, W. D., Crain, R. L., & Rossel, C. H. (1983). *Strategies for effective desegregation: Lessons from research.* Lexington, MA: Lexington Books.

Hawley, W. D., Rossell, C. H., & Crain, R. L. (1983). Directions for future research. In C. H. Rossell & W. D. Hawley (Eds.), *The consequences of school desegregation* (pp. 158–179). Philadelphia: Temple University Press

Hawley, A. H., & Zimmer, B. (1970). *The metropolitan community: Its people and government.* Beverly Hills, CA: Sage Publications.

Henig, J. R. (1989). Choice, race and public schools: The adoption and implementation of a magnet program. *Journal of Urban Affairs,* 11, 243–259.

Henig, J.R. (1994). *Rethinking school choice: Limits of the market metaphor.* Princeton, NJ: Princeton University Press.

Hess, G.A., Jr. (1990). *School restructuring, Chicago style.* Newberry Park, CA: Corwin Press.

Hess, G.A., Jr. (1994). Introduction: School-based management as a vehicle for school reform. *Education and Urban Society, 26,* 203–219.

Hill, P.T., Wise, A.E., & Shapiro, L. (1989). *Educational progress: Cities mobilize to improve their schools.* Santa Monica, CA: Rand Corporation.

Hirsch, A.R. (1983). *Making the second ghetto: Race and housing in Chicago, 1940–1960.* New York: Cambridge University Press.

Hochschild, J.L. (1984). *The new American dilemma: Liberal democracy and school desegregation.* New Haven, CT: Yale University Press.

Hogan, D.J. (1985). *Class and reform: School and society in Chicago, 1880–1930.* Philadelphia: University of Pennsylvania Press.

Homel, M.W. (1984). *Down from equality: Black Chicagoans and the public schools, 1920–41.* Urbana: University of Illinois Press.

Homel, M.W. (1990) Two worlds of race? Urban Blacks and the public schools, North and South, 1865–1940. In D. N. Plank & R. Ginsberg (Eds.), *Southern cities, Southern Schools: Public education in the urban South* (pp. 237–261). New York: Greenwood Press.

Hoyt, H. (1939). *The structure and growth of residential neighborhoods in American cities.* Washington, DC: U.S. Federal Housing Administration.

Hummel, R.C., & Nagle, J.M. (1973). *Urban education in America: Problems and prospects.* New York: Oxford University Press.

Hunter, F. (1953). *Community power structure: A study of decision-makers.* Chapel Hill: University of North Carolina Press.

Jackson, K.T. (1975). Urban deconcentration in the nineteenth century: A statistical inquiry. In L.F. Schnore (Ed.), *The new urban history: Quantitative explorations by American historians* (pp. 110–142). Princeton, NJ: Princeton University Press.

Jackson, K.T. (1985). *The crabgrass frontier: The suburbanization of the United States.* New York: Oxford University Press.

Kaestle, C.F. (1973). *The development of an urban school system: New York City, 1750–1850.* Cambridge: Harvard University Press.

Kaestle, C.F., & Vinovskis, M.A. (1979). *Education and social change in nineteenth century Massachusetts.* New York: Cambridge University Press.

Kantor, H., & Brenzel, B. (1993). Urban education and the "truly disadvantaged": The historical roots of the contemporary crisis, 1945–1990. In M.B. Katz (Ed.), *The underclass debate: Views from history* (pp. 366–401). Princeton: Princeton University Press.

Karier, C.J., Violas, P., & Spring, J. (1973). *Roots of crisis: American education in the twentieth century.* Chicago: Rand McNally.

Katz, M.B. (1968). *The irony of early school reform: Educational innovation in mid-nineteenth century Massachusetts.* Boston: Beacon Press.

Katz, M.B. (1972). *Class, bureaucracy, and schools: The illusion of educational change in America.* New York: Praeger.

Katz, M.B. (1992). School reform as history. *Teachers College Record, 94,* 58–71.

Katz, M.B. (1993). The urban "underclass" as a metaphor of social transformation. In M.B. Katz (Ed.), *The underclass debate: Views from history* (pp. 1–23). Princeton, NJ: Princeton University Press.

Katz, M.B., & Vinovskis, M.A. (1987). Forum. *History of Education Quarterly, 27,* 241–258.

Katzman, M.T. (1971.) *The political economy of urban schools.* Cambridge, MA: Harvard University Press.

Katznelson, I. (1981). *City trenches: Urban politics and the patterning of class in the United States.* New York: Pantheon Books.

Katznelson, I., & Weir, M. (1985). *Schooling for all: Class, race, and the decline of the democratic ideal.* New York: Basic Books.

Katznelson, I. (1992). *Marxism and the city.* Oxford, England: Clarendon Press.

Kirp, D. L. (1982). *Just schools: The idea of racial equality in American education.* Berkeley: University of California Press.

Kirp, D. (1992, November). What school choice really means. *Atlantic Monthly,* p. 125.

Kleppner, P. (1985). *Chicago divided: The making of a Black mayor.* DeKalb, IL: Northern Illinois University Press.

Kohl, H. (1967). *36 children.* New York: New American Library.

Kozol, J. (1967). *Death at an early age.* New York: Bantam Books.

Kozol, J. (1991). *Savage inequalities.* New York: Crown Publishers.

Kusmer, K. (1976). *A ghetto takes shape: Black Cleveland, 1870–1930.* Urbana: University of Illinois Press.

Lazerson, M. (1970). *The origins of the urban school: Massachusetts, 1870–1900.* Cambridge, MA: Harvard University Press.

Lee, V., & Bryk, A. S. (1993). Science of policy argument? A review of the quantitative evidence in Chubb and Moe's *Politics, markets, and America's schools.* In E. Rasell & R. Rothstein (Eds.), *School choice: Examining the evidence.* Washington, DC: Economic Policy Institute.

Lee, V. E., Croninger, R. G., & Smith, J. B. (1994). Parental choice of schools and social stratification in education: The paradox of Detroit. *Educational Evaluation and Policy Analysis, 16,* 434–457.

Lemann, N. (1991). *The promised land: The great Black migration and how it changed America.* New York: Alfred A. Knopf.

Levine, D., & Havighurst, R. J. (1968). Social systems of a metropolitan area. In R. J. Havighurst (Ed.), *Metropolitanism: Its challenge to education.* (67th Yearbook of the National Society for the Study of Education, pp. 5–23). Chicago: University of Chicago Press.

Levine, M. V., & Zipp, J. F. (1993). A city at risk: The changing social and economic context of public schooling in Milwaukee. In J. L. Rury & F. A. Cassell (Eds.), *Seeds of crisis: Public schooling in Milwaukee since 1920* (pp. 42–72). Madison: University of Wisconsin Press.

Lewis, D. A., & Nakagawa, K. (1995). *Race and educational reform in the American metropolis: A study of decentralization.* Albany: State University of New York Press.

Lewis, N. A. (1989, September 24). New York's new schools chief has a super decentralization plan. *New York Times,* E6.

Lewis, O. (1965). Further observations on the folk-urban continuum and urbanization with special reference to Mexico City. In P. M. Hauser & L. Schnore (Eds.), *The study of urbanization* (pp. 187–200). New York: John Wiley.

Lewis, O. (1968). The culture of poverty. In D. P. Moynihan (Ed.), *On understanding poverty: Perspectives from the social sciences* (pp. 187–200). New York: Basic Books.

Logan, J., & Molotch, H. (1987). *Urban fortunes: The political economy of places.* Berkeley: University of California Press.

Logan, J. R., & Swanstrom, T. (1990). Urban restructuring: A critical view. In J. R. Logan & T. Swanstrom (Eds.), *Beyond the city limits: Urban policy and economic restructuring in comparative perspective.* Philadelphia: Temple University Press.

London, B., & Flanagan, W. G. (1979). Comparative urban ecology: A summary of the field. In J. Walton & L. H. Masotti (Eds.), *The city in comparative perspective: Cross national research and new directions in theory* (pp. 41–66). Beverly Hills: Sage.

Long, N.E. (1972). *The unwalled city.* New York: Basic Books.
Lukas, J.A. (1986). *Common ground: A turbulent decade in the lives of three American families.* New York: Vintage.
Mark, J.H., & Anderson, B.D. (1984). Schools and the transformation of a metropolis. *The Urban Review,* 16, 3–23.
Massy, D.S., & Denton, N.A. (1993). *American apartheid: Segregation and the making of the underclass.* Cambridge, MA: Harvard University Press.
Mayer, H.M. (1965). A survey of urban geography. In P.M. Hauser & L. Schnore (Eds.), *The study of urbanization* (pp. 81–114). New York: John Wiley.
Mirel, J. (1990). Progressive school reform in comparative prespective. In D. Plank & R. Ginsberg (Eds.), *Southern cities, southern schools: Public education in the urban south* (pp. 151–174). New York: Greenwood Press.
Mirel, J. (1993a). *The rise and fall of an urban school system: Detroit, 1907–81.* Ann Arbor: University of Michigan Press.
Mirel, J. (1993b). School reform, chicago style: educational innovation in a changing urban context, 1976–1991. *Urban Education, 28,* 116–149.
Moe, T.M. (1994). School choice and the creaming problem. In T.A. Downes & W.A. Testa (Eds.), *Midwest approaches to school reform* (pp. 156–161). Chicago: Federal Reserve Bank.
Mohraz, J.J. (1979). *The separate problem: School segregation in three northern cities, 1900–1930.* Westport, CN: Greenwood Press.
Murray, C. (1984). *Losing ground: American social policy, 1950–1980.* New York: Basic Books.
Natriello, G., McDill, E., & Pallas, A. (1990). *Schooling disadvantaged children: Racing against catastrophe.* New York: Teachers College Press.
Nearing, S. (1917). Who's who on our boards of education. *School and Society,* V, 89–90.
Oakes, J. (1985). *Keeping track: How schools structure inequality.* New Haven: Yale University Press.
Oates, W.E. (1969). The effects of property taxes aqnd local public spending on property values: An empirical study of tax capitalization and the tiebout hypothesis. *Journal of Political Economy, 77,* 957–971.
Ogawa, R. (1994). The institutional sources of educational reform: The case of school-based management. *American Educational Research Journal,* 31, 519–548.
Ogbu, J.U. (1986). Structural constraints in school desegregation. In J. Prager, D. Longshore, & M. Seeman (Eds.), *School desegregation research: New directions in situational analysis* (pp. 21–45). New York: Plenum Press.
Omi, M., & Winant, H. (1994). *Racial formation in the United States: From the 1960s to the 1990s.* New York: Routledge.
Orfield, G. (1969). *The reconstruction of southern education: The schools and the 1964 Civil Rights Act.* New York: Wiley Interscience.
Orfield, G. (1977). Policy implications of White flight in metropolitan areas. In D.U. Levine & R.J. Havighurst (Eds.), *The future of big-city schools: Desegregation policies and magnet alternatives* (pp. 70–84). Berkeley: McCutchen.
Orfield, G. (1978). *Must we bus? Segregated schools and national policy.* Washington, DC: The Brookings Institution.
Orfield, G. (1983). *Public school desegregation in the United States, 1968–1980.* Washington, DC: Joint Center for Policy Studies.
Orfield, G., & Ashkinaze, C. (1993). *The closing door: Conservative policy and Black opportunity.* Chicago: University of Chicago Press.
Osofsky, G. (1963). *Harlem: The making of a ghetto.* New York: Harper & Row.
Passow, A.H. (1963). Education in depressed areas. In A.H. Passow (Ed.), *Education in depressed areas.* New York: Teachers College Press.

Peters, T.J. (1987). *Thriving on chaos: Handbook for a management revolution.* New York: Alfred A. Knopf.

Peters, T.J., & Waterman, R.H., Jr. (1982). *In search of excellence: Lessons from America's best run companies.* New York: Harper and Row.

Peterson, P. (1974). The politics of American education. *Review of Research in Education, 2,* 348–389.

Peterson, P.E. (1976). *School politics Chicago style.* Chicago: University of Chicago Press.

Peterson, P.E. (1981). *City limits.* Chicago: University of Chicago Press.

Peterson, P.E. (1985). *The politics of school reform, 1870–1940.* Chicago: University of Chicago Press.

Peterson, P.E. (1988). Economic and political trends affecting education. In R. Haskins & D. MacRae (Eds.), *Policies for America's schools: Teachers equity and indicators* (pp. 44–46). Norwood, NJ: Ablex.

Peterson, P.E. (1991). The urban underclass and the poverty paradox. In C. Jenks & P.E. Peterson (Eds.), *The urban underclass.* Washington, DC: The Brookings Institution.

Peterson, P.E. (1993). Are big-city school systems holding their own? In J.L. Rury & F.A Cassell (Eds.), *Seeds of crisis: Public schooling in Milwaukee since 1920* (pp. 269–301). Madison: University of Wisconsin Press.

Peterson, P.E., Rabe, B.G., & Wong, K. (1986). *When federalism works.* Washington, DC: The Brookings Institution.

Popenoe, D. (1977). *The suburban environment: Sweden and the United States.* Chicago: University of Chicago Press.

Prager, J., Longshore, D., & Seeman, M. (1986). Introduction: The desegregation situation. In J. Prager, D. Longshore, & M. Seeman (Eds.), *School desegregation research: New directions in situational analysis* (pp. 3–19). New York: Plenum Press.

Purkey, S.C., & Smith, M.S. (1983). Effective schools: A review. *The Elementary Schools Journal, 83,* 426–452.

Raftery, J.R. (1992). *Land of fair promise: Politics and reform in Los Angeles Schools, 1885–1941.* Stanford, CA: Stanford University Press.

Ravitch, D. (1974). *The great school wars, New York City, 1805–1973: A history of the public schools as battlefield of social change.* New York: Basic Books.

Ravitch, D. (1978). *The revisionists revised: A critique of the radical attack on the schools.* New York: Basic Books.

Ravitch, D. (1994). Somebody's children: Expanding educational opportunities for all America's children. *The Brookings Review, 12,* 4–9.

Raywid, M.A. (1992). Choice orientations, discussions, and prospects. In P. Cookson (Ed.), *The choice controversy* (pp. 3–23). Newbury Park, CA: Corwin Press.

Read, F.T. (1975). Judicial evolution of the law of school integration since Brown vs. Board of Education. *Law and Contemporary Problems, 39,* 7–49.

Reese, W.J. (1986). *Power and the promise of school reform: Grassroots movements during the Progressive Era.* Boston: Routledge and Kegan Paul.

Riessman, F. (1962). *The culturally deprived child.* New York: Harper & Row.

Rivlin, G. (1992). *Fire on the prairie: Chicago's Harold Washington and the politics of race.* New York: Henry Holt and Co.

Rogers, D. (1968). *110 Livingston Street: Politics and bureaucracy in the New York City School System.* New York: Random House.

Rossell, C.H. (1975). School desegregation and White flight. *Political Science Quarterly, 90,* 675–695.

Rossell, C.H. (1977). The mayor's role in school desegregation implementation. *Urban Education, 12,* 247–270.

Rossell, C.H. (1979). Magnet schools as a desegregation tool: The importance of contextual factors in explaining their success. *Urban Education, 14,* 303–320.

Rossell, C.H. (1983a). Applied social science research: What does it say about the effectiveness of school desegregation plans? *Journal of Legal Studies,* 12, 69–107.

Rossell, C.H. (1983b). Desgregation plans, racial isolation, White flight and community response. In C. H. Rossell & W.D. Hawley (Eds.), *The consequences of school desegregation* (pp. 13–57). Philadelphia: Temple University Press.

Rossell, C.H. (1985). What is attractive about magnet schools? *Urban Education, 20,* 7–22.

Rossell, C.H. (1987). The Buffalo controlled choice plan. *Urban Education,* 22, 328–354.

Rossell, C.H. (1988). How effective are voluntary plans with magnet schools? *Educational Evaluation and Policy Analysis, 10,* 325–342.

Rossell, C.H. (1990). *The carrot of the stick for school desegregation policy.* Philadelphia: Temple University Press.

Rossell, C., & Glenn, C.L. (1988). The Cambridge controlled choice plan. *Urban Review, 20,* 75–94.

Rossell, C.H., & Hawley, W.D. (1983). Introduction: Desegregation and change. In C.H. Rossell & W.D. Hawley (Eds.), *The consequences of school desgregation* (pp. 3–12). Philadelphia: Temple University Press.

Rubin, L.B. (1972). *Bussing and Backlash: White against White in a California school district.* Berkeley: University of California Press.

Rury, J.L. (1984). Urban structure and school participation: Immigrant women in 1900. *Social Science History, 8,* 219–241.

Rury, J.L. (1989). Urbanization and education: Regional patterns of educational development in American cities, 1900–1910. *Michigan Academician,* 20, 261–279.

Rury, J.L. (1991). *Education and women's work: Female schooling and the division of labor in urban America, 1870–1930.* Albany: State University of New York Press.

Rury, J.L. (1993). The changing social context of urban education: A national perspective. In J.L. Rury & F.A. Cassell (Eds.), *Seeds of crisis: Public schooling in Milwaukee since 1920* (pp. 10–41). Madison: University of Wisconsin Press.

Sacks, S. (1972). *City schools/Suburban schools: A history of fiscal conflict.* Syracuse: Syracuse University Press.

Saunders, P. (1981). *Social theory and the urban question.* London: Hutchinson.

Schnore, L.F. (1961). The myth of human ecology. *Sociological Inquiry, 31,* 29–43.

Schnore, L.F. (1965). *The urban scene: Human ecology and demography.* New York: The Free Press.

Schnore, L.F. (1972). *Class and race in cities and suburbs.* Chicago: Markham.

Schrag, P. (1967). *Village school downtown: Politcs and education—A Boston report.* Boston: Beacon Press

Schultz, S. (1973). *The culture factory: Public schools in Boston, 1790–1860.* New York: Oxford University Press.

Sears, D.O. (1988). Symbolic racism. In P. Katz & D. Taylor (Eds.), *Eliminating racism* (pp. 53–83). New York: Plenum.

Sears, D.O., Hensler, C.P., & Speer, L.K. (1979). Whites' opposition to "Bussing": Self interest of symbolic politics? *American Political Science Review,* 73, 369–384.

Sedler, R.A. (1975). Metropolitan desegregation in the wake of Milliken—on losing big battles and winning small wars. *Washington University Law Quarterly, 53,* 535–620.

Sexton, P. (1965). *Spanish Harlem.* New York: Harper Colophon Books.

Sjoberg, G. (1960). *The preindustrial city: Past and present.* New York: The Free Press.

Sjoberg, G. (1965). Theory and research in urban sociology. In P.M. Hauser & L. Schnore (Eds.), *The Study of Urbanization* (pp. 157–189). New York: John Wiley.

Soja, E. (1987). Restructuring and internationalization of the Los Angeles region. In M. Smith & J. Feagin (Eds.), *The capitalist city: Global restructuring and community politics* (pp. 178–198). New York: Basil Blackwell.

Spear, A. (1967). *Black Chicago: The making of a Negro ghetto.* Chicago: University of Chicago Press.

Spring, J. (1972). Education and the rise of the corporate state. Boston: Beacon Press.

Stolee, M. (1993). The Milwaukee desgregation case. In J.L. Rury & F.A. Cassell (Eds.), *Seeds of crisis: Public schooling in Milwaukee since 1920* (pp. 229–268). Madison: University of Wisconsin Press.

Sugrue, T. (1993). The structures of urban poverty: The reorganization of space and work in three periods of American history. In M.B. Katz (Ed.), *The underclass debate: Views from history* (pp. 85–117). Princeton: Princeton University Press.

Sukstorf, M.E., Wells, A.S., & Crain, R. (1993). A re-examination of Chubb and Moe's *Politics, Markets and America's Schools.* In E. Rasell & R. Rothstein (Eds.), *School choice: Examining the evidence* (pp. 209–218). Washington, DC: Economic Policy Institute.

Taeuber, K.E. (1975). Racial segregation: The persisting dilemma. *Annals of the American Academy of Political and Social Science, 422,* 87–96.

Taeuber, K.E., & Taeuber, A.F. (1965). *Negroes in cities: Residential segregation and neighborhood change.* Chicago: Aldine.

Thomlinson, R. (1969). *Urban structure: The social and spatial character of cities.* New York: Random House.

Thompson, W.R. (1965). *A preface to urban economics.* Baltimore: Johns Hopkins University Press.

Tiebout, C.M. (1956). A pure theory of local expenditures. *Journal of Political Economy, 64,* 416–424.

Timar, T.B. (1992). Urban politics and state school finance in the 1980s. In J.G. Cibulka, R.J. Reed, & K.K. Wong (Eds.), *The politics of urban education in the United States* (pp. 105–121). Washington, DC: Falmer Press.

Tyack, D. (1974). *The one best system: A history of urban education in the United States.* Cambridge, MA: Harvard University Press.

Tyack, D., Lowe, R., & Hansot, E. (1984). *Public schools in hard times: The great depression and recent years.* Cambridge, MA: Harvard University Press.

U.S. Civil Rights Commission. (1967). *Racial isolation in the public schools.* Washington, DC: U.S. Government Printing Office.

U.S. Department of Education. (1986). *What works: Research about teaching and learning.* Washington, DC: Government Printing Office.

Urbanski, A. (1991, October 23). "Real change is real hard": Lesson learned in Rochester. *Education Week,* p. 29.

Usdan, M.D. (1967). Some issues confronting school administrators in large school systems. *Educational Administration Quarterly, 3,* 218–237.

Vander Weele, M. (1994). *Reclaiming our schools: The struggle for Chicago school reform.* Chicago: Loyola University Press.

Vinovskis, M.A. (1985). *The origins of public high schools.* Madison: University of Wisconsin Press.

Vinovskis, M.A. (1995). *Education, society and economic opportunity: Some historical perspectives.* New Haven, CT: Yale University Press.

Violas, P.C. (1978). *The training of the urban working class: A history of twentieth century American education.* Chicago: Rand McNally.

Walton, J. (1979). Urban political economy: A new paradigm. *Comparative Urban Research, 7,* 374–390.

Walton, J. (1981). The new urban sociology. *International Social Science Research, 33,* 374–390.

Wegmann, R.G. (1977). Desegregation and resegregation: A review of the research on White flight from urban areas. In D.U. Levine & R.J. Havighurst (Eds.), *The future of big-city schools: Desgregation policies and magnet alternatives* (pp. 11–54). Berkeley: McCutchen Publishing.

Welch, F., & Light, A., Dong, F., & Ross, J.M. (1987). *New evidence on school desegregation.* Washington, DC: United States Commission on Civil Rights.

Wells, A.S. (1993a). The sociology of school choice: Why some win and others lose in the educational marketplace. In E. Rasell & R. Rothstein (Eds.), *School choice: Examining the evidence* (pp. 29–48). Washington, DC: Economic Policy Institute.

Wells, A.S. (1993b). *A time to choose: America at the crossroads of school choice policy.* New York: Hill and Wang.

Wells, A.S., & Cronin, R.L. (1992). Do parents choose school quality or school status? A sociological theory of free market education. In P. Cookson (Ed.), *The choice controversy* (pp. 65–82). Newbury Park, CA: Corwin Press.

Wilkerson, J.H. (1979). *From Brown to Bakke: The Supreme Court and school integration, 1954–1978.* New York: Oxford University Press.

Wilson, W.J. (1987). *The truly disadvantaged: The inner city, the underclass, and public policy.* Chicago: University of Chicago Press.

Wilson, W.J. (1991). Another look at *The Truly Disadvantaged. Political Science Quarterly, 106* (4), 639–656.

Wirth, L. (1928). *The ghetto* Chicago: University of Chicago Press.

Wirth, L. (1938). Urbanism as a way of life. *American Journal of Sociology, 44,* 1–24.

Wise, A.E. (1968). *Rich schools, poor schools: The promise of educational opportunity.* Chicago: University of Chicago Press.

Witte, J.F., & Thorn, C. (1994). Who chooses? Vouchers and interdistrict choice programs in Milwaukee. In T.A. Downes & W.A. Testa (Eds.), *Midwest approaches to school reform* (pp. 127–155). Chicago: Federal Reserve Bank.

Wolf, E. (1981). *Trial and error: The Detroit school segregation case.* Detroit: Wayne State University Press.

Wong, K. (1990). *City choices: Education and housing.* Albany: State University of New York Press.

Wong, K. (1991). The politics of education as a field of study: An interpretive aanalysis. In J.G. Cibulka, R.J. Reed, & K.K. Wong (Eds.), *The politics of urban education in the United States.* Washington, DC: Falmer Press.

Wong, K. (1993). Governance structure, resource allocation and equity policy. *Review of Research in Education, 20,* 257–289.

Wong, K., & Sunderman, G. (1994). Redesigning accountability at the systemwide level: The politics of Chicago school reform. In T.A. Down & W.A. Testa (Eds.), *Midwest approaches to school reform* (pp. 162–187). Chicago: Federal Reserve Bank.

Wrigley, J. (1982). *Class politics and public schools: Chicago, 1900–1950.* New Brunswick, NJ: Rutgers University Press.

Zorbaugh, H.W. (1929). *The Gold Coast and the slum.* Chicago: University of Chicago Press.

Zunz, O. (1983). *The changing face of inequality: Urbanization, industrial development and immigrants in Detroit, 1880–1920.* Chicago: University of Chicago Press.

Received October 12, 1995
Revision received November 26, 1995
Accepted November 29, 1995

II.
RACE AND EDUCATION

Chapter 3

Research in American Indian and Alaska Native Education: From Assimilation to Self-Determination

DONNA DEYHLE
University of Utah

KAREN SWISHER
Arizona State University

Those who have been involved in the formal education of Indians have assumed that the main purpose of the school is assimilation. The Indian would be better off, it was believed, if he could be induced, or forced, to adpot [*sic*] the white man's habits, skills, knowledge, language, values, religion, attitudes, and customs—or at least some of them. Assimilation, to be sure, is a reciprocal process, and in the course of it the white man has learned much from the Indian, so that today American culture is immeasurably enriched by items adopted from the Indian. But it was always the white man's way of life which must set the pattern. Formal education has been regarded as the most effective means for bringing about assimilation. (B. Berry, 1968, pp. 15–16).

INTRODUCTION

Nearly 3 decades have passed since Brewton Berry included this statement in his extensive review of the research literature in Indian education. At about the same time Berry completed his study, the Kennedy Report, formally known as *Indian Education: A National Tragedy—A National Challenge* (U.S. Senate, 1969), reiterated and recognized additional problems in Indian education identified previously in the Meriam Report of 1928, *The Problem of Indian Administration.* In 1991 a research report to the Commission on the Rights, Liberties, and Responsibilities of the American Indian, *The Indian: America's Unfinished Business* (Brophy & Aberle, 1966), argued that schools were failing at their jobs. Assimilation was their business, and yet there remained the "Indian problem." Twenty-six years later, *Indian Nations At Risk: An Educational Strategy for Action* reported that progress has been made; however, Indian students remain at risk, confronted with a number of barriers that impede additional

We would like to thank our contributing editors, John Tippeconnic III and Frank Margonis, for their thoughtful insights on our chapter. We would also like to thank Tarajean Yazzie and Christine Cain for their expert help on sections of the chapter. We bear sole responsibiiltiy, however, for the interpertations presented.

success. Despite unchanging economic, social, and health problems; inadequate, unequal, and unpredictable funding for K–12 schools, tribal colleges, and higher education; schools that do not promote Native language use or appropriate academic, social, cultural, and spiritual development among Native students; and curricula that do not include tribal history, culture, and language, American Indian and Alaska Native people have been successful in the development and operation of their own schools and colleges and know a great deal about effective practices.

Why Indian Education?

From its beginnings in the 17th century, formal education for American Indians and Alaska Natives developed differently than it did for other people in this country (Senese, 1991; Szasz, 1974). Based on principles of sovereignty and trust responsibility, the history of Indian education is unique, complex, and not clearly understood by the majority of mainstream America.

In exchange for nearly 1 billion acres of land, certain services, protection against invasion, and self government were to be provided in perpetuity, or "as long as the grass grows and rivers flow." More than 400 treaties solemnized the transactions—land in exchange for promises—between sovereigns for nearly 100 years (1778 to 1871), thus creating a special relationship between Indian people and the federal government.

The foundation of this unique relationship is one of trust: the Indians trust the United States to fulfill the promises which were given in exchange for land. The federal government's obligation to honor this trust relationship and to fulfill its treaty commitments is known as its *trust responsibility.* (Pevar, 1992, p. 26)

In more than 100 of the treaties, provision for educational services and facilities was included. "Thus treaties and subsequent executive orders, congressional acts, and court decisions formed the legal basis for federal recognition and responsibility for Indian education" (Tippeconnic & Swisher, 1992, p. 75). Boarding schools established by missionaries in the 1600s represented the first assimilative attempts to remove Indians from their tribal and family members, religion, language, and homeland by placing them in distant schools to learn non-Indian ways. This approach gained wide support during the 1700s and flourished in the 1800s when the federal government increased its involvement and responsibility by developing an educational system for American Indians. Viewed as a solution to the "Indian problem," the boarding school system, in essence, became the problem. Breakdown of tribal culture, alienation of Indian parents from the education of their children, and emotional, psychological, and mental anguish were the results of boarding school education. During the early 1900s, education reform efforts influenced a shift away from boarding schools to day schools located closer to Indian communities, and eventually to public schools, based on the belief that assimilation would occur more rapidly if Indian students were integrated with non-Indian students. By 1920, more Indian students were in public schools than Bureau of Indian Affairs (BIA) schools. According to Tippeconnic and Swisher (1992):

Even though the policy of attending public schools continues into the 1990s, curricular and instructional approaches in teaching Indian students have varied over time: The 1930s saw attention given to culturally related materials; the 1950s witnessed the federal government's policy of termination of services to Indians and a move away from Indian-related curriculum; the 1960s and 1970s encouraged a revival of "Indianness" in the classroom. During the 1980s the national reform movement in education questioned "Indianness" in the classroom in favor of a standard approach to education that emphasized accountability through testing. (p. 75)

For more than 100 years, the system was operated by the federal government with little or no local control; in contrast, public education was based on local control with very little assistance from the federal government (Swisher, 1994). Today, local control is a reality; there are more tribal schools than BIA-operated schools in the BIA system. Although Indian children are still "at risk" of educational failure, great strides have been made by Indian people to take control of the systems of education (and other institutions) that affect their future.

Throughout history Indian people have been characterized as "problems." Such a description necessitated finding solutions, and schools as purveyors of assimilation became natural laboratories of research. Studying the formal education of Indians was a necessary step in the many educational experiments that sprang from the first attempts to formally educate Indians in colonial America. Nearly 400 years later, assimilation may not be the explicit goal, but the perplexities in Indian educational achievement still remain as a major field of inquiry.

Researching the "Indian Problem"

As noted earlier, perhaps the most visible symbol of the assimilatory strategies and goals of the dominant society was the development of the boarding school system. The idea was that the best way for Indians to become Americans was to remove their children as far as possible from the influences of their homes, families, and culture. The use of native languages by children was forbidden under threats of corporal punishment; semiskilled vocational training was encouraged for Indians; students were placed as laborers and domestics in White families' homes during vacation time; and native religions were suppressed. In a very real sense, the schooling package that provided literacy for Indians also required becoming "White." While the structure has changed somewhat, this practice has changed very little in the past 100 years.

Research studies on boarding school experiences argued that assimilation was "complete" for very few Indians (Lomawaima, 1994; McBeth, 1983; Trennert, 1988). Indian youth, separated from their White peers, developed a strong ethnic identity with their peers from other tribes, facilitating the development of a pan-Indian identity. For the most part, Indian youth endured the schooling experience, retained a strong ethnic identity, and returned to live with their families on the reservations. In an ironic way, the boarding school experience helped create a climate that increased a sense of "Indianness." McBeth (1983) highlighted this contradiction with the voice of a Kiowa woman, a leader in her tribe, who said in 1918, "The boarding schools have their strong points and their weak points. We endure over the years despite the bad experiences, and we get stronger on account of them" (p. 148).

Assimilationists, aware of the failure of the boarding school system, argued that public school would represent the best educational experience for Indian youth. If these youth were integrated with Anglo students, their ethnic identity (which was viewed as inferior) would soon fade and the "Indian problem" would vanish (McBeth, 1983). This, too, has failed. As the research we will present in this chapter illustrates, Indian identity is as strong today as 100 years ago, and yet the "Indian educational problem" remains unsolved. Although the federal government has closed most of the boarding schools, shifting the responsibility of the education of almost 85% of Indian youth to public education, the assimilationist goals of the boarding school era are still evident in teachers' beliefs, pedagogy, and curricula.

Within this educational context researchers have investigated the "Indian problem." The purpose of this chapter is to review and discuss selected research in American Indian and Alaska Native[1] education. In our review, we will argue that, until recently, research has made little difference in the academic achievement of Indian youth. Educational research—carried out by researchers who often do not have a long-term commitment to the community—has tended to buttress the assimilatory model by locating deficiencies in Indian students and families. In part, we will argue that the kinds of questions asked, such as "How do Indian children compare with White students?" position the Indian student in a deficit category in need of "change," thus supporting an assimilation model. This "deficit model" was an especially dominant theme of research studies up until the 1960s, when community-based ethnographic or long-term research studies argued for a "cultural difference" model that addressed power relations. Different kinds of research questions were asked by cultural and critical researchers, who attempted to understand the integrity of Native cultures and argued against assimilation as a goal of schooling. Cultural and critical research has provided a valuable alternative perspective, although some of it has also been marred by assimilatory assumptions. Indian researchers, grounded in self-determination and the beliefs of cultural integrity, currently offer further insights into the kind of research directions and questions needed to assess educational success from a local perspective.

American Indians have been studied more than any other ethnic group in this country.[2] We believe that it is not within the scope of work defined for this chapter to review each of the research citations, nor are all of the citations worthy of review. In addition, the issues examined in the research were extremely broad, covering such topics as teacher education, school types (BIA, public, day, boarding, religious), tribal colleges and higher education, technology, parent involvement, curriculum development, school facilities and funding, staff training, and school reform. Instead, we have chosen to limit our review to studies focusing specifically on Indian students, their families, communities, and the influence of both culture and power relations. In our review of the literature over the past 30 years, we found that the largest body of research was grounded in educational anthropology and sociology. This research used the concept of culture as a framework for the analysis of schooling and the behaviors of Indian students, parents and their communities. With this culturally focused research, we try to capture an understanding of educational success and failure from the perspective of Indian students. Finally, we describe recent initiatives taken by Indian individuals and organizations to define and conduct relevant research.

A LEGACY OF DEFICIT THOUGHT: RESEARCH GUIDED BY ASSIMILATION IDEOLOGY

The magnitude of study in Indian education is demonstrated by several reviews, most of which were completed in the late 1960s and early 1970s and many of which overlap in content. The *Bibliography of American Indian Education Studies* completed by the Battelle Human Affairs Research Center in 1976 produced 790 citations. Trimble, Goddard, and Dinges (1977) completed the *Review of the Literature on Educational Needs and Problems of American Indians: 1971–1976*, which produced 962 articles on Indian educational research. Perhaps the most comprehensive early review of the literature was completed by Brewton Berry in 1968 for the Special Subcommittee on Indian Education of the Committee on Labor and Public Welfare of the United States Senate. Titled *The Education of American Indians: A Survey of the Literature,* his review bibliography contains 708 items from the early 1900s to the late 1960s, nearly half of the 1,500 books, articles in professional and popular journals, theses, and dissertations he uncovered. Berry described much of what was written as "polemic, apologetic, speculative, and prescriptive" (1968, p.2). What remained in his bibliography were pieces that Berry anticipated would have value for graduate students, although the quality of the items varied considerably.

Much of it represents research of a high order, but much was poorly designed and ineptly executed. However, even in a thesis where the design and methodology are questionable, there often reside a few grains of truth, an interesting fact or statistic, a descriptive paragraph or two, or reports of interviews with now-departed pioneers. Any of these would prove useful to future researchers, and are therefore included. (1968, p. 3)

Most recently, graduate students at Arizona State University, under the direction of Professor Grayson Noley, compiled a listing of 2,900 citations since 1969 from the Education Resources Information Clearinghouse (ERIC) database. This work will provide yet another valuable source for researchers and practitioners.

Our review and discussion begins with an overview of categories that emerged from these studies as a means of providing a historical backdrop—covering 60 years—to position the research in the remainder of the chapter. Specifically, the categories of research were intelligence and achievement testing, urban migrants, teachers, parents, cultural deprivation, the language barrier, school, and stereotypes, categories that remain prominent in current research. B. Berry's (1968) and Trimble et al.'s (1977) analyses took a position critical of the assimilatory model and non-Native theoretical frameworks underlying the research they reviewed, a position with which we agree. Berry (1968) was critical of deficit thought when he argued against the prevailing views in research of Native language as an educational barrier, Indian parents as apathetic and non supportive of schooling, and Indian intelligence as inferior. Instead, he suggested that the problems in Indian education are not entirely situated in the individual or her or his home, community, and culture but must be shared by schools (specifically, uncaring teachers) and society (specifically, racism and discrimination).

Intelligence and Achievement Testing: The Indian Student as a Deficit Being

Long before cultural influences on learning appeared as a research topic, deficit thought assumed that American Indian children lacked the innate intelligence to succeed in school. A great deal of the literature B. Berry (1968) and Trimble, et al. (1977) reviewed was devoted to establishing the fact that Indians did not perform as well as Whites in school. Psychological tests, normed against a middle-class Anglo population, consistently revealed that American Indian children achieved less well than non-Native children on tests measuring intelligence and innate ability. Starting in the 1920s, however, researchers began to challenge both the validity of these tests and the assumptions derived from them. Specifically, some researchers questioned these tests, all of which emphasized verbal reasoning skills, as discriminating against American Indian children, many of whom were non-English speaking (Jamieson & Sandiford, 1928). Evidence was also available from visually based intelligence tests (e.g., the Goodenough Draw-A-Man Test, which revealed exceedingly high test scores of American Indian children), to challenge the assumptions of the "lower intelligence" of these children (Goodenough, 1926; Telford, 1932). Although not without criticism, this empirical evidence pointed to the conclusion that these children were better able to successfully respond to visually loaded test items than they were to tests that emphasized verbal and auditory skills. What this discovery and subsequent investigations established was that Indians were not inherently inferior or uneducable. B. Berry (1968) stated that "the conclusion which is drawn by most social scientists from the data on Indian cultures and Indian intelligence is that the American Indians of today have about the same innate equipment for learning as have the white children of America" (p. 34). He went on to say that, unfortunately, many White people, including teachers, with whom Indians came into contact were not aware of, or refused to accept, the conclusions reached by psychologists and social scientists. Consequently, the attitudes and beliefs of inferiority contributed to a self-fulfilling prophesy for many Indian students. Several studies cited by Berry (1968) tested this theory (Anderson & Safar, 1967; Gwilliam, 1957; Jackson, 1963; Tefit, 1967). Berry concluded that

if the self-fulfilling prophecy is valid, as it appears to be, the poor academic achievement of Indian children becomes more a problem for the white man than for the Indian, and calls for a program designed to increase the knowledge and understanding of the Indian on the part of the non-Indian community. (p. 36)

Achievement testing of Indian students began with criticism expressed in the 1928 Meriam Report (a criticism of the administration of Indian affairs) that Indian schools were not making use of intelligence or achievement tests. B. Berry (1968) noted that this criticism was taken so seriously that, for the next 40 years, "no aspect of Indian education has received more attention from researchers than has achievement testing" (p. 19). This trend has continued;during its first 30 years (1961–1991), the *Journal of American Indian Education* published 78 studies on achievement or intelligence tests and the Indian student.

The database pointing to the poor achievement of Indian children began to be built in the 1930s by individual researchers working with one or more tribes. Whereas research in the 1930s was completed by individuals, the 1940s and 1950s brought "contract" research, and major universities such as the University of Chicago and the University of Kansas conducted comprehensive nationwide studies for the BIA. The most comprehensive study was summarized in a 1958 monograph titled *The Indian Child Goes to School* by Madison Coombs and associates (McCoombs, Kron, Collister, & Anderson, 1958). Testing 23,608 students in federal, mission, and public schools in 11 states, the study offered further evidence that Indian students did not achieve as well as their White peers in basic skills subjects. The study also created a hierarchy of achievement, namely, White students in public schools had higher achievement that Indian students in public schools, who in turn scored higher than Indian students in BIA schools; Indian students in mission schools were at the bottom of the hierarchy. Throughout all of the studies reviewed by B. Berry (1968), it was apparent that "regardless of the instruments or criteria used, the Indian students show poor academic achievement" (p. 20); however, there were exceptions, and in all studies some students did exceedingly well. Profiles of the students who did well added fuel to the assimilation fires; those students who were more assimilated scored higher. Although this conclusion was not profound, it established certain premises that promoted public school attendance by Indian students to hasten assimilation and therefore questioned the need for the federal government to be in the education business.

Probably the most significant phenomenon to emerge from psychologically based research in the decades up to the 1970s was what has been described as the "crossover" effect. This phenomenon suggests that, at some point in school, Indian students who had been achieving at or above the norm of their White peers "cross over" and begin doing poorly. This achievement decline is not recovered, and, in fact, the decline continues as long as students stay in school. There is variance in studies regarding the grade level at which this crossover occurs, but researchers agree that students begin doing poorly in the upper grades. The cause of this phenomenon is perplexing. Although experiences during adolescence are recognized as an explanation, Bryde (1965) proposed that psychological factors, locating the problem in the individual, represented a more plausible explanation. He suggested that alienation was central to explaining the problem in that cultural conflict comes to focus at the adolescent level when identity problems and negative self esteem are more likely to occur. The crossover effect gave identity to a phenomenon that would continue to be studied. As we will illustrate later in this chapter, more recent research on the crossover effect argued that in school contexts that are supportive of Indian students' identity, culture, and language, the phenomenon does not exist, supporting the fact that this is a complex situation that is not simply a problem of adolescent development.

Urban Migrants: Off the Reservations and on the Path to Assimilation

B. Berry (1968) labeled the category of research focused on urban Indians as urban migrant studies. Indian people were encouraged to leave the reservation at various points in history. Before and after World War II, economic conditions provided an impetus. During the 1950s when termination was the federal policy, a federally sponsored relocation program drew many people to large cities such as Los Angeles, Chicago, and Dallas where many remained, creating significant urban Indian communities in some cities and multitribal representation in the schools. Researchers wanted to know about transition and adjustment experiences, based on the assimilation ideology that once off the reservation, attending schools with Anglo students would help the Indian student "blend in," and the "Indian problem" would be solved. Berry noted that, in these studies, schooling had little to do with successful adjustment. He suggested that "if schools had achieved any success at all in preparing Indians for effective citizenship, one would expect otherwise" (1968, p. 26).

The education of Indian people in urban settings has been the subject of numerous studies in the last three decades. In *To Live on This Earth,* Fuchs and Havighurst (1972) summarized findings of the National Study of Indian Education (conducted from 1967–1971), which included three large urban areas and several small urban settings. Their observation of urban schools that Indian children attend was that they

differ from most other schools serving Indian children in that the number of Indian children attending are relatively small—indeed sometimes not even noticed by the school authoritiies. The Indian children tend to be merged into the ranks of the "disadvantaged," attend predominantly lower class schools in the inner city, and little attention is paid to their unique characterstics as Indians. (1972, p. 290)

They suggested that the federal government and state governments pay particular attention to funding special programs to improve the educational environment for Indian children. Their recommendation and those that emerged from the Kennedy Report were instrumental in establishing legislation that enacted the Indian Education Act of 1972, as well as examining existing legislation such as Johnson-O'Malley that gave public schools assistance to meet the educational needs of Indian students.

The combined ERIC database from 1966 to 1995 listed 70 studies in which urban Indians were included as ethnic groups or were the topic of a study (e.g., dropouts, substance use, adult education). Considering the steady population growth in urban areas (30% in the 1960 census to 50% in 1990), the study of educational conditions for urban Indians (including those residing in Canada) has been relatively limited in comparison with such research on reservation Indians.

Teachers: Part of the Problem or Not?

B. Berry (1968) noted the scarcity of research directed toward teachers, relative to the volume of research on other aspects of Indian education, considering that the teacher plays an extremely important role in the academic career of an Indian child. He argued that because the ideology of assimilation was driving this body of research, the "problem" was located in the students, and fewer studies were seen as needed on schools or teachers. In the studies that did focus on teachers, Berry argued that factors causing a turnover problem, parochialism or narrow mindedness, prejudiced attitudes from "bitter hatred to mild condescension" (p. 37), and lack of awareness regarding cultural differences and inadequate qualifications indicated that, indeed, teachers were part of the "problem." In addition, he cited programmatic efforts to overcome the problems through orientation, teacher training, and in-service training.

In a summary of the National Study of American Indian Education (Fuchs & Havighurst, 1972), a different teacher attitude regarding assimilation emerged. A representative sample of 634 teachers answered questionnaires (345 of these teachers subsequently were interviewed) that included four different measures of attitudes and perceptions on the issue of assimilation "into the dominant white culture versus maintenance of a separate Indian culture" (p. 196). Fuchs and Havighurst (1972) reported that the majority of teachers interviewed tended to take the "man of two cultures" position, maintaining that Indians should acquire skills and attitudes required for success in society, but they should also maintain their culture. The teachers tended to view their schools as more Anglo oriented than their preference would suggest. Fuchs and Havighurst (1972) concluded that the teachers' position on assimilation was moderate and cautious but not Anglo oriented, and they were not inclined to view the teaching of culture as a major objective for them in school. Interestingly, Indian teachers' (11% of the teacher sample) position on assimilation was similar to that of the non-Indian group, and the only difference indicated that they were slightly more inclined toward an Anglo-orientation. Fuchs and Havighurst (1972) suggested that "the Indian teachers, then, seem to be characterized as a group with close contacts to the Indian communities and a firm Anglo orientation for themselves and in their view on the role of the school" (p. 197). This finding indicates that Indian teachers of this era who participated in mainstream teacher education programs and emerged with Anglo-oriented attitudes ascribed to the "two cultures" position. They were teachers who happened to be Indian, but aspects of their culture did not play an important role in their orientation to curriculum and instruction. In a later section of this chapter, the importance of Indian teachers as a topic of inquiry is discussed.

Fuchs and Havighurst (1972) believed that teachers and schools were in the position of teaching young people "caught between two conflicting cultures" (p. 203). To be helpful, according to Fuchs and Havighurst, schools and teachers needed a better knowledge and understanding of Indian communities and the cultures in which they work, as well as the goals that are approved and supported by the Indian community.

Teachers have always been a critical—positive or negative—factor in the education of Indian children. Current research hs reaffirmed that teachers are a critical factor in the education of Indian children (Coburn & Nelson, 1989). Community control and self-determination efforts focus strongly on the training of Native teachers as a means of transmitting effective practices around language and cultural maintenance, rather than assimilation, to increase student achievement. Simultaneously, the preparation of non-Native teachers who are understanding and knowledgeable of Indian students, their families, and communities is an important aspect of self-determination and local control of schools.

Parents: An Influence to Be Avoided

Although the influence of Indian parents in the educational process is widely accepted in current research, B. Berry (1968) commented on a lack of research in this area until the late 1960s. Apathy and similar labels were the prevalent terms used in the literature to describe the attitudes and behavior of parents. This deficit view of Indian parents was guided by assimilation beliefs that the "influence" of parents was bad (because it would reinforce Indianness) and that the fewer interactions Indian parents had with the school, the better. While hostility and resistance characterized parent attitudes in some of the earlier literature, Berry noted a change over time and paraphrased three phases Indian education has passed through (according to Spicer, 1961):

1) a period of resistance, which lasted into the 1920's; 2) a period of several decades when Indians felt the need of schools for their children, but the need was not matched by white society; and 3) the period

in which we now find ourselves, when serious efforts are being made to meet the Indians' educational demands. (pp. 44–45)

A more sympathetic look into the role of Indian parents in the education of their children appeared in ethnographic research studies by Bernardoni (1962); Harkins (1968); Parmee (1968); M. Wax, Wax, and Dumont (1989); and Wolcott (1984). Rather than "apathy," these studies presented the dynamic, complex roles parents played in the education of their children. Specifically, parents supported the concept of education but strongly resisted the assimilatory goals of Eurocentric schools. The stereotype of "apathetic parents" becomes more clearly understood as "resistant parents" in these studies. Studies since Berry's (1968) review consistently have illustrated an increased school involvement of Indian parents and a consistent struggle against assimilation.

Cultural Deprivation: The Problem of a Deficit Cultural View

In the 1960s, the term *cultural deprivation* came into vogue to describe the limited experiences of poor or impoverished children as a cause for poor academic achievement. There was an assumption that Indian children had limited backgrounds upon which the schools could build. Called the "vacuum ideology" by M. Wax et al. (1989), this deficit ideology, used by non-Native teachers and administrators, suggested that Indian homes and the minds of Indian children were empty, or meager, thus rationalizing the need for "enriching" Eurocentric experiences. This position ignored and disclaimed the failure of schools to meet the academic needs of Indian students. Problems such as discipline, attitudes toward authority, motivation, achievement orientation, competition, and etiquette were attributed to differences between the home culture (values, attitudes, beliefs) of Indian children and school personnel. Citing thorough explanations of the problem by M. Wax et al. (1989), Witherspoon (1961), Wolcott (1984), and Zintz (1960), B. Berry (1968) believed that the magnitude of the problem of cultural conflict in the classroom called for considerably more research. This body of research, indicating that Indian cultures were only "deficit" remainders of their past culture, was challenged by the research of cultural difference theorists that will be presented in depth later in this chapter.

Native Languages: Barriers to Overcome

Barrier, problem, handicap, and *obstacle* are terms that B. Berry (1968) found in the research to describe the use of a native language and lack of proficiency in English. Researchers tried to determine the extent of the language problem (i.e., the "interference" of native language in the teaching of English). Throughout the literature was a prevalent belief that the Native language was a barrier to academic achievement as measured by achievement tests. Berry found numerous examples of the repressive measures taken to stamp out native languages in favor of English in the belief that English proficiency equated with academic achievement. Two important points that Berry made seem to contradict this notion. He stated:

First, even though most Indian children the country over may speak English, and often English only, it is usually a "substandard" variety of English. And, however colorful their substandard language may be, and however adequate for purposes of communication within the group, it is not the standard English of the classroom and of the textbooks. Consequently, such children also labor under a language handicap—serious certainly, but not as serious as the handicap of the non-English-speaking student. And second, even in those Indian communities where English, and English only, is the language, we still find the universal problems of low achievement, high dropout rates, absenteeism, overageness, etc. This strongly suggests that we should look for some more basic cause of these academic shortcomings. (Berry, p. 57)

Supporting Berry's assertion, the research we will report on later argues that the use of Native languages is not the cause of academic failure.

Stereotypes of the Indian Personality: Inaccurate Images of Indian Youth

B. Berry (1968) offered the following observation:

The white man has always displayed a readiness to generalize about Indians and to force them into convenient stereotypes. The fact is that Indian societies are today, and always have been, widely different, and this is made abundantly clear in the literature on Indian education. Not only does each tribe, or reservation, or community differ from the others, but there are differences within each group. (p. 45)

Citing stereotypes of American Indians as proud, courageous, independent, stoical, and self-sufficient, Berry pointed to the Spindlers' (1957) review of psychologically oriented studies and autobiographies that reached a conclusion regarding American Indian personality types. According to the Spindlers, certain features such as "positive valuation of bravery and courage, reserve and self-control, ability to endure pain, and a sort of fatalistic dependence upon supernatural power" were widely distributed among American Indians (Berry, 1968, p. 66). And yet many of the studies in Berry's survey pointed to the presence of other personality traits indicating a negative self-concept, such as alienation, hopelessness, powerlessness, rejection, depression, anxiety, estrangement, and frustration. A poor, negative, or damaged self-concept was reported to be a major factor in the academic failure or underachievement of Indian children in the studies Berry reviewed. Trimble et al.'s (1977) review found that most of the studies focused on negative outcomes, such as drug addiction, alcoholism, and suicide, while few addressed the positive competent Indian adolescents, who represent the majority of Indian youth.

Trimble and Medicine (1976) argued that this "deficit" portrait of Indian youth was constructed by non-Native researchers and non-Native Eurocentric theoretical models. Trimble (1977) characterized this body of research on Indian adolescence as "ethnocentric, narrow in focus, and full of misunderstanding. If research on American Indians is to continue, accuracy of content from a native viewpoint should guide efforts" (p. 162). B. Berry (1968) suggested that in the final analysis, self-concept reflects the attitudes and opinions of the dominant non-Indian society with whom the Indian child interacts directly or indirectly. He located the problem outside of the individual in the hostile and racist attitudes about Indians in school and society. Attributed to lack of knowledge, inadequate knowledge, or inaccurate knowledge, Berry cited references that influenced him to conclude that "there is much evidence to prove that prejudice yields to education, and, while the schools alone are not equal to the task of changing the white man's concept of the Indian, they are in a position to make significant contributions to that end" (1968, p. 70).

Schools: The Focus of the Problem

Reviewing the research on schools B. Berry (1968) stated:

Further evidence that the schools have failed to meet the Indian's needs, or to help him find his place in American society, is to be seen in the school itself, where the figures on under enrollment, absenteeism, tardiness, retardation, overageness, and dropouts are distressingly large. (p. 27)

Clearly, of the conditions about which figures have been recorded, dropping out was the most severe. According to Berry, "No report on Indian education fails to note its wide extent" (1968, p. 28). Although "statistics on the extent of absenteeism and dropouts are readily available, . . . the causes are elusive and complex" (p. 29). Meriam (1928), M. Wax et al. (1989), and Wolcott (1967) were among those cited by Berry who were critical of the school rather than parents, children, teachers, community, or cultural barriers as causes of poor academic achievement. Asking questions about facilities, the curriculum and program, and the social environment, these researchers wanted to know, "What's wrong with the schools?" Reports of the curriculum as a serious source of controversy were evident in Berry's review, but the discussion, especially in early years, focused on whether the curriculum ought to be academic or vocational. Berry pointed out, however, that researchers were not attracted to the curriculum as a problem to be studied. The social environment or atmosphere was the subject of study for several investigators, most notably, M. Wax et al. (1989). Although not numerous, studies of the social environment of the school and the classroom established causal references suggesting that the structure of schooling presented obstacles to learning. The classrooms in which Indian students were members were not conducive to feelings of security and acceptance or to scholastic achievement. Shyness of Indian students and reluctance to participate in classroom activities characterized much of the literature, thus indicating the power of the peer group to control the social interactions of individuals in an alien environment.

Berry's review of the voluminous literature on more than 60 years of research on Indian education established a cogent thesis: The structure and purpose of schools and society must be carefully considered in evaluating the success or failure of American Indian and Alaska Native students in their K–12 and postsecondary experiences.

Dropout Studies: A Deficit Model

In the following sections, we examine the research literature focusing on American Indian and Alaska Native school leavers. In almost all of the studies Berry (1968) reviewed, dropout or "failure" was a central theme. A focus on the "dropout" is itself a deficit positioning of the Indian child (Trueba, Spindler, & Spindler, 1989). In contrast, Indian youth often position themselves differently, as "pushouts" from an uncaring, rejecting institution. We argue that perhaps the research on dropouts produces ambivalent conclusions. On one hand, the very problem of dropouts assumes a deficit orientation. On the other hand, the dropout rate is an indicator that education for Indian students is not working, and it is from these studies that some sympathetic understanding of Indian students has arisen. For many Indian youth, leaving school before graduation is the ultimate expression of academic "failure"; much of the research argued that Indian youth were to blame for their failure, a position we reject. According to the dropout studies reviewed in this section, educational models that seek assimilation as the "solution" to Indian school achievement and "success" are misguided at best and destructive at worse. Rather than a barrier to overcome, research suggest that a strong cultural identity enhances school success. These Indian youth spoke of pressures and problems that lie outside of their individual control, specifically the racially restricted "place" reserved for Indians in the dominant society. These institutionalized "problems" are the focus of the ethnographic research we will discuss later in the chapter. Although the body of research on dropouts is substantial, we found very few studies that asked Indian students, "Why did you leave school?" The voices presented in these particular studies, however, provide a powerful critique of non-Native controlled schools that discriminate against Indians with either overt racism or a dull, vocationalized curriculum.

The U.S. General Accounting Office's 1986 report, *School Dropouts,* presented the findings of several major studies on the correlates of dropping out in the general population that have been applied to studies of Native youth as well. All of these studies used a deficit model that positioned youth and their family as "the problem." The following correlates were identified: being 2 or more years behind grade level, being pregnant, coming from a household where the mother or father was not in the home when the youth was 14 years of age, having relatively little knowledge of the labor market, low classroom grades, negative school attitudes, and delinquent behavior in junior high school. Using the High School and Beyond (HS&B) database, Ekstrom, Goertz, Pollack, and Rock (1986) found significant correlations among socioeconomic status, ethnicity, and dropout rates; in addition, they identified dropouts as less active in sports and other extracurricular activities and in non-school-related social activities with peers and as having lower self-esteem, along with a feeling that they do not have a great deal of control over their lives and futures. Analyzing the four best known national longitudinal studies, Wehlage and Rutter (1986) identified the following correlates for dropping out of school: low socioeconomic status, poor performance leading to low grades and course failures, and disciplinary problems. In addition, they identified low educational-occupational aspirations, weak sociability, negative school attitudes, and low self-esteem as possible correlates.

Dropping out of school is a serious problem, and a logical line of inquiry into the condition naturally inspires identification of correlates as well as reasons given by students for leaving school. Swisher, Hoisch, and Pavel (1991) believe that discussions of correlates of dropping out become confounded by overuse of the term *cause*. They suggested that "identified correlates are just that and although they have predictive power, they cannot be treated as causal factors. Even where relationships between variables are highly correlated, examples abound of the exceptions . . ." (p. 53). They cautioned researchers to use care in discussing "causes" or making causal arguments and urged that the term not be used interchangeably with "correlates."

Studies generally look at the student characteristics that correlate with dropping out and rarely examine the characteristics of schools producing dropouts (Wehlage & Rutter, 1986). In mainstream research, the phenomenon of dropping out is commonly defined as an issue of individual failure. Youth "fail," either academically or socially, to make it through school. The problems exist not because of deficiencies in the schools but because of deficiencies in individuals and families. Youth who leave school are described as deviant, dysfunctional, or deficient because of individual, family, or community characteristics. Solutions reside in remediating or changing youth and families to better fit in. After all, most youth do succeed in school, suggesting evidence of the school as an effective institution. A similar understanding exists in districts that educate American Indian and Alaskan Native children. Deyhle (1995) reported a district-wide meeting on the Navajo reservation where non-Indian administrators identified the following causes for their Navajo students' school failure: lack of self-esteem, inadequate homes, inadequate preparation for school, lack of parenting skills, poor communication between home and school, poor school attendance, limited vocabulary and language development, limited cultural enrichment opportunities, too academic a curriculum, poor attitude and motivation, and fetal alcohol syndrome (p. 416). All of these "causes" place the blame on deficits of the students and their families. In contrast, only three causes listed found fault with the schools: questionable teacher support, lack of counseling, and nonrelevant curriculum. Lipka (1994) described the same reasoning in a superintendent's remarks to a Yup'ik bilingual committee: "I can assume that the school is doing the best it can. What are the elements that keep the scores down?" (p. 81). Lipka argued that the administrator's question located community and bilingualism as the problematic "elements" that limited Yup'ik student achievement.

Like Deyhle (1995) and Lipka (1994), Platero, Brandt, Witherspoon, and Wong's (1986) study of Navajo reservation student dropouts reported that administrators and staff identified a lack of parental-family support and encouragement, poor academic skills and performance, home and family problems, and a lack of interest in education as the most important reasons for school failure. This line of research, or thinking, ignored the barriers institutions themselves created for youth. As both Platero et al. (1986) and Deyhle (1995) pointed out, factors associated with school environment, racial mistreatment, and interactions within the school were not cited as significant reasons Indian students left school; rather, external factors and the responsibility of the student were emphasized. As described subsequently, a different picture was painted by Indian youth who left school.

The Institutional Portrait: American Indian Dropouts

On the national level, there is very little information about overall dropout rates for American Indians, in part because American Indians, unlike African Americans, Whites, or Hispanics, are not differentiated as a separate cohort. However, there are numerous Indian-specific studies that indicate the extent of the dropout problem. In 1969, the Kennedy Report, *Indian Education: A National Tragedy—A National challenge,* (U.S. Senate, 1969), found that dropout rates for Indian students were twice the national average in both public and BIA schools, with some schools approaching a 100% dropout rate. Testimony before the U.S. Senate in 1969 placed the national dropout rate at 60%. Several studies in the 1970s (American Indian Policy Review Commission, 1976; Fuchs & Havighurst, 1972) reported that Indian students drop out at higher rates than Anglos but offered no specific figures. A 1983 national impact evaluation of Title IV, Part A, found that the dropout rates contained in a number of studies ranged from 14% to 60% (Development Associates, 1983). More recent estimates of the problem include dropout rates ranging from 35.5% (National Center for Educational Statistics, NCES, 1988) to more than 50% (Wells, 1991) and, in undocumented cases, between 80% and 90%. The HS&B study, sponsored by NCES, is probably the best-known and most often cited research on dropouts in the United States. Although the HS&B study did not provide specific data on American Indian students, some data sets available from NCES specify that of the 1980 cohort of (public school) sophomores surveyed, 29.2% of the American Indian students dropped out before graduation (BIA, 1988, pp. 135–136). Not only did Indian students tend to have the highest dropout rates of any of the major racial/ethnic groups, they also had the lowest rate of returning to eventually complete high school or an equivalent program (NCES, 1988).

The Center for Indian Education at Arizona State University recently completed a research project for the National Education Association Office of Human and Civil Rights (Swisher et al., 1991). The extensive state of the art study examined the available dropout literature on American Indian students and surveyed all 50 states and the largest urban school districts with a considerable Indian population across the nation. Individual studies of dropout rates they reviewed varied as to specific figures, although the studies were consistent in reporting the magnitude of the problem. For example, Coladarci (1983) reported a dropout rate of 60% for Indian youth in Montana, Platero et al. (1986) calculated the Navajo Nation's dropout rate to be 31%, Eberhard (1989) reported a 29% dropout rate among urban American Indian students, and Deyhle (1992) reported a 34% dropout rate for Navajo students that increased to 44% when only students who graduated on time in the traditional high school program were included.

Acknowledging the difficulty of determining the overall or national dropout rate for American Indian populations, Swisher et al. (1991) urged readers to examine the reported figures with caution, not only because of demographic exclusion, but for the following reasons. First, Indian students attend several types of schools operated by the BIA or by state, or private agencies, and there is no one repository for data, making "total" figures suspect. Second, the definition of dropouts varied from state to state, and dropout data are gathered and calculated according to several different methods, making aggregation very difficult. Third, the mobility of Indian students suggested that transferring is as serious a problem as dropping out in some parts of the country. Finally, dropout data have not been collectively reported and gathered in a comprehensive database. With these qualifiers, the study concluded:

The best estimate of an American Indian/Alaskan Native rate at this time can be derived from those longitudinal studies, including those conducted between 1962–1989 which calculated the rate to be between 24 and 28%, and the longitudinal studies completed in the 1980s which established a rate between 29 and 36%. However, with the exception of NCES (1988) which reported [a] 35.5% dropout rate, other studies are limited to a specific population or region, and are not national in scope. (Swisher et al., 1991, p. 86)

A comprehensive review of the educational literature regarding American Indian dropouts revealed, literally, hundreds of reports: individual school evaluation or annual reports; local, state, or national reports; senate hearings; task force proceedings; descriptions of dropout intervention programs; and individual scholarly research studies (Ledlow, 1992; Swisher, et al. 1991). Some reports provided specific dropout rates; most focused on descriptions of the "problem." Almost without exception, these individual studies suffered from the same problems mentioned for the national level studies. However, what is most revealing is that few studies actually focused on the causes of dropping out, and even fewer provided the "voices" of American Indian youth as to why they leave school. In the following section, we will focus on the few research studies that systematically sought from Indian youth the answer to the question "Why did you leave school before graduation?"

American Indian Youth Self-Portrait: "Why We Left School"

Navajo and Oglala Sioux youth, Indian youth from various tribes in Montana, and urban Indian youth from Phoenix had similar messages. They felt "pushed out" of schools and mistreated by teachers and administrators, and, in turn, they rejected the schools' academic offerings as dull and unconnected to their lives. Students acknowledged the importance of parental and home support; however, problems with schools and teachers were equally as important.

Coladarci's (1983) interview study of dropouts from several reservations in Montana provided evidence from dropouts that pointed toward social relationships, especially relationships with teachers, as well as academic problems in school as factors related to dropping out of school. Almost 40% of the dropouts complained that teachers did not care about them and did not provide enough assistance with their school assignments. One third cited conflict with teachers that led to their decision to leave school. A little less than half of the school leavers stated that school was not important for what they wanted to do in life, and approximately one fourth indicated that school was not important to them as American Indians. Lack of parent support and problems at home were important factors in the dropout decision for approximately 40% of the students. The Coladarci (1983) study also pointed to the desire of students to be with other dropouts and/or some degree of peer pressure as salient factors in these students' decisions to drop out. The image of the school from the perspective of these youth was one of a cold and personally unrewarding place.

In contrast, Milone's (1983) survey of 31 urban American Indian dropouts from the Phoenix Union High School District revealed "surprisingly" positive attitudes toward school at the same time students reported feeling that they were "pushed out" of school by academic problems, discipline problems, or pregnancy (pp. 55–57). This is similar to R. H. Wax's (1976) study of Sioux dropouts who felt that they were "kicked out" of school. Eberhard's (1989) study of urban American Indian students also identified rejection and "cultural insensitivity" as structural problems cited by students and parents as having "pushed" the students out of schools.

In a dropout study commissioned by the Navajo Nation, Platero et al.'s (1986) evidence from nearly 900 interviews also revealed a student critique of schools. Administrators cited lack of familial encouragement, academic problems and performance, and home and family problems (all based on a deficit view of the home and family) as the three most likely reasons why students dropped out. In contrast, Navajo students claimed that boredom with school, problems with other students, and being retained a grade because of absenteeism were the top three reasons that most of them actually dropped out. Platero et al. (1986) noted that dropouts' own reports diverged sharply from the opinions of the administrators and staff: "The students and dropouts were more likely to focus on interactions (between peers, between students, and teachers) and school environmental factors in response to the question of what causes Navajos to drop out" (p. 61).

In her ethnographic study, Deyhle (1992) used Coladarci's (1983) student questionnaires, school records, and ethnographic data to examine not only what Navajo and Ute students who left school said about their school experience but also the economic and political climate of the communities in which the students lived. As found by Coladarci (1983) and Platero et al. (1986), the relationship between students and their teachers was important for retaining Navajo and Ute youth in school; more than half of the Navajo and 80% of the Ute dropouts felt that their teachers did not care about them or help them with their work. Deyhle reported that when youth experienced minimal individual attention or personal contact with teachers (which she observed in classrooms), they translated this into an image of teacher dislike and rejection. Indian students, many with reading difficulties requiring extra help from their teachers, were seen as an added burden by some of the teachers. She also argued that "lack of attention" was rooted in racist views of Indians:

Mistrust of teachers was often justified. A past superintendent explained the "cultural problem" to me, "Some of our older teachers hold traditional views of Indians, and 'wiping the slate clean' of these teachers would help the Indian students. . . . Our Indian students learn which teachers don't like them and avoid them." (p. 31).

Deyhle concluded that

Indian students didn't trust their teachers, even good teachers who deeply cared about their students. The teacher represented a member of the outside Anglo community, a community that has actively controlled the economic, religious, and political lives of the Navajo community. Tensions in the larger community were often mirrored inside classrooms. . . . The only path to "success" for Indians was to become "non-Indian." It was a path many Indian youth rejected. (p. 32)

The content of what was taught in school also emerged as an important issue in both the Coladarci (1983) and Deyhle (1992) studies. In both studies, the school curriculum, perceived as not connected to students' life goals, was an important reason for leaving school. This did not mean that youth left school because the content was not subject specific enough to American Indian cultures; rather, because school simply was not an avenue to obtain the knowledge or skills they desired. Some students in Deyhle's study resisted the emphasis on basic, remedial, or vocational tracking in the high schools, which they saw as limiting their opportunities, even with a high school degree. One said,

I didn't care to finish high school. It was not that important. You see, I was just learning the same thing over and over. Like the teachers didn't expect anything of you because you were an Indian. They put you in general education, basic classes, and vocation. They didn't encourage college bound classes. (Deyhle, p. 37)

In addition, a significant number of students Deyhle interviewed mentioned the economic necessity of finding a job or working at home, long distance commutes to school, pregnancy, reading problems, and feelings of being "unwanted" as contributing to their decisions to leave school. These students spoke of dissatisfaction with school, feelings of mistrust and alienation, academic difficulties, and the importance of family responsibilities, which often required students to leave school to work at home or at a job.

Two significant dropout studies were gender specific. Rosalie H. Wax (1976) studied young Oglala Lakota men, and Bowker (1993) studied Indian women across the nation. In both studies (even though 25 years apart), youth reported feelings of rejection from teachers and schools. The article "Oglala Sioux Dropouts and Their Problems With Educators" (Wax, 1976), represented results from one of the earliest ethnographic studies that contained data on the reasons young Indian men say they left schools. Wax's research, using ethnographic data and an interview sample that included 153 youth between the ages of 13 and 21, 35% of whom had dropped out before the end of the ninth grade, focused on social as well as cultural reasons as factors that lead to leaving school. Rarely did the young men mention trouble with studies, but about half found school a lonely place or unbearable for other reasons, such as abuse by experienced students. Many of the youth said that school was "all right," but conforming to school regulations was too difficult. Focusing on value differences between Sioux culture and the Anglo school system, Wax stated that most of the young men

arrived at adolescence valuing elan, bravery, generosity, passion, and luck, and admiring outstanding talent in athletics, singing, and dancing. While capable of wider relations and reciprocities, they function at their social best as members of small groups of peers or relatives. (1976, p. 223).

These values were seen as contrary to those required by the school,

a respect for humdrum diligence and routine, for "discipline" (in the sense of not smoking in toilets, not cutting classes, and not getting drunk), and for government property. In addition, they are expected to compete scholastically on a highly privatized and individualistic level, while living in large dormitories, surrounded by strangers who make privacy impossible. (p. 223)

One of Wax's most revealing findings showed how these youth did not define themselves as the "problem"; rather, the required structure of the school system "forced" them out of school. Presenting the voices of these youth, she reported that "Many state explicitly that they do not wish to leave school and see themselves as 'pushouts' or 'kickouts' rather than 'dropouts.' As a Sioux youth in our sample put it, 'I quit, but I never did *want* to quit!' " (p. 216).

The Female American Indian: Dropout or Pushout?

Research on female American Indians within the educational setting is almost nonexistent. Peng and Takai (1983), using the HS&B database, reported that whereas American Indians have the highest dropout rate in the country, American Indian girls have the highest dropout rates of all groups, whether male or female. They reported the dropout rate for American Indian girls at 31.8%, followed by Hispanic girls at 18%, African American girls at 14.1%, White girls at 11.5%, and Asian American girls at 2.7%. The dropout rate for American Indian boys was 27.2%. Current estimates place the overall dropout rate of American Indians at 50% or higher (Bowker, 1993). It has also been estimated that American Indian girls constitute approximately 54 to 60% of those statistics (Chavers, 1991). According to data from the 1980 census, 25% of American Indian women in 1980 had not completed high school or a GED, as compared with 16% of White women. Given research that demonstrates the correlation between high school graduation and future income, it is not surprising that most American Indian women fall below the poverty level (Bowker, 1993). Statistics from the 1970s showed that 86% of American Indian women, more than any other racial or ethnic group, earned less than $5,000 per year (Sargent, 1977). Whereas White women in America earned 59 cents for every dollar a man earned, according to the 1980 census, American Indian female earned only 89% of what White women earned. Only 35% of American Indian women were employed in the work force, the lowest rate for any racial/ ethnic group.

We found few studies on American Indian students that distinguished between male and female attitudes, achievement, or perceptions. In these studies, American Indian youth, when positioned against other minority groups and Anglos, were at a deficit. Fuchs and Havighurst (1972) found that although American Indian adolescents felt slightly more favorable toward their teachers than Anglo-American adolescents, American Indian girls were more critical of teachers than boys. Other researchers (Delk, 1974; Owens & Bass, 1969; Selinger, 1968) reported that Indian girls were more likely to drop out than boys, and pregnancy was a major factor for dropping out among Indian girls. In the area of self-concept, American Indian girls appeared more likely to show a significant decrease in self-esteem from preadolescence to adolescence than boys, to rate themselves less favorably on self-concept measures than Anglo girls, to be more self-critical and self-doubting than Indian boys, and to report more negative self-esteem than White and Mexican youth (Burnap, 1972; Fuchs & Havighurst, 1972; Mason, 1969). Coladarci's (1983) dropout study indicated that American Indian female dropouts reported more frequently than boys that teachers did not care about them, and 48% of the girls reported problems at home as an important factor in dropping out. Some researchers maintained that the major factor contributing to dropping out among American Indian girls was the abuse of alcohol (Cahalan & Crossley, 1969; Clawson, 1990; Whittaker, 1963). However, Bowker (1993) reported that more males (60%) than females (40%) drink, that strong community sanctions for young Indian women mitigates displays of drunkenness, and that Indian parents maintain more restrictive standards for their daughters than for their sons.

Unlike the studies mentioned earlier, the studies by Deyhle and Margonis (1995) and Bowker (1993) rejected an assimilationist position and attempted both to hear from American Indian women as to why they left school and to place these experiences within the larger social, political and economic context surrounding these women. In both the Deyhle and Margonis and Bowker studies, young Indian women left school because of an accumulation of negative experiences, such as uncaring teachers and racism against Indians. Bowker (1993) wrote of these experiences:

Many women reported negative experiences with teachers who put them down. They were called "dumb," "squaws," "baby factories," or "wild Indians." They reported teachers who "yelled," "screamed," or "hit." They described teachers who humiliated them, nagged them, and lost control when students didn't understand something. . . . Others spoke quite eloquently about racism, prejudice, and stereotyping. They felt helpless and confused as to why school boards did not protect them from teachers who obviously held contempt for Indian people and their cultures. (pp. 269–270)

A majority of the 991 women in Bowker's study related negative school experiences (oppressive school policies and poor school climate), and as these experiences accumulated they outweighed any positive experiences. Deyhle and Margonis (1995) also found that feelings of rejection from their teachers and racial hostilities in schools were central reasons that lead young Navajo women to leave school. As one young woman explained, "Those white kids don't like us . . . I think that most of them think Navajos are disgusting. That is what I think" (p. 145). With the following example, Deyhle and Margonis argued that racism was an ever-present force facing these young women in schools:

The yearbook exemplified the "place" for Indians in the school. Jan and her friends were signing each other's yearbooks. "Look. Here on the first page is the homecoming queen." The full-page, glossy, color photograph showed a smiling blond wearing a crown and a pink formal. "Now look at us." She flipped to the last page of the yearbook. A matte, black-and-white photograph showed a smiling "Indian princess." "It's still the Indians at the back of the bus. That's what they think of us." (pp. 145–146)

A deficit perspective, evident in many studies that connect pregnancy to dropping out, positions the young woman as having "caused" school failure because of pregnancy. Teen pregnancy was an important reason to leave school in both studies. What is significant, however, is what schools do to girls who become pregnant: They push them out of school because they no longer "fit" rather than accepting them as their families do. In the Bowker (1993) study, teen pregnancy was reported by slightly more than half of the women as a concrete reason to leave school or as "the straw that broke the camel's back" (p. 272). In the Deyhle and Margonis study (1995), 42% of Navajo women dropped out of high school, and 40% of those who left did so as a result of pregnancy. Having a child, however, was not a final barrier to finishing school; both studies revealed that the Indian extended family often shared child-care responsibilities, which allowed the young women to return to school. Deyhle and Margonis (1995) argued that, for young Navajo women, surrounded by a racially restricted economy that limited the value of educational credentials, having a baby and assuming a secure position within Navajo matriarchal and economic networks on the reservation was a sound choice for many women. Although these women's motherhood was accepted in their homes and community, it was unacceptable in school. Young women reported that after having a child, they felt "pushed out" by teachers and school authorities.

One Navajo woman said, "The teachers, you know, they look at you differently. They know you have had a baby, and they stay away from you. I didn't like the way they looked at me" (Deyhle & Margonis, 1995, p. 146). What was significant in both of these studies was that what the schools—both teachers and Anglo peers—did to these young mothers "pushed" them out and ensured that they stayed out of school.

The Navajo women in the study by Deyhle and Margonis (1995) reported that an irrelevant vocationalized curriculum, designed to prepare women for semi-skilled, low-paying jobs off the reservation, and the primacy of the family, requiring young women to be a cooperative member of the extended family, were pivotal reasons for them to leave school prematurely. At present, most Navajo women pursue life as mothers and daughters on the reservation, and schools—as currently conceived—offer little to that life course. In fact, functioning with an assimilation model, the schools do everything they can to "break up" Navajo culture and families. Deyhle and Margonis argued, "The vision of economic mobility paid tribute to by educators and the larger educational discourse is most possible if Navajo women leave the reservation, but such a decision threatens Navajo women's most basic values while promising them very little" (p. 163). Again, they described Navajo women's decisions to leave school as sound when placed within the larger political, economic, and social discrimination surrounding their lives.

As Navajo women enter white-dominated schools and businesses, they trade a powerful respected role for the subordinate role that Anglos reserve for both Navajos and women. While many Navajo parents want their kids to experience the best of both worlds—wedding school achievement with living a Navajo life on the reservation—differences of culture and Anglo power make such a task difficult. The ethic of cooperation embodied in family networks is so sharply at odds with the individualism promoted in the Anglo schools and economy that "success" would, in many cases, require an abandonment of basic Navajo attitudes and beliefs. (p. 163)

Bowker (1993) found, in addition, that young women who left school had experienced difficulty adjusting to school and suffered negative peer pressure, which worked against school success and, in some cases, resulted in dropping out. Bowker argued:

Further, peer groups seemed to set the standards for identification of who was "Indian" and who was "white." "Going along with a teacher," "not participating in some plot against a teacher," "getting good grades," or "not skipping school" could be interpreted by the peer group as "being white." . . . Even many of those who were of "mixed heritage" sought to prove their "Indianness" by conforming to group standards when their ethnicity or loyalties were tested by the group. Only those women who had a strong support group of family or friends, were involved in school activities, and had a firm sense of their own personal identity seemed not to fall prey to such pressure. (pp. 274–275)

The last significant factor that contributed to young women leaving school prematurely in Bowker's (1993) study was poverty. "Growing up poor places American Indian girls at high risk of dropping out of school. . . . Poverty involves living in communities where alcoholism, drug abuse, lack of job opportunities, welfare, and inadequate housing are often the norm, rather than the exception" (p. 275). Inadequate nutrition, clothing, and shelter contributed to both personal and family problems. This deficit talk, however, can easily lead, again, to locating the "problem" in Indian students and their homes. The language of poverty fits well into deficit thought with terms such as *culturally deprived* and *culture of poverty*. Bowker argued that rather than confronting the problems of poverty, researchers have often mislabeled the conditions of poverty as the conditions of culture or "the Indian thing," and, hence, this distortion of "cultural conflict" deflected attention from the poverty conditions that created the problems in the first place. Young Indian women—and men—reported dropping out to combat the problems of poverty by aiding the family with jobs at home or in the workplace (Deyhle, 1992). Poverty must also be viewed as a result of job discrimination and the absence of opportunities. Although the majority of the Navajo women lived within poverty conditions, Deyhle and Margonis (1995) argued that school success did not necessarily lead to greater economic prosperity in the context of a racially restricted job market in the community. The ways in which schools dismissed Navajo culture and language and provided only training for marginal jobs, in fact, worked to ensure the conditions of poverty in the community. Instead, economic stability in the lives of the women they studied was achieved by the economic networks established by extended families on and off the reservation, regardless of school credentials.

Debunking Deficit Myth: Traditionality and Success

At the core of an assimilatory model is the belief that Native languages and cultures are the reasons for Indian school failure. The research reviewed here suggested a contrary position: Native languages and cultures correlate positively with school success. In the Platero et al. (1986) study, there was little difference in grades or retention rates between dropouts and persisters (p. 66). Early exposure to English correlated with persistence, but both stayers and dropouts reported approximately equal participation in traditional Navajo culture and fluency in Navajo language. Given assimilation arguments that lay the blame of the "Indian problem" on Native languages and cultures, this was an important finding.

A case study of 24 Navajo adolescents by Chan and Osthimer (1983) supported the findings of Platero et al.(1986) that traditionalism was not a negative factor correlated with dropping out. They found that students' first language was not as important a determinant to their success in school as the successful transition to English. Students who were English dominant or bilingual were less likely to drop out, regardless of their first language. Bilinguals were most likely to be college bound (Chan & Osthimer, 1983, pp. 24–27). One of the most significant findings was that students from less traditional homes dropped out at higher rates. Students who reported their families as "moderate," meaning that they observed Navajo traditions while having adopted certain Anglo conveniences, were most likely to be college bound (pp. 27–30). According to Chan and Osthimer, "Successful youths came from moderate homes that valued many of the Navajo traditions while adhering to many modern notions. Dropouts perceived themselves as more contemporary" (1983, p. 1). In a study of southwestern Indian college students, a majority of which were Navajo, Schwartz (1985) also found similar results. Out of five groups, students described as the most traditional were the most success-ful, and the most acculturated group was found to be the least successful. Again, these are important findings that refuted the long-held assimilationist's assump-tion that American Indian youth failed in school because of their language and culture.

Of particular interest in Deyhle's (1992) work is her discussion of "cultural dis-continuity," for which evidence to refute "Indianness" as the reason for academic failure is clearly provided. She found that those students who came from the most traditional Navajo homes, spoke their native language, and participated in tradi-tional religious and social activities did not feel that the school curriculum was inappropriate to them as Indians, and they were among the most successful stu-dents in school (p. 42). This was in contrast to the Ute students who came from the least traditional homes and felt that the curriculum was not important to them as Indians. These students experienced the highest dropout rates and the greatest number of academic and social problems in school. Deyhle concluded, "A cultur-ally non-responsive curriculum is a greater threat to those whose own cultural 'identity' is insecure" (p. 42). She argued that although the inclusion of language, history and cultural information was important, a "culturally sensitive" curricu-lum was not the solution or sole key to increasing school success. She also argued that most youth who left school did so with concrete and stable reasons when these decisions were framed by the larger socio-political structures surrounding them and that culturally "secure" Indian youth were more successful in schools. As Deyhle (1995) concluded

For Navajo students, one of the most life-affirming strategies is to embrace reservation life and tradi-tional Navajo culture. Indeed, the students in my study who were able to maintain Navajo/reservation connections gained a solid place in Navajo society and were more successful in the Anglo world of school and workplace. (p. 404)

Findings from both the Bowker (1993) and Deyhle and Margonis (1995) stud-ies suggested that the most successful young women were those who had the sup-port of their community and families and who had a strong ethnic identity. Bowker stated, "It appears that American Indian women who strongly identify with their Indian heritage and those who strongly identify with the white culture do better in school than those who have no strong ethnic identity" (p. 182). Acceptance of their "Indianness" and support of families contributed to their school success. Deyhle and Margonis (1995) make it clear that, in Navajo society, women were at the core of both beliefs and practices and that this positioning of

women was central to understanding their lives. Describing women who had successfully navigated through schools, they said

> Their success relied upon a familial commitment to their education, for the family helped put them
> through school and looked after their children. Correspondingly, their motivation was not for individ-
> ual mobility but for the good of the family, and more generally, in Christine's words, it is "an invest-
> ment in the community." (p. 164)

This "investment" in the community speaks to the strength of Navajo culture as an
asset for school success.

Studies by Bowker (1993), Chan and Osthimer (1983), Deyhle (1992), Deyhle
and Margonis (1995), and Schwartz (1985) have provided evidence that a strong
sense of traditional identity, such as speaking the native language fluently and
engaging in traditional religious and social activities, provides students with an
advantage in school. This body of research would seem to challenge the assimilationist argument that the more "Indian" a student is, the worse he or she will do in
school and the idea presented by some cultural difference theorists that the more
different the culture of the home and school, the more problems students will
experience.

CHALLENGES TO ASSIMILATION AND DEFICIT THOUGHT

Understanding Cultural and Ethical Differences Shaping
Educational Interaction

An alternative view to the deficit portrait in the previous sections is the research
presented in this section, which draws from cultural difference theory derived
from anthropological and sociological studies of American Indians and schooling.
This body of research disputes cultural vacuum and cultural deficit positions by
suggesting that difficulties in schools and classrooms are linked to the differences
between the home and school culture. At the very basis of these differences is the
socialization of children or the child-rearing practices that occur before the child
goes to school. In other words, the styles and methods used by parents/caregivers
determine how children learn to learn. When children enter kindergarten and first
grade, these cultural differences become evident. Schools follow a model that is
little changed from its beginnings in colonial America 400 years ago; it is a
Eurocentric model that is compatible with the ways of life and cultural practices
of the majority of mainstream America. Cultural differences in beliefs, attitudes,
and behaviors are usually manifested in communication patterns, interactional
styles, and social values. Many Indian students come to school with learning and
interactional styles that are very different from the style of learning and interaction they encounter in the classroom. Not only are Indian students faced with
learning new concepts, but they must also become participants in a new cultural
context, a context whose social organization is often not in congruence with the
students' cultural and/or community norms (Collier, Jr., 1973; Deyhle, 1995;

Dumont, 1972; Erickson & Mohatt, 1982; Lipka & Ilutsik, 1995; Macias, 1987; Philips, 1972, 1983).

We believe that an environment that communicates the fact that cultural differences are strengths and not deficiencies is the first step in addressing the educational needs of American Indian/Alaskan Native and Canadian Indian students. If educators are equipped with this culturally specific information on how Indian students have come to view and learn of their world, test results, classroom behavior, and the communication and interaction patterns educators confront in classrooms will be more meaningful. It is our argument that this understanding can lead to educational practices that are more sympathetic and effective with American Indian students. A cultural difference perspective will aid the effort to avoid assimilation; it gives clues to the ways in which some Indian students think and communicate that are not supported in the analytic-competitive model of the public schools. However, as we argue at the end of this section, a cultural difference theory can also support the effort to define Indian students in a deficit fashion, in that the Indian student is not seen as exhibiting the "norm." We will also argue that "understanding" the cultural context is not enough. The structure of school and society that harbors institutional racism and an assimilationist educational model limits both educational and economic opportunities and must be analyzed as a critical problem to be addressed in the education of American Indian youth.

Childrearing Practices: The Influence of Culture

A significant body of research has documented the ways in which parents from various Indian tribes have socialized their children, and these methods are often in contrast to the concept of "childhood" and child-rearing practices in Anglo-American families (Annahatak, 1994; Bennett deMarrais, Nelson, & Baker, 1992; Chilcott, 1985; Chisholm, 1983; Condon, 1987; Crago, Annahatak, & Ningiuruvik, 1993; Deyhle & LeCompte, 1994; Dozier, 1970; Joe, 1994; Okakok, 1989; Pettit, 1946; Philips, 1988; Riley, 1993; Suina & Smolkin, 1994; Tafoya, 1989; Tharp, 1994; Whiting, Chasdi, Antonovsky, & Ayres, 1975). In all societies, specific forms of child rearing provide each child with the social and linguistic skills necessary to "fit" into the group. Different sociocultural environments result in behaviors that differ from culture to culture. This theoretical framework (Ramirez & Castaneda, 1974) suggests that cultural values influence socialization practices, which, in turn, influence the ways in which children learn to learn or approach learning. Although American Indian communities have experienced tremendous social, cultural, and economic changes over the past 100 years—resulting in "traditional" versus "nontraditional" communities—ethnographic evidence suggests that child-rearing practices continue to be much the same as they have been in the past. (Cazden & John, 1971; Hilger, 1951; Joe, 1994; Rohner, 1965).

A recent special issue of *Family Perspective* (1993) was devoted to Native American families. Ward, the guest editor, explained that the research contained therein addressed several issues of family research by exploring them in new ways. Past research, while instrumental in reporting social, political, and economic conditions that presented barriers to the health and well-being of families, often created new stereotypes of Americans Indians as victims who were passive and in need of interventions to correct their problems. According to Ward, citing Yellowbird and Snipp:

> American Indian families have been able to perpetuate the American Indian population, sustain tribal organization, and preserve native culture precisely because they were capable of changing to meet the needs of the population. It should surprise no one that American Indian families today are as different from their ancestors of 100 years ago as those Indians were different from their ancestors 100 years earlier. (p. 306)

Yellowbird and Snipp, both Native scholars, also suggested that despite changes affecting American Indians, traditional elements such as the roles of men, women, and the elderly are often retained in families today.

Experiencing the World Through Observation

An abundance of research has illustrated that Native children learn by observing and imitating the actions of their parents, elders, and older siblings. The child is both a spectator of and participant in all types of family and community affairs. In close proximity to family members during home chores, community meetings, and religious ceremonies the child has the opportunity to observe and learn simple tasks such as cooking and carrying water and more complex tasks such as beading, weaving, or planning and organizing a ceremony. Children are raised to be careful listeners and thoughtful observers. Learning through observation was reported in studies on Navajo children (Cazden & John, 1971; Guilmet, 1979; John, 1972; Swisher & Deyhle, 1989), Pueblo children (John-Steiner & Osterreich, 1975; Suina & Smolkin, 1994), Eskimo children (Briggs, 1970), Yaqui children (Appleton, 1983), Warm Springs children (Philips, 1972, 1983), Northern Alaska Inupiat Eskimo children (Okakok, 1989), Yup'ik Eskimo children (Bennett deMarrais et al., 1992), and Kwakuitl children (Philion & Galloway, 1969; Rohner, 1965; Wolcott, 1984). These practices resulted (and still result to some extent) in visually acute perceptual skills, children acquiring the ability to organize their observations and form concepts from them. These skills have been reported in the results of psychological tests with Navajo and Pueblo children (Garber, 1968), Sioux children (Kuske, 1969), children from the Flathead Reservation in western Montana (Downey, 1977), Inuit and White children in Labrador (Taylor & Skanes, 1975), Canadian Inuit children (Berry, 1966), Alaskan Inuit children (Kleinfeld, 1973), urban Inuit children (Berry, 1971), Yakima children (Diessner & Walker, 1989), and Mississippi Choctaw children (Greembaum & Greenbaum, 1983). In all of these studies, the American Indian and Inuit children were most successful at processing visual information and had the most difficulty performing well on tasks saturated with verbal content.

It can be argued that all children—regardless of ethnicity or culture—are encouraged to learn by observation and the imitation of others' actions. Research evidence, however, reveals an important difference between the child-rearing practices of many American Indian/Alaska Native societies and those of adult members of the dominant White society: the use of verbal instruction (Eggan, 1976; Greenbaum & Greenbaum, 1983; R. Scollon & Scollon, 1982; S.B. Scollon & Scollon, 1988). In a synthesis of the research, Kaulback (1984) stated,

> Much of the informal learning that takes place in Native societies is non-verbal in nature. The children learn the customs and skills of their society by sharing directly in the activities of others. In such situations, verbal instruction is neither offered nor required because the child's close proximity to the observable action makes instruction-giving quite redundant. (p. 33)

Modeling, requiring little verbalization, was also reported by Suina and Smolkin (1994) who explained that, "learning by example is central to traditional Pueblo education" (p. 117). It appears that Native children best acquire much of the information to which they are exposed and expected to learn through observation rather than verbalization.

The conditions in Native communities where observation is an essential tool of learning are less prevalent in the dominant White society. In this mainstream context, siblings often play and interact with a peer group separate from each other; parents may be absent from the home for extended periods for employment and other adult activities; young children are frequently cared for by non-family members; and children rarely accompany their parents to "adult" social activities. Under these circumstances, learning occurs without a shared contextual framework, and the use of language, such as question asking, and verbal interaction becomes a critical means of communication within the Euro-American family. In a review of the verbal/nonverbal research, Kaulback (1984) cautiously concluded that

> although far from conclusive, there is a growing body of research to suggest that distinctively different child rearing practices—one stressing observational learning and other emphasizing learning through verbalization—has [sic] fostered the development of very different styles of learning among Native and white children. Whereas many white children, by virtue of their upbringing and their linguistic exposure, are oriented towards using language as a vehicle for learning, Native children have developed a learning style characterized by observation and imitation. (p.34)

Respect and Control: Egalitarian Relationships

Parenting philosophies reflect cultural values of appropriate roles for both the individual child and the adult. Research has illustrated that Navajo young children are respected as independent-thinking adults at a very early age. Viewed as adults, youth are respected, and interfering or intruding into their lives would be inappropriate behavior. This positions parents and children within egalitarian frameworks, in which relationships are negotiated, rather than authoritarian frameworks. The autonomy of the individual regarding possessions and actions is strongly maintained, while at the same time the consensus and cooperation of the group are desired (Deyhle & LeCompte, 1994; Kluckhohn & Leighton, 1974; Lamphere, 1977; Leighton & Kluckhohn, 1948). For example, Joe (1994) explained that the meaning of the Navajo term *nila*, which translates into "it is up to you," embodies the value of an unwillingness to make a controlling or "expert" decision for someone else. This ethic of "noninterference" has been reported in studies on the Sioux (M. Wax et al., 1989) Navajo (Deyhle, 1991; Joe, 1994), and Sac and Fox (Gearing; 1970) and as a general cultural pattern among North American Indian tribes (Good Tracks, 1976). Respectful behavior in relationships does not involve the control of others (Deyhle & Margonis, 1995; Suina & Smolkin, 1994; M. Wax et. al., 1989). Among the Pueblos, a reciprocal balance in traditional hierarchical age relations results in a situation in which both youth and adults have the authority to assist in correcting inappropriate behavior (Suina & Smolkin, 1994). A Northern Alaska Inupiat researcher provided a native's perspective on these differences in child-rearing practices: "Our perspective is that Western child-rearing practices are overly directive and controlling, essentially interfering and intruding in the development of the child. The development of individuality is constrained and childhood is prolonged in Western society" (Okakok, 1989, p. 414).

It has been argued that this cultural value of noninterference has led to a deficit view when it has been misunderstood by teachers and administrators (Deyhle, 1991; Deyhle & LeCompte, 1994; R.H. Wax, 1976). Deyhle (1991) reports that school personnel viewed this culturally specific behavior among Navajos as "permissive" and were critical of Navajo parents' "lack of control" or "apathy" over their children. At the very least, these cultural differences in terms of appropriate behaviors, when manifested in Eurocentric classrooms, become defined as deficit simply because of their opposition to the governed norms in the classroom.

Communication Patterns: Cultural Values and Speech

Cultural values and practices in child rearing influence the respective ways in which American Indian/Alaska Native children learn to learn and display that learning. Ethnographic research reports an avoidance or dislike of individual public performance, such as answering questions publicly, and an economy of speech or purposeful use of silence among Warm Springs children (Philips, 1983), Western Apache children (Basso, 1970), Canadian Cree children (Darnell, 1979; 1988), Indian students in a Canadian boarding school (King, 1967), Alaska Native youth (R. Scollon & Scollon, 1981), Ojibwa children in Minnesota and Ontario (Black, 1973), Eskimo children (Cline, 1972; Collier, Jr., 1973), Oglala Sioux children (Wax, et al. 1989), and Navajo children (Guilmet, 1979, 1978). In examinations of the issue of interactional styles or the demonstration of knowledge in classroom studies on Native children, a focus has emerged that centers on the conflict arising when these children's styles are at odds with those required for successful participation in the classroom (Cazden, 1982; Dumont, 1972; Erickson & Mohatt, 1982; Philips, 1972, 1983; Swisher & Deyhle, 1987; Van Ness, 1981).

In typical American classrooms, one way in which children are expected to demonstrate competence is by publicly responding to direct questions from the teacher. This style or approach stresses performance as a means of gaining competence. In other words, "If at first you don't succeed, try, try again." Research suggested that in many Indian societies competence precedes performance. Werner and Begishe (1968) and Longstreet (1978) reported that Navajo children observed an activity repeatedly and reviewed the performance in their heads before attempting any kind of public performance. Suina and Smolkin (1994) described this "private practice" among Pueblo children: "Children try out, through enactments [privately], thinking, and feeling, that which is seen or heard in order to make the knowledge or skill their own" (p. 118). Brewer (1977), in describing learning by Oglala Sioux children, said that observation, self-testing in private, and then demonstration of a task for approval were essential steps in learning. "Learning through public mistakes was not and is not a method of learning which Indians value" (p. 32). M. Wax et al. (1989) also described a cultural pattern among Oglala Sioux in which performance did not precede competence and an individual should not attempt an action until observations have produced an understanding that will lead to an accurate performance. Deyhle (1986b) illustrated how classroom practices designed to assess individual knowledge through either public display (classroom questioning) or a test were not effective with elementary-aged Navajo children who had learned to learn at home without the use of public, individual displays of knowledge. Without socialization that praised individual achievement as measured on testlike events or tests, Navajo children did not approach testing seriously or respond with remorse toward deficient grades. Teachers' interpretations of students' apparent lack of respect, acceptance, or understanding of personal failure on tests led them to a deficit view of Navajo children as somewhat lacking and in need of being brought up to the "norm."

Research illustrated that distinct communication patterns developed from values that respected egalitarian relationships and the autonomy of the individual. One of the most frequently-cited sociolinguistic studies was conducted by Philips (1972, 1983) on the Warm Springs (Oregon) Indian Reservation community. She argued that Warm Springs children were raised in a context in which authority was shared and participation was voluntary. Philips (1972) stated:

The Indian social activities to which children are early exposed outside the home generally have the following properties: (1) they are community-wide, in the sense that they are open to all Warm Springs Indians; (2) there is no single individual directing and controlling all activity, and to the extent that there are "leaders," their leadership is based on the choice to follow [which is] made by each person; (3) participation in some forms is accessible to everyone who attends. No one need be exclusively an observer or audience, and there is consequently no sharp distinction between audience and performer. And each individual chooses for himself the degree of his participation during the activity. (p. 390)

Eurocentric organizational school structures and Indian community cultural norms for participation and communication differed significantly in the classrooms Philips observed. Structures that required large-and small-group recitation (public performance) brought reluctant participation from Warm Springs children, whereas these children were more talkative than non-Indian children when they initiated the interaction with the teacher or they were working in student-led group projects. However, large-and small-group recitation directed by the teacher occurred more frequently in the classrooms. Philips argued that Indian students were socialized into a conversational pattern quite different from the behaviors expected of them in classrooms.

Philips (1972) concluded that culturally constructed speech patterns may help to explain a reluctance of Warm Springs Indian children to speak in front of their classmates. An incongruency existed in that the acquisition of knowledge and demonstration of knowledge in the classroom were "collapsed into the single act of answering questions or reciting when called upon to do so by the teacher, particularly in the lower grades" (p. 388).

Philips's insight was critical for understanding not only how but why Warm Springs students performed the way they did in the classroom. This was missing from previous, psychologically driven research that ignored the cultural context of the Indian child. Rather than accepting the "cultural vacuum" ideology (Wax et al., 1964; B. Berry, 1968), her training as an ethnographer led her to respect the cultural background of the Warm Springs students and placed her in a position of learner, rather than expert, in the community. This approach also presents an understanding of student behavior as a form of self-determination or resistance to assimilation in that students chose to follow community norms rather than school norms.

Other ethnographic research suggested that the communication difficulty experienced by the Warm Springs Indian children when participant structures were teacher dominated and required public recitations may be generalized to other groups of American Indian children. Dumont (1972) found a similar situation in a study that compared two Cherokee classrooms. In one classroom, teacher-dominated recitations were a predominant structure, and the children were silent. In the other classroom, the children were observed talking excitedly and productively about all of their learning tasks because they had choices of when and how to participate and the teacher encouraged small-group, student-directed projects. The landmark research by Philips (1972) and Dumont (1972) places behavior within a cultural frame of reference, which then clarifies why some Indian children may be more apt to participate actively and verbally in group projects, and in situations in which they have control in volunteering participation, and less apt to perform on demand when asked a question individually in a large group.

The Individual and the Group: Cooperation Within the Community

A body of research points to socialization practices that highlight, by emphasizing an ethic of cooperation, group or community commitment over that of the individual (Deyhle, 1995; Joe, 1994; Lamphere, 1977; Suina & Smolkin, 1994; Swisher, 1990). Among relatives and in the community, extensive sharing, generosity, and cooperation surround Native children as they grow into adulthood among the Mistassini Cree (Sindell, 1987), Zuni (Whiting et al., 1975), Eskimo (Briggs, 1970), Navajo (Leighton & Kluckhohn, 1948), and Tohono O'odham (formerly Papago) (Macias, 1987). In this cultural frame of reference, excelling differs considerably from the competitive stance found in mainstream society. Suina and Smolkin (1994) illustrated this concept among Pueblo society, "To shine as an individual in the Pueblo world is to have done so on behalf of the extended family and the community; such excellence brings pride and cohesion to the group" (p. 118). C. Barnhardt (1994) reported the comments made to a group of Alaska educators by a Yup'ik Eskimo man:

> Don't expect to see Native students [in university classrooms] shooting their hands in the air with the "I know, I know" look. And don't think less of them for not doing so. It is not our way. Our culture teaches modesty. For us success means not to stand out from the crowd but to live in harmony with everything around us. (p. 116)

Eggan (1976) described a childrearing technique that assured the individual Hopi would remain emotionally connected to the group as a result of "the early and continued conditioning of the individual in the Hopi maternal extended family, which was on every level an inculcation of *interdependence* as contrasted with our [Eurocentric] training for *independence* " (p. 142). And Ovando (1994) described a similar value of social interdependence in an Athapaskan Indian community in Alaska.

Along with individual achievement as connected to the betterment of the group, was the ethic of cooperation that avoided unnecessary competition among peers. This ethic manifested itself in studies that reported Indian student preference for cooperative behavior in the learning context. Using the Madsen Cooperation Board, in which cooperative and competitive behaviors were examined, Miller and Thomas (1972) found dramatic differences between Blackfoot Indian children, who behaved cooperatively, and White Canadian children, who behaved competitively even when it was maladaptive to do so. A. Brown (1980), using the same instrument, found Cherokee children to be more cooperative and less competitive than Anglo-American children and found a negative relationship between the cooperative behavior of Cherokee children and their school achievement. Brown's analysis centered on the children following traditional Cherokee cultural norms such as maintaining harmonious relations, which requires children "to hold fast to group standards of achievement that all of the children are capable of meeting" (p. 70). High-ability students who did not want to violate this norm kept from displaying their competence, and the result, according to Brown, was lowered achievement for many members of the classroom society.

Similarly, the focus on the group rather than the individual in the classroom was also described by Wolcott (1984), who was both a teacher and a researcher, among the Kwakiutl in the Northwest. When he gave an assignment, his students interpreted their tasks as a matter of group as well as individual concerns.

Although he acknowledged the benefit of pairs of students working together in an informal, noncompetitive way, he also expressed frustration with the "leveling" of achievement, noting that "no pupil, however, worked in such a way that another peer was *too* much slower," and "the instant after the teacher posed any such question to a group of younger pupils the answer would be whispered somewhere else in the classroom by the older ones" (p. 104).

Ethnographic research also confirmed that many Indian students avoided competition, which they viewed as unfair in its composition (Dumont, 1972; Sindell, 1987; Swisher, 1990; M. Wax et al., 1989). Havighurst (1970) observed that "Indian children may not parade their knowledge before others nor try to appear better than their peers" (p. 109). In looking at competition and the peer society of Sioux Indian youth, M. Wax (1971) stated:

It has frequently been observed that Indian children hesitate to engage in an individual performance before the public gaze, especially where they sense competitive assessment against their peers and equally do not wish to demonstrate by their individual superiority the inferiority of their peers. On the other hand, where performance is socially defined as benefiting the peer society, Indians become excellent competitors (as witness their success in team athletics). (p. 85)

This research suggests that Indian children who have learned to learn in a cooperative way experience conflicts when they enter the competitive, individualistic world of the classroom. This literature also suggests that, for Indian children from certain groups, a public display of knowledge that is not in keeping with cultural or group norms may be an uncomfortable experience, one that often causes Indian children to withdraw and act out the prototype of the "silent Indian child."

Institutional Parenting: Cultural Disruption

We have discussed the role and influence of parents in the education of their children by presenting B. Berry's (1968) review of the literature, which characterized parents as a negative influence on the assimilation of their children. We have also discussed the importance of child-rearing practices that influence the way in which children learn to learn. We would be remiss if we did not discuss the intergenerational effects of boarding schools on parenting and child rearing, a topic that has appeared in the mental health literature more so than in educational research literature. One of the most profound effects of boarding schools on generations of Indian people has been the deprivation of culturally appropriate socialization and child-rearing models. With the overt aim of "helping" Indian children enter the mainstream of American life, children as young as 6 years old were sent to distant boarding schools. According to Mindell and Gurwitt (1977), "this educational practice has had a devastating effect on several generations of Indian children. It has affected their family life, their native culture, their sense of identity, and their parenting abilities" (p. 62). Devoid of the influence of their families, children were raised—in many cases, for their entire school lives—by institutional parents. Outing systems in which children were placed with White families during summer vacations, more often than not as domestic help, falsely substitute for family life back home and were intended to hasten assimilation. In *The Destruction of Indian Families* (1977), Merriam wrote about the effects of boarding schools on Indian family life. He noted the effects of early deprivation of family life on the development, health, and personality of the institutional children relative to those in families. Parents were also deprived of the care of their children, creating unnatural conditions in which their development as parents to full adult responsibility was also affected. Merriam (1977) concluded that "under normal conditions the experience of family life is preparation for future parenthood. Without the parent-child relationship experience, youth have serious disability in their relationships with their own children" (p. 17). Attneave (1977), in "Destruction of American Indian Families," wrote about her work with Indian parents.

I recall vividly how often each year worried sets of parents would come to the clinic begging for help in securing placement in a boarding school for their eight or nine year old child. This puzzled me, and it soon became clear that although it was heartbreaking for them to part with their child, they knew of nothing else to do. Neither they nor their own parents had ever known life in a family from the age they first entered school. The parents had no memories and no patterns to follow in rearing children except for the regimentation of mass sleeping and impersonal schedules that they had known. How to raise children at home had become a mystery. (p. 30)

While there is an abundance of research on boarding schools, the effect of institutional parenting is an area of inquiry that is relatively new. Can affected parents of this generation recapture the socialization skills and child-rearing patterns they have been deprived of from generations past? One effort to do just that is the program operating in several schools funded by the BIA. The Family and Child Education (FACE) program seeks to nurture parents along with their preschool and school-aged children. The FACE program is characterized by furthering the education of the parent while the child is in school. The parent or caregiver takes classes on parenting skills and is given an opportunity to practice the skills in a supportive instructive environment and in the home. The philosophical base for the program draws from culturally appropriate parenting of the respective tribal groups. Early anecdotal evidence indicates that this approach is highly successful. The important point of this initiative is that it is grounded in self-determination. Communities are taking back their right to socialize their children according to values and traditions of their respective cultures.

Cultural Influences, Learning, and Institutional Barriers: What Is the Meaning for Educators?

If the relationship between culture and the impact culture has on the approach to learning were understood, a teaching and learning situation could exist wherein the learner would no longer be solely responsible for adjustment to the situation.

This implies that traditional power relations—in which the teacher controls the means of participation, pacing of instruction, and organization of teacher-dominated instruction—would have to be modified to adjust to the culture of the students. Unfortunately, this rarely happens in classrooms for American Indian students. We believe that what teachers *do* to students—how power relations are negotiated in the classroom—is critical in understanding American Indian student performance in school. And we believe that culture is the lens through which these events must be viewed.

Ethnographic research reveals a great deal about cultural influences on student learning, which, in turn, leads to suggestions for teachers' instructional accommodation to these patterns (Cazden & Leggett, 1981; Kaulback, 1984; Reyhner, 1992; Sawyer, 1991; Swisher & Deyhle, 1989). The suggestions are based on the educational position of accepting cultural differences rather than ascribing to an assimilatory position of dissolving these differences. For example, Macias's (1987) research illustrated how local knowledge of children's culture by Tohono O'odham (formerly Papago) teachers enabled them to construct a smooth path for Papago students. In choosing methods for a particular situation, there are many variables to consider that will lead to optimal learning. Only recently, however, has the culture of the learner been considered among those variables, as a strength to be built upon rather than a deficit to be remedied (Burgess, 1978). Philips (1983) capsulized this attitude when she said:

Surprisingly little attention has been given to the teaching methods used in teaching ethnic minority students in this country. Particularly when the notion of culturally relevant curriculum materials has been around so long as it has. It is as if we have been able to recognize that there are cultural differences in what people learn, but not in how they learn. (pp. 132–133)

Leacock (1976) also provided a strong rationale for understanding culture and its influence on instruction. She believed that "true cultural insight" enables one to look beyond differences that are superficial and socially determined to the integrity of the individual; it prevents misinterpretation of behaviors that do not follow an accustomed pattern. Leacock (1976) cited as an example teachers' misinterpretation of the pervading "cooperative spirit" in Indian societies and a reluctance of Indian children to compete with peers as a lack of desire and motivation. In essence, Leacock was saying that cultural differences are often misinterpreted and that the lens through which the teacher views behavior is colored by the atypical behavior used as a prototype in the teacher training process. For example, "timidity" or shyness is often interpreted as lack of initiative, motivation, or the competitive spirit. If the behavior were viewed through a more culturally relativistic lens, the timid behavior might reveal a reluctance to compete with one's peers or a reluctance to display learning in a way incongruent with the child's lifestyle.

Researchers such as Dumont (1972) and Philips (1983) have concluded that the cultural incongruity between the home and school—especially the school's tendency to isolate control in the hands of the teachers—causes resistance and lack of participation on the part of American Indian students. According to Dumont (1972), classroom teachers are more effective with Indian students when they share social control and use warmer and more personal teaching styles. Philips's (1983) study of participant structures in the classroom revealed that Indian students' level of participation was highest in activities in which students worked either in small student-led groups or individually (participant structures in which power is shared) and lowest during teacher-directed groups and lecturing (participant structures in which power is localized in the teacher). Tierney (1992) argued that effective teachers in higher education altered the authority relationship—teacher as expert—to position themselves as colearners with Indian students. Other researchers, such as Collier (1979), F. Erickson and Mohatt (1982), and R. Barnhardt (1981), identified teacher pacing (the instructor's adaptation to the speed and movements of students) as an important factor in working successfully with American Indian students. Erickson and Mohatt (1982) also identified other cultural "adaptations," such as accepting silence, using more small group instruction, avoiding spotlighting (singling students out for praise, criticism, or recitation), and being sensitive to nonverbal clues, as being important for effective instruction with American Indian students. In describing effective instructors of American Indian and Alaska Native students, Kleinfeld (1975) identified two primary characteristics: personal warmth (vs. professional distance) and active demandingness (vs. passive understanding). She referred to this type of teacher as a "warm demander" (in other words, one who can balance humanistic concerns with high expectations for achievement).

Mohatt and Erickson's (1981) study of cultural differences in teaching styles in an Odawa school supports the differences regarding participant structures Philips (1972) found in Warm Springs. In their study, an Indian and a non-Indian teacher were observed to determine whether there were differences in their teaching styles. Although both teachers were effective and experienced, they varied as to the strategies they used with students. The Indian teacher paused longer for answers and did not single out individuals in the total classroom group but, rather, focused on children in more intimate, private situations and exerted control over the whole class at once, proceeding slowly and deliberately. The non-Indian teacher gave short pauses for answers, called out directions to individual children across the room and generally moved more rapidly around the whole room, giving directions to the total classroom group and small reading groups at the same time. Mohatt and Erickson (1981) believed that these different teaching strategies reflected cultural patterns of what is appropriate in ordinary social relations between adults and children:

Differences in the teachers' style of interaction seem to be related to characteristic Odawa Indian participation structures, in contrast to non-Indian ones. At issue, then, is not the general effectiveness or efficiency of either style of teaching, in terms of final results, but the cultural congruence of each style with the patterns of interaction customary for Indian children in everyday life. (p. 117)

What is also important about the Mohatt and Erickson (1981) study was the way in which the non-Native teacher adapted to the ways of acting used by the Indian teacher next door.

He was developing a more culturally congruent teaching style by making more use of Odawa participant structures. He increased the amount of time he spent with individual children and small groups,
and decreased the amount of contact he had with children in the public arena of large group instruction. (pp. 117–118)

Much of the research in this section discussed the instructional relationship between non-Indian teachers and Indian students. Positive impact on the educa-tion of American Indian and Alaska Native students is implied through two approaches. One is the development and use of culturally appropriate and relevant curricula and methodology. Another is increasing teacher sensitivity to and skill at dealing with cultural differences during preservice and in-service teacher train-ing programs. A third approach scarcely researched is the impact of Indian teach-ers teaching Indian students. It is anecdotally argued that successful Indian teachers understand and relate to the history, culture, and language of Indian stu-dents more favorably and serve as positive role models for Indian students, thereby increasing self-esteem and ulitmately their academic achievement. In addition, there is a belief that increasing the number of Indian graduates who return to Indian communities to teach would help reduce the turnover rate referred to in the literature. Although there is a perceived need for more Indian teachers, little is known about the attributes or behaviors and attitudes of Indian teachers, but there are many questions. Do Indian teachers who are trained in mainstream university teacher education programs teach differently than their non-Indian counterparts? In what ways do they retain their ethnicity and demonstrate it in the classroom? How are Indian students affected by having an Indian teacher? These questions are the focus of inquiry in case studies in progress at the Center for Indian Education at Arizona State University.

The research in this section is not as much about "teaching styles" adapted to "Indian learning styles" as it is about student-teacher relationships. Specifically, the construction of a mutually respectful relationship is central to educational success. For teachers who care enough to watch and listen and who have high expectations of their Indian students, the educational experience is a positive one for both teachers and students. This "cultural accommodation" implies respect for the Indian child's culture and home life. A review of the research, however, reveals that too few Indian students have these kinds of educational experiences.

Deficit Thought in a Cultural Differences Model

The concept of an "American Indian learning style" has not been without criti-cism. Several reviews in the 1980s examined the research on how cultural values have influenced students' behavior, resulting in distinct learning styles in the class-room. This thinking challenged prevailing beliefs of cultural deprivation as an explanatory model for school failure (Kaulback, 1984; Swisher & Deyhle, 1987). In our review (Swisher & Deyhle, 1987), we examined 52 studies on the cultural influences of learning—some empirical and others anecdotal—and argued that the cultural influences of the home resulted in different learning styles in the classroom. The original work in 1987 was revised twice (1989, 1992), reprinted in a textbook (Johnson, Dupuis, & Johansen, 1991), and widely distributed. As more and more research reported on American Indian learning styles, the *Journal of American Indian Education* devoted a special issue to the topic in August 1989.

We believe that this information is important in order to understand how Indian children are prepared to learn when they come to school. Knowledge of group tendencies presents a framework through which to observe and understand individual behaviors. In our reviews we discussed research, some from 20–30 years ago, that presented compelling evidence that Indian students from several groups were visual learners who were reluctant to perform without private practice and preferred cooperative rather than competitive learning situations. While we were careful to caution readers of the diversity among tribes (more than 500 different tribes speaking more than 200 languages), we presented research that was generalized to suggest that there is an American Indian learning style. Although this research has been useful in focusing attention on differences in learning styles, we are convinced that it has also been used to stereotype students into specific group styles and to ignore both individual and tribal differences. In this light, we have sought to report only tribal-specific research in this chapter. Researchers and educators now know a great deal more about learning and culture than 10 years ago; however, there is still a tendency to view the cultural knowledge and strengths with which Indian children come to school as deficits because they are not the same predispositions that Anglo children have.

The conflict regarding an Indian learning style exists, in part, because of the ill-defined and ambiguous terms that fall under "learning styles" in the research. A wide assortment of abilities, modes of processing information, and labels has been used to define and describe learning styles (e.g., spatial abilities, right-brain hemispheric dominance, visual memory, field independence, holistic or successive rather than sequential patterns of information processing, and cooperative learning). Some researchers argue that such discussions result in dangerous stereotypes that can, in effect, limit the educational opportunities of American Indian youth. For example, discussions of right-brain hemispheric dominance have led researchers to urge teachers of American Indian students to develop a "right-brained curriculum" (Ross, 1989). On the basis of anecdotal evidence and generalizations from neuropsychology and anthropology—such as "The right hemisphere cannot think in words, it only thinks in symbols" (Ross, 1989, p. 73) and "The right hemisphere hasn't a good sense of time and doesn't seem to comprehend what is meant by the term 'wasting time' as does the left hemisphere" (p. 74)—teachers are urged to focus on the "inherent" strengths of their American Indian students. According to Chrisjohn and Peters (1989), not only are these "facts" suspect, but they can result in disastrous implications for the education of American Indian children: "Once the educator has been convinced that the Indian is right-brained, it may be decided that some of the skills that are thought to be 'left-brain' skill should not be emphasized. Why bother to teach Indian children things that they are not capable of learning anyhow?" (p. 78). These researchers cautioned about the use of "anatomical" proof for the differences between the brains of Whites and non-Whites, which has historically been twisted and manipulated to prove the superiority of Whites in general and certain nationalities in particular and of the ethnocentric assumptions built into this body of research:

The emphasis on training the right-brained child with a right-brain curriculum, incidentally, is rather peculiar. If there were any substance to this entire issue one might expect the educator to focus on so-called "left-brain" skills, under the assumption that the right-brain skills are sufficiently developed. (Chrisjohn & Peters, 1989, p. 78).

Chrisjohn and Peters (1989) argued that this information has been misused to justify remedial, nonacademic, and nonchallenging curricula for American Indian students. Kleinfeld, whose own research among the Alaskan Inuit (1973) revealed culturally influenced learning patterns, recently challenged the effectiveness of the concept of learning style:

Good teachers always adapt to the culture of the child and the culture of the school. Nothing is lost by using the term "learning style" to denote such teaching adaptation, but little is gained. "Learning style" becomes a vague and ambiguous concept without significant heuristic value. (Kleinfeld, 1988, p. 95)

Kleinfeld and Nelson (1991) acknowledged, however, that empirical research supported the existence of cultural patterns in learning: "Psychological research on the performance of native American groups on various tests indicates a cognitive ability pattern characterized by higher spatial and visual skills and lower verbal skills," and "a similar conclusion about the strength of visual as opposed to verbal skills appears to follow from ethnographic research on the characteristic mode of learning among Native American children outside the context of formal schooling" (p. 275). In reviewing three studies (D. Erickson, 1972; McCartin & Schill, 1977; Shears, 1970) that attempted to demonstrate that a visual instructional approach would enhance student achievement, Kleinfeld and Nelson (1991) found that "the few studies of teaching methods adapted to Native American students' visual learning styles provide virtually no support for the hypothesis that this type of culturally adapted instruction will increase achievement" (p. 279). While not dismissing the importance of culturally patterned learning styles, Kleinfeld (1988) argued that this information is important not for "matching" instruction to high or low verbal or visual abilities; its importance "lies rather in helping teachers understand the cultural context in which they are working so that they can respond with better judgment" (p. 95).

A study by McCarty, Wallace, Lynch, and Benally (1991) also challenged the learning style research we have presented here when it is used by educators to restrict classroom instruction to "accommodate" to the explicit cultural behaviors of the Indian child pictured in this body of research. As did Chrisjohn and Peters (1989), McCarty, Wallace, Lynch, & Benally (1991) argued that the learning style literature has been used to stereotype Indian students, in particular, as nonverbal learners who will not speak or answer questions because this action is "culturally inappropriate." This assumption was even internalized by the staff at their research site, one of whom said, "But Navajo students won't *respond* to questions" (p. 42). These authors argued that the context of the classroom setting—where communicative interaction between student and teacher takes the form of a "face-to-face assault"—itself contributes to or creates the "silent Indian child" (p. 53). Foley's (1996) research among the Mesquakis also challenges a sociolinguistic explanatory model that ignored racism and resistance. The power relations in the classroom, rather than the Indian child as culturally or inherently "nonverbal" are central to understanding the nonparticipatory behavior observed in many Indian classrooms. In these "silent" classrooms, communication is controlled by the teacher, who accepts only one correct answer and singles out individuals to respond to questions for which they have little background knowledge. Many of these educators expect passivity and fail to provide Indian students with enriched opportunities for open-ended discussions about challenging academic content.

In the McCarty et al. (1991) study, an experimental, bilingual social studies curriculum, using content information from the local Navajo community and emphasizing open-ended questioning, inductive/analytical reasoning, and student participation and verbalization in both small-and large-group settings, was developed for Navajo students in Grades K-9. The researchers reported a dramatic increase in Navajo students' involvement and interactions in their classroom and concluded:

In classrooms where talk is shared between teacher and students, where the expression of students' ideas is sought and clearly valued, where students' social environment is meaningfully incorporated into curricular content, and where students are encouraged to use their cultural and linguistic resources to solve new problems, Native American students respond eagerly and quite verbally to questioning, even in their second language. . . . The point is that the variables which facilitate this are dispositions [cultural learning experiences] *and* context which lie behind the performances labeled as "style" . . . this requires a thorough, deep local knowledge . . . that goes beyond labels and overt manifestations of the local culture, and that also includes an understanding of the sociohistorical experiences of the local population with formal schooling. (McCarty et al., 1991, pp. 53–54)

Linking microlevel processes and cultural variables with macrolevel forces, McCarty et al. (1991) illustrated the importance of critically examining the interplay between cultural differences and power relations as we study the school performance of American Indian students.

As we have illustrated, early psychological tests, normed against a middle-class Anglo population, consistently revealed that American Indian and Alaska Native children achieved less well than non-Native children on tests measuring intelligence and innate ability. Challenging conclusions that these children were "intellectually inferior," researchers started using "culture" as a factor to explain these achievement differences. Early "cultural difference" researchers used the general concept of "culture" with little empirical research that looked at the process of the development of cultural patterns. With broad claims, (e.g., "Indians are keen observers"), this research ignored the specific values that lead to certain behaviors. It was also assumed that cultural differences, by themselves, caused academic difficulties. Although research clearly illustrated the cultural inconsistency faced by American Indian students in classrooms, there is a danger in that this can be used to both further stereotypes and locate the problem in "them." What was missing was an examination of how cultural differences might intertwine with power relations. Cultural differences studies that ignored the larger political, social, and economic context provided only a partial picture of Indian students' academic achievement in the classroom. Cultural resistance and the power struggle between Anglos and Indians—specifically, the relationships between Anglo-controlled schools (functioning with a model of assimilation) and Indian societies—do help explain academic success and failure.

Resistance Research: Institutional Racism and Student Resistance

Research grounded in critical theory focuses on institutional inequities, moving the analysis away from a deficit perspective while capturing the dominant group's role in creating educational inequities. Resistance theory allows us to consider the educational results of assimilatory policy, because the legacy of assimilation has been understood by students, and assimilation has consistently produced resistant students. Critical studies also provide an explanation of the problematic teacher-student relations that occur in these studies: Whether students resist passively or actively, and whether teachers are racists or anthropologists (like Wolcott), they are unable to create good student-teacher relations because of the political meaning of being educated in an assimilatory, White-dominated institution.

There has been little research conducted on racism, discrimination, and prejudice within and/or among American Indian groups or American Indians and non-Indians within the school setting; yet, racism, prejudice, and discrimination clearly exist and may, in fact, be contributors to students' lack of success in the school setting. In this section, we highlight ethnographic or longitudinal studies that implicitly and explicitly examine community and institutional racism and the effects of this treatment on school performance. These studies illustrate how cultural differences become politicized within dominated and subordinated power relations. They also demonstrate how Indian students respond, often resisting, to the assimilatory practices of their educators.

The ethnographic research conducted by M. Wax et al. (1989) has been consistently cited; the information on cultural differences they identified among Oglala Sioux students, not their structural analysis, is most frequently discussed. With this use of their data, once again, cultural differences are positioned as "deficits," hence locating the problem in the "Indian" culture. Although Wax et al. (1989) provided a rich account of the cultural differences between the Oglala Sioux community and the community's Anglo-controlled schools, they located the problem in racism and the assimilatory model used in school, which produced "passive resistance" in the students.

In summarizing their research findings, Wax et al. (1989) acknowledged that when they started their research they were unconvinced of the assumption that cultural disharmony or cultural shock as an explanatory model for Oglala Sioux school failure was critical in and of itself. They noted that many other culturally different families had reared their children in a warm and relaxed atmosphere and sent them to impersonal and competitive school contexts; although the transition may have been uncomfortable, these children were able to profit from their educational experience.

The history of the immigrants to this nation demonstrates how people of the most varied ethnic backgrounds adapted themselves to the American economic and educational system, sometimes with outstanding success and virtuosity. . . . The educational and social problems of Pine Ridge do not stem either from a cultural lack or from the simple fact of cultural difference. (Wax et al., 1989, p. 104)

In their analysis, power relations, specifically cultural resistance and racism, were central to understanding the school failure of Oglala Sioux children. They concluded: "The educators believe the Sioux children are so lacking in culture that they cannot master scholastic materials, and the children regard the teachers and their subject matters as 'White' and hence legitimate targets of their hostility and indifference" (p. 104).

With evidence of more than an 80% dropout rate on the Pine Ridge Sioux reservation, Wax et al. (1989) examined cultural differences and resistance as possible causes of this extremely high rate. Their "cultural disharmony" hypothesis suggested that because these Indian youth were reared in traditional homes, the atmosphere of a normal, American school would be painful, incomprehensible, and even immoral; and teachers would view the behavior of these students as undisciplined, lacking in scholastic initiative, and immoral. These authors presented evidence of extreme cultural differences between traditional Oglala Sioux homes and the cultural values expected in the school, however, what was important was not the existence of these differences but how they were used by teachers and administrators. These differences were ignored by teachers to create a "cultural vacuum" ideology. According to this ideology, Oglala Sioux students were lacking in the knowledge, morals, and manners necessary for school success because of an inadequate home life. They provided the following quote from a school administrator as an example of an attitude that is frequently cited in current research:

The Indian child has such a meager experience. When he encounters words like "elevator" or "escalator" in his reading, he has no idea what they mean. But it's not just strange concepts like those. Take even the idea of water. When you or I think of it, well, I think of a shining, stainless steel faucet in a sink, running clean and pure. . . . But the Indian child doesn't think of water as something flowing into a bath tub . . . guess the Indian child would think of a creek . . . or of a pump, broken down and hardly working. (Wax et al., 1989, pp. 67–68)

Wax et al. argued that the Oglala Sioux did not suffer from an absence of culture but from a situation of isolation and a lack of political power to control or counter these racist assumptions about Oglala Sioux students. Although they acknowledged cultural differences as a reality, they identified the critical problem as one of power relations.

> Teachers do encounter difficulties in conducting their classes, because some pupils do not wish to recite publicly or do not wish to be placed in a competitive situation with their classmates, but the difficulty here was not one of direct conflict of White and Indian values, so much as a struggle between school and Indian peer society. (Wax et al., 1989, p. 114).

According to the authors, what teachers *do* to students (such as degrading or dismissing Native culture) is critical to understandings Oglala Sioux school failure. In this case, Indians simply shut themselves off from any interactions or compliance with teachers, who were the symbol of assimilation.

Wax et al.'s "preservation of identity" questions hypothesized that traditional Indians' identity was the last and most valuable "treasure" remaining to them. If education was seen as a means to turn children into "Whites"—the goal of assimilation—this would result in emotional complications and the rejection of schooling. Their findings revealed that educators thought the school was designed to make the Oglala Sioux student "less Indian." Indian parents, on the other hand, thought of their "Indianness" as an intrinsic part of their being and viewed school pragmatically as a means of qualifying them for better paying employment. Indians strongly resisted the efforts of Anglos to make "White men" out of their children: "In their judgment, the White is the alien, the enemy, and the intruder, who has brought the Indian people only misery. 'Acting White' is the most stinging epithet in their vocabulary" (p. 11). Given this resistance, Wax et al. cautioned that "insofar as the educators orient themselves toward rendering their pupils 'less Indian,' they tend to foster a situation that, aggravated by the 'cultural disharmony' of the first theory, tends to gravely handicap the operation of the school system" (pp. 113–114).

The children in this community clearly understood that their teachers harbored negative assumptions and feelings about them and their parents. Rather than being eager to "leave" a community that outsiders viewed as inferior or repulsive, these children formed a peer society that solidified their resistance to the school's regimes and effectively limited or sabotaged the educational efforts of their teachers. Wax et al. (1989) described this "passive resistance":

> As the pressure of the teacher becomes greater, the resistance of the pupils becomes more grotesque, so that like plantation slaves, they appear stupid or infantile. This, in turn, provokes the teacher into treating these adolescents with a condescension that only little children could tolerate. (p. 99)

This combination of student resistance and derogatory teacher treatment created a dismal opportunity for educational success for these Oglala Sioux students.

Like the Wax et al. (1989) study of Oglala Sioux youth, Wolcott's (1984) ethnography of a Canadian Kwakiutl village and school also revealed resistance and a deep distrust of formal schooling by Kwakiutl youth and their families and a dismissal of Kwakiutl culture by Anglo educators who taught with an explicit model of assimilation. Wolcott, who was both an anthropologist and a teacher, sought to identify the influence of cultural barriers to classroom performance and determine why Indian pupils failed in school. At the conclusion of his research, his orientation had changed to a critique of the institution (viz., "How do the schools fail their Indian pupils?") (p. 131).

Wolcott discovered a firmly entrenched pattern of student hostility toward the teacher and nearly every nonmaterial aspect of the way of life the teacher represented. He argued that the critical issue was not of a classroom origin but what he called "antagonistic acculturation":

Frequent antagonisms are aggravated by a contradiction between the ideal of assimilation and the reality of prejudicial treatment accorded to minority groups within the dominant society. . . . Indian schools run by the federal governments of both countries [the United States and Canada] consciously directed their efforts toward replacing Indian ways with ways more acceptable to and characteristic of the dominant white middle class, although the respective societies have at the same time responded prejudicially to the Indian who attempted to assimilate. (Wolcott, 1987, p. 137)

The antagonism he found was not a consequence of cultural, psychological, or personal incompatibility but an antagonism rooted in social forces outside the classroom. When the goal of schooling was assimilation, youth were faced with two difficult decisions: to "defect" and try to enter a racially restricted position in the dominant society or to "reject" the school system that was trying to change them. Wolcott used a war metaphor to illustrate the seriousness of the conflict. He referred to students as "prisoners of war" and urged teachers to understand their students' resistance because of their role as "enemy," whose purpose of instruction was to recruit new members into their society. This positioning allowed for more sensitivity on the part of teachers to the resistance of their students. According to Wolcott,

Most important, the teacher realizes the meaning that accepting his teaching may have for those prisoners who do not accept it. It may mean selling out, defecting, turning traitor, ignoring the succorance and values and pressures of one's peers, one's family, one's own people. It can require terrible and anxious decisions for the prisoner, and it may even require him to sever his most deeply-rooted human ties. The teacher needs constantly to review what these costs mean to any human. As a consequence, the teacher interested in his enemy pupils as humans may find himself less inclined to act as a cultural brainwasher and more inclined to weigh both the difficulties of cultural transition and the ultimate consequences of change. (1987, p. 147)

Wolcott believed that his Kwakiutl students' orientation to school was one of patient endurance: "What my pupils wanted most to get out of school was to get out of school " (1987, p. 138). The classroom perceived by his students revealed an institutional picture of harsh, uncaring teachers. His study speaks to institutionally framed student-teacher relations that yielded in no way to establish trust, rapport, and learning. Students, writing to the assigned topic "If I Were the

Teacher," mimicked their Anglo teachers by emphasizing middle-class values of cleanliness, quiet, punctuality, and obedience. Discipline and punishment were frequent themes. These students painted a picture of the classroom as an orderly, severe, and punishing place and contrasted the pseudowork and satisfaction of the classroom from the real work and real rewards of adult life. Students accurately saw Wolcott as a symbol of assimilation and effectively shut him and the school out of their lives.

The study by Dumont and Wax (1976) in a Cherokee community also identified the complexities of both cultural differences and student resistance in classrooms whose goals are "to shape and stamp them into becoming dutiful citizens, responsible employees, or good Christians" (p. 205). Cherokee students were oriented toward the world of their elders, where learning and other cooperative efforts were to occur without friction. Within their homes, they learned that restraint and caution were the proper modes of relating to others. In the classroom, they learned to sustain, order, and control the relationships of a Cherokee community as they proceeded toward adult maturity and responsibility. According to these norms, the educational exchange was voluntary for both students and teachers and was governed by a mutual respect. From the perspective of their teachers, Cherokee students were described as model students who were patient, diligent, and quiet, and who loved to "play school." The silence of the students was seen as timidity or shyness, and their control and restraint were seen as docility. The silence, in fact, was the sound of nonviolence and passive resistance as the students created a "Cherokee school society" to block out the inappropriate intrusion of the Anglo teachers. Student-teacher relations were framed by community tension and resistance to assimilatory practices.

What typically happens is that, by the seventh and eighth grades the students have surrounded themselves with a wall of silence impenetrable by the outsider, while sheltering a rich emotional communication among themselves. The silence is positive, not simply negative or withdrawing, and it shelters them so that, among other things, they can pursue their scholastic interests in their own style and pace. (Dumont & Wax, 1976, p. 211)

In the classrooms they studied, the role of the teacher (specifically, the respect teachers accorded the Cherokee students) was central to constructing intercultural bridges for communication and instruction. Effective teachers created "two-way learning paths" that positioned teachers on a more equal level such that they had to learn from Cherokee youth the most basic cultural prescriptions. The role of the teacher was a "scholastic assistant rather than classroom tyrant" (Dumont & Wax, 1976, p. 213). This respect built trust, and, within these classroom contexts, some Cherokee youth were engaged learners. In most, however, "the war within the classrooms was so cold that its daily battles were not evident, except at the close of the day as the teachers assessed their lack of pedagogical accomplishment" (p. 209).

Like the previous ethnographic studies, Wilson's (1991) study of Canadian Sioux high school students identified racial prejudice, rather than cultural differences, as central in understanding their lack of success and subsequent rejection of schooling. Wilson described elementary school experiences on the reserve, including warm, caring, and respectful Native teachers who had high expectations for Indian students. Students thrived, and test scores were high. Educational success turned to failure when students left the reserve for high school in the city. Teachers were cold to the Indian students, frequently facing away from Indian students throughout entire class periods, and had low expectations of them. In the teachers' views, Indian students could not speak proper English, could not read, would not mix with other students, and just did not fit into the system. Indian students were isolated in an institution that did not want them. "In the space of one day they faced racism, behavior patterns different from their own, alien cultural norms, and economic stress. The structure appeared to them to have been designed for their failure, and they failed, practically overnight" (Wilson, 1991, p. 377). The Indian students were aware of racial prejudice in the school and, fulfilling the low expectations of their teachers, they undervalued their academic ability, taking boring, undemanding courses to minimize their engagement with the hostile school. One student said, "The work I am taking now is so simple that it is ridiculous. I took this stuff in about grade four. I look at it now and my mind goes blank. I wasn't dumb before I got here, but I soon will be if I stay in this place" (p. 378). Of the 23 students from the reserve in the high school, 18 had dropped out before the end of the school year. To cope with the trauma of the high school experience, and rejecting an underclass status, students chose the adaptive strategy of dropping out of school. Wilson (1991) concluded that, in the face of cultural conflict and psychological trauma, these students maintained a sense of dignity and choice.

It is true that the initial reaction was one of hopelessness, but then that hopelessness spurred them on to action. The action that they chose was that of dropping out or of abandoning school for a time. To them, staying in school would have been an unwise choice. Their adaptive strategies required withdrawal because the setting was impossible. They chose psychological survival. (p. 378)

After Dumont and Wax (1976), M. Wax, et al. (1989), and Wolcott (1984) had conducted their research, Deyhle (1995) undertook an ethnographic study of Navajo youth in and out of school. For more than a decade, she followed Navajo youth and their families through high school, to the job market, and into life as young mothers and fathers. Like the student resistance and assimilatory practices reported in previous studies—Wax et al.'s (1989) "cultural resistance and racism," Wolcott's (1987) "antagonistic acculturation," Dumont and Wax's (1976) "cold war," and Wilson's (1991) "racial trauma"—Deyhle (1995) painted a disturbingly similar picture of "cultural warfare." She argued that the teachers and administrators in the school district, who have defied a court order to provide a bilingual and bicultural program for Navajo students for 27 years, framed their understanding of Navajo students with a century-old model of assimilation that viewed Navajo culture and language as the reasons for school failure. This assimilationist belief was used to rationalize the need to "change" Navajos—an educational goal of taking the "Navajoness" out of their Navajo students—to fit into the outside world. As one English as a Second Language teacher explained, "These kids we get are learning disabled with their reading. Because they speak Navajo, you know. The Indian students need to learn English and basic skills to survive in the Anglo world. That bilingual and bicultural stuff is not important for them" (Deyhle, 1995, p. 418). These racially driven views were also used to adjust educational and economic opportunities downward—providing a vocationalized curriculum for semi-skilled job opportunity—so as to be "appropriate" for Navajo culture. Explaining a 75% vocational curriculum in one high school, a career education teacher said, "Well, I mean, they are good in spatial things. Working hands on. They don't learn theoretically. You can talk until you are blue in the face. It's much better if there is practical hands-on application" (p. 415).

Similar to M. Wax et al. (1989) and Wolcott (1984), the teachers and administrators in Deyhle's (1995) study saw only a "cultural vacuum" when they looked at their Navajo students. This view allowed educators to ignore substantial value differences between Navajos and Anglos and how these differences interacted with the schools and the educational goals they constructed for Navajo students. For example, traditional Anglo notions of "success"—school credentials, individual careers, and individual economic prosperity—did not reflect those of the Navajo. The successful Navajo was judged in terms of intact extended familial relations, where individual jobs and educational success were used to enhance the family and the community, and aggressive individualism was suppressed for the cooperation of the group. These cultural characteristics in themselves did not necessarily result in school failure, although they contributed to the tension and misunderstandings between Navajos and Anglos.

Deyhle (1995) argued that racism and misguided cultural assumptions about Navajos intertwined in the schools and worked to limit educational and economic opportunities for Navajos while maintaining political and economic power for Anglos in the community. Navajo students spoke of daily racial conflict and a resistance to accept the inferior status assigned them by their educators. Many left school, while others simply faded into the background of their classrooms. The Anglo community viewed assimilation as a necessary path to school success. Deyhle's data revealed the opposite:

The more academically successful Navajo students were more likely to be those who were firmly rooted in their Navajo community. . . . Failure rates were more likely for youth who felt disenfranchised from their culture and at the same time experienced racial conflict. Rather than viewing the Navajo culture as a barrier, as does an assimilation model, "culturally intact" youth are, in fact, more successful students. (1995, pp. 419–420).

For many, school was "resisted," in part, by moving through high school as a short "interruption" in their progression to lives as adult Navajo men and women.

For them, high school was something one tolerated and sometimes enjoyed; school success did not pose a serious threat to them when their cultural identity was firmly grounded. Deyhle found that almost 70% of Navajo youth remained on or near their homes on the reservation, where they were provided social and economic networks that were unavailable in the Anglo community beyond the reservation. Specifically, the choice to remain on the reservation and the insistence on maintaining culturally different values were central to the power struggle in the larger community because these choices were defined as impoverished by Anglos. These choices, however, worked well for most of the young Navajo men and women.

Only one long-term ethnographic study, *Official Encouragement, Institutional Discouragement: Minorities in Academe—the Native American Experience,* by Tierney (1992), has examined young American Indian's experiences beyond high school into institutions of higher education. Like the other studies we have covered in this section, Tierney provided a critical analysis of how both cultural issues and structural factors intertwined to thwart these young people's achievement in higher education. As was the case with Indian youth in the other studies, these college students were told that they had problems "adjusting" because of their culture. The issue of cultural differences (e.g., a lack of competitive ethic) was viewed as a barrier to overcome. As one school official explained, "The major problem is that they have a foot in each culture that draws them back to their roots. They are drawn back to their culture and it's a difficult transition to make" (Tierney, 1992, p.109). As Tierney pointed out, the assumptions embedded in this statement point to the students culture as problematic; school success will come only when these roots are "cut," or, in other words, the assimilation process is complete.

The portrait Tierney presented of Indian students, however, was more complex. Students spoke of isolation, academic deficiencies and fears, and the difficulties of incorporating their cultural life into the social life of the institutions. On the surface, institutions of higher education encouraged the participation of Indian students. However, institutional practices and circumstance such as large impersonal classes, instructors unknowledgable about American Indians, inflexible admittance procedures, and financial aid requirements, created a "draining out of hope" for Indian students, especially when they faced an institution that either ignored them or sought to remake them into a different people (Tierney, 1992, p. 137). From a critical perspective, linking relations of power to concepts such as knowledge and authority, Tierney argued that knowledge presented to Indian students was limited to factual information or skill development rather than being "dispositional knowledge," which would include the values and ethics that guide community life, shape social justice, and acknowledge racial heritages. It is this kind of knowledge that is necessary to reconceptualize authority and pedagogy to incorporate a politics of difference and emancipation that does not assume assimilation as its goal.

Empowerment is not the learning of specific rules of the "culture of power" because it is a process rooted in social relations and contexts. Rituals of empowerment use the experience of people who have been marginalized to produce an aggressive critique of the prevailing social system. (p. 149)

In an ironic sense, this is just the kind of knowledge pursuit the institutions did not want to provide students, because students then would begin to challenge assimilatory models and unequal power relations between Indians and Anglos.

Tierney's recommendations regarding directions of change focused on the institutions, not the Indian students and their communities, and he provided the example of tribal community colleges as a movement in the correct direction, a path leading to self-determination and empowerment as the means to academic success. This is the same kind of control over schools that other researchers have argued, based on data from tribally controlled bilingual-bicultural schools, resulted in increased student achievement in elementary and secondary schools (R. Barnhardt, 1991; Collier, 1973; Holm & Holm, 1995; McLaughlin, 1995;) And this is the same kind of school control that other Indian communities are struggling to gain (Deyhle, 1995; Freeman, Stairs, Corbier & Lazore, 1995).

School Failure: Cultural Discontinuity or Sociostructural Conflict?

The discussion of "why" American Indian youth drop out or do poorly in schools centers around two general frameworks used to explain school failure of minority youth in general: "cultural discontinuity theory" and "sociostructural theory." The cultural discontinuity hypothesis assumes that culturally based differences in the communication styles, behaviors, and values of the minority students' home and the Anglo culture of the school lead to conflicts, misunderstandings, and ultimately, failure for those students. The research focuses on microlevel processes and interactions in the classroom, rather than macrolevel racial stratification of the U.S. society and the economy, and often concludes that making the classroom more culturally appropriate will result in a higher rate of achievement. Although few studies directly address this issue as a research question, many do contain both explicit and implicit assumptions about the importance of cultural relevance in the curriculum. The issue of cultural discontinuity, or the importance of cultural relevance or sensitivity, was asserted as a cause of school failure in the dropout studies by Giles (1985), Coladarci (1983), Eberhard (1989), and Platero et al. (1986). This explanatory model was also evident in the research studies we reviewed in the Understanding Cultural And Ethical Differences Shaping Educational Interaction section.

Sociostructural theorists, such as Ogbu, argue that the explanations for minority school failure lie outside of the school itself, specifically in the racial stratification of U.S. society and the economy (1978, 1993). This "structured inequality" creates a job ceiling for minority youth, and the ideal that hard work and achievement in school lead to economic success is contradicted by the poverty surrounding minority youth. Ogbu argues that this leaves minority youth disillusioned and that they therefore exhibit a lack of effort, optimism, and perseverance. Specifically, "castelike minorities" (which include American Indians) develop resistance to schooling to help them cope with the social, economic, political, and psychological history of rejection by the dominant group and its institutions. Ogbu argues that to say that minority students experience failure merely as a result of cultural differences between their homes and the school is to deny the historical and structural context in which those differences are embedded.

Using these two theoretical frameworks, cultural difference and sociostructural conflict, Ledlow (1992) argued that there is simply not enough evidence to conclude that cultural discontinuity plays a significant role in American Indian students dropping out, but there is overwhelming evidence that economic and social issues that are not culturally specific to being Indian (and other minorities) are very significant in causing students to drop out of school. Bowker (1993), mirroring Ledlow (1992), also is wary of the cultural discontinuity theory as an explanatory model for American Indian women school leavers. She argues that, in her study, cultural differences did not play the primary role in young women's decisions to leave school.

For most educators, the solution to cultural discontinuity has been the development of a culturally relevant curriculum, which is generally undefinable and at best couched in vague descriptive terms. Without question, this focus on a culturally relevant curriculum draws attention away from some of the more pressing political and economic issues faced by Indian students. (Bowker, 1993, p. 174)

Distrust of school personnel resulting from years of negative experiences and or giving up on school because it had no relevancy to their futures were much more likely to cause young women to drop out out of school than the fact that the school's language and culture differed from the home's. According to Bowker, "The bottom line appears to be this: the content of the curriculum is not nearly so important as the interaction between teacher and student and the bond the student develops with the school" (p. 173). Given additional comments that job discrimination provided little way out of poverty, even with school credentials, and that schools were corrupt and unjust and promoted an Anglo culture that was in opposition to students' values and those of their parents, there was little reason for these women to "bond" with their schools.

One of Ledlow's (1992) concerns is that, based on limited empirical research, educators have used the cultural discontinuity theory to argue for a "culturally compatible curriculum" to solve the dropout problem. Cultural relevance is rarely defined and almost always assumed to be significant. This exclusive focus on culture and curricular innovation draws attention from the very real possibility that economics and social structure may be more important. While we agree with Ledlow's analysis, we argue that the results of the research she reports, as well as subsequent research, do not so neatly fall into "either/or" categories; rather, cultural differences intertwine with sociostructural conflict to create an educational context that ensures failure for many Indian students. Of particular importance is how cultural differences are treated within the schools Indian students attend. While we will not argue that a "culturally relevant" curriculum will "solve" the dropout problem, we take the position that within the large social and economic climate that discriminates against Indian students, the inclusion of culturally specific information, Native languages, and culturally matched pedagogy can have an impact on what teachers *do* to Indian students and *how* students react to their schooling. Peter McLaren's (1989) words ring true for the situation faced by American Indian students: "School failure is structurally located and culturally mediated" (Ledlow, 1992, p. 34). Or, as F. Erickson (1984) argued, "it may be that culturally congruent instruction depoliticizes cultural differences in the classroom, and that such depoliticization has important positive influences on the teacher-student relationship. Such a situation in the classroom might prevent the emergence of student resistance" (p. 543).

In the previous sections, we reviewed research that focused on cultural differences factors or structural factors as models to explain the academic failure of American Indian students. Both models are based on empirical research. Structural factors, such as discrimination in the labor market, and culturally based conflictual student-teacher interactions can both be seen as barriers that influence academic performance. These bodies of research give legitimacy to looking both outside the school, into the local community and the broader society, and inside the school, within classroom interactions, to identify the roots of educational failure or success. In doing so, we believe that the issue of "trust," specifically the power relationships between students and teachers and American Indian communities and the Anglo community, is pivotal in understanding why some students "learn" and others do not.

As F. Erickson (1993) argued, learning involves a trust relationship between learner and teacher. A teacher asks a student to move into an "unknown" or new area, which involves risk. If the student does not trust the teacher or has reason to fear humiliation, rejection, or being revealed as incompetent, the risk to "learn" is too great. M. Wax et al. (1989) described this situation among the Oglala Sioux students they observed: "Indian children perceive very early what most Whites think of their parents and themselves. Once past the primary grades, they approach each teacher with caution, testing her response to them; if it is negative, they quickly retreat" (p. 102). Deyhle (1992) also reported that trusting teachers was a key factor in Navajo students' responses to their schools. Students described a "good teacher" as one who cares; the subject a teacher taught was rarely connected to what made a teacher good or not. A "bad teacher" was one who displayed antagonism toward Indians. As one student said, "Some of them are all right, but they have prejudice against Indians. Like they look at us when we ask questions like, 'Oh, I'm tired of trying to help you.' They care about the students [Anglos] who don't need help" (Deyhle, 1992, p. 31). These students were then labeled as "failures" when they did not learn what school authorities, teachers, and administrators intended for them to learn. An examination of the ethnohistorical relationships between Indians and Anglos, however, showed clear reasons for Indian students to "not trust" the goals of schools or some of their individual teachers. Viewed from this perspective, Indian students' lack of school performance can also be seen as a form of resistance. As Erickson pointed out, "Learning what is deliberately taught can be seen as a form of political assent. Not learning can be seen as a form of political resistance" (1993, p. 36). From this view, school failure can be seen as a form of resistance to assimilation or to a racially inferior identity presented by the schools.

Complex Worlds and Multiple Choices: American Indian Youth

The metaphor "walking in two worlds" frequently appears in the research to describe in a bipolar, dichotomous manner the world of the Anglo society on one side and the world of Indian societies on the other, which Indian students must "straddle," "walk between," or "cross." This implies that there are clear-cut choices—one stays "Indian" (traditional), becomes "Anglo" (assimilates), or chooses the "best of both worlds" (bicultural/bilingual). In an insightful article, Henze and Vanett (1993) argued that this metaphor, although appealing and used by both Indians and non-Indians to describe the "plight" of Indian youth, itself positions youth incorrectly in a deficit manner.

The reality of many diverse worlds coalesces to become two idealized worlds, and the implicit assumption that it is possible to "walk" in both sets students up for failure. Ironically, the metaphor becomes a barrier rather than a model of how to live in the world today. (p. 123)

Specifically, it masks the complexity of lived situations and multiple loyalties and may work to limit the options of Indian youth.

This flat and static view of "two worlds" also ignores complex cultural shifts in American Indian societies, creating a stereotypic "traditional culture." Indian youths' lives reflect a variety of cultural contexts, and often the "traditional life" of their grandparents is of the past. The assumption that Indian youth can merge these worlds and become bicultural/bilingual individuals also ignores that the world of the "Anglos" is only marginally available to these young people as a choice because of poverty, racism, discrimination, and lowered teacher expectations of their potential for success. Also overlooked are the tremendous internal conflicts that occur when youth try to live according to two value systems that in some ways contradict each other. And, finally, this metaphor shuts down the possibility of yet a "third world" reflected in Indian youths' contemporary lives and, therefore, works to deny them a firm sense of cultural identity. This was illustrated by Sarris (1993), a Pomo researcher, in an article about a teacher on his reservation. This teacher used a "traditional" story about Slug Woman to try to engage her Pomo students, who responded with either open hostility or stone silence. Sarris argued that not only were relationships, the central meaning of the story, left out of the translation, but students saw the event as one more attempt to set them up for failure by superficially "admitting" a limited, static view of their culture into the classroom. In their classroom, the Slug Woman story represented neither the world they knew, nor the world in which they lived. According to Henze and Vanett (1993) the language of the two worlds metaphor, "is part of the systematic political and social inequity that keeps them in a powerless position" (p. 131). They simply cannot "fit" in either idealized world. Henze and Vanett (1993) offered the following critical assessment from a Yup'ik woman that more correctly positions Indian youth: "My people must learn from both worlds as they collide" (p. 118).

Offering an Indian perspective in a speech titled "Between Two Worlds," noted Hopi engineer and artist Al Qîyawayma presented his view of the balance that must exist. He described today's generation, half of whom live in urban areas but travel back and forth to the reservation, as "horizon children" who are caught at the horizon, neither sky nor earth, and suspended between two worlds. He believes "that is why we struggle with alcoholism, suicide, high school dropouts, unemployment and low wages. We now strive to find out who we are" (Qöyawayma, 1991). In an eloquent manner he said,

Indian people today have a foot in two worlds, but we live one life. Our footing is often uncertain because each world is in continuous state of change. The Indian people need to evaluate the best that is in our own culture and hang onto it; for it will always be foremost in our life. But we also need to take the best from other cultures to blend with what we already have. (Qöyawayma, 1991)

His thoughts echo those of Sitting Bull, who advised that his people must select the good aspects and reject the bad of both worlds.

Framed by "colliding worlds," Indian youth make choices. Most succeed in schools (as measured by graduation rates) and continue their lives as young adults in their various tribes and communities. While we agree that the intertwining of cultural and structural factors, as captured by the two worlds metaphor, often works to thwart Indian students' efforts at success in school, our analysis cannot ignore the 50% to 75% of Indian students who successfully complete traditional high school programs. Indian students are not monolithic in their response to schooling, and these differences are central to our understanding of why some youth succeed and others give up trying. From the studies presented in this chapter, three different "profiles" of Indian youth are revealed: the adapter, the passive resister, and the resister. We propose this framework to understand the condition of school persistence and school leaving among American Indian and Alaska Native students. This framework suggests that students make choices regarding their participation in high school. Some choose to adapt to the system and succeed by Anglo-enforced criteria, others drift through school, and still others choose to view the goal of graduation as unimportant in their lives. We insert a cautionary note here about "choice." As much of the research has illustrated, Indian students do not face a level playing field. Discrimination, racism, vocationalized curricula, and boring classes are experiences that frame their school years. Given this context, Indian students "choose" from the limited set of options constructed for them by society and schooling.

Many Indian students choose to "adapt" to the educational system and "succeed." These adapters have exercised their inherent right to self-determination in choosing to persist and graduate. They recognize that the structure of schooling is not fair, and they see little of themselves or their culture, history, and language included in the system of curriculum and instruction. They accept this segment of their lives as a short interruption on their way to meeting life goals as adults participating in existing Indian societies or the dominant society. Caring teachers are critical to their success (Deyhle, 1992; Kleinfeld, 1975; McCarty, 1989; Swisher et al., 1991; Wilson, 1991). Much of the research suggests that these student are the ones who have strong traditional identities that serve as a firm foundation on the road through school (Bowker, 1993; Chan & Osthimer, 1983; Deyhle, 1992, 1995; Deyhle & Margonis, 1995; Kleinfeld, 1979; McLaughlin, 1995; Platero, et al., 1986). These studies provide evidence against an assimilationist model that assumes that success is possible only after Indian languages and cultures are eliminated. Adapters can also be viewed as resisters in that they choose to retain their culture and language.

Indian students are also passive resisters. They reject the notion of dropping out and attend school, although not as seriously as those who have decided to persist. Their attendance is poorer than average, and they passively sit in classrooms and participate in school activities. They enjoy peer interaction, and this becomes their reason for staying in school. Unfortunately, time runs out for these students, their lack of attention to grades and credits for graduation catches up with them, and they must drop out or make other choices such as a fifth-year or alternative program of high school completion (Deyhle, 1992; Platero et al., 1986; R.H. Wax, 1976; M. Wax et al., 1989). Many of these students voice the opinion that they have been "pushed out" or "kicked out" of school, placing the blame for their condition on institutional norms that would not "adapt" to their needs or circumstances.

Students who have made the decision to drop out of school are resisters. These students are the subject of myriad studies, and their voices reflect the resistance they are exhibiting (Wolcott, 1984, 1987) They speak of rejecting a system that has systematically rejected them. Wilson (1991) argued that the Canadian Sioux students in her study who dropped out of school made a sound decision because of the psychological "trauma" they experienced in schools. In Deyhle's study (1986a) the resisters were often the ones who had minimal traditional cultural experiences outside of school. She describes one group of these youth, Navajo breakdancers, who clearly understood the larger race war surrounding them in and outside of school. As one said, "It used to be cowboys and Indians. Now its cowboys and breakers" (p. 124).

As the research has illustrated, even the most successful students have had to experience some kind of adaptation, often enduring humiliating experiences in silence. In the following section, we shift to examine research on school programs for American Indian youth that have been successful. Most successful programs are ones that do not require "adaptation" in quite the same way as mainstream public schools. In these schools, Native languages and culture exist side by side with English and the dominant culture.

COMMUNITY-BASED EDUCATIONAL RESEARCH

Our review of the literature on language programs revealed very few data-driven studies that show the efficacy of teaching in and through American Indian languages. Over the past 30 years, 58 studies of language and bilingual education have been published in the *Journal of American Indian Education*. With titles such as "Helping Navajo Children change pronunciation habits," "Teachers Tackle Speech Problems," and "When Is a Disadvantage a Handicap?" almost 80% of the studies in the 1960s positioned Native languages as deficits and barriers to overcome. With a metaphor expressing this assimilatory thought, one study suggested the introduction of the television in order to "flood" the Indian child with American English. Over the past two decades, however, almost 60% of the researchers have been informed, in part, by cultural difference theory and self-determination. Their research has moved the explanatory model away from a deficit view of the individual to a view of Native languages as an asset in the schooling process.

Most language studies were descriptions of existing programs, with little or no systematic investigation into the specific effects of such programs. In part, this was because most of these "studies" consisted of short term visits to the programs by outside (to the community) researchers or program evaluators. Several ethnographic or long-term studies, however, provided data-driven research that was developed over time and deeply embedded in the context of Indian communities. As a result, the political and economic self-determination of the community framed the language and schooling experiences and became part of the analysis of educational "success." It is important to note that the articles we highlight here represent research that has often followed the development of Native community education throughout the 1980s and, in some cases, since the 1970s. This long-term picture reflects both a commitment on the part of the researchers (many of whom were Native researchers) and a means to a more accurate understanding of the complexities of local controlled schooling that rejects assimilation as an educational goal. Most of the programs described in these studies are located in either the southwestern United States, where some 26 indigenous languages and more than 40 tribal groups coexist (Martin & McCarty, 1990), or Alaska, where more than 15% of the residents are American Indians or Alaska Natives living in 200 village groups (Pavel, Swisher, & Ward, 1995). Tribal governments and schools are actively involved in developing bilingual-bicultural education programs in these communities, where issues of cultural and linguistic identity remain strong.

Since the passage of the Indian Education Act in 1972 and the Indian Education and Self-Determination Act in 1975, Indian people have put back their languages and culture into the schools they control. As Indian people have gained a voice in the schools that educate their children, the issue of Native language literacy, or bilingual education, has become of paramount importance as a key to increasing academic achievement and maintaining language and cultural traditions. Some Indian parents and communities have hesitated to embrace bilingual education after having been told for decades that ancestral language and culture are the primary obstacles to educational advancement (Ahler, 1994; Leap, 1991; Watahomigie & McCarty, 1994). The research that we present in this section, however, illustrates the positive social-educational outcomes associated with programs among the Navajo, Yup'ik, Hualapai, Northern Ute, and Eskimo that systematically use local linguistic and cultural knowledge (Begay, Dick, Estell, Estell, & McCarty, 1995; Holm & Holm, 1995; Lipka, 1994; Lipka & McCarty, 1994; Lipka & Stairs, 1994; McCarty, 1989; McCarty, Lipka & Dick, 1994; McLaughlin, 1989, 1995,; Ovando, 1994). Questions framing much of this research have to do with the intertwining of language and power (e.g., "Whose knowledge is legitimate?" and "What should be the language or languages of instruction?") (Lipka, 1994). Most of these studies appeared in three special journal theme issues on American Indian languages and schooling: the *Bilingual Research Journal*, "Indigenous language education and literacy," 1995, *19* ; the *Journal of American Indian Education*, "Local knowledge in indigenous schooling: Case studies in American Indian/Alaska Native education," 1994, *33;* and the *Peabody Journal of Education*, "Negotiating the culture of Indigenous schools," 1994, *69.* Although some studies claimed that Native language instruction enhanced academic success as measured on tests, others claimed that positive results were evident in the very existence (or revitalization) of Native languages in Indian communities and schools. As a symbol of sovereignty and a visible sign of the lack of successful assimilation, results of this body of research argued that bilingual education and use of local knowledge and language are important for empowerment, and empowerment is important for educational success. Writing about the empowerment of Indian students, Cummins (1992) stated,

In programs where minority students' home-language skills are strongly reinforced, school success appears to reflect both the more solid cognitive or academic foundation developed through intensive first-language instruction and also the reinforcement of their cultural identity. . . . Educators who see their role as encouraging their students to add a second language and culture to supplement rather than supplant their native language and culture are more likely to create conditions in which students can develop a sense of empowerment. (p. 6)

Local Knowledge, Local Control: Effective Practices

Historically, by federal policy, Native languages were outlawed in schools and students were punished severely for speaking their home languages (McCarty, 1994; Szasz, 1974). With the exception of the educational reform movements in the 1930s, when Congress passed the Bilingual Education Act (BEA) in 1967, bilingual education was virtually unknown in schools serving American Indian students. McCarty (1994) argued that this legislative act allowed for community-controlled bilingual programs and that these macrolevel changes "represent a fundamental rejection of past educational policies that have failed Indian students and a reclamation of indigenous languages, cultural resources, and education rights" (p. 31). Although the federal government has taken steps in the 1990s to move away from the support of bilingual education programs, the 1992 Native American Languages Act strengthened the call for the preservation and protection of indigenous languages and cultural resources. The act recognized "the right of Indian tribes and other Native American governing bodies to use the Native American languages as a medium of instruction in all schools funded by the Secretary of the Interior" (Reyhner, 1992, p. 62). At the local community level, these federal policies have given rise to language programs that have successfully increased student participation (Holm & Holm, 1995; McCarty, 1991) and achievement (Ahler, 1994; McLaughlin, 1995; Watahomigie, 1988), parent participation (Deyhle, 1991), Native language development (Holm & Holm, 1995; McLaughlin, 1995), and graduation rates (McCarty, 1994; McLaughlin, 1995; Watahomigie, 1992). Unlike the researchers reported by B. Berry (1968), who argued that the use of Native languages was detrimental to student success, the researchers working with Native language programs over the past 20 years are arguing that the use of Native languages has positive social, political, economic, and educational outcomes.

One of the first and best-known American Indian bilingual programs to both develop a written form of the native language and develop certified Native-speaking personnel was the Hualapai project at Peach Springs in northwestern Arizona (Watahomigie & McCarty, 1994). Started in 1975, the Yuman language program used thematic curriculum content organized around the local language and social environment, affirmed students' identities as Hualapai, and capitalized on their prior knowledge, specifically their bilingualism, as a means of enhancing their school experience. At Peach Springs, Hualapai students increased their mean scores on the Language Assessment Scale (a test of oral English) by more than 12 percentile points between 1986 and 1989 (McCarty, 1991; Watahomigie, 1988). Countering the "crossover" effect phenomena described by other researchers (B. Berry, 1968; Bryde, 1965; Dinges, Trimble, & Hollenbeck, 1979), program evaluation data showed that the longer students remained in the program, the greater their achievement gains (Watahomigie & Yamamoto, 1987). Since bilingual education began at Peach Springs in 1976, student attendance has significantly improved, and Hualapai students now graduate from eighth grade (when the program ends) and from high school in far greater numbers than their peers in conventional school programs. In 1989, 100% of Hualapai students who had completed the eighth grade went on to graduate from high school (McCarty, 1991; Watahomigie, 1992). These instructional changes, in which the Hualapai language and culture were authentic and integral parts of the school, along with an increase of Native teachers that enhanced the integration of the school with the community, resulted in Indian students'

increased success in school. According to McCarty (1994), "These transformations—grounding education in local personnel and knowledge—are arguably the
most significant and lasting outcomes of BEA policies and programs to date. . . .
It thus serves as a direct challenge to the various language restrictionist proposals currently before Congress" (p. 31). The equalization of power relations was
critical for the program's success.

From negotiations about the way Hualapai would be represented in its written form, to the elaboration of
instructional content and the method of its delivery, local people played the decisive roles. As a result,
Peach Springs now has a school of *the community's* choice" (Watahomigie & McCarty, 1994, p. 40).

McLaughlin's (1989, 1991, 1992) ethnographic study of one of the first bilingual schools on the Navajo reservation also speaks of a community that decided
Native language and culture would aid its children's school success. More than 30
years ago, school administrators, teachers, and community members designed K–12
instruction in Navajo to reinforce the cultural and linguistic resources of the students who, at that point, had the lowest test scores in the Navajo nation. Although
there are no standardized texts for measuring Native language proficiency, these
Navajo students now consistently score higher than other comparable reservation
children on tests of reading, language, and math in English. McLaughlin found the
use of Navajo print in schools and homes, individuals using letters, journals, lists,
and notes to express themselves in Navajo, and argued that "Navajo print is useful
for maintaining traditional culture and for promoting self-understanding" (1989, p.
275). Although there was initial reluctance to use Navajo in school, in part because
most official and school documents are produced in English, most local parents
and students viewed Navajo literacy as a vehicle for self-understanding and
empowerment. A recent graduate who was attending an Ivy League university in
the East wrote back to her fellow students to express her feelings about the use of
Navajo in the high school. Her voice spoke to the issue of empowerment.

If you think learning Navajo is going to make you less Navajo, you are mistaken. No matter how much
we know English, we are still going to be intimidated because of our ethnic background. No matter
how much you try, your color is never going to change. . . . We need to learn how to deal with this
assimilation process yet maintain our identity as Navajos. We have to learn that just going out into the
Whiteman's world doesn't mean that we have to lose our identity. Be appreciative that Mesa Valley is
trying to provide a medium so transitions from red to white and white to red will be easier. . . . We
need to educate ourselves so we can decide what is good for us. We cannot let others decide for us any-
more. They know what they want—not what we need. (McLaughlin, 1989, p. 286)

McLaughlin's research suggested that educators of Navajo children need to
reinforce, not neglect, the cultural identities of children to stop the widespread
pattern of school failure. Active collaboration of parents and Navajo language
should be integrated into all aspects of classroom life. In turn, these actions of
self-determination, specifically with bilingual education, "locate the source of
students' difficulties in structural conditions in society rather than in innate processing deficits of the children" (McLaughlin, 1989, p. 287).

Like McLaughlin, McCarty's (1994) ethnographic study of Rough Rock Demonstration School, the first Navajo controlled school on the reservation, argued for the critical importance of local knowledge and control to counter a "language and culture as the problem" perspective. She also illustrated that a constellation of political and economic factors made student achievement scores or graduation rates a limited means of assessing the school's success. The community was extremely poor and dependent on federal funding. Curriculum and pedagogical approaches varied with high teacher turnover and unstable federal funds, factors that pointed to problems in the institution, not the students. Over the course of the program, trained Native teachers have dramatically stabilized the staff, and locally developed instructional and curricular efforts maintain the use of Navajo language and culture in the school. Beyond student school success, McCarty argued that the control of the school has not only brought economic benefits, but it has also created a school of and by the community.

Other studies of long-term bilingual programs on the Navajo reservation support McLaughlin's (1992) and McCarty's (1989) position of long term positive effects from such programs. Begay et al. (1995) examined the transformations in curriculum and pedagogy at the Rough Rock Community School. On locally developed criterion-referenced measures, students' end-of-the-year scores consistently showed substantial improvements in oral English and reading; in 1992–1993, 88% of all K–3 students mastered objectives for English listening comprehension and 71 percent mastered objectives for English reading. Overall, the K–3 group improved its mean listening score by 15 percentage points. Begay et al. argued that, in addition to enhanced student achievement, the bilingual program altered larger power structures by developing and employing local community educators teaching according to community norms and using local cultural and linguistic knowledge.

Holm and Holm (1995) also reported positive student gains, when measured against other students on the reservation, in the bilingual program at Rock Point Community School. Of particular significance was the finding that instances of the crossover phenomenon decreased the longer students stayed in school.

It would be incorrect to claim that the students met or exceeded national averages on standardized achievement grades. Some grade levels did so on some tests. But the students did do better than comparable students in nearby schools at all grade levels, and the margin of differences tended to be larger at each succeeding grade. Just as important—though harder to gauge—was that students had considerable more self-confidence and pride. (Holm & Holm, 1995, pp. 147–148).

In 1976, shortly after the bilingual program started, Rosier and Farella (1976) had argued that Navajo language had a "prestige problem" and that emphasizing it on an equal basis with English in school would increase student self-esteem. Twenty years later, their predictions that bilingual education, local control, and Native teachers would increase self-confidence and achievement seem to have been correct.

Another bilingual program Holm and Holm (1995) evaluated was the Navajo Immersion Program (NIP) at Fort Defiance Elementary School. Unlike the goal of the program at Rock Point, which was higher academic achievement, this program sought Navajo literacy "without cost" (i.e.,, the students in the program would be doing as well in English as those not in the program). Holm and Holm reported:

The NI [Navajo Immersion] students did considerably better on local assessments of writing-in-English. They did better on math in the computer lab. On standardized tests, they still were slightly behind (but catching up) in English reading; slightly ahead on some and slightly behind in other so-called language subtests; and way ahead in math. (1995, p. 150)

Leap (1991, 1993) described a bilingual program on the Northern Ute reservation that has achieved some success, although not measured by test scores, in Ute language development. In 1984, the Northern Ute Tribal Business Committee passed a resolution to affirm the importance of retaining the Northern Ute language and teaching it in schools. It declared:

The Ute language is a living and vital language that has the ability to match any other in the world for expressiveness and beauty. Our language is capable of lexical expansion into modern conceptual fields such as the field of politics, economics, mathematics and science. . . . We assert that our students are fully capable of developing fluency in our mother tongue and the foreign English language and we further assert that a higher level of Ute mastery results in higher levels of English skills. (p. 17)

The program, Wykoopah ("two paths"), used supplemental instruction in Ute language and culture as a means of strengthening English language skills and academic achievement levels of Ute students. Over the course of 10 years, this Ute language program resulted in a practical writing system for the Northern Ute language, a cadre of Ute people familiar with the writing system, language teaching/learning materials, and classes teaching Ute reading skills to schoolchildren, parents, and other members of the tribe (Leap, 1991). Like McLaughlin (1989), Leap argued that the use of native language, in both print and oral forms, enhanced students' academic opportunities as it built a foundation for literacy development. Regardless of what language the students used, they became the "actors" necessary for becoming fluent readers and writers of standard English.

Lipka's (1994) research also argued against the assumption that "ridding" Native children of their home language would increase student achievement by showing that although Alaska Native students are losing their home language to learn English, they are not learning English up to academic norms. Lipka described a program in the Yup'ik village of Manokotak designed to reverse first language loss and strengthen English language competence through local control, Native speakers as teachers, Native language instruction, and community initiatives. For more than a decade, Lipka collaborated with Yup'ik teachers and elders as they worked with administrators and teachers who believed that English is and ought to be the language of instruction. After a 20-year struggle, in 1991 a Yup'ik language of instruction program was established. Students are now exceeding the mean on the Yup'ik version of the Stanford Early School Achievement Test (Lipka, 1994) and are beginning to learn and read with ease (Sharp, 1994). The operation of the program is now in the hands of the community, which rejected assimilation and intuitively knew its children needed both Yup'ik and English to thrive in the educational setting. As a Yup'ik school board member stated, "Our language is part of our identity: [It is] a part of ourselves. We can work out ways to keep the language and be successful in the Western world" (Lipka, 1994, p. 82).

As documented in *Indian Nations at Risk: An Educational Strategy for Action*, regional hearings of the Indian Nations At Risk Task Force, parents, educators, and tribal leaders described a number of successful practices throughout the United States. The Denver Indian Center developed Circle of Learning a prekindergarten culturally-based curriculum model that involved home visits focused on learning activities, nutrition, safety, child growth, family literacy, support groups, and positive parenting skills. The Circle of Learning program has evidence that its approach works. Children performed in kindergarten at levels comparable to their classmates; by the first grade, 90% had risen to the top of their class; and it was not uncommon for students to skip first or second grade. Success was attributed to the program's focus on cultural instruction that fosters positive self-esteem. Another successful program highlighted in the report was I WA'SIL, an adult education and dropout reentry program sponsored by the The United Indians of All Tribes Foundation in Seattle to address adult educational needs in the greater Seattle metropolitan area. The philosophy of the program is based on a whole person approach to helping youth make positive transitions in their lives. I WA'SIL means "to change." The program served homeless youth (12 to 20 years of age) with tutoring for reentry to public schools or GED testing, personal counseling, alcohol and drug prevention counseling and treatment, juvenile justice advocacy, medical and dental service, and recreational and cultural activities. With a 90% successful placement rate, the placement activities included returning students to their local school, preparing them to pass the GED, placing them in higher education or vocational training, and helping them find employment.

We end this section with a review of Kleinfeld's (1979) ethnographic study, *Eskimo School on the Andreafsky: A Study of Effective Bicultural Education*. The Eskimo students who graduated from St. Mary's, a small Catholic boarding school, succeeded in college much more frequently than comparable Eskimo students, even though the school did not provide bilingual instruction. As Cummins (1992) pointed out, effective schools for Indian students can exist without instruction in the Native language when these schools respect and support the students and do not try to "erase" the students' home culture or language. This is the kind of school Kleinfeld described. The model of bicultural education developed at St. Mary's was "cultural fusion" across three critical dimensions of schooling: curriculum content, social relationships, and value structure. The curriculum emphasized the majority culture but included cultural elements from contemporary (rather than historic) village life. Social patterns from both modern society and local village culture were fused throughout the school. Thus, while students were taught behavioral patterns needed to succeed in the dominant society, such as asking and answering questions before a group, occupying leadership roles, and talking easily to strangers, the Eskimo social relations connected to group opinion and control were equally represented in the school. For example, students and teachers developed indirect forms of communication to avoid face-to-face situations in which one person told another what to do, a form of communicative control unacceptable in Eskimo culture. In the area of values, the school emphasized the fundamental cultural ethic on which students' primary identity framework was based. Achievement was viewed not as an individual accomplishment but as preparing oneself to accomplish group goals, and leadership was defined not as putting oneself above others, but as working hard for the benefit of the group.

Kleinfeld argued that while Eskimo families did not have political control over the school, on a more fundamental level the school was pursuing parental values and goals. Because a model of cultural infusion that accepted Native culture and language on an equal footing with the majority culture was used, acquiring the skills necessary for success in the majority culture did not come at the expense of cultural identity. The youth were successful both in school and in their home community. According to Kleinfeld,

St. Mary's students clearly identified themselves as Eskimo and were comfortable with this identity. Most students returned to the villages and adapted with little difficulty, often holding the unassuming leadership roles congruent with cultural patterns. In contrast to many Indian and Eskimo children who schooling leaves stranded between two cultures, what was impressive about St. Mary's students was their integrated identity and psychic well-being. (1979, p. 129)

Ten years later, after boarding schools such as St. Mary's were closed and replaced by small, local high schools, Kleinfeld, McDiarmid, and Hagstrom (1989) reported a dramatic decrease of the dropout rate for Alaska Natives, to about half the national average. They argued that the increase in graduation rates was due to the characteristics of the schools: small size, a community atmosphere, and individualized academic work tailored to students' backgrounds, all characteristics shared with St. Mary's.

What the schools and programs in this section were able to achieve, from our analysis, was the successful integration of both the cultural difference position (with the inclusion of culturally specific behavior patterns and a culturally relevant curriculum) and the sociostructural position (with the equalizing of power relations between Natives and Anglos). Rather than "cultural" as an add on to the curriculum, it became part of the structure of the schools themselves. In turn, this form of empowerment, in which the school was closely in rhythm with the community, increased the school success of children. What this body of research is telling us is that effective schooling for American Indian and Alaska Native students embraces Native culture and language as a resource to work from, rather than a barrier to overcome, and that local communities are effective agents in shaping this process. Or, as Stairs (1994) said, "The optimistic proposal of cultural negotiation is the potential for evolving cultural identities as a rich range of alternatives to assimilation and culture loss, or even to indigenization and cultural isolation or anomie between the two" (p. 155).

SELF-DETERMINATION AND RESEARCH: RESEARCH ABOUT INDIANS BY INDIANS

Early researchers of American Indian education were primarily Anglo-Americans with a Eurocentric perspective that guided them in not only what to look for but also how to look at the Indian child and community; both were guided by a vision of assimilation. Now there are new challenges to the traditional Eurocentric ways of knowing, seeing, and understanding. These perspectives are presented here through the voices of Indian scholars, researchers, and tribal members.

We started this chapter with voices that spoke of assimilation as the goal of Indian education. We end this chapter with the voices of Indian people who propose a different goal, one that envisions equal coexistence and the maintenance of languages and cultures as effective means of achieving success in schools and communities. These Indian voices also call for an increase of both Indian researchers and perspectives.

In 1994 Swisher wrote, "Over the past two decades, the voices of Indian people have echoed consistent rhetoric, some of it going back as far as fifty years ago: Indian people want the opportunity to determine all aspects of their children's education" (p. 861), including, we would add, research. A forthcoming issue of the *American Indian Quarterly* is devoted to the topic "Who should be writing about Indians?" a concern about which there is serious discussion among Indian scholars. In discussing the question as it relates to education, Swisher cited the recent National Dialogue Project on American Indian Education as an example of authentic research conducted on Indians by Indians. The project was sponsored jointly by the American Indian Science and Engineering Society (AISES) and the College Board's Educational Equality Project (EQ). The research project determined what educational changes American Indians across the country want for American Indian youth. As Swisher (1996) stated, "Indian people were not only the informants, but the principal investigators as well." The project involved seven regional dialogues facilitated by Indian regional dialogue directors, Indian parents, students, tribal leaders, and educators who discussed issues of educational change. Central to the discussions was the belief that American Indians "have many educational needs that differ from those of mainstream society . . . and the assimilation objectives of American education are detrimental to the social, economic, and political well-being of their communities" (College Board and AISES, 1989, p. 1). The report of the national dialogues, *Our Voices, Our Vision: American Indians Speak Out for Educational Excellence* (College Board and AISES, 1989), was developed by AISES and written by the Indian staff and graduate students of the American Indian Studies Center at UCLA. A strong statement expressed attitudes toward past and current research and writing.

Just as the exploitation of American Indian land and resources is of value to corporate America, research and publishing is valuable to non-Indian scholars. As a result of racism, greed, and distorted perceptions of native realities, Indian culture as an economic commodity has been exploited by the dominant society with considerable damage to Indian people. Tribal people need to safeguard the borders of their cultural domains against research and publishing incursions (College Board and AISES, 1989, p. 6).

The writers of the report made it clear that research on Indian history and culture must consider Indian perspectives and that American Indian scholars need to "become involved in producing research rather than serving as subjects and consumers of research" (College Board and AISES, 1989, p. 7). Swisher (in press) notes that the distinguishing feature of the EQ/AISES report is the self-determination perspective. From conception and initiation of the dialogue format to formulation of data and publication, Indian people were in charge and guided the project; voices and concerns of the people were clearly evident.

On the heels of the National Dialogue Project on American Indian Education, two other significant events occurred in the early 1990s. The Indian Nations At Risk Task Force and the White House Conference on Indian Education were convened to describe the condition of American Indian and Alaska Native education nationwide and to seek solutions to the problems that were identified.

The Indian Nations At Risk Task Force, established in early 1990, held hearings, visited schools, commissioned papers, and compiled a final report titled *Indian Nations At Risk: An Educational Strategy for Action.* The White House Conference on Indian Education, authorized by Congress in 1988, took place in January of 1992 after more than a year of state and regional hearings and meetings. *The Final Report of the White House Conference,* published in two volumes, included 113 resolutions adopted by the delegates to the conference. The conference delegates and task force members made several recommendations regarding the need for basic research, applied research, and development of new programs and materials. A summary of the research and development needs were compiled into an ERIC digest blueprint for Indian education by the Clearinghouse on Rural Education and Small Schools (Cahape, 1993; these needs are summarized later in this section).

Like many other aspects of Indian life affected by the policy of self-determination, research is increasingly controlled by Indian people. Tribal councils have established review processes for research requests by non-Indian and Indian researchers. According to Swisher (1993),

As we approach the twenty-first century there is a strong collective and collaborative voice of Indian (and non-Indian) people speaking about the role of research in the lives of Indian people. Included in this voice are professors at tribal, public and private colleges and universities; teachers and administrators in tribal, public and private schools; policy-makers at the local, state and national levels; and last but not least, the tribal leaders who envision the lives of their people being improved by research." (p. 4)

Indian people have become active researchers in order to find solutions to critical issues facing Indian societies. "Once purveyors of research, Indian people have become leaders in defining, discovering, constructing and explaining their reality" (Swisher, 1993, p. 4). In the essay "From Passive to Active: Research in Indian Country," Swisher asked, "So what?" now that Indians are involved in conducting research from an insider perspective. Will the research paradigms change? Should they change? Who will be setting the research agendas at the local, state, and national levels?

Appropriate Paradigms

Recent work by Mary E. Romero of Cochiti Pueblo demonstrates a new paradigm. In addressing the issue of underrepresentation of American Indian students in gifted programs in New Mexico, Romero and colleagues at the Santa Fe Indian School initiated a study to determine perceptions of giftedness among the Keresan Pueblos in New Mexico. Romero was able to define giftedness within the Keresan Pueblo cultural context. She also discovered that the research protocol must defer to the Pueblo protocol. She said,

A skepticism towards research and Pueblo cultural norms have limited the breadth and kind of information obtained in many previous research endeavors in Native communities. In this community-based research study, the direct involvement of Keresan community members in every aspect of the study assured cultural sensitivity to Pueblo people and recognition and adherence to proper Native protocol which assisted in the attainment of rich and vital data and yielded new and culturally appropriate research methodology in the Keresan Pueblos. Although sensitivity to Pueblo protocol and etiquette required extensive time investment, valuable data was produced, but more importantly, a trust of research in general was established within the seclusive Keresan Pueblo communities." (1994, p. 57)

Swisher (1986), who is also Standing Rock Sioux, also addressed the issue of protocol and time, as well as bias and the advantage of being an "insider" when she wrote about her experience of completing a dissertation on her home reservation.[3] Because she knew the people in her sample and where they lived and worked, she was able to complete her survey of 50 parents in an unprecedented amount of time. Being an enrolled tribal member—an "insider"—did not guarantee access to individuals; however, familiarity and knowledge of proper protocol did positively affect the research procedure.

Brown (1980), who is Cherokee, cited his own research experience, and that of Trimble and Medicine, who are both Lakotas, when he wrote about the research role of American Indian social scientists. Critical of the experimental paradigm as a deficit hypothesis approach, Brown supported a matrix model proposed by Trimble and Medicine (1976). The matrix, according to Trimble and Medicine, consists of three categories: human activities, environmental factors, and levels of analysis. Brown (1980) agreed with the authors "that research utilizing the matrix approach to studying Indians will produce problem-solving studies instead of the data-gathering, theory-testing studies that traditionally have characterized research on Indian behavior" (p. 53). Likewise, Argyris (1980) believes that conventional methodology (i.e., manipulation and control of subjects) tends to produce results that are invalid and/or work against the self-determination of Indian people. Trends toward multimethod and multidisciplinary research would be compatible with Trimble's (1977) belief that mixed method approaches are closely aligned to the Native view of people in their environments, but such research has been used infrequently in Indian communities.

On the basis of collaborative research with Indian communities, Trimble (1977) suggested a procedure of at least four steps: (a) formation of an advisory committee, (b) selection of trained indigenous, bilingual interviewers, (c) preparation of culturally sensitive instrumentation, and (d) consent from tribal officials representing target communities. The research projects that were conducted in this manner "left groups with the sense of participation and accomplishment that eventually promoted beneficial exchanges" (p. 162). The research questions were initiated by Indian people and stemmed from their growing concern for obtaining some reasonable answers that could be put to use to effect change (p. 162).

It appears that the thoughts and concerns of Indian researchers (such as Trimble) 15 years ago are still being echoed today. Conducting research in Indian communities can be complicated, and understanding the community is essential if research is to be valid, based on the needs of the people and not just the researchers, and something more than fleeting contact or a quick foray in and out of the community. History suggests that Indian people recognized that some research was designed to meet the needs of the researchers and not the researched and that they were deliberately misleading in their role as information givers (Brown, 1980).

Self-Determination in Defining Research Needs

Research needs have been identified in several recent documents. Most recently, an ERIC digest, *Blueprints for Indian Education: Research and Development Needs for the 1990s* (Cahape, 1993), summarized the research, development, evaluation, and dissemination needs embedded in the reports of the Indian Nations At Risk Task Force (1990) and the White House Conference on Indian Education (1992), respectively. Both the conference delegates and the task force members recommended basic research in two areas: (a) bilingualism and language development and (b) fetal alcohol effects and fetal alcohol syndrome. They called for applied research in the following areas: extent of adult illiteracy and adequacy of current adult literacy funding and programs; unmet needs in higher education; progress in higher education, including enrollment, retention, and graduation; elementary and secondary enrollment and achievement; identification of gifted and talented individuals; and demographic characteristics. The development work proposed included: alternative assessment or unbiased standardized tests to assess student achievement and abilities; effective parent support programs; instruction, curriculum, and program administration for exceptional students of all ages; and alcohol and substance abuse issues.

Conference delegates and task force members were clear about who ought to be conducting research and evaluation. They urged the Department of Education to support a range of research by American Indian and Alaska Native scholars committed to addressing the educational needs of their communities. Cahape (1993) summarized their concern: "Much research about natives—research that presents an 'insider' view—is essential to future progress" (p. 1). The conference and task force participants, however, urged a variety of organizations and individuals to be involved in the development of new programs, methods, and materials. For example, colleges and universities should be involved in research-driven needs defined by Indian communities and linked by electronic networks. Research on pedagogy should be conducted with Native education departments and tribal colleges, and research designed to improve education programs and academic achievement should be funded and made available through a national research and school improvement center specifically for Native education.

Similar areas of research were identified by Tippeconnic and Robbins (1985) and Tippeconnic and Swisher (1992). They included intertribal communication, learning styles, alcohol and drug abuse among families, development of industry on the reservation, efficiency at the university for Indian professionals/professors, possible educational relations between American Indian tribes and other sovereign countries, leadership power in education, and cognitive skills (Tippeconnic & Robbins, 1985), as well as pedagogy, curriculum, teachers, achievement scores, dropout rate, higher education, and parental involvement (Tippeconnic & Swisher, 1992).

Fearing that reports developed by the Indian Nations at Risk Task Force and the White House Conference on Indian Education would again go unheeded, the National Indian Education Association, the National Advisory Council on Indian Education, and the National Congress of American Indians have joined together to keep the issues on the forefront of tribal agendas as well as the legislative and executive branches of the federal government. An American Indian and Alaska Native education summit was sponsored by the three organizations in March of 1994, and updates at respective conferences and conventions have kept the issues before the constituencies with the goal of translating the issues into a national educational policy statement.

The Role of Indian Scholars

As the Lakota scholar Vine Deloria, Jr., argued, the shift to the Indian "voice" was critical to accurate scholarship and to reach an understanding of Indian societies. He acknowledged the difficulties facing Indian scholars.

The realities of Indian belief and existence have become so misunderstood and distorted at this point that when a real Indian stands up and speaks the truth, at any given moment, he or she is not only unlikely to be believed, but will probably be contradicted and "corrected" by the citation of some non-

Indian and totally inaccurate "expert." . . . This is not only a travesty of scholarship, but it is absolutely devastating to Indian societies (Deloria, cited in Rose, 1992, p. 404)

Deloria spoke to the concerns of self-determination; however, as Rose (1992) said, this does not mean that non-Native researchers—given the right intent and integrity—cannot be an aid in the empowerment process.

The fear exists among non-native writers that we are somehow trying to bar them from writing about Indians at all, that Indian people might be "staking a claim" as the sole interpreters of Indian cultures, most especially of that which is sacred, and asserting that only Indians can make valid observations on themselves. Such fears are not based in fact; I know of no Indian who has ever said this. Nor do I know of any who secretly thinks it. We accept as given that whites have as much prerogative to write and speak about us and our cultures as we have to write and speak about them and theirs. The question is how this is done and, to some extent, why it is done. (Rose, 1992, p. 316)

Recent reports such as *Our Voices, Our Vision: American Indians Speak Out for Educational Excellence, Indian Nations At Risk: An Educational Strategy for Action,* and *The Final Report of the White House Conference on Indian Education* are example of comprehensive reports that define research needs in Indian education based on the voices of Indian people. Individual Indian scholars have produced volumes of materials in which different perspectives are presented. Some of this stellar work includes essays by Vine Deloria Jr. (Standing Rock Sioux, 1991), and G. Mike Charleston (Choctaw, 1994); tribal histories by Grayson Noley (Choctaw, 1979, 1981) and Clara Sue Kidwell (Choctaw, 1995); boarding school histories by Paulette Fairbanks Molin (White Earth Chippewa, 1988); Brenda Child (Red Lake Chippewa, 1993); Devon A. Mihesuah (Choctaw, 1993); Jeffery Hamley (Turtle Mountain Chippewa, 1994); K. Tsianina Lomawaima (Creek, 1994); research on language and culture issues by Lucille Watahomigie (Hualapai, 1988, 1992), Galena Sells Dick (Navajo, with Estell and McCarty, 1994), and Esther Ilutsik (Yup'ik, 1994); a history of tribal colleges by Wayne Stein (Turtle Mountain Chippewa, 1992); higher education research by D. Michael Pavel (Skokomish, 1992, 1994 with Swisher & Ward); research and policy issues by John W. Tippeconnic III (Comanche, 1991, 1992); and curriculum and instruction and research issues by Karen Gayton Swisher (Standing Rock Sioux, 1990, 1994).

The words of a great Indian scholar, Rupert Costo (1970), offered 25 years ago, are appropriate:

Among us, traditionally, the scholars are the servants of the people. The "people" reign supreme, by virtue of their rights to approve or disapprove actions in all areas of life, and by reason of their prerogative to protect individual and tribal rights. And so we say . . . let people come for help to their own scholars. And let the scholars spend "their very days" and energies to the service of their people. (p. 4)

CONCLUSIONS

The 1960s seem to define a point of demarcation in Indian education. This decade marked the emergence of strong Indian leadership that led to a policy of self-determination. Consistently over the past two decades, the voices of Indian people have become stronger in determining all aspects of their children's education, including educational research. More schools on reservations are now locally controlled, and research, once the domain of university researchers, has been demystified to include research partnerships with local people asking their own questions and constructing appropriate paradigms for finding solutions. Work in progress on the Gila River Indian Community, for example, has partnered the Tribal Council with the Center for Indian Education at Arizona State University to determine the conditions that cause a high dropout rate among adolescents on the reservation.

We began this chapter by stating that, until recently, research into the education of Indian students has not made a difference, especially in two areas of nagging concern: school leaving before graduation and low achievement levels. Recent research based on cultural strengths and cultural integrity has yielded significant sustainable results for some schools and communities. The examples we cited in Alaska and Arizona are grounded in the cultural capital of their respective communities. These examples have demonstrated that local knowledge, with Native language playing a prominent role, can have an impact on schooling. The forming of study groups that included Native teachers and community elders resulted in discussions of how the curriculum, when infused with cultural or local knowledge, led to transformation of literacy in English only to biliteracy including the Native language. The Native language and inclusion of local knowledge were key components in the transformation of schooling for the Hualapai community in Peach Springs, Navajo communities in Rough Rock and Rock Point, and the Yup'ik community in Alaska.

Research has made a difference in other areas of inquiry as well. We are now more aware of cultural differences. We now know more about the learning styles of Indian students. We know that caring teachers make a difference in the decisions students make to persist or leave school before graduation. We know that strong grounding in culture and language does not interfere with, but instead enhances, achievement for young Indian people. Research suggests that for those individuals who have strong cultural identities and know their language, a culturally relevant curriculum is less important. Conversely, for those who are less well grounded, cultural integration of the curriculum is more important. Still needed, however, is the interpretation of what this research means in the way teachers are trained, schools are organized, curriculum is designed, and instruction is delivered.

Basic and applied research is still needed to find out more about several conditions. Is the crossover effect still operating, and, if so, why? What are the effects of competition and cooperation in classrooms? Do culturally appropriate parenting classes combat the effects of boarding school or institutional parenting? Has the research on learning styles been too general and instead limited the opportunities for Indian students to be fulfilled? How are the social, economic, and political structures of society affecting the postschool opportunities of young Indian people?

Still troublesome is the condition of education among the large population of Indian students in urban and off-reservation public schools. Current statistics indicate that there are more than 400,000 American Indian and Alaska Natives in kindergarten through Grade 12. Of that number more than 40,000, or about 10%, are in 187 schools funded by the BIA. The multitribal nature of the urban population makes it more difficult to do what the communities in Alaska and Arizona have done. There is clearly a need to involve Indian teachers, parents, and elders in urban and off-reservation communities to improve schooling for children. Both Indian and non-Indian researchers must more vigorously work with these multitribal communities to improve schooling for this large population of students.

The role of researchers, both Indian and non-Indian, has never been more important than it is now. A clear message in the last sections of this chapter is that when research is perceived as a partnership between the researcher and the community, sustained over time, the research that emerges benefits both parties in the partnership.

NOTES

[1] We prefer to describe the indigenous peoples of this country as American Indians or Alaska Natives, the term used in legislation and by organizations such as the National Congress of American Indians and the National Indian Education Association. In Canada, First Nations is the preferred term. When a particular tribe is not designated, American Indian and Alaska Native, First Nations, Indian, or Native will be used throughout the chapter except when otherwise noted in quotations.

[2] The notion that anthropologists have studied North American Indians more than any other group in the world is liberally attributed to George and Louise Spindler, notable educational anthropologists who themselves conducted studies among Menominee and Ojibway peoples.

[3] The "insider" doctrine, according to Merton (1972), maintains that researchers are singularly effective in studying their own reference group; therefore, in this case, only a tribal member can understand other tribal members.

REFERENCES

Ahler, J.G. (1994). The evolution of bilingual education in an American Indian community: A decade of evaluation as applied anthropology. *Great Plains Research, 4,* 293–303.

American Indian Policy Review Commission. (1976). *Final report: Indian education.* Washington DC: U.S. Government Printing Office.

Anderson, J.G. & Safar, D. (1967). The influence of differential community perspectives on the provision of equal education opportunities. *Sociology of Education, 3,* 219–230.

Annahatak, B. (1994). Quality education for Inuit today? Cultural strengths, new things, and working out the unknowns: A story by an Inuk. *Peabody Journal of Education, 69,* 12–18.

Appleton, N. (1983). *Cultural pluralism in education.* New York: Longman.

Argyris, C. (1980). *The inner contradictions of rigorous research.* New York: Academic Press.

Attneave, C. (1977). The wasted strengths of American Indian families. In S. Unger (Ed.), *The destruction of Indian families* (29–33). New York: Association on American Indian Affairs.

Barnhardt, C. (1994). Life on the other side: Native students survival in a university world. *Peabody Journal of Education, 69*, 115–139.

Barnhardt, R. (1981). *Culture, community and the curriculum.* Fairbanks: Center for Cross Cultural Studies, University of Alaska.

Barnhardt, R. (1991). Higher education in the fourth world: Indigenous people take control. *Canadian Journal of Native Education, 18*, 199–231.

Basso, K. H. (1970). To give up on words: Silence in Western Apache culture. *Southwestern Journal of Anthropology, 26*, 213–230.

Battelle Human Affairs Research Center. (1976). *A bibliography of American Indian education studies.* Seattle, WA: Author.

Begay, S., Dick, G. S., Estell, D. W., Estell, J., & McCarty, T. (1995). Change from the inside out: A story of transformation in a Navajo community school. *Bilingual Research Journal, 19*, 121–139.

Bennett deMarrais, K., Nelson, P., & Baker, J. (1992). Meaning in mud: Yup'ik Eskimo girls at play. *Anthropology & Education Quarterly, 23*, 120–144.

Bernardoni, L. C. (1962). *Critical factors influencing the stated vocation preference of male, White-Mountain-Apache students.* Unpublished doctoral dissertation, Arizona State University.

Berry, B. (1968). *The education of American Indians: A survey of the literature.* Washington, DC: U.S. Government Printing Office.

Berry, J. (1966). Temne and Eskimo perceptual skills. *International Journal of Psychology, 1*, 207–229.

Berry, J. (1971). Ecological and cultural factors in spacial perceptual development. *Canadian Journal of Behavioural Science, 3*, 324–336.

Black, M. B. (1973). Ojibwa questioning etiquette and use of ambiguity. *Studies in Linguistics, 23*, 13–29.

Bowker, A. (1993). *Sisters in the blood: The education of women in Native America.* Newton, MA: WEEA Publishing Center.

Brewer, A. (1977). An Indian education. *Integrateducation, 15*, 21–23.

Briggs, J. L. (1970). *Never in anger: Portrait of an Eskimo family.* Cambridge, MA: Harvard University Press.

Brophy, W., & Aberle, S. (1966). *The Indian: America's unfinished business.* Norman: University of Oklahoma Press.

Brown, A. (1980). Research role of American Indian social scientists. *Journal of Educational Equity and Leadership, 1*, 47–59.

Brown, A. D. (1980). Cherokee culture and school achievement. *American Indian Culture and Research Journal, 4*, 55–74.

Bryde, J. F. (1965). *The Sioux Indian student: A study of scholastic failure and personality conflict.* Unpublished doctoral dissertation, University of Denver.

Bureau of Indian Affairs. (1988). *Report on BIA education: Excellence in Indian education through effective school process.* Washington, DC: U.S. Department of the Interior.

Burgess, B. (1978). *Native American learning styles.* Washington, DC: U.S. Office of Education.

Burnap, A. (1972). *An analysis of self-esteem in reservation Indian youth as measured by Coopersmith's Self-Esteem Inventory.* Unpublished master's thesis, Northern State College, Aberdeen, SD.

Cahalan, D. L., & Crossley, H. M. (1969). *American drinking practices: A national study of drinking behaviors and attitudes.* New Brunswick, NJ: Rutgers Center for Alcohol Studies.

Cahape, P. (1993). *Blueprints for Indian education: Research and development needs for the 1990s.* Charleston, WV: ERIC/CRESS, Appalachia Educational Laboratory.

Cazden, C.B. (1982). Four comments. In P. Gilmore & A. Glatthkorn (Eds.), *Children in and out of school* (pp. 4–18). Washington, DC: Center for Applied Linguistics.

Cazden, C.B., & John, V.P. (1971). Learning in American Indian children. In M.L. Wax, S. Diamond, & F. Gearing (Eds.), *Anthropological perspectives on education* (pp. 253–257). New York: Basic Books.

Cazden, C.B., & Leggett, E. (1981). Culturally responsive education: Recommendations for achieving Lau remedies II. In H. Trueba, G. Guthrie, & K. Au (Eds.), *Culture and the bilingual classroom* (pp. 69–86). Rowley: Newbury House.

Chan, K.S., & Osthimer, B. (1983). *Navajo youth and early school withdrawal: A case study.* Los Alamitos, CA: National Center for Bilingual Research.

Charleston, G.M. (1994). Toward true Native education: A treaty of 1992 final report of the Indian Nations At Risk Task Force, Draft 3. *Journal of American Indian Education, 33,* 1–156.

Chavers, D. (1991). Indian education: Dealing with a disaster. *Principal, 70,* 28–29.

Chilcott, J.H. (1985). Yaqui world view and the school: Conflict and accommodation. *Journal of American Indian Education, 24,* 21–32.

Child, B. (1993). Homesickness, illness, and death: Native-American girls in government boarding schools. In B. Bair & S.E. Cayleff (Eds.), *Wings of gauze: Women of color and the experience of health and illness* (pp. 169–179). Detroit: Wayne State University Press.

Chisholm, J.S. (1983). *Navajo infancy: An ethnological study of child development.* Albuquerque: University of New Mexico Press.

Chrisjohn, R.D., & Peters, M. (1989, August). The right-brained Indian: Fact or fiction? *Journal of American Indian Education,* pp. 77–83.

Clawson, R. (1990). Death by drink: An Indian battle. *Montana Standard, 7,* 5.

Cline, M.S. (1972). Village socialization of the bush teacher. *The Northian, 9,* 19–27.

Coburn, J., & Nelson, S. (1989). *Teachers do make a difference: What Indian graduates say about their school experience.* Portland, OR: Northwest Regional Educational Laboratory.

Coladarci, T. (1983). High school dropout among Native Americans. *Journal of American Indian Education, 23,* 15–22.

College Board and American Indian Science and Engineering Society. (1989). *Our voices, our vision: American Indians speak out for educational excellence.* New York: College Entrance Examination Board.

Collier, J., Jr. (1973). *Alaskan Eskimo education: A film analysis of cultural confrontation in the schools.* New York: Holt, Rinehart & Winston.

Collier, J. (1979). *A film study of classrooms in western Alaska.* Fairbanks: Center for Cross Cultural Studies, University of Alaska.

Condon, R. (1987). *Inuit youth: Growth and change in the Canadian arctic.* New Brunswick, NJ: Rutgers University Press.

Coombs, M., Kron, R.E., Collister, E.G., & Anderson, K.E. (1958). *The Indian child goes to school.* Lawrence, KS: Haskell Press.

Costo, R. (1970). Moment of truth for the American Indian. In J. Henry (Ed.), *Indian voices: First convocation of American Indian scholars* (pp. 1–14). San Francisco: Indian Historian Press.

Crago, M., Annahatak, B., & Ningiuruvik, L. (1993). Changing patterns of language socialization in Inuit homes. *Anthropology & Education Quarterly, 24,* 205–223.

Cummins, J. (1992). The empowerment of Indian students. In J. Reyhner (Ed.), *Teaching American Indian Students* (pp. 3–12). Norman: University of Oklahoma Press.

Darnell, R. (1979). *Reflections on Cree interactional etiquette: Educational implications* (Working Papers in Sociolinguistics No. 57). Austin, TX: Southwestern Educatinal Development Laboratory.

Darnell, R. (1988). The implications of Cree interactional etiquette. In R. Darnell & M. Foster (Eds.), *Native North American interaction patterns* (pp. 69–77). Quebec: National Museums of Canada.

Delk, J.L. (1974). Dropouts from an American Indian reservation: A possible prevention program. *Journal of Community Psychology, 2,* 15–17.

Deloria, V., Jr. (1991). *Indian education in America.* Boulder, CO: American Indian Science and Engineering Society.

Development Associates. (1983). *Academic performance, attendance and expectations of Indian students in public schools.* Arlington, VA: Author. (ERIC Document Reproduction Service No. ED 237–277)

Deyhle, D. (1986a). Break dancing and breaking out: Anglos, Utes, and Navajos in a border reservation high school. *Anthropology & Education Quarterly, 17,* 111–127.

Deyhle, D. (1986b). Success and failure: A micro-ethnographic comparison of Navajo and Anglo students' perceptions of testing. *Curriculum Inquiry, 16,* 365–389.

Deyhle, D. (1991). Empowerment and cultural conflict: Navajo parents and the schooling of their children. *Qualitative Studies in Education, 4,* 277–297.

Deyhle, D. (1992). Constructing failure and maintaining cultural identity: Navajo and Ute school leavers. *Journal of American Indian Education, 31,* 24–47.

Deyhle, D. (1995). Navajo youth and Anglo racism: Cultural integrity and resistance. *Harvard Educational Review, 65,* 403–444.

Deyhle, D., & LeCompte, M. (1994). Cultural differences in child development: Navajo adolescents in middle schools. *Theory into Practice, 33,* 156–166.

Deyhle, D., & Margonis, F. (1995). Navajo mothers and daughters: Schools, jobs, and the family. *Anthropology & Education Quarterly, 26,* 135–167.

Dick, G.S., Estell, D., & McCarty, T.L. (1994). Saad Naakih Bee'enootiiji Na'alkaa: Restructuring the teaching of language and literacy in a Navajo community school. *Journal of American Indian Education, 33* (3), 31–46.

Diessner, R., & Walker, J.L. (1989). A cognitive pattern of the Yakima Indian students. *Journal of American Indian Education,* 84–88.

Dinges, N., Trimble, J.E., & Hollenbeck, A. (1979). American Indian adolescent socialization: A review of the literature. *Journal of Adolescence, 2,* 259–296.

Downey, M. (1977). *A profile of psycholinguistic abilities of grades one, two and three students of the Flathead Reservation.* Unpublished doctoral dissertation, University of Montana.

Dozier, E. (1970). *The Pueblo Indians of North America.* New York: Holt, Rinehart & Winston.

Dumont, R.V., Jr., (1972). Learning English and how to be silent: Studies in Sioux and Cherokee classrooms. In C. Cazden, V. John & D. Hymes (Eds.), *Fuctions of language in the classroom* (pp. 334–369). New York: Teachers College Press.

Dumont, R.V., Jr., & Wax, M.L. (1976). Cherokee school society and the intercultural classroom. In J. Roberts & S. Akinsanya (Eds.), *Schooling in the cultural context: Anthropological studies of education* (pp. 205–216). New York: David McKay.

Eberhard, D. (1989). American Indian education: A study of dropouts, 1980–87. *Journal of American Indian Education, 29,* 32–40.

Eggan, D. (1976). Instruction and affect in Hopi cultural continuity. In J. Roberts & S. Akinsanya (Eds.), *Schooling in the cultural context: Anthropological studies of education* (pp. 140–155). New York: David McKay.

Ekstrom, R.B., Goertz, M.E., Pollack, J.M., & Rock, D.A. (1986). Who drops out of high school and why? Findings from a national study. *Teachers College Record, 87,* 356–373.

Erickson, D. (1972). *Verbal and diagram-supplemented instructional strategies and achievement for Eskimo students.* Unpublished manuscript.

Erickson, F. (1984). School literacy, reasoning and civility: An anthropologist's perspective. *Harvard Educational Review, 54*, 525–546.

Erickson, F. (1993). Transformation and school success: The politics and culture of educational achievement. In E. Jacob & C. Jordan (Eds.), *Minority education: Anthropological perspective* (pp. 27–51). Norwood, NJ: Ablex.

Erickson, F., & Mohatt, G. (1982). Cultural organization of participation structures in two classrooms of Indian students. In G. Spindler (Ed.), *Doing the ethnography of schooling* (pp. 132–174). New York: Holt, Rinehart & Winston.

Foley, D. (1996). The silent Indian as a cultural production. In A. Levinson, D. Foley, & D. Holland (Eds.), *The cultural production of the educated person* (pp. 79–91). New York: State University of New York Press.

Freeman, K., Stairs, A., Corbiere, E., & Lazore, D. (1995). Ojibwe, Mohawk, and Inuktitut alive and well? Issues of identity, ownership, and change. *Bilingual Research Journal, 19*, 39–69.

Fuchs, E., & Havighurst, R.J. (1972). *To live on this earth: American Indian education.* Albuquerque: University of New Mexico Press.

Garber, M. (1968). *Ethnicity and measures of educability.* Unpublished doctoral dissertation, University of Southern California.

Gearing, F. (1970). *The face of the fox.* Chicago: Aldine.

Giles, K.N. (1985). *Indian high school dropouts: A perspective.* Milwaukee, WI: Midwest National Origin Desegregation Assistance Center.

Goodenough, F.L. (1926). Racial differences in the intelligence of school children. *Journal of Experimental Psychology, 9*, 388–395.

Good Tracks, J.G. (1973). Native American noninterference. *Social Work, 18* (6), 30–34.

Greenbaum, P., & Greenbaum, S. (1983). Cultural differences, nonverbal regulation, and classroom interaction: Sociolinguistic interference in American Indian education. *Peabody Journal of Education, 61*, 16–33.

Guilmet, G.M. (1978). Navajo and Caucasian children's verbal and non-verbal visual behavior in the urban classroom. *Anthropology & Education Quarterly, 9*, 196–215.

Guilmet, G.M. (1979). Maternal perceptions of urban Navajo and Caucasian children's classroom behavior. *Human Organization, 38*, 87–91.

Gwilliam, R.F. (1957). *The relationship of the social acceptance of a Navajo minority and teacher attitudes on the dominative-supportive dimensions.* Unpublished master's thesis, Brigham Young University.

Hamley, J. (1994). An introduction to the federal Indian boarding school movement. *North Dakota History, 61* (2), 2–9.

Harkins, A.M. (1968). *Public education on a Minnesota Chippewa reservation.* Washington, DC: Department of Health, Education, and Welfare.

Havighurst, R. (1970). *The education of Indian children and youth.* Chicago: University of Chicago Press.

Henze, R., & Vanett, L. (1993). To walk in two worlds—Or more? Challenging a common metaphor of Native education. *Anthropology & Education Quarterly, 24*, 116–134.

Hilger, M.I. (1951). *Chippewa child life and its cultural background.* Washington, DC.: Government Printing Office.

Holm, A., & Holm, W. (1995). Navajo language education: Retrospect and prospects. *Bilingual Research Journal, 19*, 141–167.

Ilutsik, E.A. (1994). The founding of Ciulistet: One teacher's journey. *Journal of American Indian Education, 33* (3), 6–13.

Indian Nations At Risk Task Force. (1990). *Indian Nations at risk: An educational strategy for action.* Washington, DC: U.S. Department of Education. (ERIC Document Reproduction Service No. ED 339 578)

Jackson, E.E. (1963). *The teaching of English as a second language to Alaskan Native children of non-English speaking backgrounds on the kindergarten and first grade levels.* Unpublished master's thesis, University of Washington, Seattle.

Jamieson, E., & Sandiford, P. (1928). The mental capacity of Southern Ontario Indians. *Journal of Educational Psychology, 19,* 313–328, 536–551.

Joe, J.R. (1994). Revaluing Native-American concepts of development and education. In P. Greenfield & R. Cocking (Eds.), *Cross-cultural roots of minority child development* (pp. 107–113). Hillsdale, NJ: Lawrence Erlbaum.

John, V.P. (1972). Styles of learning—styles of teaching: Reflections on the education of Navajo children. In C. Cazden, D. Hymes & V.P. John (Eds.), *Functions of language in the classroom* (pp. 331–343). New York: Teachers College Press.

Johnson, J.A., Dupuis, V.L., & Johansen, J. (1991). *Reflections on American education, classic and contemporary readings.* Boston: Allyn and Bacon.

John-Steiner, V., & Osterreich, H. (1975). *Learning styles among Pueblo children.* Unpublished manuscript, Department of Educational Foundations, University of New Mexico.

Kaulback, B. (1984). Styles of learning among Native children: A review of the research. *Canadian Journal of Native Education, 2* (3), 27–37.

Kidwell, C.S. (1995). *Choctaws and missionaries in Mississippi, 1818–1918.* Norman: University of Oklahoma Press.

King, R.A. (1967). *The school at Mopass: A problem of identity.* New York: Holt, Rinehart & Winston.

Kleinfeld, J. (1973). Intellectual strengths in culturally different groups: An Eskimo illustration. *Review of Educational Research, 43,* 341–359.

Kleinfeld, J. (1975). Effective teachers of Eskimo and Indian students. *School Review, 83,* 301–344.

Kleinfeld, J. (1979). *Eskimo school on the Andreafsky.* New York: Praeger.

Kleinfeld, J. (1988). Adapting instruction to Native Americans' learning style: An iconoclastic view. In W. Lonner & V. Tyler (Eds.), *Cultural and ethnic factors in learning and motivation: Implications for education* (pp. 83–101). Bellingham, WA: Western Washington University.

Kleinfeld, J., McDiarmid, G.W., & Hagstrom, D. (1989). Small local high schools decrease Alaska Native drop-out rates. *Journal of American Indian Education, 28,* 24–30.

Kleinfeld, J., & Nelson, P. (1991). Adapting instruction to Native Americans' learning styles: An iconoclastic view. *Journal of Cross-Cultural Psychology, 22,* 273–282.

Kluckhohn, C., & Leighton, D. (1974). *The Navajo.* Cambridge, MA: Harvard University Press.

Kuske, I. (1969). *Psycholinguistic abilities of Sioux Indian children.* Unpublished doctoral dissertation, University of South Dakota.

Lamphere, L. (1977). *To run after them: Cultural and social bases of cooperation in a Navajo community.* Tucson: University of Arizona Press.

Leighton, D., & Kluckhohn, C. (1948). *Children of the people.* Cambridge, MA: Harvard University Press.

Leacock, E. (1976). The concept of culture and its significance for school counselors. In J.I. Roberts & S.K. Akinsanya (Eds.), *Schooling in the cultural context* (pp. 418–426). New York: David McKay Co.

Leap, W. (1991). Pathways and barriers to Indian language literacy-building on the Northern Ute. *Anthropology & Education Quarterly, 22,* 21–41.

Leap, W. (1993). *American Indian English.* Salt Lake City: University of Utah Press.

Ledlow, S. (1992). Is cultural discontinuity an adequate explanation for dropping out? *Journal of American Indian Education, 31,* 21–36.

Lipka, J. (1994). Language, power, and pedagogy: Whose school is it? *Peabody Journal of Education, 69,* 71–93.

Lipka, J., & Ilutsik, E. (1995). Negotiated change: Yup'ik perspectives on indigenous schooling. *Bilingual Research Journal, 19,* 195–207.

Lipka, J., & McCarty, T.L. (1994). Changing the culture of schooling: Navajo and Yup'ik cases. *Anthropology & Education Quarterly, 25,* 266–284.

Lipka, J., & Stairs, A. (1994). Editors' introduction. *Peabody Journal of Education, 69,* 1–5.

Lipka, J., & Stairs, A. (1994b). Negotiating the culture of indigenous schools [Special issue]. *Peabody Journal of Education, 69.*

Lomawaima, K.T. (1994). *They called it prairie light: The story of Chilocco Indian School.* Lincoln: University of Nebraska Press.

Lombardi, T. (1970). *Psycholinguistic abilities of Papago Indian school children.* Unpublished doctoral dissertation, University of South Dakota.

Longstreet, E. (1978). *Aspects of ethnicity.* New York: Teachers College Press.

Macias, J. (1987). The hidden curriculum of Papago teachers: American Indian strategies for mitigating cultural discontinuity in early schooling. In G. Spindler & L. Spindler (Eds.), *Interpretative ethnography of education at home and abroad* (pp. 365–380). Hillsdale, NJ: Erlbaum.

Martin, J.F., & McCarty, T. L. (1990). The greater Southwest culture area: Diverse life-ways in a varied environment. In D.L. Boxberger (Ed.), *Native North Americans: An ethnohistorical approach* (pp. 215–264). Dubuque, IA: Kendall & Hunt.

Mason, E.P. (1969). Cross-validation study of personality characteristics of junior high students from American Indian, Mexican, and Caucasian ethnic backgrounds. *Journal of Social Psychology, 77,* 15–24.

McBeth, S.J. (1983). *Ethnic identity and the boarding school experience of west-central Oklahoma American Indians.* Washington, DC: University Press of America.

McCartin, R., & Schill, W.J. (1977). Three modes of instruction. *Journal of American Indian Education,* 14–20.

McCarty, T.L. (1989). School as community: The Rough Rock demonstration. *Harvard Educational Review, 59,* 484–503.

McCarty, T.L. (1991). *Hualapai bilingual academic excellence program: Blending tradition with technology, guide for replication site administrators.* Peach Springs, AZ: Peach Springs School District No. 8.

McCarty, T.L. (1994). Bilingual education policy and the empowerment of American Indian communities. *Journal of Educational Issues of Language Minority Students, 14,* 23–40.

McCarty, T.L., Lipka, J. & Dick, G.S. (1994a). Introduction to the theme issue. *Journal of American Indian Education, 33,* 2–4.

McCarty, T.L., Lipka, J., & Dick, G.S. (1994b). Local knowledge in indigenous schooling: Case studies in American Indian/Alaska Native education [Special issue]. *Journal of American Indian Education, 33* (3).

McCarty, T.L., Wallace, S., Lynch, R.H., & Benally, A. (1991). Classroom inquiry and Navajo learning styles: A call for reassessment. *Anthropology & Education Quarterly, 22,* 42–59.

McCarty, T.L., & Zepeda, O. (1995). Indigenous language education and literacy [Special issue]. *Bilingual Research Journal, 19* (1).

McLaren, P. (1989). *Life in schools: An introduction to critical pedagogy in the foundations of education.* New York: Longman.

McLaughlin, D. (1989). The sociolinguistics of Navajo literacy. *Anthropology & Education Quarterly, 20,* 275–290.

McLaughlin, D. (1991). Curriculum for cultural politics: Literacy program develolpment in a Navajo school setting. In R. Blomeyer, Jr., & D. Martin (Eds.), *Case studies in computer aided learning* (pp. 151–164). New York: The Falmer Press.

McLaughlin, D. (1992). *When literacy empowers: Navajo language in print.* Albuquerque: University of New Mexico Press.

McLaughlin, D. (1995). Strategies for enabling bilingual program development in American Indian schools. *Bilingual Research Journal, 19,* 169–178.

Meriam, L. (1928). *The problem of Indian administration.* Baltimore: Johns Hopkins Press.

Merriam, L. (1977). The effects of boarding schools on Indian family life. In S. Unger (Ed.), *The destruction of Indian families* (pp. 14–17). New York: Association on American Indian Affairs.

Merton, R. K. (1972). Insiders and outsiders: A chapter in the sociology of knowledge. *American Journal of Sociology, 78* (1), 9–47.

Mihesuah, D. (1993). *Cultivating the rosebuds: The education of women at the Cherokee seminary: 1850–1909.* Urbana: University of Illinois Press.

Miller, A.G., & Thomas, R. (1972). Cooperation and competition among Blackfoot Indian and urban Canadian children. *Child Development, 43,* 1104–1110.

Milone, D.E. (1983). *American Indian student reasons for dropping out and attitude toward school.* Unpublished master's thesis, Arizona State University, Tempe.

Mindell, C., & Gurwitt, A. (1977). The placement of American Indian children–The need for change. In S. Unger (Ed.), *The destruction of Indian families* (pp. 61–66). New York: Association on American Indian Affairs.

Mohatt, G., & Erickson, F. (1981). Cultural differences in teaching styles in an Odawa school: A sociolinguistic approach. In H. Trueba, G. Guthrie, & K. Au (Eds.), *Culture and the bilingual classroom* (pp. 105–119). Rowley, MA: Newbury House.

Molin, P.F. (1988). "Training the hand, the head, and the heart": Indian education at Hampton Institute. *Minnesota History, 51,* 82–98.

National Center for Educational Statistics. (1988). *Dropout rates in the United States.* Washington, DC: U.S. Department of Education, Office of Educational Research and Improvement.

Noley, G.B. (1979). Choctaw bilingual and bicultural education in the 19th century. In *Multicultural education and the American Indian* (pp. 25–39). UCLA: American Indian Studies Center.

Noley, G.B. (1981). Historical research and American Indian education. *Journal of American Indian Education, 20,* 13–18.

Northern Ute Tribe. (1985). Ute language policy. *Cultural Survival Quarterly, 9,* 16–19.

Ogbu, J.U. (1978). *Minority education and caste: The American system in cross-cultural perspective.* New York: Academic Press.

Ogbu, J.U. (1993). Variability in minority school performance: A problem in search of an explanation. In E. Jacob & C. Jordan (Eds.), *Minority education: Anthropological perspective* (pp. 83–111). Norwood, NJ: Ablex.

Okakok, L. (1989). Serving the purpose of education. *Harvard Educational Review, 59,* 405–422.

Ovando, C. (1994). Change in school and community attitudes in an Athapaskan village. *Peabody Journal of Education, 69,* 43–59.

Owens, C.S., & Bass, W.P. (1969). *The American Indian high school dropout in the Southwest.* Albuquerque, NM: Southwest Cooperative Lab.

Parmee, E.A. (1968). *Formal education and culture change: A modern Apache Indian community and government education programs.* Tucson: University of Arizona Press.

Pavel, D.M. (1992). *American Indians and Alaska Natives in higher education: Research on participation and graduation.* EDO-RC-92-2.

Pavel, M., Swisher, K., & Ward, M. (1995). Special focus: American Indian and Alaska Native demographics and educational trends. *Minorities in Higher Education*, 13th annual status report, 33–60.

Peng, S.S., & Takai, R.T. (1983). *High school dropouts: Descriptive information from High School and Beyond*. Washington, DC: National Center for Educational Statistics.

Pettit, G.A. (1946). *Primitive education in North America*. Berkeley: University of California.

Pevar, S. (1992). *The rights of Indians and tribes*. Carbondale: Southern Illinois University Press.

Philion, W.E., & Galloway, C.E. (1969). Indian children and the reading program. *Journal of Reading*, *12*, 553–560, 598–602.

Philips, S. (1972). Participant structures and communicative competence: Warm Springs children in community and classroom. In C. Cazden, D. Hymes & V. John (Eds.), *Functions of language in the classroom* (pp. 370–394). New York: Teachers College Press.

Philips, S. (1983). *The invisible culture: Communication in classroom and on the Warm Springs Indian reservation*. New York: Longman.

Philips, S. (1988). Similarities in North American Indian groups non-verbal behavior and their relation to early child development. In R. Darnell & M. Foster (Eds.), *Native North American interaction patterns* (pp. 150–164). Quebec: National Museums of Canada.

Platero, P., Brandt, E.A., Witherspoon, G., & Wong, P. (1986). *Navajo students at risk: Final report for the Navajo area dropout study*. Window Rock, AZ: Navajo Nation.

Qöyawayma, A. (1991, January). *Between two worlds*. Speech presented at the Heard Museum, Phoenix, AZ.

Ramirez M., III, & Castaneda, A. (1974). *Cultural democracy, bicognitive development, and education*. New York: Academic Press.

Reyhner, J. (1992). Bilingual education. In J. Reyhner (Ed.), *Teaching American Indian students* (pp. 59–77). Norman: University of Oklahoma Press.

Riley, P. (1993). *Growing up Native American: An anthology*. New York: Morrow.

Rohner, R.P. (1965). Factors influencing the academic performance of Kwakiutl children in Canada. *Comparative Education Review*, *9*, 331–340.

Romero, M.E. (1994). Identifying giftedness among Keresan Pueblo Indians: The Keres study. *Journal of American Indian Education*, *34*, 35–58.

Rose, W. (1992). The great pretenders: Further reflections on Whiteshamanism. In M.A. Jaimes (Ed.), *The state of Native America* (pp. 403–421). Boston: South End Press.

Rosier, P., & Farella, M. (1976). Bilingual education at Rock Point—Some early results. *TESOL Quarterly*, *10*, 379–388.

Ross, A.C. (August, 1989). Brain hemispheric functions and the Native American. *Journal of American Indian Education*, 72–76.

Ryan, R.A. (1980). A community perspective for mental health research. *Social Casework*, *61*, 507–511.

Sargent, A.G. (1977). *Beyond sex roles*. St. Paul, MN: West.

Sarris, G. (1993). Keeping Slug Woman alive: The challenge of reading in a reservation classroom. In J. Boyarin (Ed.), *The ethnography of reading* (pp. 238–269). Los Angeles: University of California Press.

Sawyer, D. (1991). Native learning styles: Shorthand for instructional adaptations? *Canadian Journal of Native Education*, *18*, 99–105.

Schwartz, J. (1985). *Native Americans in a southwestern university: A study of the impact of traditionality in higher education*. Unpublished master's thesis, Northern Arizona State University.

Scollon, R., & Scollon, S. (1981). *Narrative, literacy and face in interethnic communication*. Norwood, NJ: Ablex.

Scollon, R. & Scollon, S. (1982). *Athapaskan-English interethnic communication*. Fairbanks: Alaska Native Language Center.

Scollon, S.B., & Scollon, R. (1988). Face in interethnic telecommunicaton at the University of Alaska: Computer conferencing as non-focused interaction. In R. Darnell & M. Foster (Eds.), *Native North American interaction patterns* (pp. 188–193). Quebec: National Museums of Canada.

Selinger, A.D. (1968). *The American Indian high school dropout: The magnitude of the problem.* Portland, OR: Northwest Regional Educational Laboratory.

Senese, G. (1991). *Self-determination and the social education of Native Americans.* New York: Praeger.

Sharp, N. (1994). Caknernarqutet. *Peabody Journal of Education, 69,* 6–11.

Shears, B.T. (1970). *Aptitude, content and method teaching word recognition with young American Indian children.* Unpublished doctoral dissertation, University of Minnesota.

Sindell, P. (1987). Some discontinuities in the enculturation of Mistassini Cree children. In G.D. Spindler (Ed.), *Education and cultural process* (pp. 378–400). Prospect Heights, IL: Waveland Press.

Spicer, E.H. (1961). *Perspectives in American Indian culture change.* Chicago: University of Chicago Press.

Spindler, G.D., & Spindler, L.S. (1957). American Indian personality types and their sociocultural roots. *Annals of the American Academy of Political and Social Science, 311,* 147.

Stairs, A. (1994). The cultural negotiation of indigenous education: Between microethnography and model-building. *Peabody Journal of Education, 69,* 154–171.

Stein, W.J. (1992). *Tribally controlled colleges making good medicine.* New York: Lang.

Suina, J., & Smolkin, L.B. (1994). From natal culture to school culture to dominant society culture: Supporting transitions for Pueblo Indian students. In P. Greenfield & R. Cocking (Eds.), *Cross-cultural roots of minority child development* (pp. 115–130). Hillsdale, New Jersey: Erlbaum.

Swisher, K. (1986). Authentic research: An interview on the way to the ponderosa. *Anthropology & Education Quarterly, 17,* 185–188.

Swisher, K. (1990). Cooperative learning and the education of American Indian/Alaskan Native students: A review of the literature and suggestions for implementation. *Journal of American Indian Education, 29,* 36–43.

Swisher, K.G. (1993). From passive to active: Research in Indian country. *Tribal College, 4,* 4–5.

Swisher, K. (1994). Primary and secondary U.S. Native education. In D. Champagne (Ed.), *The Native North American Almanac* (pp. 855–868). Detroit: Gale Research.

Swisher, K.G. (1996). Who should be writing about Indians in education? *American Indian Quarterly, 20,* 83–87.

Swisher, K., & Deyhle, D. (1987). Styles of learning and learning styles: Educational conflicts for American Indian youth. *Journal of Multilingual and Multicultural Development, 8,* 345–360.

Swisher, K., & Deyhle, D. (1989). The styles of learning are different, but the teaching is just the same: Suggestions for teachers of American Indian youth. *Journal of American Indian Education,* 1–14.

Swisher, K., & Deyhle, D. (1992). Adapting instruction to culture. In J. Reyhner (Ed.), *Teaching American Indian students* (pp. 81–95). Norman: University of Oklahoma Press.

Swisher, K., & Hoisch, M., & Pavel, D.M. (1991). *American Indian/Alaska Natives dropout study 1991.*Washington, DC: National Education Association.

Swisher, K., & Pavel, D.M. (1994). American Indian learning styles survey: An assessment of teacher knowledge. *Journal of Educational Issues of Language Minority Students, 13,* 59–77.

Szasz, M.C. (1974). *Education and the American Indian: The road to self-determination since 1928.* Albuquerque: University of New Mexico Press.

Tafoya, T. (1989). Coyote's eyes: Native cognition styles. *Journal of American Indian Education,* 29–42.

Taylor, L., & Skanes, G. (1975). Psycholinguistic abilities of children in isolated communities in Labrador. *Canadian Journal of Behavioural Science, 7,* 30–39.

Tefit, S.K. (1967). Anomy, values and culture change among teen-age Indians: An exploratory study. *Sociology of Education, 60,* 145–157.

Telford, C.W. (1932). Test performance of full and mixed blood North Dakota Indians. *Journal of Comparative Psychology, 14,* 123–145.

Tharp, R. (1994). Intergroup differences among Native Americans in socialization and child cognition: An ethnogenetic analysis. In P. Greenfield & R. Cocking (Eds.) *Cross-cultural roots of minority child development* (pp. 87–105). Hillsdale, NJ: Erlbaum.

Tierney, W.G. (1992). *Official encouragement, institutional discouragement: Minorities in academe—the Native American experience.* Norwood, New Jersey: Ablex Publishing Corporation.

Tippeconnic, J.W. III & Robbins, R. (1985). *Research in American Indian education.* Tempe, AZ: Center for Indian education, Arizona State University.

Tippeconnic, J.W., III. (1991). The education of American Indians: Policy, practice, and future direction. In D.E. Green & T.V. Tonneses (Eds.), *American Indians: Social justice and public policy.* Milwaukee, WI: Institute on Race and Ethnicity.

Tippeconnic, J.W., III & Swisher, K. (1992). American Indian education. In M.C. Alkin (Ed.), *Encyclopedia of education research* (pp. 75–78). New York: Macmillan.

Trennert, R., Jr. (1988). *The Phoenix Indian School: Forced assimilation in Arizona, 1891–1935.* Norman: University of Oklahoma Press.

Trimble, J.E. (1977). The sojourner in the American Indian community: Methodological issues and concerns. *Journal of Social Issues, 33,* 159–174.

Trimble, J. E., Goddard, A., & Dinges, N. (1977). *Review of the literature on educational needs and problems of American Indians: 1971–1976.* Seattle, WA: Battelle Human Affairs Research Center.

Trimble, J.E., & Medicine, B. (1976). Development of theoretical models and levels of interpretation in mental health. In J. Westermeyer (Ed.), *Anthropology and mental health* (pp. 161–200). The Hague, The Netherlands: Mouton.

Trueba, H.T., Spindler, G,. & Spindler, L. (Eds.). (1989). *What do anthropologists have to say about dropouts?* New York: Falmer Press.

U.S. General Accounting Office. (1986). *School dropouts: Survey of local programs.* Washington, DC: Author.

U.S. Senate. (1969). *Indian Education: A national tragedy—a national challenge.* Washington, DC: U.S. Government Printing Office.

Van Ness, H. (1981). Social control and social organization in an Alaskan Athabaskan classroom: A microethnography of `getting ready' for reading. In H. Trueba, G. Guthrie, & K. Au (Eds.), *Culture and the bilingual classroom* (pp. 120—138). Rowley, MA: Newbury House.

Ward, C.J. (Ed.). (1993). Native American families [Special issue]. *Family Perspective, 27,* 305–503.

Watahomigie, L. (1988). *Hualapai bilingual academic excellence program: Blending tradition and technology model replication training manual.* Peach Springs, AZ: Peach Springs School District No. 8.

Watahomigie, L. (1992, April). *Discussant's comments: The power of American Indian communities.* Paper presented at the annual meeting of the American Educational Research Association, San Francisco, CA.

Watahomigie, J., & McCarty, T.L. (1994). Bilingual/bicultural education at Peach Springs: A Hualapai way of schooling. *Peabody Journal of Education, 69*, 26–42.

Watahomigie, L., & Yamamoto, Y. (1987). Linguistics in action: The Hualapai bilingual/bicultural education program. In D. D. Stull & J. J. Schensul (Eds.), *Collaborative research and social change: Applied anthropology in action* (pp. 77–98). Boulder, CO: Westview Press.

Wax, M. (1971). *Indian Americans: Unity and diversity.* Englewood Cliffs, NJ: Prentice Hall.

Wax, M., Wax, R., & Dumont, R., Jr. (1964). Formal education in an American Indian community [Special supplement]. *Social Problems, 11* (4).

Wax, M., Wax, R. & Dumont, R., Jr. (1989) *Formal education in an American Indian community.* Prospect Heights, IL: Waveland Press. (Original work published 1964)

Wax, R.H. (1976). Oglala Sioux dropouts and their problems with educators. In J. Roberts & S. Akinsanya (Eds.), *Schooling in the cultural context: Anthropological studies of education* (pp. 216–226). New York: David McKay.

Wehlage, G.G., & Rutter, R. (1986). Dropping out: How much do schools contribute to the problem? *Teachers College Record, 3*, 374–392.

Wells, R.H., Jr. (1991). *Indian education from the tribal perspective: A survey of American Indian tribal leaders.* Unpublished manuscript.

Werner, O., & Begishe, K. (1968, Augus). *Styles of learning: The evidence from Navajo.* Paper presented at the Conference on Styles of Learning in American Indian Children, Stanford, CA.

White House Conference on Indian Education. (1992). *The final report of the White House Conference on Indian Education (executive summary).* Washington, DC: Author.

Whiting, J.W., Chasdi, E.H., Antonovsky, H.F., & Ayres, B.C. (1975). The learning of values. In E. Vogt & E. Albert (Eds.), *People of Rimrock: A study of values in five cultures* (pp. 83–125). New York: Atheneum, 83–125.

Whittaker, J.O. (1963). Alcohol and the Standing Rock Sioux tribe: Psychodynamic and cultural factors in drinking. *Quarterly Journal of Studies of Alcohol, 24*, 80–90.

Wilson, P. (1991). Trauma of Sioux Indian high school students. *Anthropology & Education Quarterly, 22*, 367–386.

Witherspoon, Y.T. (1961). Measurement of Indian children's achievement in the academic tool subjects. *Journal of American Indian Education, 1*, 5–9.

Wolcott, H. (1967). *A Kwakiutl village and school.* New York: Holt, Rinehart & Winston.

Wolcott, H. (1984). *A Kwakiutl village and school.* Prospect Heights, IL: Waveland Press. (Original work published 1967)

Wolcott, H. (1987). The teacher as an enemy. In G. Spindler (Ed.), *Education and cultural process: Anthropological approaches* (pp. 136–150). Prospects Heights, IL: Waveland Press.

Yellowbird, M., & Snipp, C.M. (1994). American Indian families. In R.L. Taylor (Ed.), *Minority families in the United States* (pp. 179–201). Englewood Cliffs, NJ: Prentice Hall.

Zintz, M. (1960). *The Indian research study: The adjustment of Indian and non-Indian children in the public schools of New Mexico.* Albuquerque: College of Education, University of New Mexico.

Manuscript received October 27, 1995
Revision received December 1, 1995
Accepted December 6, 1995

Chapter 4

Critical Race Theory and Education: History, Theory, and Implications

WILLIAM F. TATE IV
University of Wisconsin—Madison

In 1993 President Clinton nominated Professor Lani Guinier of the University of Pennsylvania Law School to be assistant attorney general in charge of the Civil Rights Division. Her nomination for this government post resulted in a large controversy centering on her scholarship (Guinier, 1991a, 1991b). Guinier's research, which examined voting systems, asked the following question: Are there factors that guarantee winners and losers? She contended that such factors do exist and that race is too often an important factor in the construction of voting districts, the outcome of elections, and ultimately political influence, including the control of educational systems. Guinier (1989) argued that the political system must be rejuvenated to be more inclusive. Specifically, she called for the creation of electoral schemes that would allow Blacks to elect candidates representing their interests. These schemes—proportional voting, in particular—were already a reality in many southern localities and had received endorsement from the Reagan-Bush Justice Department and the Supreme Court. Professor Guinier also was critical of political bargaining between leading civil rights groups, African American politicians, and Republicans that resulted in the construction of guaranteed African American legislative districts and conservative White districts in adjacent jurisdictions. Guinier's position sparked great controversy among both liberals and conservatives.

In the epilogue of *Racial Formation in the United States*, Omi and Winant (1994) posited that this controversy had little to do with Guinier's position on the issue of voting districts; rather, her "sin" was her eagerness to discuss the changing dimensions of race in contemporary U.S. politics. Omi and Winant (1994) remarked:

Guinier's recognition that, in the post-civil rights era as previously, racial injustice still operates, that it has taken on new forms, and that it needs to be opposed if democracy is to advance, in our view located her in a far more realistic position. Guinier understood the flexibility of *racial identities and*

I would like to thank Michael Apple (editor) and Gloria Ladson-Billings (editorial consultant) for their feedback on this chapter. Also, a special thanks to Carl Grant, Ron Jetty, Kimberly Tate, and Jessica Trubek for their valuable assistance with this project.

politics [italics added], but also affirmed that racism still shapes the U.S. social structure in a wide-spread fashion. She resisted the idea of closing Pandora's box; in fact she denied the possibility of closing it, arguing the racial dimensions of U.S. politics are too complex, too basic, and too subtle to be downplayed for long. (p. 156)

Ladson-Billings and Tate (1995) asserted that, despite the salience of race in U.S. society, it remains untheorized as a topic of scholarly inquiry in education.[1] Over the past three decades, theoretical and philosophical considerations of gender have been delineated and debated (Chodorow, 1978; Damarin, 1995; DeBouvoir, 1961; Harding, 1986; Hartsock, 1979). Similarly, Marxist and neo-Marxist analyses of class continue to frame many explanations of social inequality (Apple, 1992; Bowles & Gintis, 1976; Carnoy, 1974; Frankenstein, 1987).[2] Although gender-and class-based analyses continue to struggle for legitimacy in academe, educational studies conceptualized on these theoretical precepts abound (see reviews by Ewert, 1991; B. M. Gordon, 1995; Noddings, 1990; Schmitz, Butler, Rosenfelt, & Guy-Sheftall, 1995).

Ladson-Billings and Tate (1995) recognized the importance of gender-and class-based analyses; however, they asserted that the significance of race in the United States, and more specifically "raced" education, could not be explained with theories of gender or class.[3] Similarly, McCarthy and Crichlow (1993) argued that

the subject of racial domination has, to say the least, been treated problematically in modern educational and social theories. Racial logics and mechanisms have been difficult to specify, their persistence difficult to explain, and their dynamics and trajectories difficult to predict. Indeed, the very slippery nature of what has come to be known in the educational literature as the "race question" challenges in fundamental ways the entire tapestry of curriculum and educational thought, particularly with respect to nonclass social antagonisms and domination relations in general. That is to say, the race question brings into the foreground omissions and blind spots. (p. xvii)[4]

These omissions and blind spots suggest the need for theoretical perspectives that move beyond the traditional paradigmatic boundaries of educational research to provide a more cogent analysis of "raced" people and move discussions of race and racism from the margins of scholarly activity to the fore of educational discourse. King (1995) stated:

Conceptual intervention in the educational research literature is needed to facilitate a systemic examination of scholarship that addresses ideological influence on knowledge in curriculum and education practice, particularly with regard to the education of Black people. (p. 270)

To this end, one important question for scholars interested in educational equity and the politics of education is, In what theoretical framework did Lani Guinier embed her analyses of race, voting systems, and political equality?[5] The answer to this question can be found in an emerging literature in legal discourse referred to as critical race theory (CRT). Calmore (1992) remarked:

As a form of oppositional scholarship, critical race theory challenges the universality of white experience/judgement as the authoritative standard that binds people of color and normatively measures, directs, controls, and regulates the terms of proper thought, expression, presentation, and behavior. As represented by legal scholars, critical race theory challenges the dominant discourses on race and racism as they relate to law. The task is to identify values and norms that have been disguised and subordinated in the law. As critical race scholars, we thus seek to demonstrate that our experiences as people of color are legitimate, appropriate, and effective bases for analyzing the legal system and racial subordination. This process is vital to our transformative vision. This theory-practice approach, a praxis, if you will, finds a variety of emphases among those who follow it. . . .

From this vantage, consider for a moment how law, society, and culture are texts—not so much like a literary work, but rather like the traditional black minister's citation of text as a verse or scripture that would lend authoritative support to the sermon he is about to deliver. Here, texts are not merely random stories; like scripture, they are expressions of authority, preemption, and sanction. People of color increasingly claim that these large texts of law, society, and culture must be subjected to fundamental criticism and reinterpretation. (pp. 2161–2162)

This chapter is structured around the exposition of various sources (authors of CRT articles and philosophers who influenced these authors), followed by commentaries that summarize and critique the more descriptive discussions. The reason for this unusual structure relates to the twofold purpose of the chapter. The first purpose is to describe the major theoretical elements undergirding CRT. The second purpose is to discuss the potential implications of this body of literature for the scholarly articulation of race and equity in educational policy and research. This discussion will offer a critique of CRT writing that asks whether the methods of analysis and argument, and the research agenda represented by the CRT scholarship described here, are valuable in two ways. First, do they provide insights capable of radically transforming educational policy or the study of education? Second, do they provide insights into equity issues in education that are substantial and novel?

OUTLINE OF THE DISCUSSION

This chapter does not include a comprehensive review of the wide range of topics analyzed by scholars employing tenets of CRT; rather, it attempts to outline elements of this theory especially relevant to educational researchers. With this in mind, the first topic explored is the paradigmatic kinship of educational research and the legal structures of U.S. society. The intent of this discussion is to describe how both educational research and legal structures contribute to existing belief systems and to legitimating social frameworks and policy that result in educational inequities for people of color. The section concludes with a call for conceptual intervention.

In the next section, the historical origins and shifting paradigmatic vision of CRT are discussed. CRT is a product of and response to one of the most politically active and successful eras of social change in the United States and cannot be divorced from it without losing analytical insight. The CRT movement in legal studies is rooted in the social missions and struggles of the 1960s that sought justice, liberation, and economic empowerment; thus, from its inception, it has had both academic and social activist goals. Furthermore, the movement is a response to the retrenching of civil rights gains and a changing social discourse in politics.

Fixing the origin of the CRT movement in the 1970s does not deny the pre-movement intellectual history and legal strategies that served as its foundation. Rather, this pre-1970s history both provides a rich resource of data on which to build and reflects an intellectual continuity central to the movement's mission.

The intellectual continuity of CRT should also be viewed as a shift in paradigm from critical legal studies (CLS). The distinctions between CRT and CLS are important for those interested in how race and racism are framed in intellectual discourse. Scholars using both methods of legal analysis have concurred that the law serves the interests of powerful groups in society; however, scholars in the CRT movement have argued that civil rights discourse in CLS does not adequately address the experiences of people of color. Ultimately, this argument serves as a point of departure between the two theoretically driven movements.

EDUCATIONAL RESEARCH AND THE LAW: RACED REPRESENTATIONS

The purpose of this section is to briefly describe how the law and educational research have been influenced by a paradigmatic view that characterizes people of color as inferior. Considerable debate has centered on the appropriateness of quantitative and qualitative research methodologies in educational research (Gage, 1989; Jacob, 1987; Schrag, 1992; Shulman, 1986). This debate has focused largely on ideology and conceptions of social science. Shulman argued that some of the ideological differences developed as a result of contrasting conceptions of education in general and teaching in particular; others developed in relation to views on acceptable forms of research; and yet others developed around political commitments. Research programs often are developed and accepted because of their consistency with favored ideological positions (Shulman, 1986). Earlier, Durkheim (1965) made a similar point when describing the role of theory in scholarly thought and society:

It is not at all true that concepts, even when constructed according to rules of science, get their authority uniquely from their objective value. It is not enough that they be true to get believed. If they are not in harmony with other beliefs and opinions, or, in a word, with a mass of other collective representations (the concepts taken for granted by most people in a given time and place), they will be denied; minds will be closed to them; consequently it will be as though they do not exist. (p. 486)

Durkheim's (1965) analysis suggests that, for a theory to become acceptable, it must be consistent with other representations or belief systems that reflect the prevailing cultural ethos of a people. Wynter (1995) argued that belief systems are mechanisms by which human orders are integrated on the basis of artificial or symbolic modes rather than on the basis of genetic modes of classification. Wynter stated that the systemic goal of belief systems is to motivate culture-specific ensembles of behavior rather than to deal with truth. Instead, truth is found in the behavior motivated by belief systems and the systemic effects to which the behaviors collectively lead.

The theories and belief systems predominant in education related to people of color and the representations of these citizens in American jurisprudence have shared a common trait. Both have been premised upon political, scientific, and religious theories relying on racial characterizations and stereotypes about people of color that help support a legitimating ideology and specific political action (Allport, 1954; Bullock, 1967; Cone, 1970; Marable, 1983; Takaki, 1993). Some of the earliest studies with educational implications centered on the intellectual assessment and school achievement of African American and other ethnic minority students (Hilliard, 1979; Kamin, 1974; Madaus, 1994). This research legacy, referred to as the inferiority paradigm, is built on the belief that people of color are biologically and genetically inferior to Whites (Carter & Goodwin, 1994; Gould, 1981; Selden, 1994).[6] The inferiority paradigm is characterized by its fluidity and dynamic nature, an ever-changing hegemonic discourse. However, despite its fluid nature, some scholars have attempted to describe elements of the inferiority paradigm.

Padilla and Lindholm (1995) argued that a set of identifiable characteristics inherent in the inferiority paradigm—particularly IQ studies—are still apparent today in educational research involving ethnic minorities. These complex, connected assumptions conform to a societal disposition that makes them appear natural and appealing. The identifiable assumptions of this paradigm are as follows: (a) The White middle-class American (often male) serves as the standard against which other groups are compared; (b) the instruments used to measure differences are universally applied across all groups, with perhaps slight adjustments for culturally diverse populations; and (c) although we need to recognize sources of potential variance such as social class, gender, cultural orientation, and proficiency in English, these factors are viewed as extraneous and can later be ignored (Padilla & Lindholm, 1995). Other scholars also have recognized these assumptions and viewed them as biased against African Americans, Latinos, and other ethnic minorities (Lightfoot, 1980; Pang, 1995; Rodrìguez, 1995).

In *Minority Students: A Research Appraisal*, Weinberg (1977) argued that educational research studies should move beyond the conceptual frameworks associated with the inferiority paradigm. Moreover, he contended that educational research concerning children of color should include (a) pertinent historical and legal background, (b) the ideology of racism, (c) a continuing reexamination of prevailing views of the role of race and social class in learning, and (d) the influence of minority communities on schools.

Although many scholars have called for a change in the way educational research is conducted in communities of color, the influence of past research is persistent (e.g., Lomawaima, 1995; Moran & Hakuta, 1995). Carter and Goodwin (1994) stated:

The conventional belief in the intellectual inferiority of visible racial/ethnic individuals has had a powerful impact on educational policy and curriculum development since before the 1800s. Because differences in achievement between White and non-White students were assumed to be genetically based, the inferiority paradigm allowed slavery to be condoned, which resulted in racial/ethnic groups, particularly Blacks and Indians, being considered uneducable and barred from formal or adequate schooling. . . . The inferiority paradigm continues to manifest itself in the quality of education offered non-White children. (p. 296)

The assumptions of the inferiority paradigm have not been limited to discussions by the educational research community. The assumed intellectual inferiority of African Americans, Native Americans, Latinos, and other people of color also has a long history in the legal discourse of the United States (Clay, 1993; Takaki, 1993). In fact, a relationship exists between educational research built on assumptions of the inferiority paradigm and the construction of education-related policy and law (Elliot, 1987). For example, Arthur Jensen (1969) illustrated the interrelationship between science and public policy in an article in the *Harvard Educational Review*. Charged by the editors of the journal to consider why compensatory education programs of the "War on Poverty" had not produced better results, Jensen argued that the programs were bound to have disappointing results because the target population of students—disproportionately African American—had relatively low IQ scores. Similarly, Hernstein and Murray (1994) argued that society has experienced and continues to experience a dramatic transformation resulting in a group of largely White cognitive elite:

The twentieth century dawned on a world segregated into social classes defined in terms of money, power, and status. The ancient lines of separation based on hereditary rank are being erased, replaced by a more complicated set of overlapping lines. . . . Our thesis is that the twentieth century has continued the transformation, so that the twenty-first will open on a world in which cognitive ability is the decisive dividing force. The shift is more subtle than the previous one but more momentous. Social class remains the vehicle of social life, but intelligence now pulls the train. (p. 25)

Herrnstein and Murray (1994) posited that low intelligence is at the root of society's social ills, and policy formulation must take this into consideration. The arguments of both Jensen (1969) and Herrnstein and Murray (1994) have been subjected to considerable scholarly critique (e.g., Fraser, 1995; Gould, 1994; Hilliard, 1984; Hirsch, 1975); however, their position reflects an ideology with a long history in Western civilization (Gould, 1981). Of importance here is the binary opposition of White-Black (Allen, 1974; Anderson, 1994; Crenshaw, 1988): Whites are an intelligent, diligent, and deserving people; Blacks are a simple, lazy, and undeserving people. These socially constructed representations of subjective identity have categorized specific groups of society in terms of perceived abilities to think logically and justified the construction of oppressive social policy and law that reflect these categories (Jefferson, 1954).[7]

Perhaps nowhere is this reality more obvious than in the development of the Constitution (Black, 1988). It would be difficult to understand the construction of law without understanding the individual and collective mind-set of the original framers of American law. Anderson (1994) argued that the men who constructed the Constitution formed the foundation for the subordination and exploitation of African Americans. In 1786, the framers of the Constitution laid the legal groundwork for a White-Black binary opposition by (a) counting Blacks as three fifths of a person, (b) delaying for 20 years the effective date for outlawing the slave trade, and (c) obligating the government to uphold fugitive slave laws and to use its troops to end Black insurrections and violence. Thus, by constitutional law, the federal government was legally empowered to support a cultural ethos of African American inferiority manifested as slavery.[8] Harold Cruse (1984) stated:

> The legal Constitution of American society recognizes the rights, privileges and aspirations of the individual, while America has become a nation dominated by the social powers of various ethnic and religious groups. The reality of the power struggles between competing ethnic or religious groups is that an individual has few rights and opportunities in America that are not backed up by the political and social power of one group or another. (pp. 7–8)

Cruse's (1984) argument is consistent with the laws, policies, and folkways that have regulated education. For a majority of the 1800s, laws in many states prohibited the education of African Americans. For instance, teaching a Black person to read would lead to fines, imprisonment, or flogging for the educator. These laws were partly a product of White capitalists attempting to secure control over an important means of their economic growth: slavery (Marable, 1983). However, these laws cannot be separated from the inferiority paradigm in education. The following excerpt from the *Dred Scott v. Sanford* decision of 1857 illustrates the relationship between American jurisprudence and the inferiority paradigm:

> They had for more than a century before been regarded as . . . so far inferior . . . that the negro might justly and lawfully be reduced to slavery for his benefit. . . . This opinion was at that time fixed and universal in the civilized portion of the white race. It was regarded as an axiom of morals as in politics, which no one thought of disputing . . . and men in every grade and position in society daily and habitually acted upon it . . . without doubting for a moment the correctness of this opinion. (p. 407)

The power and danger of the inferiority paradigm, and paradigms in general, is that its adherents often fail to seek different conceptions. Oh and Wu (1996) stated:

> A conservative Congress or an electorate voting on a ballot proposition might believe the arguments and accept the public policy proposals advanced in *The Bell Curve* and *Alien Nation*, which argue, respectively, that race determines intelligence which in turn, determines socioeconomic success, and that the nation has been and should remain racially White and culturally homogeneous. With enough social science and empirical data, courts could sustain those [discriminatory] laws. Moreover, the courts may be compelled to sustain those laws because they would lack authority to take an approach that was more critical or that deviated from legal ratification of statistical data. The courts are *limited* [italics added] by the data. (p. 186)

Instead, the concepts and theories of the "accepted" paradigm influence social problem solving, policy development, policy interpretation, and policy implementation. For example, in his analysis of the *Brown* decision, Lawrence (1993) argued that *Brown* should be viewed as an attempt to regulate societal conceptions of African American inferiority:

The key to this understanding of *Brown* is that the practice of segregation, the practice the Court held inherently unconstitutional, was *speech*. *Brown* held that segregation is unconstitutional not simply because the physical separation of Black and white children is bad or because resources were distributed unequally among Black and white schools. *Brown* held that segregated schools were unconstitutional primarily because of the *message* segregation conveys—the message that Black children are an untouchable caste, unfit to be educated with white children. Segregation serves its purpose by conveying an idea. It stamps inferiority upon Blacks, and this badge communicates a message to others in the community, as well as to Blacks wearing the badge, that is injurious to Blacks. Therefore, *Brown* may be read as regulating the content of racist speech. As a regulation of racist speech, the decision is an exception to the usual rule that regulation of speech content is presumed unconstitutional. (p. 59)

Carter and Goodwin's (1994) review of social scientific paradigms revealed that social scientists have historically used race as a determinant of intellectual and educational aptitude. Similarly, the framers and interpreters (i.e., policymakers) of our legal system have used race as a factor in the construction and implementation of laws influencing education (Bell, 1987; Omi & Winant, 1994). Both educational research and law have often characterized "raced" people as intellectually inferior and raised doubts about the benefit of equitable social investment in education and other social services (Ford & Webb, 1994; Herrnstein & Murray, 1994). This paradigmatic kinship built on conceptions of inferiority suggests the need for a theory that explicates the role of race in education and law.

A GENESIS OF CRITICAL RACE THEORY

It is important to view the origins of CRT from both a historical and philosophical perspective. A historical perspective is required to provide a context for understanding the origins of contemporary legal debates concerning the effectiveness of past civil rights strategies in today's political climate. For example, current discussions of equal opportunity and "color blindness" have little meaning unless framed historically (Culp, 1991). Over the years, both concepts were guiding principles for a model of equality closely aligned with the dominant view of justice (Aleinikoff, 1991; Ming, 1948). However, the complexity of civil rights doctrine can be seen by examining the concept of color blindness.

Justice Harlan's dissenting opinion in the case of *Plessy v. Ferguson* (1896) reflects a normative principle of color blindness that runs deep in American civil rights discourse:

In view of the Constitution, in the eye of the law, there is in this country no superior, dominant, ruling class of citizens. There is no caste system here. Our Constitution is *color-blind* [italics added], and neither knows nor tolerates classes among citizens. In respect of civil rights all citizens are equal before the law. (p. 559)

From Justice Harlan's dissent to Martin Luther King's desire that his children be judged by the "content of their character" rather than the "color of their skin," the color-blind principle has existed in civil rights discourse. Moreover, despite what may appear to be an obvious tension between race-conscious and color-blind principles, individual supporters of race-conscious measures may actually be guided by logic associated with a color-blind philosophy. For example, many liberal advocates of race-conscious measures justify the implementation of affirmative action policy on the basis of past violations of the color-blind principle (Aleinikoff, 1991). One example is Justice Blackmun's dissenting opinion in the *Bakke* decision (*Regents of the University of California v. Bakke*, 1978). He argued, "In order to get beyond racism [to color blindness], we must first take account of race. There is no other way" (p. 407).

Similarly, many conservative advocates of color-blind measures cannot ignore the importance of race. For example, Speaker of the House Newt Gingrich, an outspoken supporter of color-blind policy, argued that Blacks, like the Irish, Italians, and Jews before them, must overcome oppression with hard work (Pitts, 1995). When asked what he would tell a Black child growing up in America, Gingrich responded: "If you're black, you have to work harder, and if you're black and poor, you have to work twice as hard" (Pitts, 1995, p. 3A). In his remarks, Speaker of the House Gingrich acknowledged the reality of racial inequality; however, his color-blind approach to policy-making impeded him from moving beyond the recommendation of "pulling yourself up by your boot-straps." Congressman Gingrich's remark reflects a paradox by many who assert strongly they are color blind: To be color blind in this way requires race consciousness; one must notice race. Aleinikoff (1991) described the process:

It is apparently important, as a matter of widespread cultural practice, for whites to assert that they are strongly colorblind, in the sense that they do not notice or act on the basis of race. One can see this at work in such statements as: "I judge each person as an individual." Of course, it cannot be that whites do not notice the race of others. Perhaps what is being said is that the speaker does not begin her evaluation with any preconceived notions. But this too is difficult to believe, given the deep and implicit ways in which our minds are color-coded. To be truly color blind in this way . . . requires color-consciousness: one must notice race in order to tell oneself not to trigger the usual mental processes that take race into account. (p. 1079)

Many legal and political scholars of color question whether the philosophical underpinnings of traditional liberal civil rights discourse—a color-blind approach—are capable of supporting continued movement toward social justice in a climate of retrenchment (e.g., Lawrence, 1987; Wilkins, 1995; P. J. Williams, 1991). In fact, some critical race theorists argue that there is little difference between conservative and liberal discourse on race-related law and policy. Crenshaw and colleagues (1995) remarked:

Liberals and conservatives seemed to see issues of race and law from within the same structure of analysis—namely, a policy that legal rationality could identify and eradicate the biases of race-consciousness in social decision-making. Liberals and conservatives as a general matter differed over the degree to which racial bias was a fact of American life: liberals argued that bias was widespread where conservatives insisted it was not; liberals supported a disparate effect test for identifying discrimination, where conservatives advocated a more restricted intent requirement; liberals wanted an expanded state action requirement, whereas conservatives wanted a narrow one. The respective visions of the two factions differed only in scope: they defined and constructed "racism" the same way, as the opposite of color-blindness. (Crenshaw, Gotanda, Peller, & Thomas, 1995, p. xvii)

Critical race scholars find themselves questioning the philosophical underpinnings of civil rights discourse during a period of ideological attack from the right by neoconservatives seeking to eliminate past civil rights gains. Thus, to understand CRT within legal discourse it is important to recognize this scholarship as a critique of both liberal and conservative legal ideologies.

ONE HISTORICAL OVERVIEW[9]

The United States has a long history of attempting to use the courts and legal remedies to resolve racial injustice (Allen, 1974; *Roberts v. City of Boston*, 1850). However, by the turn of the 20th century the doctrine of "separate but equal" was the law of the land (*Plessy v. Ferguson*, 1896). The separate-but-equal doctrine reflected the prevailing social temperament, a belief in the inherent inferiority of African Americans that made it impossible for Whites to see themselves sharing public accommodations with Blacks (Bogle, 1989; *Dred Scott v. Sandford*, 1857; Jefferson, 1954; Peters, 1982; Selden, 1994). African Americans in the South were required by law to use racially segregated schools, trains, streetcars, hotels, barbershops, restaurants, and other public accommodations. The job market was also segregated, resulting in low-paying employment opportunities for African Americans (Margo, 1990). Moreover, African Americans were denied political equality by restrictive voting laws. The flawed legal concept of separate but equal resulted in the maintenance of African American subordination (Tate, Ladson-Billings, & Grant, 1993).

The need for legal remedies to address this subordinate position was articulated by Carter G. Woodson (1933/1990).[10] However, he argued that many African American lawyers were not prepared to litigate and resolve issues of race and American law:

There are, moreover, certain aspects of law to which the white man would hardly address himself but to which the Negro should direct special attention. Of unusual importance to the Negro is the necessity for understanding the misrepresentations in criminal records of Negroes, and race distinctions in the laws of modern nations. These matters require a systemic study of the principles of law and legal procedure and, in addition thereto, further study of legal problems as they meet the Negro lawyer in the life which he must live. This offers the Negro law school an unusual opportunity. (p. 174)

Woodson was not the only intellectual to recognize the need for African American professionals capable of fighting racial injustice (see, e.g., Bullock, 1967).[11] A case in point is that of Mordecai W. Johnson. In 1926, Dr. Johnson was appointed to the presidency of Howard University, a historically Black college. He brought a set of strict academic standards to the position and a commitment to fight social inequities (Davis & Clark, 1992). Johnson recruited some of the nation's finest scholars. Moreover, on the advice of Supreme Court Justice Louis Brandeis, the new president moved to develop a first-rate law school to address racism and the law. Brandeis remarked, "Build a law school and train men to get the constitutional rights of [your] people. Once you train lawyers to do this, the

Supreme Court will have to hand your people their civil rights" (as cited in Davis & Clark, 1992, p. 47).

Johnson responded by hiring Charles Hamilton Houston to rebuild the law school with a focus on creating a cadre of lawyers capable of challenging racial injustice. An outstanding legal scholar, Houston was credited with the development of a social engineering approach to achieving racial equality (McNeil, 1983). Nathaniel Jones, judge of the United States Court of Appeals for the Sixth Circuit and former general counsel of the NAACP, remarked:

> It was Charles Hamilton Houston who persuasively argued that one of the most effective means of educating the public, of building political coalitions, and thereby obtaining meaningful change, was through litigation. Moreover, it was his view that litigation under the Fourteenth Amendment could be a powerful means of racial minorities to confront governmental authorities with their duty to act on behalf of those whose constitutional rights were being denigrated. He initiated litigation on a broad front and carried it forward. (as cited in Jones, 1993, p. 98)

After rebuilding Howard University's Law school, Houston resigned his deanship to assume the position of chief counsel of the NAACP, with responsibility for organizing the NAACP's campaign against legalized racial discrimination. Incorporating the meta-strategy of social engineering vis-à-vis litigation, Houston and his colleagues at the NAACP won impressive legal victories that led to changes in the nature of race relations in the United States (e.g., *Brown v. Board of Education*, 1954; *McLaurin v. Oklahoma State Regents for Higher Education*, 1950; *Missouri ex rel. Gaines v. Canada*, 1938; *Sipuel v. Board of Regents of the University of Oklahoma*, 1948).

During his tenure as chief counsel of the NAACP, Houston hired Thurgood Marshall, his former student at Howard University Law School and a protégé in the NAACP, to assist with the implementation of the social engineering litigation strategy. In 1938, Houston's health forced him to leave the NAACP (Davis & Clark, 1992). At the age of 30, Thurgood Marshall replaced Charles Houston as chief counsel of the NAACP. Marshall continued the path charted by Houston of using carefully planned lawsuits to challenge the doctrine of separate but equal. The social engineering strategy ultimately led to the *Brown* (1954) lawsuit and a decision that helped legally overturn *Plessy v. Ferguson* (1896).

A few years after the *Brown* decision, Thurgood Marshall, then director-counsel of the NAACP Legal Defense Fund, visited Pittsburgh, where Derrick Bell, a lawyer by training, was serving as executive director of an NAACP branch (Bell, 1993). Marshall offered Bell a position on his staff, and Bell accepted. From Marshall and from NAACP general counsel Robert L. Carter, Bell (1993) learned that "the role of the civil rights lawyer was not simply to understand the legal rules but to fashion arguments that might change existing laws" (p. 75). Thus, Derrick Bell received first-hand experience in Charles Houston's meta-strategy of using litigation to socially engineer civil rights. Moreover, it is this experience that Bell brought to his academic career in law.

The connection between Derrick Bell the civil rights lawyer and Derrick Bell the academic is important in chronicling the origins and philosophical undergirdings of CRT. In 1969, Bell accepted a position on the law faculty of Harvard University. In his negotiations with the dean of the law school, Bell (1994) made it clear that he viewed teaching as an opportunity to continue his civil rights work in a new arena. His legal scholarship was greatly influenced by his perspective as a Black man and his experience as a practicing civil rights lawyer. Bell (1994) noted, "Practitioners, often through storytelling and a more subjective, personal voice, examine ways in which the law has been shaped by and shapes issues of race" (p. 171). His methods of writing about race and law were at the forefront of a new school of scholarly thought in law: critical race theory. However, it is not possible to separate Bell's scholarship and CRT from the African American scholarship that emerged during and after the civil rights movement.

Although no identifiable date can be assigned to the conception of CRT, its foundation is linked to the development of African American thought in the post—civil rights era: the 1970s to the present (Bell, 1980a, 1980b; Matsuda, Lawrence, Delgado, & Crenshaw, 1993). The civil rights movement of the 1960s had slowed, and many opportunities associated with the movement were under attack (e.g., *Regents of the University of California v. Bakke*, 1978). Many scholars and activists of this era noted the limitations of achieving justice using dominant conceptions of race, racism, and social equality. For example, Ladner (1973) in sociology, Cone (1970) in theology, Allen (1974) in political science, and Banks (1971) in education all moved beyond the traditional paradigmatic boundaries of their fields to provide a more cogent analysis of the African American experience. This boundary crossing represents a significant contribution of the Black studies movement to the academic community.

This intellectual movement permeated the boundaries of legal education as law professors and teachers committed to racial justice began to correspond, meet, talk, and engage in political action in an effort to resist institutional structures that facilitated racism while claiming the objective of racial harmony and equality (Matsuda et al., 1993). Thus, the foundation of CRT as a movement and as an intellectual agenda was connected to the development of the new approach to examining race, racism, and law in the post—civil rights period (Barnes, 1990; Crenshaw, 1988). Matsuda and colleagues (1993) stated, "Both the movement and the theory reflected assertions of a community of values that were inherited from generations of radical teachers before us" (p. 3). CRT should be understood as an effort to build upon and extend the legal scholarship and activism that led to the civil rights movement rather than an attack on the thinking and efforts associated with the legal scholarship and strategies of that era (Crenshaw, 1988).

SHIFTING PARADIGMS: BEYOND CRITICAL LEGAL STUDIES

The development of CRT cannot be fully understood without a description of its relationship to the CLS movement.[12] According to Matsuda and colleagues

(1993), many legal scholars of color sought refuge within this intellectual community. The CLS movement emerged in the late 1970s as a small group of academics devoted their scholarly efforts to reappraising the merits of the realist tradition in legal discourse. Livingston (1982) described realism as a dominant philosophical influence on American legal thought for most of the 1920s and 1930s (see also White, 1972). The realist movement developed out of dissatisfaction with tenets of classical legal thought that cast judicial decision as the product of reasoning from a finite set of determined rules (White, 1972).[13] In contrast, the realists argued that legal rules were limited and could not guide courts to definite answers in specific cases (Llwellyn, 1931). Moreover, the realists contended that legal scholarship failed to recognize the impact of social forces on legal change and discourse.

Legal realists built on the philosophical traditions of pragmatism, instrumentalism, and progressivism. Closely connected to the New Deal, the realists supported the notion of identifying a coherent public interest and aligning political strategies to further it (Lasswell & McDougal, 1943). To support the development of political strategy, the realists advocated removing the dogmas of legal theory that obstructed law reform and substituting a "rational, scientific" method of legal scholarship (Livingston, 1982). Specifically, the realists asserted that the application of behavioral sciences and statistical method to legal analysis would lead to better and more creative forms of legal thought and, ultimately, social policy.

Livingston (1982) provided insight into the connection between the realist tradition and CLS:

Legal Realism was not simply a clarion call for energetic empiricism, however, but also the herald of a characteristic critical methodology oriented toward pragmatic policy reform. Today's critical legal scholar can claim a particularly close kinship to Realist forebears in adoption of the Realists' twin orientations toward an iconoclastic historiography and a rigorous analytic jurisprudence. The work of critical legal scholars can be understood as the maturation of these Realist methodologies—maturation in which critical scholars explore incoherences at the level of social or political theory and critical scholarship is linked, not to reformist policy programs, but to a radical political agenda. (pp. 1676–1677)

In broadest terms, scholars within the CLS movement have attempted to analyze legal ideology and discourse as a mechanism that functions to re-create and legitimate social structures in the United States. Critical legal scholars constructed their view of legal ideology in part from the scholarship of Antonio Gramsci, an Italian neo-Marxist theorist who conceptualized a framework to analyze domination that transcended the perceived limitations of traditional Marxist analyses (Collins, 1982).[14] More traditional Marxist accounts described the law as a vehicle that supports oppression and assists in the pacification of the working class. Borrowing from Gramsci, CLS scholars argued that this instrumental perspective is limited because it fails to account for the significant support the state and legal system receive from the dominated classes.[15]

According to Unger (1983), scholarship within the CLS movement is distinguished by two main tendencies.[16] The first tendency views past or contemporary legal doctrine as a particular perspective of society while illustrating its internal contradictions (usually by exposing the incoherence of legal arguments) and its external inconsistencies (often by describing the contradictory political views embedded in legal doctrine). The second tendency developed out of the social theories of Marx and Weber and the mode of political analysis that combines functionalist methods with radical goals (Unger, 1983).[17]

Both tendencies undergird the theoretical challenges to the dominant style of legal doctrine and the legal theories that support this style. More specifically, CLS is a critique of formalism and objectivism. Unger (1983) described formalism as a belief in the possibility of a method of legal justification that can be contrasted to open-ended debates that are philosophical or ideological. Although philosophical debates may not totally lack criteria, they fail to maintain the level of rationality that the formalist claims for legal reasoning. Formalism is characterized by impersonal purposes, policies, and principles that serve as the foundation for legal reasoning. According to Unger, formalism in the traditional sense—the search for a method of deduction from a coherent system of principles—is only the "anomalous, limiting case of this jurisprudence" (p. 564). Objectivism is the belief that the legal system—statutes, cases, and accepted legal concepts—represents and sustains a defensible framework of human association (Unger, 1983). It provides, although not infallibly, an intelligible moral order.

The CLS critique of formalism and objectivism has led to a far-ranging attack on American legal and social institutions, including the bar, legal reasoning, rights (including civil rights), precedent, doctrine, hierarchy, meritocracy, the prevailing liberal vision, and conventional views of the free market (Brosnan, 1986; Delgado, 1987; R. W. Gordon, 1984; Hutchinson & Monahan, 1984; Stick, 1986). The focus and method of CLS critique have been seen as positive to scholars within the CRT movement. However, many critical race scholars have noted the limitations of the CLS critique for matters of race and the law.

Delgado (1987) and P. J. Williams (1987) argued that the CLS critique of the social order demonstrates that current configurations and distributions of power are neither necessary nor natural and that hierarchy irrationally results in part from judicial support and authority. Similarly, critical race scholarship has employed critiques of formalism. For example, Greene (1995) argued that a series of 1989 Supreme Court decisions involving civil rights issues were built on formalistic interpretations that ignored contextual reality and the impact on traditional victims of racial discrimination. Thus, Greene illustrated the importance and appeal of critiquing formalism within the critical race movement. However, both Delgado (1987, 1988a) and Williams (1987) posited that the CLS position on rights-based theory is especially problematic for people of color seeking justice. Williams (1987) stated:

There are many good reasons for abandoning a system of rights which are premised on inequality and helplessness; yet despite the acknowledged and compelling force of such reasons, most blacks have not turned away from the pursuit of rights even if what CLS scholars say about rights—that they are contradictory, indeterminate, reified and marginally decisive—is so. I think this has happened because the so-called "governing narrative," or metalanguage, about the significance of rights is quite different for whites and blacks. (p. 404)

Williams (1987) argued that for most Whites, including the mostly White elite of CLS, social relationships are influenced by a world view that links achievement to committed self-control. In contrast, for many Blacks, including academics, lawyers, and legal clients, relationships are viewed frequently as a function of historical patterns of physical and psychic dispossession. According to Williams (1987), this difference is both semantic and substantive; moreover, it is reflected in how the CLS critique has ignored the extent to which rights assertion and the benefits of rights have helped people of color and the underclass of society. Williams (1987) was careful not to idealize the importance of rights in a society in which rights often are selectively employed to create boundaries. However, she contended that to condone analyses that symbolically diminish the significance of rights is to participate in one's own disempowerment.

Delgado (1987) contended that much of the misfit between the CLS program and the agenda of people of color is a product of the informality of the CLS program. According to Delgado (1987), CLS themes and methods criticize formal structures such as rights, rules, and bureaucracies while promoting informal processes that build on goodwill, intersubjective understanding, and community. Delgado (1987) argued that the danger of structureless processes is an increased likelihood of prejudice, a threat CLS theorists avoided reckoning with given their lack of political or psychological theory concerning race and racism (see also Crenshaw, 1988; Delgado, 1984). Instead, CLS theory simply assumes that racism is analogous to other forms of class-based oppression, largely a function of hierarchal social structure (Bell, 1984; Crenshaw, 1988; Delgado, 1987).

Delgado (1987) named three other elements of the CLS movement that were a threat to people of color. First, he objected to the rejection by some CLS scholars of incremental reform. This rejection of incremental reform is built on the theoretical premise that an unfair society uses piecemeal reform as a disguise to legitimize oppression. Delgado (1987) argued that this critique was imperialistic in that it tells people of color how to interpret events in their lives. Moreover, it diminishes the role incremental change can play in catalyzing more revolutionary change. It is worthy to note that, in a later article, Delgado (1990) argued that a theme of CRT was to question the basic premises of moderate/incremental civil rights law. However, the CRT argument against incremental civil rights law is often based on experiential knowledge and personal interpretation by people of color rather than on strictly theoretical proposition.

Second, Delgado (1987) asserted that the CLS program is idealistic; that is, it assigns a large role to reason and ideology. However, reason and ideology alone do not explain all evil. Specifically, racism will not be understood or go away because critical legal scholarship shows that legalisms are indeterminate, rights are alienating and legitimizing, and the law reflects the interest of the power structure.

Third, Delgado (1987) challenged the CLS concept of false consciousness. The notion of false consciousness suggests that workers and people of color buy into a system that degrades and oppresses them and defend the system with a kind of false honor. Delgado (1987) questioned whether the concept of false consciousness holds true for people of color. Much of the CLS argument concerning false consciousness represents a distrust of liberal legalism and evasive promises of court victory. Delgado posited that many minorities have already acquired this distrust, a product of life's lessons. The aforementioned arguments represent important points of departure between the CLS and CRT movements.

CRITICAL RACE THEORY

The elements that characterize CRT are difficult to reduce to discrete descriptions, largely because critical race theorists are attempting to integrate their experiential knowledge into moral and situational analysis of the law. Delgado (1990) argued that people of color in our society speak from experience framed by racism. This framework gives their stories a common structure warranting the term *voice*. For the critical race theorist, social reality is constructed by the creation and exchange of stories about individual situations (Bell, 1989; Matsuda, 1989; P. J. Williams, 1991). Much of the CRT literature tacks between situated narrative and more sweeping analysis of the law. Many of the arguments found in CRT are best described as an enactment of hybridity in their texts, that is, scholarship that depicts the legal scholar as minimally bicultural in terms of belonging to both the world of legal research and the world of everyday experience.[18] Barnes (1990) stated:

Minority perspectives make explicit the need for fundamental change in the ways we think and construct knowledge. . . . Exposing how minority cultural viewpoints differ from white cultural viewpoints requires a delineation of the complex set of social interactions through which minority consciousness has developed. Distinguishing the consciousness of racial minorities requires acknowledgement of the feelings and intangible modes of perception unique to those who have historically been socially, structurally, and intellectually marginalized in the United States. (p. 1864)

The notion of voice in the critical race literature and the form of legal analysis associated with this scholarship have implications for the organization of this section of the chapter. To understand the CRT literature, it is important to understand the voice of a particular contributor within the critical race conversation.[19] Thus, three legal scholars who employ CRT methods will be reviewed: Derrick Bell, Richard Delgado, and Kimberlé Crenshaw. Each of these scholars has made a significant contribution to the CRT literature. Moreover, each was chosen because his or her scholarship uniquely intersects with important issues raised in debates of race and the politics of education. However, the review will not be limited to these three scholars. Scholarship that is a part of the CRT conversation and builds on or is critical of the arguments made by Bell, Delgado, and Crenshaw will be incorporated to provide a more comprehensive view of the theoretical underpinnings of CRT.

Derrick Bell and the Critical Race Theory

The ideas of Derrick Bell are key to understanding the CRT movement because, within this group of scholars, Bell is arguably the most influential source of thought critical of traditional civil rights discourse and a premier example of CRT. Bell's critique of civil rights laws and efforts to implement them was stimulated by a recognition of their importance and a challenge to rethink dominant liberal and conservative positions on these matters. Bell's (1984) description of the goal of his book *Race, Racism and American Law* provides insight into the purpose of his scholarship:

It is, though, not the goal of *Race, Racism* to provide a social formula that would solve either all or any of the racial issues that beset the country. Rather, its goal is to review those issues in *all* [italics added] their political and economic dimensions, and from that vantage point enable lawyers and lay people to determine where we might go from here. The goal for us, as it was for all those back to the slavery era who labored and sacrificed for freedom, was not to guarantee an end to racism, but to work forcefully toward that end. (p. 14)

Bell's (1984) remark reveals the dual purpose of his scholarship. His first purpose has been to contribute to intellectual discussions concerning race in American society. However, unlike many mainstream legal scholars who often have declared that certain aspects of a legal problem are not relevant—for example, particular stories of individuals—Bell (1987, 1994) has sought to use allegory as a method to examine legal discourse in an ironically situated fashion. In his critique of narrative and law, and more specifically the scholarship of Derrick Bell, Winter (1989) posited:

The attraction of narrative is that it corresponds more closely to the manner in which the human mind makes sense of experience than does the conventional, abstracted rhetoric of law. The basic thrust of the cognitive process is to employ imagination to make meaning out of the embodied experience of the human organism in the world. In its prototypical sense as storytelling, narrative, too, proceeds from the ground up. In narrative, we take experience and configure it in a conventional and comprehensible form. This is what gives narrative its communicative power; it is what makes narrative a powerful tool of persuasion and therefore, a potential *transformative* [italics added] device for the disempowered. (p. 2228)

A second purpose of Bell's scholarship has been to promote political activism to achieve racial justice. This goal can be found throughout his chain of inquiry (e.g., Bell, 1987, 1989, 1992, 1994). For instance, in the preface to *Confronting Authority: Reflections of an Ardent Protester*, Bell (1994) stated:

This book does not aim to convince readers that a passive response to harassment and ill treatment is always wrong, a confrontational one always appropriate. Few, if any, of us could survive in modern society by challenging every slight, every unfairness we experience or witness. I do believe, though, that most people are too ready to accept unwarranted and even outrageous treatment as part of the price of working, of getting along, even of living. (p. x)

After warning the reader about the difficulty of a protester's life, Bell (1994) remarked: "Of course, I will be pleased if my experiences encourage readers to consider openly confronting wrongs that afflict their lives, and the lives of others" (p. xi). Many scholars associated with CRT have attributed Bell's scholarly methods, political activism, and mentorship as pivotal to the movement's development (Barnes, 1990; Calmore, 1992; Crenshaw, 1988; Delgado, 1991). His work provides a model and a standard by which to discuss CRT.

For example, Bell's (1987) *And We Are Not Saved*, an expansion of his 1985 *Harvard Law Review* essay, "The Civil Rights Chronicles," is about the legal barriers to racial justice in the United States.[20] Bell employed a scholarly method to express matters of jurisprudence in a language and style more usual in literature than in legal discourse. Through the vehicle of 10 "chronicles," metaphorical tales devised to illuminate society's treatment of race, combined with discussions of those tales by the book's protagonist and his alter ego, Geneva Crenshaw, Bell explored societal tendencies with respect to race-remedy law.

To understand the discussions that take place between Geneva and the narrator, it is important to know Geneva's background. As depicted in the book, Geneva had been a civil rights lawyer at the NAACP Legal Defense Fund. She is described as one of the most gifted of the fund's litigators until she suffered a mental breakdown caused by a heavy workload, racist violence, and the pressure of battling for legal remedies that often seemed to recede. Geneva was committed to a mental institution for 20 years, during which her thinking raced, out of touch with reality. As the book begins, Geneva regains her mental faculties. She leaves the mental institution and searches for Bell's narrator in an attempt to become current with, and come to terms with, race-related civil rights law.

The book develops by having Geneva revisit visionary chronicles (she presents 9 of the 10) and then debate them with Bell's narrator. The chronicles and subsequent debate between Geneva and the narrator provide the reader an opportunity to explore the progress of race relations law in the United States. For instance, in "The Chronicle of the Constitutional Contradiction," Geneva journeys back to the Constitutional Convention of 1787. Addressing the delegates, she introduces herself as a Black woman from the 21st century. The delegates listen to her compelling argument about the historical legacy of slavery and the compromises they are prepared to enact, but in the end they compromise the rights of Blacks on the basis of national economic interests and White unity.

The narrator and Geneva then discuss how these compromises frame current racial politics:

The men who drafted the Constitution, however gifted or remembered as great, were politicians, not so different from the politicians of our own time and, like them, had to resolve conflicting interests in order to preserve both their fortunes and their new nation. What they saw as the requirements of that nation prevented them from substantiating their rhetoric about freedom and rights with constitutional provisions—and thus they infringed on the rights and freedom not only of slaves, who then were one-fifth of the population, but ultimately, of all American citizens. (Bell, 1987, p. 50)[21]

In another chapter, "The Chronicle of the Sacrificed Black Schoolchildren," Bell (1987) considers the influence of litigation, specifically the *Brown* decision, on the educational experiences of African American children. At the completion of the tale, Geneva and the narrator discuss the limitations and strengths of the NAACP litigation strategy, the goal of racial integration that led to *Brown*, and the failure of court-mandated school desegregation to achieve educational equality. The debate between the narrator and Geneva represents a long-standing argument in the African American community: Is segregated or desegregated education best for African American children? This question, never stated yet implicit in the subtext of the chronicle, results in a dialogue on the philosophy undergirding various positions taken on the question.

The narrator defends the position taken by civil rights litigators in the pre-*Brown* era who sought to eliminate the social doctrine of separate but equal by attacking segregation in public schools. The narrator and Geneva agree that the doctrine was morally wrong; however, Geneva is convinced a better desegregation policy was possible. She contends that if we recognize that the motivation of segregation was White domination of public education, then the Supreme Court should have given priority to desegregation of money and control rather than students. Moreover, Geneva argues that although separate but equal no longer fulfilled the constitutional equal protection standard, the court should have required immediate equalization of all school facilities and resources. Also, Geneva posits that the court should have required African American representation on school boards and other policy-making bodies to reflect the proportion of African American students in each school district. This final point would have been intended to give African American parents access to the formal decision-making process, a condition still not realized in many predominantly African American school systems (Bell, 1987).

Similarly, each of the other eight chronicles—"Celestial Curia," "Ultimate Voting Rights Act," "Black Reparations Foundation," "DeVine Gift," "Amber Cloud," "Twenty-Seventh-Year Syndrome," "Slave Scrolls," and "Black Crime Cure"—describes the tensions for both Blacks and Whites in the construction, interpretation, and implementation of race-related civil rights law. In the context of each chronicle, Bell (1987) builds on three arguments that appear in his earlier legal writings and that reoccur throughout his subsequent scholarship and that of other legal scholars building on CRT.

One argument, the constitutional contradiction, is based on the U.S. Constitution and subsequent legal decisions. This argument is more specifically an analysis of property in American society and the role of government in protecting property interests. In his discussions with Geneva Crenshaw, Bell (1987) examines the events leading up to the Constitutional Convention and concludes that the framers of U.S. law grappled with the tension between property rights and human rights. This tension was apparent in the debate over slavery. Bell (1987) contends that the slavery provisions in the original Constitution reflected pragmatic, political compromises by the framers. When confronted with the decision between White racism and justice, the framers of the Constitution chose racism and the rewards of property. Bell (1987) relates this constitutional contradiction to later political debates and policy by asking, "Does slavery have any value in analyzing contemporary racial policies and civil rights doctrine?" (p. 260). For Bell (1987), race and property are linked in complex ways that often result in racial oppression (see also P. J. Williams, 1991).[22] Advancing this argument, Harris (1993) posited that racial identity and property are deeply interrelated concepts:

Even after the period of conquest and colonization of the New World and the abolition of slavery, whiteness was the predicate for attaining a host of societal privileges, in both public and private spheres. Whiteness determined whether one could vote, travel freely, attend schools, obtain work, and indeed, defined the structure of social relations along the entire spectrum of interactions between the individual and society. Whiteness then became status, a form of racialized privilege ratified in law. Material privileges attendant to being white inhered in the status of being white. After the dismantling of legalized race segregation, whiteness took on the character of property in the modern sense in that relative white privilege was legitimated as the status quo. In *Plessy v. Ferguson* and the case that overturned it, *Brown v. Board of Education*, the law extended protection to whiteness as property, in the former instance, as traditional status-property, in the latter, as modern property. (pp. 1745–1746)

A second argument found throughout Bell's scholarly writing is the interest-convergence principle (e.g., Bell, 1979, 1980a, 1980b, 1987, 1992). The interest-convergence principle is built on political history as legal precedent and emphasizes that significant progress for African Americans is achieved only when the goals of Blacks are consistent with the needs of Whites. Bell (1980b) stated:

Translated from judicial activity in racial cases both before and after *Brown*, this principle of "interest convergence" provides: The interest of blacks in achieving racial equality will be accommodated only when it converges with the interests of whites. However, the fourteenth amendment, standing alone, will not authorize a judicial remedy providing effective racial equality for blacks where the remedy sought threatens the superior societal status of middle and upper class whites. (p. 523)

As an example of the interest-convergence principle, Bell (1987) offered:

I often cite the NAACP and government briefs in the *Brown* case, both of which maintain that the abandonment of state-supported segregation would be a crucial asset as we compete with Communist countries for the hearts and minds of Third World people just emerging from the long years of colonialism. As far as I'm concerned, the Court's decision in the *Brown* case cannot be understood without considering the decision's value to whites in policy-making positions who are able to recognize the economic and political benefits at home and abroad that would follow abandonment of state-mandated racial segregation. (p. 62)

Dudziak (1988) conducted a historical study designed to develop additional insight into the *Brown* case and Bell's interest-convergence principle. Dudziak carefully detailed the international attention given to U.S. racial discrimination in the era following World War II. She documented the Soviet Union's exploitation of poor U.S. race relations and the State Department's concern with this serious foreign policy problem. Dudziak described the Truman administration's response, particularly the Justice Department's arguments in civil rights amicus briefs that racial segregation was a detriment to U.S. foreign policy interests. Dudziak described the positive foreign policy benefits that accrued after *Brown*:

After *Brown*, the State Department could blame racism on the Klan and the crazies. They could argue that the American Constitution provided for effective social change. And, most importantly, they could point to the *Brown* decision as evidence that racism was at odds with the principles of American democracy. This foreign policy angle, this Cold War imperative, was one the critical factors driving the federal government's postwar civil rights efforts. (p. 119)

Dudziak (1988) concluded that Bell's interest-convergence theory characterized correctly the events leading up to and following the *Brown* decision.

A third major argument found in Bell's scholarship—a corollary to the interest-convergence theory—is that many Whites will not support civil rights policies that appear to threaten their superior social status (Bell, 1979, 1987, 1989). Bell (1979) referred to this argument as the "price of racial remedies." For example, in an analysis describing the commonalities between the *Brown* and *Bakke* cases, Bell (1979) stated:

The Court did not overestimate the time needed for the country to accept the *Brown* decision as law. But there were compensatory aspects of the case overlooked by the Court, cost issues that have been framed in sharper relief by the *Bakke* litigation. In *Brown*, the focus was on the South. At issue was the constitutionality of the most onerous kind of educational apartheid. The nation was more than ready to blame white Southerners, traditionally the country's scapegoat when there is a need to assign responsibility for racial injustice. . . . When the school desegregation efforts moved north, the attitude toward the South changed from condemnation to complicity, with Northerners rallying to preserve neighborhood assignment patterns, avoid busing, and maintain the "educational integrity" of white schools. Although there has been violence in Boston and Pontiac, most Northern whites do not oppose desegregation in the abstract. What they resist is the *price* of desegregation. They fear that their children will be required to scuffle for an education in schools that for decades have been good enough only for blacks. . . . The problem of cost is aggravated when the issue is college and professional school admissions. As opponents of minority admissions take pains to point out, no one is totally excluded from school under public school desegregation plans. Under preferential admissions programs, however, minority applicants are admitted to college and graduate schools *in place of* whites. Moreover, most public school desegregation plans do not affect upper middle-class white families who live in suburbs or whose children attend private schools. . . . There is a pattern to all this. It is recognizable in the opposition of New York City school teachers to community control. It is apparent in the resistance of unions to plans that require that they stop excluding minority workers. And it is reflected in suburban zoning and referendum practices designed to keep out low-income housing. In each instance, the principle of nondiscrimination is supported, but its implementation is avoided and, necessarily, opposed. The important question, of course, is whether the debilitating effects of racial discrimination can be remedied without requiring whites to surrender aspects of their superior social status. (pp. 11–12)

Bell's analysis of *Bakke* and his subsequent scholarship provide a full-scale structural theory combined with the detail required for microlevel analysis of the individual story. It is this quality that makes his scholarship a unique contribution to academic writing on issues of race, law, and society.

A Commentary on Derrick Bell

The three major arguments found in Bell's analyses of racial patterns in American law—the constitutional contradiction, the interest-convergence principle, and the price of racial remedies—convey a different message than that found in traditional race scholarship, that is, civil rights or antidiscrimination scholarship.

Bell's scholarship represents an effort to dismantle traditional civil rights language—for example, color blindness and equal opportunity—to provide a more cogent historical and legal analysis of race and law. Moreover, his scholarship is directly connected to educational policy analysis of such issues as school desegregation, admissions and financial aid, school choice, school finance, and university recruitment (Bell, 1979, 1980b, 1987, 1989; Ladson-Billings & Tate, 1995). Elsewhere, I crossed the paradigmatic boundaries of mathematics education—mathematics and psychology—to illustrate the limitations of recent school mathematics reform proposals calling for opportunity-to-learn standards and a national assessment (Tate, 1995a, 1995b). These boundary-crossing analyses were built with theoretical tools found in the scholarship of Derrick Bell and other critical race theorists.

Another area of educational policy that seems especially relevant for the kind of critical race critique found in Bell's writings is school finance.[23] For example, Clune (1993) argued that the standards-based vision of educational policy-making requires a change in school finance structures (see also Moskowitz, Stullich, & Deng, 1993; O'Day & Smith, 1993; Odden, 1992). Clune posited that school finance discussions should shift from fiscal equality to fiscal adequacy and from debates about financial inputs to a focus on standard-based outcomes as the objective of both educational policy and school finance. A shift in federal and state policy from fiscal equality to adequacy is part of a larger federal program that is moving attention away from traditionally underserved students (Chapter 1, special education, and bilingual) toward a discourse on high standards for all students (National Governors Association, 1993; Tate, 1995a). This shift in policy warrants further analysis by scholars interested in equity, and Bell's interest-convergence principle could provide insightful conceptual guidance.

The shift in policy direction from fiscal equality to a call for fiscal adequacy and high standards for all represents an attempt to converge the interests of more affluent suburban communities that wish to limit their tax burden and benefit directly from tax contributions with classical ideas of government and taxation of serving the common good. However, this shift has the potential to create even greater educational inequality. For example, Harp (1996) reported that Governor Christine Todd Whitman of New Jersey plans to address deep inequities between wealthy and poor schools by establishing new education standards rather than by providing new money from the state. Note that New Jersey has been ordered to resolve its school finance problems by the 1997–1998 school year. Governor Whitman remarked (in her state of the state address), "We must stop chasing dollars and start creating scholars" (as cited in Harp, 1996, pp. 1, 25). Governor Whitman's remarks reflect a shift in political rhetoric from equalizing spending and resources to adopting standards. However, those employing this rhetoric rarely have a plan for addressing equity problems.

The scholarship of Derrick Bell has provoked an alternative method of legal analysis of race and U.S. society. Moreover, his scholarship has important relevance to issues of educational equity. However, his work has not gone without criticism. The legal writings of Derrick Bell and many other CRT scholars are associated with a growing genre of narrative research in the academy (Scheppele, 1989; P. J. Williams, 1991); however, the narrative movement has not been universally accepted in academe. The criticism of narrative research varies depending on the paradigmatic perspective of the writer. Some scholars argue against the form; others challenge the absence of neutrality and objectivity. Still other scholars question the validity and power of narrative research given the institutional stories that may counter the narrative developed by the legal storyteller. For example, Winter (1989) stated:

Narrative is not the primary medium for the kind of institutionalized meaning that is necessary if a prevailing order is to make persuasive its claims of legitimation and justification. Narrative does not meet the threefold demands of generality, unreflexivity, and reliability that are necessary if a prevailing order is credibly to justify itself. The more limited role of narrative in the processes of social construction is as a link between experience and the effective crystallization of social mores. (It is just this prefiguring role that makes narrative a potentially effective transformative device.) But, although narrative may also be employed on behalf of the existing order, this use of narrative as authority is persuasive precisely because it evokes meaning that is already institutionalized. Accordingly, legal narratives of this sort are constrained by preexisting social processes. (p. 2228)

Winter's (1989) critique of Bell's use of legal story telling, as well as narrative scholarship in general, is important for education scholars interested in equity and policy-making. Winter recognized narrative as a persuasive tool to catalyze legal and social change. Furthermore, Winter acknowledged the role of narrative scholarship in the social construction of meaning. However, he warned that narrative is not the only means by which social meaning is institutionalized.[24]

Despite Winter's criticism of Bell and other narrative scholars, education scholars and policymakers should examine the power of legal story telling to illuminate educational equity issues in public debates. Perhaps no recent example from education illustrates this point better than Jonathan Kozol's (1991) detailed chronicle of school inequity, *Savage Inequalities.* The power of this volume is the story. The statistics on school finance inequality have a long history in educational research literature and the popular press. However, they often have lacked the ability to catalyze democratic deliberation. Reich (1988) described the importance of democratic deliberation:

The reigning American philosophy of policy making has drawn on these three currents of thought—bureaucratic expertise, democratic deliberation, and utilitarianism—but in unequal parts. Especially in this century, beginning with the Progressives' efforts to insulate policy making from the politics and continuing through the modern judiciary's oversight of policy making, there has been a tendency to subordinate democratic deliberation to the other themes. As the "administrative state" has grown, its legitimacy has increasingly rested on notions of neutral competence and procedural regularity. The "public interest" has been defined as what individual members of the public want for themselves—as such wants are expressed through opinion surveys, data on the public's willingness to pay for certain goods, and the special pleadings of interest groups. The ideal of public policy has thus become almost entirely instrumental—designed to maximize individual satisfactions. (p. 10)

Critical race theorists recognize that the way public problems are defined can influence how laws and policies are constructed and interpreted. One purpose of legal story telling by Bell and other critical race scholars is to engage the reader in democratic deliberation concerning the ironies and contradictions associated with laws constructed to appease White self-interest rather than address notions of equity.

Another scholar, Haney Lopez (1996), noted the importance of Bell's scholarship, yet offered a criticism. Specifically, Haney Lopez argued that Bell's (1992) casebook, *Race, Racism and American Law*, treated "Black" and "White" as natural categories rather than concepts created through social construction and, at least partially, through legal strategies. Despite this criticism of Bell's casebook, Haney Lopez acknowledged that critical race scholars have generated a movement to rethink race, law, and U.S. society. Haney Lopez (1996) remarked:

The tendency to treat race as a prelegal phenomenon is coming to an end. Of late, a new strand of legal scholarship dedicated to reconsidering of the role of race in U.S. society has emerged. Writers in this genre, known as critical race theory, have for the most part shown an acute awareness of the socially constructed nature of race. Much critical race theory scholarship recognizes that race is a legal construction. (p. 12)

The importance of examining the social construction of race through the law is a paramount consideration in CRT. As such, Richard Delgado's scholarship has contributed to theoretical methods that provide insight into the interrelationship between the construction of race and the law.

Richard Delgado and Critical Race Theory

The scholarship of Richard Delgado is pivotal to understanding CRT. Crenshaw et al. (1995) placed Delgado and his scholarship at the historical and conceptual origins of CRT. Delgado has engaged in extensive debate with other scholars in the legal community regarding the merits and potential contribution of CRT to legal analysis. Delgado (1990) argued that critical race scholarship is characterized by the following themes:

(1) an insistence on "naming our own"; (2) the belief that knowledge and ideas are powerful; (3) a readiness to question basic premises of moderate/incremental civil rights law; (4) the borrowing of insights from social science on race and racism; (5) critical examination of the myths and stories pow-

erful groups use to justify racial subordination; (6) a more contextualized treatment of doctrine; (7) criticism of liberal legalisms; and (8) an interest in structural determinism—the ways in which legal tools and thought-structures can impede law reform. (p. 95)

The CRT themes delineated by Delgado can be seen in his scholarship. Building on theories found in the sociology of knowledge, Delgado (1990) argued:

Sociologists of knowledge know that knowledge is power, and power is something that people fight to obtain and struggle to avoid giving up. Physical scientists, for example, have strenuously resisted "paradigm changes" even in their ostensibly objective, value-free world. Legal change comes freighted with even more meaning than the scientific version, for it often portends changes in power and well-being for specific persons or groups. It is thus not surprising that the New Race Theorists, who are raising such ideas as that civil rights doctrine perpetuates and legitimizes discrimination, meet fierce resistance. (p. 110)

A significant portion of Delgado's scholarship is devoted to explaining and clarifying the role of story, counterstory, and "naming one's own reality" in CRT (see also Ross, 1989; Russell, 1995; Torres & Milun, 1990; P.J. Williams, 1987). Delgado (1988a) identified a structural feature of human experience that separates people of color from White friends and colleagues. Simply stated, "White people rarely see acts of blatant or subtle racism, while minority people experience them all the time" (p. 407). Similarly, Lawrence (1987) stated:

Americans share a common historical and cultural heritage in which racism has played and still plays a dominant role. Because of this shared experience, we also inevitably share many ideas, attitudes, and beliefs that attach significance to an individual's race and induce negative feelings and opinions of nonwhites. To the extent that this cultural belief system has influenced all of us, we are racists. At the same time, most of us are unaware of our racism. We do not recognize the ways in which our cultural experience has influenced our beliefs about race or the occasions on which those beliefs affect our actions. In other words, a large part of the behavior that produces racial discrimination is influenced by unconscious racial motivation. (p. 322)

According to Delgado (1988a), most minorities, in contrast to Whites, live in a world dominated by race (see also Clark, 1963; Comer & Poussaint, 1976). Moreover, the exchange of trade stories among people of color concerning racial treatment and ways of dealing with racism is common (Delgado, 1987). These stories are important histories that help illustrate the irony and contradiction of traditional legal analysis and argument.

Delgado (1989) posited four reasons as justification for legal analysis and scholarship that incorporate stories or voice chronicling the experiences of people of color: (a) Reality is socially constructed, (b) stories are a powerful means for destroying and changing mind-sets, (c) stories have a community-building function, and (d) stories provide members of out-groups mental self-preservation. Elsewhere, Delgado (1990) linked this justification for voice scholarship to CRT.

The first reason critical race theorists use stories or voice scholarship is to address the manner in which political and moral analysis is conducted in traditional legal scholarship (Delgado, 1989, 1990). Many legal scholars embrace universalism over particularity. Legal analysis and reasoning in Anglo-American legal jurisprudence is characterized by the acceptance of transcendent, acontextual, universal truths (P. J. Williams, 1991). This paradigmatic perspective tends to minimize anything that is historical, contextual, or specific with the unscholarly descriptors "literary" or "personal." In contrast, critical race theorists argue that political, legal, and moral analysis is situational. Delgado (1989) stated:

> Reality is not fixed, not a given. Rather, we construct it through conversations, through our lives together. Racial and class-based isolation prevents the hearing of diverse stories and counterstories. It diminishes the conversations through which we create reality, construct our communal lives. Deliberately exposing oneself to counterstories can avoid that impoverishment, heighten "suspicion," and can enable the listener and the teller to build a world richer than either could make alone. On another occasion, the listener will be the teller, sharing a secret, a piece of information, or an angle of vision that will enrich the former teller; and so on dialectically, in a rich tapestry of conversation, of stories. (p. 2439)

The second reason for the voice theme in CRT is the potential of story to change mind-set (Delgado, 1989). Most oppression does not seem like oppression to the oppressor (Lawrence, 1987). The dominant group of society justifies its position with stock stories (Delgado, 1989, 1990; R. A. Williams, 1989). These stock stories construct realities in ways that legitimize power and position. Stories by people of color can counter the stories of the oppressor. Furthermore, the discussion between the teller and listener can help overcome ethnocentrism and the dysconscious way many scholars view and construct the world. Delgado (1989) posited:

> Stories and counterstories can serve an equally important destructive function. They can show that what we believe is ridiculous, self-serving, or cruel. They can show us the way out of the trap of unjustified exclusion. They can help us understand when it is time to reallocate power. They are the other half—the destructive half—of the creative dialectic.
>
> Stories and counterstories, to be effective, must be or must appear to be noncoercive. They invite the reader to suspend judgement, listen for their point or message, then decide what measure of truth they contain. They are insinuative, not frontal; they offer a respite from the linear, coercive discourse that characterizes much of legal writing. (p. 2415)

The third reason offered by Delgado (1989) for incorporating story into CRT is the role story telling can play in community building. Stories help to build consensus, a common culture of shared understandings, and a more vital ethics. Despite the potential for building consensus, Delgado (1989) warned of the dangers in story telling, particularly for the first-time storyteller. The listener to an unfamiliar counterstory may reject it, as well as the storyteller, because the story reveals hypocrisy and increases discomfort.[25] Moreover, the hearer may consciously or unconsciously reinterpret the new story, framing the content of the story within the hearer's own belief system, thus muting or reversing the meaning.

Delgado (1989) explained that the fourth reason for incorporating voice into legal analysis is to help ensure the psychic preservation of marginalized groups. A factor contributing to the demoralization of members of out-groups is self-condemnation. People of color may internalize the stock stories that various groups of society promote to maintain their influence (Crenshaw, 1988). Historically, people of color have used story telling to heal wounds caused by racial discrimination.[26] Delgado (1989) stated: "Along with the tradition of storytelling in black culture there exists the Spanish tradition of the picaresque novel or story, which tells of humble folk piquing the pompous or powerful and bringing them down to more human levels" (p. 2414). According to Delgado (1990), the story of one's condition leads to greater insight into how one came to be oppressed. Moreover, Bell (1987) argued that this allows the oppressed to stop inflicting mental violence on themselves.

Delgado (1984) not only wrote about the philosophical underpinnings of voice scholarship; he also questioned whose voice is heard in legal discourse addressing civil rights. In "The Imperial Scholar: Reflections on a Review of Civil Rights Literature," Delgado (1984) showed that an inner circle of 26 legal scholars, all male and White, occupied the key venues of civil rights scholarship to the exclusion of scholars of color. Delgado (1984) noted that when a member of this inner circle wrote about civil rights issues, he referenced almost exclusively other members of the inner circle for support while ignoring the scholarship of minorities in the field. Delgado (1984) offered the following explanation for this practice:

In explaining the strange absence of minority scholarship from the text and footnotes of the central arenas of legal scholarship dealing with civil rights, I reject conscious malevolence or crass indifference. I think the explanation lies in a need to remain in *control*, to make sure that legal change occurs, but not too fast. The desire to shape events is a powerful human motive and could easily account for much of the exclusionary scholarship I have noted. The moment one makes a statement, however, one is reminded that it is these same liberal authors who have been the strongest supporters of affirmative action in their own university communities, and who have often been prepared to take chances (as they see it) to advance the goal of an integrated society. Perhaps the two behaviors can be reconciled by observing that the liberal professor may be pleased to have minority students and colleagues serve as figureheads, ambassadors of good will, and future community leaders, but not necessarily happy with the thought of a minority colleague who might go galloping off in a new direction. (p. 574)

Several years later, Delgado (1995a) revisited the "Imperial Scholar" debate. He argued that a new breed of imperialists had emerged in legal discourse who deploy a different set of strategies to mute, devalue, and/or co-opt the voice of critical race theorists. Delgado (1995a) identified 13 mechanisms used by these "neo-imperialists" to marginalize critical race scholarship.[27] One mechanism discussed by Delgado (1995a) is the co-option of another person's experience that leads to a refocusing of the original story:

Some of the new writers [neo-imperialists] make an effort to identify with the stories and accounts the outsider narrativists are offering, but in a way that co-opts or minimizes these stories. The majority-race author draws a parallel between something in the experience of the outsider author and something that happened to him. There is nothing wrong with using analogies and metaphors to deal with the experience of others, for that is how we extend our sympathies. If, however, we analogize to refocus a conversation or an article towards ourselves exclusively, something is wrong, especially if the experience to which we liken another's is manifestly less serious. For example, the author of one article on

campus racial harassment observes that everyone experiences "insulting" or "upsetting" speech at one
time or another, so what is so special about the racist version? (p. 406)

According to Delgado (1995a), a second mechanism to minimize the critical
race critique is to praise the writing for its emotional or passionate quality, ultimately classifying the article in a category of its own—for example, individual
soul searching—and thus selectively ignoring the uncomfortable truths about
race, society, and injustice. A third mechanism is for the neo-imperialist to
translate a novel, hard-edge, and discomforting thesis by a critical race scholar
into a familiar, safe, and tame conceptual state. Here the neo-imperialist scholar
often forces the critical race critique into a discourse of liberal-legalist terms that
the critical race scholar has intended to avoid. The other 10 mechanisms are
equally as troubling; however, they have not deterred Delgado from exploring
voice scholarship and other nontraditional methods of analyzing race, law, and
U.S. society.

Another theme found in the scholarship of Delgado and other critical race
scholars is the examination of structural determinism (see also Bell, 1992;
Greene, 1995). Critical race scholars examine the legal system for categories,
methods of legal analysis, and doctrines to help illuminate ways the legal system
maintains the status quo. For example, Delgado and Stefancic (1989) described
how three important resources that lawyers use in legal research—the Library of
Congress subject heading, the *Index of Legal Periodicals*, and the West Digest
System—function like DNA; that is, they allow the current system to replicate
itself. Delgado and Stefancic (1989) asserted that the three information systems
function like a double helix in molecular biology: They reconstruct preexisting
ideas, arguments, and methods. Within the boundaries of the three systems, moderate, incremental legal change is possible, whereas structural, transformative
innovation is much more difficult. Delgado and Stefancic (1989) stated:

A glance at the standard categories shows why; each system bears a strong imprint of the incremental
civil rights approach these writers decry. The *Index to Legal Periodicals* and *Decennial Digest*, for
example, lead the reader to works on civil rights, employment discrimination, and school integration
or desegregation, but contain no entry for hegemony or interest convergence. The *Index to Legal
Periodicals* lacked an entry for critical legal studies until September 1987, nearly a decade after the
movement began. The *Decennial Digest* contains entries on slums and miscegenation. To find cases
on ghettos, one must look in the Descriptive Word Index under slums, which refers the searcher to
public improvements under the topic municipal corporations. Another index contains an entry labeled,
simply, races. None of the major indexes contains entries for legitimation, false consciousness, or
many other themes of the "new" or critical race-remedies scholarship. Indeed, a researcher who confined himself or herself to the sources listed under standard civil rights headings would be unlikely to
come in contact with these ideas, much less invent them on his or her own. (pp. 218–219)

Delgado and Stefancic (1992) have not limited their analysis of structural
determinism to legal information systems. Building on postmodern insights about
language and the social construction of reality, Delgado and Stefancic (1992)
argued that conventional First Amendment doctrine is most helpful in resolving

small, clearly bounded disputes. However, free speech is less able to deal with systemic problems such as racism or sexism and, thus, is least helpful with some of society's most difficult dilemmas. Delgado and Stefancic (1992) offered two interrelated reasons for the bounded range of free speech in resolving matters of racial discrimination. First, their review of 200 years of ethnic depiction in the United States revealed that society simply does not see many forms of discrimination at the time they are occurring. Delgado and Stefancic (1992) posited:

> This time-warp aspect of racism makes speech an ineffective tool to counter it. . . . Racism forms part of the dominant narrative, the group of received understandings and basic principles that form the baseline from which we reason. How could these be in question? Recent scholarship shows that the dominant narrative changes very slowly and resists alteration. We interpret new stories in light of the old. Ones that deviate too markedly from our pre-existing stock are dismissed as extreme, coercive, political, and wrong. The only stories about race we are prepared to condemn, then, are the old ones giving voice to the racism of an earlier age, ones that society has already begun to reject. We can condemn Justice Brown for writing as he did in *Plessy v. Ferguson*, but not university administrators who refuse remedies for campus racism, failing to notice the remarkable parallels between the two. (pp. 1278–1279)

Delgado and Stefancic (1992) described a second, related insight from modern scholarship that focuses not on how existing narratives limit reform but, rather, on the relationship between ourselves and those narratives. Specifically, they argued that individuals are confined to their own preconceptions from which escape is difficult. Delgado and Stefancic (1992) offered:

> The emphatic fallacy holds that through speech and remonstrance we can surmount our limitations of time, place, and culture, can transcend our own situatedness. But our examination of the cultural record, as well as postmodern understandings of language and personhood, both point to the same conclusion: The notion of ideas competing with each other, with truth and goodness emerging victorious from the competition, has proven seriously deficient when applied to evils, like racism, that are deeply inscribed in the culture. We have constructed the social world so that racism seems normal, part of the status quo, in need of little correction. It is not until much later that what we believed begins to seem incredibly, monstrously wrong. How could we have believed that? (p. 1281)

One implication of structural determinism is that it limits how individuals and society at large are able to analyze and critique oppression. Critical race theorists have attempted to address this tunnel vision by examining the law through multiple lenses. One of the newer trends in CRT has been the examination of race, gender, and class and how they operate in society and the law. For example, building on the writings of such scholars as hooks (1991), hooks and West (1991), and Harris (1990), Delgado (1993) constructed and narrated a story between himself and his alter ego, Rodrigo. The story explores the tensions that exist when a group—that is, all women—attempts a singular, unitary movement to catalyze change. Specifically, Delgado examined the essentialist debate in legal scholarship and the broader academy.[28]

Delgado (1993) constructed a story that illustrates how the scholarly focus and action of a women's law caucus to achieve its goals of gender equality could potentially result in their failure to address other forms of oppression (e.g., racial). After the story, Delgado, along with his alter ego, Rodrigo, offered a theory of social change and small groups that represents an effort to explain the process of social reform. Delgado (1993) borrowed from Dewey (1933) and other American pragmatists who argued that human intelligence and progress spring from adversity, that is, the notion that the society is not providing the individual with what he or she needs to survive. Similarly, Delgado argued that subgroups within a social movement recognize that the larger group lacks the vision to include their agenda within the movement. Thus, the subgroup develops its own agenda and moves on to continue the process of social change. Delgado (1993) theorized that social change is, by its nature, an iterative process with reform and retrenchment coming in waves.

A theme that permeates critical race scholarship is the concept of cultural nationalism (e.g., Bell, 1987; Calmore, 1992; Delgado, 1992; Johnson, 1993). Rooted in DuBois's (1906/1990) philosophy of double consciousness and the Black power movement of the 1960s and 1970s, cultural nationalism is defined by the belief that Black and Brown communities should develop their own schools, colleges, and businesses.[29] Cultural nationalism served as one philosophical underpinning of Delgado's (1995b) critique of affirmative action.

Delgado (1995b) challenged the way affirmative action is framed in policy debates. He argued that affirmative action debates typically structure the issue of minority representation with the following question: Should we as a country sanction the appointment of some specific number of people of color to achieve certain political objectives, such as social stability, a diverse workforce, and integration? According to Delgado (1995b), the political objectives are always forward looking: Affirmative action is seen as a tool for socially engineering society from state A to state B. The process ignores the fact that minorities have been treated unfairly in employment practices, deprived of their land, and enslaved. Moreover, the affirmative action debate often frames the issue so that even small accomplishments are seen as painful, requiring careful thinking by liberals and conservatives alike about the opportunity being denied White citizens. Delgado (1995b) called for careful analysis of affirmative action by people of color. He concluded with an analysis of one aspect of affirmative action mythology: the role model argument.

The role model argument is a story that exists in current discourse on affirmative action; its major premise is that if a person of color is hired now and this person is a good role model, things will be better for the next generation of minorities. Delgado (1995b) posited that the role model argument is instrumental and forward looking, like the larger program of affirmative action. Delgado's (1995b) assessment of the role model argument as being instrumental and forward looking is a criticism. He provided five reasons a person of color should avoid employment linked to this argument. Two of these reasons are especially relevant to scholars interested in educational equity. The first is that, to be a good role model, one must be an assimilationist, never a cultural or economic nationalist, separatist, radical reformer, or anything connected to any of these.[30] The second is that the job of the role model requires one to lie. Delgado (1995b) suggested that promoting an academic law career to children of color is akin to promoting a career in the National Basketball Association. He argued that the current educational conditions for children of color—diminishing federal and state support for scholarships devoted to these children and increasing campus harassment—have limited real opportunity.[31]

A Commentary on Richard Delgado

Delgado (1990) argued that scholars of color and female scholars are able to provide insights and stories different from those traditionally heard in legal discourse. Moreover, he contended that stories have a community-building function and the potential to change mind-set.[32] Delgado's scholarship has combined analytical discussions of the philosophical undergirdings of narrative methods with arguments against structural determinism, essentialism, and academic neoimperialism. Furthermore, Delgado described the function of cultural nationalism in the critical race critique. Delgado's scholarship, like Bell's, is characterized by texts that weave together lively narrative and rigorous theoretical analyses of legal constructs. Moreover, Delgado's scholarship, like Bell's, has been subject to criticism.

Randall Kennedy (1989) noted the contributions of critical race theorists such as Derrick Bell, Richard Delgado, and Mari Matsuda to the literature on race and law; however, he argued that they tended to evade or suppress complications that render their conclusions problematic. Kennedy (1989) specifically challenged (a) the notion that, on intellectual grounds, White scholars are entitled to less standing to engage in race-related civil rights discourse than scholars of color; (b) the argument that, on intellectual grounds, the racial status of scholars of color should serve as a positive credential for the purposes of analyzing their writings; and (c) arguments that contend the current position of minority scholars has been influenced by prejudiced decisions of White colleagues.

In a *Virginia Law Review* article, Delgado (1990) responded to Kennedy's criticisms. He remarked that Kennedy is a believer in dominant discourse: the collection of ideas, arguments, and concepts that compose liberal legalism. Delgado (1990) described dominant discourse as incremental and cautious. Moreover, Delgado (1990) argued that dominant discourse is a homeostatic device by which our society ensures that most race-related reform will last a short time. What is clear from Kennedy's argument and Delgado's response is that they operate in very different paradigms. Delgado (1990) stated:

The Critical Race Theorists are impatient with that discourse [dominant], and the outlook associated with it. It neither squares with our experience nor permits us to hope for the kind of future we want for ourselves and our communities. Unlike a natural language, which simply adds new concepts and words when its speakers need them, dominant legal discourse resists expansion. Indeed, one of its principal functions is to make reform difficult to achieve or even to imagine. Kennedy's opposition to alternative voices and insistence that we speak in the current idiom therefore is not merely about legal style or manners. It is about things that matter. In seeking to confine us to a single mode of thought and expression even in law reviews, a traditional forum for experimenting with new ideas, he verges close to intolerance. (pp. 103–104)

Despite the criticism of Delgado's scholarly methods, the implications of his writings for research on education and equity are far-reaching. I will discuss three potential areas in which Delgado's arguments inform equity-related debates in educational literature.

First, Delgado and Stefancic's (1989) critique of structural determinism and librarianship in legal scholarship is applicable to educational research. Scholars in education should ask, Are educational information classification systems assisting in the replication of preexisting thought? If so, what can be done to expand beyond indexing and research systems that confine thought to the traditional categories of educational discourse to include boundary-crossing scholarship related to civil rights and education? This question has been, in part, examined by Apple (1993):

While there is a formal right for everyone to be represented in the debates over whose cultural capital, whose knowledge 'that,' 'how,' and 'to,' will be declared legitimate for transmission to future generations of students, it is still the case that . . . a *selective tradition* operates in which only specific groups' knowledge becomes official knowledge. Thus, the freedom to help select the formal corpus of school knowledge is bound by power relations that have very real effects. (pp. 65–66)

Second, Delgado's (1995b) discussion of cultural nationalism is part of a larger program of scholarship within the critical race movement. This theme of CRT has important applications for the education of students of color. For example, in his analysis of the *Fordice* case, Johnson (1993) concluded that the case represented a quest for equality through an assimilationist version of integration, without respect for the culture of African Americans. Similarly, Brown (1993) argued that, on cultural and educational grounds, a powerful case exists for African American immersion schools; however, he illustrated how the abstract, individualistic nature of the legal system is an impediment. The cultural and educational grounds found in Brown's analysis are strengthened by additional educational research that illuminates the importance of culturally relevant pedagogy for children of color (Deyhle, 1995; Ladson-Billings, 1994, 1995; Nieto, 1992; Perry, 1993). However, Brown's (1993) most important contribution to the literature on educational equity is, arguably, his ability to examine the nexus of K–12 pedagogy, policy, and law. Some educational researchers whose scholarship is centered on equity have been less inclined to grapple with this combination, instead focusing on one of the three. For example, James Banks (1992), known for his important work in multicultural education, remarked:

The radical critics can maintain their innocence because many of them are professors in educational policy studies and foundations departments. Consequently, they have the luxury to write, talk, and dream about schools without having to confront directly the daily challenges that teachers, students teachers, and students must experience each day. By contrast, most multicultural theorists are former teachers and are curriculum and instruction professors. They generally are among those who construct lesson plans and units and teach methods courses for use by their students who must take their places on the firing line in the schools. The curriculum and instruction orientation of most multicultural theorists is a major factor that explains why they cast their lot with schools and teachers, and try to bring change within the system. (p. 283)

Banks's (1992) argument is compelling, yet somewhat reductive. The change process requires a theoretical lens capable of examining classroom-level and more macrolevel aspects of the educational system and society. Educational systems are built on laws, policies, and folkways requiring macrolevel analyses that overlap with microlevel issues such as curriculum and pedagogy. Thus, the need to build on and expand beyond the theoretical tenets associated with multicultural classroom practice is a paramount consideration for scholars interested in equity-related research (Grant & Tate, 1995; Ladson-Billings & Tate, 1995).

Third, Delgado (1993) posited a theory of social change and explained the role of race, class, and gender in oppositional groups. His theory provides important insight into the essentialism debate. Specifically, Delgado (1993) and other critical race scholars such as Angela Harris argue that some of the feminist legal theorists (e.g., Catharine MacKinnon and Robin West) at times rely on a unitary, essential women's experience that is described independently of race, class, and other experiences of reality. C. I. Harris (1993) offered two reasons that gender essentialism is problematic:

First, the obvious one: As a black woman, in my opinion the experience of black women is too often ignored both in feminist theory and in legal theory, and gender essentialism in feminist legal theory does nothing to address this problem. A second and less obvious reason for my criticism of gender essentialism is that, in my view, contemporary legal theory needs less abstraction and not simply a different sort of abstraction. To be fully subversive, the methodology of feminist legal theory should challenge not only law's content but its tendency to privilege the abstract and unitary voice, and this gender essentialism also fails to do. (p. 585)

This insight is timely given that scholars interested in equity in education have called for scholarship that recognizes the relevance of multiple group memberships for an issue (e.g., Grant & Sleeter, 1986; Secada, 1995). Moreover, an education problem may be analyzed with constructs that build on race, class, and gender positions. Here is where the scholarship of Kimberlé Crenshaw makes a significant contribution to the critical race literature and potentially to educational research.

Kimberlé Crenshaw and Critical Race Theory

Matsuda and colleagues (1993) placed the social origins of CRT as a scholarly movement to a student boycott and alternative course organized in 1981 at Harvard Law School. The purpose of the boycott was to convince the administration to increase the number of tenured faculty members of color. Derrick Bell, Harvard's first African American professor, had left Harvard to assume the deanship at the University of Oregon's law school. Harvard students requested that the university hire a person of color to teach Race, Racism and American Law, a course organized and taught by Bell, the author of a ground-breaking book on the topic (Bell, 1980a). The administration failed to meet the student demand, and students responded by organizing an alternative course on the topic. Kimberlé Crenshaw, a Harvard Law School student, was one of the primary organizers of the alternative course (Matsuda et al., 1993). The students invited legal scholars and activists to lecture on sections of Bell's book. This action led to collaboration and discussion among a small cadre of legal scholars about different ways to conceptualize race and law. Over time, members of this initial group—for example, Richard Delgado, Charles Lawrence, and Mari Matsuda—became instrumental in the development of critical race scholarship (Delgado, 1990; Lawrence, 1987; Matsuda, 1989). Another contributor to this new genre of scholarship is Kimberlé Crenshaw.

Crenshaw's 1988 *Harvard Law Review* article challenged both the neoconservative and CLS critiques of the civil rights movement. Crenshaw (1988) described the neoconservative critique of the New Right as a set of arguments that reduced civil rights to mere special-interest politics.[33] The New Right view law and politics as essentially distinct; they presume that illustrating that the civil rights vision is largely political renders the vision illegitimate (Crenshaw, 1988). For example, the neoconservative argument that more recent leaders of the civil rights movement have shifted the movement's focus on equal treatment under the law to a demand for equal results delegitimized the movement in a democratic society (Sowell, 1984). According to Crenshaw (1988), neoconservatives like Thomas Sowell built on

a formalistic, color-blind view of civil rights that had developed in the neoconservative "think tanks" during the 1970's. Neoconservative doctrine singles out race-specific civil rights policies as one of the most significant threats to the democratic political system. Emphasizing the need for strictly color-blind policies, this view calls for the repeal of affirmative action and other race-specific remedial policies, urges an end to class-based remedies, and calls for the Administration to limit remedies to what it calls "actual victims" of discrimination. (p. 1337)

However, Crenshaw (1988) argued that the neoconservative critique failed to identify the "real" law and instead embraced language from antidiscrimination texts while ignoring contradictory purposes and interpretations. For example, Crenshaw (1988) identified two distinct rhetorical visions of equality in the body of antidiscrimination law: one termed the *expansive view* and the other the *restrictive view*. The expansive view stresses equality as an outcome and seeks to enlist the power of the court to eliminate the effects of racial oppression. In contrast, the restrictive view of equality, which coexists with the expansive view, treats equality as a process (Crenshaw, 1988). The primary goal of antidiscrimination law, according to the restrictive view, is to stop future acts of wrongdoing rather than correct present forms of past injustice.

According to Crenshaw (1988), the tension between the expansive and restrictive visions of equality is present throughout antidiscrimination law; however, the neoconservative critique often dismisses the full complexity of the dual interpretation by simply stating that equal process is unrelated to equal results. Unsatisfied with this declaration, Crenshaw (1988) remarked:

As the expansive and restrictive views of antidiscrimination law reveal, there simply is no self-evident interpretation of civil rights inherent in the terms themselves. Instead, specific interpretations proceed largely from the world view of the interpreter. For example, to believe, as Sowell does, that color-blind policies represent the only legitimate and effective means of ensuring a racially equitable society, one would have to assume not only that there is only one "proper role" for law, but also that such a racially equitable society already exists. In this world, once law had performed its "proper" function of assuring equality of process, differences in outcomes between groups would not reflect past discrimination but rather real differences between groups competing for societal rewards. Unimpeded by irrational prejudices against identifiable groups and unfettered by government-imposed preferences, competition would ensure that any group stratification would reflect only the cumulative effects of employers' rational decisions to hire the best workers for the least cost. The deprivations and oppression of the past would somehow be expunged from the present. Only in such a society, where all other societal functions operate in a nondiscriminatory way, would equality of process constitute equality of opportunity. (pp. 1344–1345)

A belief in color blindness and equal process, according to Crenshaw (1988), is illogical in a society in which specific groups have been treated different historically and in which the outcomes of this differential treatment continue into the present. Moreover, society's adoption of antidiscrimination law is subject to the condition that it does not overly burden majority interests (see also Bell, 1987, 1992).

Crenshaw (1988) also conducted a critique of CLS. She interpreted CLS as an attempt to examine legal ideology and discourse to determine how it re-creates and legitimates American society. Specifically, to discover the composition of the law, CLS scholars deconstruct legal doctrine to illuminate both its internal inconsistencies (often by exposing illogical legal arguments) and its external inconsistencies (generally by noting the paradoxical political perspectives embedded within legal doctrine) (see, e.g., R.W. Gordon, 1984; Livingston, 1982; Unger, 1983). The CLS analysis exposes the ways in which legal ideology has helped construct, maintain, and legitimate America's present class structure.

Moreover, Crenshaw (1988) argued that CLS provides a useful analysis in understanding the limited transformative potential of antidiscrimination discourse. However, Crenshaw identified difficulties in attempting to employ critical themes and ideas to analyze the civil rights movement and to describe possible policy options the civil rights constituency could possibly pursue. More specifically, Crenshaw offered three reasons the CLS critique is inadequate for people of color.[34]

First, many CLS scholars failed to ground their analyses in the realities of the racially oppressed. This deficiency, according to Crenshaw (1988), is especially apparent in critiques related to racial issues. Thus, the CLS literature shares a characteristic with mainstream scholarship: It fails to speak to or about African Americans and other people of color.

Second, the CLS critique fails to analyze the hegemonic role of racism, thus rendering its prescriptive analysis unrealistic (Crenshaw, 1988).

> The Critics' principal error is that their version of domination by consent does not present a realistic picture of racial domination. Coercion explains much more about racial domination than does ideologically induced consent. Black people do not create their oppressive worlds moment to moment but rather are coerced into living in worlds created and maintained by others. Moreover, the ideological source of this coercion is not liberal legal consciousness, but racism. If racism is just as important as, if not more important than, liberal legal ideology in explaining the persistence of white supremacy, then the Critics' single-minded effort to deconstruct liberal legal ideology will be futile. (p. 1357)

Third, according to Crenshaw (1988), the CLS critique, while exaggerating the role of liberal legal consciousness, minimizes the potential transformative power that liberalism offers. Crenshaw supported her claim by reexamining the civil rights movement. She noted that Blacks challenged their exclusion from political society by using methods recognized and reflected in U.S. society's institutional logic: legal rights ideology. Specifically, civil rights activists articulated their demands through legal rights ideology by exposing a series of contradictions, the most important being the constitutional guarantee of citizenship and the public practice of racial subordination. Crenshaw (1988) remarked:

> Rather than using the contradictions to suggest that American citizenship was itself illegitimate or false, civil rights protestors proceeded as if American citizenship were real, and demanded to exercise the "rights" that citizenship entailed. By seeking to restructure reality to reflect American mythology, Blacks relied upon and ultimately benefited from politically inspired efforts to resolve the contradictions by granting formal rights. Although it is the need to maintain legitimacy that presents powerless groups with the opportunity to wrest concessions from the dominant order, it is the very accomplishment of legitimacy that forecloses greater possibilities. In sum, the potential for change is both created and limited by legitimation. (p. 1368)

In conclusion, Crenshaw (1988) argued that the task at hand is to develop methods to engage in ideological and political struggle while minimizing the costs of waging in an inherently legitimating legal discourse. Central to this process is the creation of a distinct political thought that is the product of the lives and conditions of Black people.

In an effort to create this kind of political thought, Crenshaw has sought to theorize about race and apply this theory to social problems. Crenshaw (1993) argued that social issues emphasizing gender often minimized the interaction of gender and race and class. She contended that this practice is largely consistent with doctrinal and political discourses that construct racism and sexism as mutually exclusive. In response, Crenshaw (1993) called for an intersectional framework to address multiple systems of subordination:

> On the simplest level, an intersectional framework uncovers how the dual positioning of women of color as women and as members of a subordinated racial group bears upon violence committed against

us. This dual positioning, or as some scholars have labeled it, double jeopardy, renders women of color vulnerable to the structural, political, and representational dynamics of both race and gender subordination. A framework attuned to the various ways that these dynamics intersect is a necessary prerequisite to exploring how this double vulnerability influences the way that violence against women of color is experienced and best addressed. (p. 112)

Crenshaw's (1993) argument for an intersectional framework builds on her examination of rhetorical strategies that characterize antiracist and feminist politics merging in ways that construct new problems for women of color. The intersectional critique is important for discovering the methods in which reformist interventions of one discourse establish and reinforce subordinating aspects of another.

Crenshaw (1993) developed an intersectionality framework that explored race and gender while noting that the concept can and should be expanded by including issues such as class and age. She described intersectionality as a provisional concept that links contemporary politics with postmodern theory. The specific purpose of intersectionality is to frame the following inquiry: "How does the fact that women of color are simultaneously situated within at least two groups that are subjected to broad societal subordination bear upon problems traditionally viewed as monocausal—that is, gender discrimination or race discrimination" (Crenshaw, 1993, p. 114).

In her analysis, Crenshaw (1993) used three constructs or metaphors to guide her examination of race and gender in U.S. law and popular culture: (a) the structural dimensions of domination (structural intersectionality), (b) the politics engendered by a specific system of domination (political intersectionality), and (c) the representations of the dominated (representational intersectionality). The intersectionality metaphors attempt to map the space in which women of color are situated: between categories of race and gender when the two are treated as mutually exclusive.

Crenshaw (1993) describes *structural intersectionality* as the way in which women of color are often situated within overlapping structures of subordination. Any area of vulnerability is sometimes exacerbated by yet another set of constraints emerging from a separate system of subordination. According to Crenshaw (1993), scholarly analysis built on the examination of structural intersections would provide insights into the lives of those at the bottom of complex layers of social hierarchies to determine how the interactions within each hierarchy influence the dynamics of another. For Crenshaw (1993), the material outcomes of these interconnected dynamics both within and across hierarchies in the lives of women of color are the essence of structural intersectionality. Crenshaw (1993) provided an example of how structural intersectionality limits legal protection and political intervention:

Structural intersectionality is the way in which the burdens of illiteracy, responsibility for child care, poverty, lack of job skills, and pervasive discrimination weigh down many battered women of color who are trying to escape the cycle of abuse. That is, gender subordination—manifested in this case by battering—intersects with race and class disadvantage to shape and limit the opportunities for effective intervention. (p. 115)[35]

According to Crenshaw (1993), the term *political intersectionality* refers to the various ways in which political and discursive practices associated with race and gender interrelate, often minimizing women of color. On some political issues, the arguments focusing on race and those focusing on gender work at odds. Manifestations of this oppositionality are found in antiracist and feminist discourse that supports the dynamics of either racial or gender subordination. Crenshaw (1993) remarked that a common example of political intersectionality is the practice of "protecting" the political and cultural integrity of the Black community by silencing public discussions of domestic violence. In other cases, women of color are overlooked when gender politics fail to recognize the plight of women of color. Crenshaw (1993) argued that this was the case with rhetorical appeals made by sponsors of the Violence Against Women Act.

White male senators eloquently urged passage of the bill because violence against women occurs everywhere, not just in the inner cities. That is, the senators attempted to persuade other whites that domestic violence is a problem because "these are *our* women being victimized." White women thus come into focus, and any authentic, sensitive attention to our images and our experience, which would probably have jeopardized the bill, faded into darkness. (Crenshaw, 1993, p. 116)[36]

Political intersectionality, as it relates to issues affecting women of color, reveals the methods in which politics built on mutually exclusive notions of race and gender provide women of color an inadequate political framework that fails to contextualize their experiences and realities (Crenshaw, 1993). Thus, tokenistic, objectifying, voyeuristic inclusion within a political discourse is at least as harmful to women of color as exclusion because both fail to adequately contextualize their lived realities and concerns (Crenshaw, 1993).

The final metaphor of the intersectional framework is *representational intersectionality*, which describes the manner in which race and gender images, abundant in our culture, merge to construct unique narratives considered appropriate for women of color (Crenshaw, 1993). Representational intersectionality is significant for the exploration of issues involving women of color because it seeks to understand the subtle and explicit ways their experiences are weighed against counternarratives that build on stereotypes.

Crenshaw (1993) suggested that media images provide insights into understanding the ways Latina, African American, Asian American, and Native American women are constructed through permutations of accessible racial and gender stereotypes. Crenshaw (1993) conducted an analysis using the intersectionality framework of cultural images widely disseminated in four mainstream movies, a video game, and a rap album.[37] A goal of her analysis was to determine whether cultural artifacts such as media images can influence legal and political thinking. In Crenshaw's (1993) words, "Whatever the relationship between imagery and actions is, it seems clear that these images do function to create counternarratives to the experiences of women of color that discredit our claims and render the violence we experience unimportant" (p. 120).

A Commentary on Kimberlé Crenshaw

Kimberlé Crenshaw's scholarship characterizes the interdisciplinary and eclectic nature of CRT. Like other critical race scholars, Crenshaw borrows from several traditions, including cultural nationalism, postmodernism, CLS, and black feminist thought, to provide a more comprehensive examination of race, society, and U.S. law. For example, Crenshaw's (1988) critique of neoconservative and CLS arguments in antidiscrimination law provides unique insight into how both groups, for different reasons, have failed to address the complexity of race in U.S. society and the laws governing the society. Instead, Crenshaw (1988) called for scholarship that demonstrates the racist nature of ostensibly neutral norms—a response to neoconservative arguments—and the development of proactive strategies for change that include the pragmatic use of legal rights, a position that differs from that of scholars in the CLS movement. Crenshaw's call for a different approach to antidiscrimination law and related scholarship has more recently been applied to scholarship in education.

In Tate et al. (1993), two colleagues and I built on Crenshaw's notion of expansive and restrictive forms of equality. Specifically, we argued that many policymakers are unaware of the potential for divergent constructions of equality; thus, the implementation of policy and law derived from the restrictive interpretation of antidiscrimination law continues to inhibit African American students' opportunity to learn. We concluded with a description of a more expansive vision of desegregated schooling that considered student diversity, curriculum, instruction, and parent-community involvement. This article represents an effort to negotiate macrolevel policy issues with pragmatic classroom-level concerns, a challenge for all scholars concerned with equity in education. The critical race critique provided important conceptual intervention in this effort, and, more specifically, Crenshaw's (1988) analysis of antidiscrimination law was central. Other potential areas of education and related scholarship where Crenshaw's perspective on antidiscrimination law would be applicable include (a) school choice and voucher plans, (b) standards-based reform efforts, and (c) school desegregation efforts, including those in higher education (see Ladson-Billings & Tate, 1995; Tate, 1995a).

Another way Crenshaw's (1993) scholarship can make a potentially unique contribution to educational research on equity is with her intersectionality framework. Recently, many progressive scholars have called for or actually included a close examination of the intersection of race, class, and gender in their research programs (Apple, in press; Grant & Sleeter, 1986; Morrow & Torres, 1995; Reid, 1995; Secada, 1995). The three variants on the intersectional theme—structural, political, and representational—provide a conceptual framework for analyzing the interplay of race, class, and gender in educational contexts.

Despite the potential of the intersectionality framework, its postmodern roots have been subject to criticism. Apple (in press) warned of the problems inherent in

the tendency by *some* postmodernists and poststructuralists to see *any* focus on political economy and class relations to be somehow reductive, to analyze the state as if it floats in air, to expand the linguistic turn until it encompasses everything, to embrace overly relativistic epistemological assumptions, and the stylistic arrogance of some its writings.

This warning is worth noting. However, it is Crenshaw's careful attention to structural artifacts, the political economy, and cultural representations that makes her intersectional framework most appealing to education scholars seeking to build on postmodern and critical traditions to better understand the role of race in U.S. schools and society.

FINAL REMARKS: THE DEFINING ELEMENTS OF CRITICAL RACE THEORY

One purpose of this review is to answer the question, What is CRT? A major goal of CRT is the elimination of racial oppression as part of the larger goal of eradicating all forms of oppression (Matsuda et al., 1993). To this end, several defining elements emerge from the CRT literature. Although these elements are distinct, they each reflect the goal of achieving racial justice. In this sense, the elements of CRT are interrelated. Moreover, each of these elements provides guidance for the development of questions related to the systematic inquiry of the political dimensions of equity in education. My literature review of CRT revealed the following defining elements and related questions.

1. CRT recognizes that racism is endemic in U.S. society, deeply ingrained legally, culturally, and even psychologically. Thus, the question for the education scholar employing CRT is not so much whether or how racial discrimination can be eradicated while maintaining the vitality of other interests linked to the status quo such as federalism, traditional values, standards, established property interests, and choice. Rather, the new question would ask how these traditional interests and cultural artifacts serve as vehicles to limit and bind the educational opportunities of students of color.

2. CRT crosses epistemological boundaries. It borrows from several traditions, including liberalism, law and society, feminism, Marxism, poststructuralism, CLS, cultural nationalism, and pragmatism, to provide a more complete analysis of "raced" people. This element of CRT suggests that scholars in education interested in equity research must begin to question the appropriateness and potential of their theoretical and conceptual frameworks. For example, does functionalism, a particular multicultural perspective, or critical theory provide the most cogent analysis of the experiences of students of color in education or the many "raced" representations?

3. CRT reinterprets civil rights law in light of its limitations, illustrating that laws to remedy racial inequality are often undermined before they can be fully

implemented. Interestingly, multicultural education and some multicultural perspectives are built on or closely associated with the civil rights laws developed in the 1960s. Thus, an important question from a critical race theoretical perspective is, What limitations do these perspectives have and how can they be reinterpreted to the advantage of traditionally underserved students of color? Moreover, this question can be applied to each theoretically driven movement in education.

4. CRT portrays dominant legal claims of neutrality, objectivity, color blindness, and meritocracy as camouflages for the self-interest of powerful entities of society. Do currently employed theoretical perspectives in education address these practices? If not, how do they fail, and what does CRT offer to remedy this lack of conceptual depth?

5. CRT challenges ahistoricism and insists on a contextual/historical examination of the law and a recognition of the experiential knowledge of people of color in analyzing the law and society. Do we in education challenge ahistorical treatment of education, equity, and students of color? Moreover, what role should experiential knowledge of race, class, and gender play in educational discourse?

These elements of CRT represent a beginning point. Critical race scholars are engaged in a dynamic process seeking to explain the realities of race in an ever-changing society. Thus, their theoretical positions and, more specifically, these elements should be viewed as a part of an iterative project of scholarship and social justice.

Secada (1989) argued that there are three areas into which research on educational equity might move. First, future scholarship should seek to set equity apart from equality of education while building on the important contributions that have emerged from that paradigmatic view. It is here that CRT makes a direct contribution to equity-related research in education. Critical race scholars have reinterpreted civil rights law and dominant legal claims of equality, color blindness, and meritocracy as part of an interest-convergence ploy. They have described in detail the origin and intent of these claims of neutrality and offered alternative solutions to difficult social problems.

Second, Secada (1989) called for equity research in education that focused on the individual and on the group case. This is where the power of legal story telling is most illuminating. The voice of the individual can provide insight into the political, structural, and representational dimensions of the legal system, especially as they relate to the group case. Similarly, narrative research in education can provide comparable insights into the educational system (see Casey, 1995).

Finally, Secada (1989) argued that the link of educational equity to justice needs examining with respect to how changing notions of justice may give rise to different interpretations of educational equity. A central part of the critical race critique is to examine ever-changing conceptions of justice. Thus, scholars interested in educational equity should benefit from the CRT literature.

Throughout this chapter, I have attempted to delineate the possibilities and limitations of CRT, specifically for debates concerning equity in education. A challenge for those interested in the politics of education and related research in equity is to find theoretical frameworks that allow for an expansive examination of race that moves beyond those associated with the inferiority paradigm. Such inquiry must begin with the recognition that this paradigm is a tool for the maintenance of racial subordination. The defining elements of CRT suggest that this theoretical perspective can provide novel and innovative ways of exploring educational policy, research, and practice.

NOTES

[1] Despite the ground-breaking work of such scholars as Woodson (1933/1990) and DuBois (1919), many researchers have continued to use race as only a categorical variable to compare and contrast social conditions rather than a theoretical lens or analytical tool.

[2] Race and gender have more recently emerged as important considerations to scholars in this tradition. For example, Apple (1992) remarked:
We cannot marginalize race and gender as constitutive categories in any cultural analysis. If there is indeed basic cultural forms and orientations that are specifically gendered and raced, and have their own partly autonomous histories, then we need to integrate theories of patriarchal and racial forms into the very core of our attempt to comprehend what is being reproduced and changed. At the very least, a theory that allows for the contradictions within and among these dynamics would be essential. (p. 143)

[3] Historians, social scientists, and other scholars have argued that race is not a natural cultural artifact but, rather, a social construction (see, e.g., Apple, 1992; Apple & Weis, 1983). Thus, people are "raced" based on certain characteristics and for different reasons (Harris, 1993; McCarthy & Crichlow, 1993; Morrison, 1992; Roediger, 1991).

[4] Haney Lopez (1996) provided an insightful description of race:
Race can be understood as the historically contingent social systems of meaning that attach to elements of morphology and ancestry. This definition can be pushed on three interrelated levels, the physical, the social, and the material. First, race turns on physical features and lines of descent, not because features or lineage themselves are a function of racial variation, but because society has invested these with racial meanings. Second, because the meanings given to certain features and ancestries denote race, it is the social processes of ascribing racialized meanings to faces and forbearers that lie at the heart of racial fabrication. Third, these meaning-systems, while originally only ideas, gain force as they are reproduced in the material conditions of society. The distribution of wealth and poverty turns in part on the actions of social and legal actors who have accepted ideas of race, with the resulting material conditions becoming part of and reinforcement for the contingent meanings understood as race. (p. 14)

[5] Another important question is, What was it about Guinier's thinking and writing that alarmed both liberal and conservative writers and critics? Although this chapter will not specifically deal with this question, Stephen L. Carter's foreword in Lani Guinier's (1994) *The Tyranny of the Majority* provides excellent insight into the issue.

[6] Despite the effort to associate intelligence testing with genetic classification, this movement is more consistent with Wynter's (1995) notion of artificial/symbolic modes of classification. I contend that one goal of intelligence testing is to create a symbolic mode (i.e., test score) that affirms a belief system and justifies and motivates political action. Hernstein and Murray (1994) illustrated this point when they raised the following question: "How should policy deal with the twin realities that people differ in intelligence for reasons that are not their fault and that intelligence has a powerful bearing on how well people do in life?" (p. 535).

The authors argued that the interrelationship between race and intelligence is a fixed genetic reality. One limitation of this argument is captured in the following statement:

"Race" is not a biological category that can serve as a justifiable scientific tool for representing and comparing human populations. Rather, it is a *marker* [italics added] for historically oppressed groups whose domination was perpetuated and reproduced through reference to accidental phenotypical features, those of "visible" minorities. (Morrow & Torres, 1995, p. 385)

[7] Walker (1991) argued that race has evolved beyond being an ideological construct:
To most nineteenth-century white Americans the Negroes' racial difference and inferiority were not mere abstractions. Race was a physical fact. To argue as one recent student of southern history has that for nineteenth-century whites race was a pure "ideological notion" is arrant, ahistorical nonsense. Those American historians who have noted that racial antipathy was a major factor in the history of the United States have not been engaged in some sort of exceptionalism, as has sometimes been alleged. Nor have they accorded race a transhistorical, almost metaphysical, status that removes it from all possibility of analysis and understanding. On the contrary, what scholars such as Carl Degler, George Fredrickson, Wintrop Jordon, Leon Litwack, Michael Rogin, Richard Slotkin, and Joel Williamson have done is to pay close attention to race and racial thinking, as it evolved in Euro-American thought. (p. 5)

[8] Fields (1990) provides additional insight into the relationship between racial oppression and inferiority:
Race as a coherent ideology did not spring into being simultaneously with slavery, but took even more time than slavery did to become systematic. A commonplace that few stop to examine holds that people are more readily oppressed when they are already perceived as inferior by nature. The reverse is more to the point. People are more readily perceived as inferior by nature when they are already seen as oppressed. Africans and their descendants might be, to the eye of the English, heathen in religion, outlandish in nationality, and weird in appearance. But that did not add up to an ideology of racial inferiority until a further historical ingredient got stirred into the mixture: the incorporation of Africans and their descendants into a polity and society in which they lacked rights that others not only took for granted, but claimed as a matter of self-evident natural law. (p. 106)

[9] According to Anderson (1994), "As a general rule, the category of race has been distorted or omitted in the writing and teaching of American history" (p. 87). To avoid contributing to this problem, I use the heading "One Historical Overview" to indicate that my historical interpretation of the origins of critical race theory is subject to critique and debate. Moreover, the heading reflects my belief that it is possible to construct more than one history of this scholarly movement.

[10] Woodson's argument extended beyond legal education. He argued that schools and universities, in general, taught about European civilization and from European perspectives while ignoring the Black experience. He contended that this practice was harmful to the esteem and thinking of African American youth.

[11] For a discussion of educators who participated in this struggle, see Banks (1993).

[12] The purpose of this section of the chapter is to provide the reader insight into the thinking of critical race legal scholars about scholarship associated with critical legal studies. Thus, I am not attempting to represent the critical legal studies movement as a scholar in that movement might; rather, the intent is to present the conceptual similarities and differences as interpreted by individual scholars within the critical race group.

[13] According to Unger (1982):
Classical legal thought which flourished between approximately 1885 and 1940, conceived of law as a network of boundaries that marked off distinct spheres of individual and governmental power. Judicial authorities were thought to arbitrate conflict through impartial elaboration of a mechanical legal analytic. (p. 1670)

[14] I am not attempting to suggest that every scholar associated with the CLS movement borrows from the work of Gramsci. Instead, I suggest that this is a tendency within the movement (see, e.g., Gordon, 1984).

[15] Gramsci (1971) conceptualized the notion of hegemony, the method by which a network of attitudes and beliefs, influencing both popular values and the ideology of powerful members of society, sustains existing social configurations and convinces dominated groups that existing social relationships are natural.

[16] Unger's (1983) use of the word *tendencies* is more appropriate than *tenet* or *methodology*. CLS scholarship is closely associated with a variety of currents in contemporary radical social theory but does not reflect any agreed upon set of political tenets.

[17] Livingston (1982) contended that these two tendencies distinguished realist tradition from CLS. Whereas the realists employ analytic critique to discredit legal arguments and suggest specific methods of legal reform, critical legal scholars are more focused on the entire framework of liberal thought, exploring the tension between normative ideals and social structure.

[18] Narayan (1993) provided important insight into the enactment of hybridity:
One wall stands between ourselves as interested readers of stories and as theory-driven professionals; another wall stands between narrative (associated with subjective knowledge) and analysis (associated with objective truths). By situating ourselves as subjects simultaneously touched by life-experience and swayed by professional concerns, we can acknowledge the hybrid and positioned nature of our identities. Writing texts that mix lively narrative and rigorous analysis involves enacting hybridity, regardless of our origins. (p. 682)

[19] I use the term *conversation* to indicate the dialogue that exists between critical race theorists and other scholars outside this genre of legal analysis.

[20] For an excellent review and critique of *And We Are Not Saved*, see Delgado (1988b).

[21] Throughout this chronicle, Bell (1987) builds his arguments on research conducted by constitutional scholars (e.g., Beard, 1913; Wiecek, 1977). His analysis differs in that he uses story to introduce ideological contradiction and raise questions.

[22] The notion of property as "thing" is the popular conception. A second conception of property as the relationship between various entities is the more sophisticated conception. In this analysis, I am discussing the latter.

[23] I am using the terms *critical race theory* and *critical race critique* interchangeably in this chapter.

[24] See Casey (1995) for a review of narrative research in education.

[25] For additional discussion of this issue, see Tatum (1992).

[26] For a powerful example of this, see Sara Lawrence-Lightfoot's (1994) *I've Known Rivers*.

[27] Each of these mechanisms should be read and understood by scholars interested in equity and education. They provide a power mirror for self-reflection and a lens for critiquing the scholarship of colleagues in the field.

[28] Harris (1990) provided an excellent summary of the tension created by gender essentialism in political action and scholarly writing:
The notion that there is a monolithic "women's experience" that can be described independent of other facets of experience like race, class, and sexual orientation is one I refer to in this essay as "gender essentialism." A corollary to gender essentialism is "racial essentialism"—the belief that there is a monolithic "Black Experience," or "Chicano Experience." The source of gender and racial essentialism (and all other essentialisms, for the list of categories could be infinitely multiplied) is the second voice, the voice that claims to speak for all. The result of essentialism is to reduce the lives of people who experience multiple forms of oppression to addition problems: "racism + sexism = straight

black women's experience," or "racism + sexism + homophobia = black lesbian experience." Thus, in an essentialist world, black women's experience will always be forcibly fragmented before being subjected to analysis, as those who are "only interested in race" and those who are "only interested in gender" take their slices of our lives. (pp. 588–589)

[29] DuBois (1990) stated:

After the Egyptian and Indian, the Greek and Roman, the Teuton and Mongolian, the Negro is a sort of seventh son, born with a veil, and gifted with second-sight in this American world—a world which yields him no true self-consciousness, but only lets him see himself through the revelation of the other world. It is a peculiar sensation, this double-consciousness, this sense of always looking at one's self through the eyes of others, of measuring one's soul by the tape of a world that looks on in amused contempt and pity. One ever feels his two-ness—an American, a Negro; two souls, two thoughts, two unreconciled strivings; two warring ideals in one dark body, whose dogged strength alone keeps it from being torn asunder. (pp. 8–9)

For additional reading on DuBois and implications for the law, see Barnes (1990). For a discussion of DuBois's philosophy and African American education, see, for example, Lee, Lomotey, and Shujaa (1990) and Shujaa (1993).

[30] Delgado's argument is grounded in reality. For example, an article in *USA Today* naming the newspaper's academic all-star team described an African American student who, despite mediocre schooling and an unstable family structure, was able to maintain outstanding grades and admission to Stanford (della Cava, 1996). The article casts the young woman as a leader and role model for other students in similar social conditions. However, a remark by the student's counselor was confirming of Delgado's argument. The counselor stated, "Tonya has *grown* [italics added] in the last four years, moving from being a black nationalist to being less ethnocentric" (p. 8E). It appears that, in the eyes of the school counselor, Tonya's growth and role model status were predicated on more than overcoming her personal hurdles and included Tonya's view of the world.

[31] See Bell (1994) for a detailed description of the resistance he encountered when attempting to get a woman of color on the Harvard law faculty. The process described confirms Delgado's NBA analogy. See Frierson (1990) and Tate (1994) for similar discussions about the academy and education faculty.

[32] Similarly, Gordon (1992) argued that biographical information about scholars of color helps to forge relationships between minority scholars across the academy.

[33] Crenshaw (1988) used the term *New Right* to reflect the significant changes in the social and political fabric that have influenced the rhetoric and composition of tradition political coalitions.

[34] Recall that Delgado (1987, 1988a) and Williams (1987) offered additional reasons the CLS critique does not meet the needs of people of color. However, Delgado, Williams, and Crenshaw (1988) remarked that CLS provided important insights into civil rights discourse.

[35] This illustration of structural intersectionality provided by Crenshaw (1993) is especially relevant to the way children of color are labeled "at risk." Often, school systems label children of color "at risk" if they are the products of illiterate parents, poverty, and/or homes where abuse is present. This label is often a signal to school systems to offer limited intervention and then abandon responsibility, claiming the role of schools is to educate and not mediate social "dysfunction" (see Jackson, 1993).

[36] This point is consistent with Bell's (e.g., 1979, 1987, 1992) interest-convergence argument. However, Crenshaw provides a unique framework for understanding multiple intersections of a woman of color's reality.

[37] The four movies were "Angel Heart," "Colors," "Year of the Dragon," and "Tales from the Darkside." The video game and rap album were "General Custer's Revenge" and 2 Live Crew's "Nasty as They Wanna Be."

REFERENCES

Aleinikoff, A. T. (1991). A case for race-consciousness. *Columbia Law Review, 91,* 1060–1123.

Allen, R.L. (1974). *Reluctant reformers: The impact of racism on American social reform movements.* Washington, DC: Howard University.

Allport, G.W. (1954). *The nature of prejudice.* Garden City, NY: Doubleday Anchor.

Anderson, C. (1994). *Black labor and White wealth: The search for power and economic justice.* Edgewood, MD: Duncan & Duncan.

Apple, M.W. (1982). *Education and power.* New York: Routledge.

Apple, M.W. (1992). Education, culture and class power. *Educational Theory, 42,* 127–145.

Apple, M.W. (1993). *Official knowledge: Democratic education in a conservative age.* New York: Routledge.

Apple, M.W. (in press). Power, meaning, and identity: Critical sociology of education in the United States. *British Journal of Sociology of Education.*

Apple, M.W., & Weis, L. (1983). *Ideology and practice in schooling.* Philadelphia: Temple University Press.

Banks, J.A. (1971). Relevant social studies for Black pupils. In J.A. Banks & W.W. Joyce (Eds.), *Teaching social studies to culturally different children* (pp. 202–209). Menlo Park, CA: Addison-Wesley.

Banks, J.A. (1992). African American scholarship and the evolution of multicultural education. *Journal of Negro Education, 61,* 273–286.

Banks, J.A. (1993). Multicultural education: Historical development, dimensions, and practice. In L. Darling-Hammond (Ed.), *Review of research in education* (Vol. 19, pp. 3–49). Washington, DC: American Educational Research Association.

Barnes, R.D. (1990). Race consciousness: The thematic content of racial distinctiveness in critical race scholarship. *Harvard Law Review, 103,* 1864–1871.

Beard, C. (1913). *An economic interpretation of the Constitution of the United States.* New York: Macmillan.

Bell, D.A. (1979). *Bakke,* minority admissions, and the usual price of racial remedies. *California Law Review, 76,* 3–19.

Bell, D.A. (1980a). *Race, racism and American law* (2nd ed.). Boston: Little, Brown.

Bell, D.A. (1980b). *Brown v. Board of Education* and the interest-convergence dilemma. *Harvard Law Review, 93,* 518–533.

Bell, D.A. (1984). The hurdle too high: Class-based roadblocks to racial remediation. *Buffalo Law Review, 33,* 1–34.

Bell, D.A. (1985). The civil rights chronicles. *Harvard Law Review, 99,* 4–83.

Bell, D.A. (1987). *And we are not saved: The elusive quest for racial justice.* New York: Basic Books.

Bell, D.A. (1989). The final report: Harvard's affirmative action allegory. *Michigan Law Review, 87,* 2382–2410.

Bell, D.A. (1992). *Race, racism and American law* (3rd ed.). Boston: Little, Brown.

Bell, D.A. (1993). Remembrances of racism past: Getting beyond the civil rights decline. In H. Hill & J.E. Jones (Eds.), *Race in America: The struggle for equality* (pp. 73–82). Madison: University of Wisconsin Press.

Bell, D.A. (1994). *Confronting authority: Reflections of an ardent protester.* Boston: Beacon Press.

Black, E. (1988). *Our Constitution: The myth that binds us.* Boulder, CO: Westview Press.

Bogle, D. (1989). *Toms, coons, mulattoes, mammies, and bucks: An interpretive history of Blacks in American films.* New York: Continuum. (Original work published 1973).

Bowles, S., & Gintis, H. (1976). *Schooling in capitalist America.* New York: Basic Books.

Brosnan, D.F. (1986). Serious but not critical. *Southern California Law Review, 60,* 259–396.

Brown, K. (1993). Do African-Americans need immersion schools? The paradoxes created by the legal conceptualization of race and public education. *Iowa Law Review, 78,* 813–881.

Brown v. Board of Education, 347 U.S. 483 (1954).

Bullock, H.A. (1967). *A history of Negro education in the South: From 1619 to the present.* New York: Praeger.

Calmore, J.O. (1992). Critical race theory, Archie Shepp and fire music: Securing an authentic intellectual life in a multicultural world. *Southern California Law Review, 65,* 2129–2230.

Carnoy, M. (1974). *Education and cultural imperialism.* New York: McKay.

Carter, R.T., & Goodwin, A.L. (1994). Racial identity and education. In L. Darling-Hammond (Ed.), *Review of research in education* (Vol. 20, pp. 291–336). Washington, DC: American Educational Research Association.

Casey, K. (1995). The new narrative research in education. In M.W. Apple (Ed.), *Review of research in education* (Vol. 21, pp. 211–253). Washington, DC: American Educational Research Association.

Chodorow, N. (1978). *The reproduction of mothering.* Berkeley, CA: University of California Press.

Clark, K. (1963). *Prejudice and your child* (2nd ed.). New York: Simon & Schuster.

Clay, W.L. (1993). *Just permanent interests: Black Americans in Congress 1870–1992.* New York: Amistad.

Clune, W.F. (1993). The shift from equity to adequacy in school finance. *The World and I, 8,* 389–405.

Collins, H. (1982). *Marxism and law.* New York: Oxford University Press.

Comer, J., & Poussaint, A. (1976). *Black child care: How to bring up a healthy Black child in America.* New York: Simon & Schuster.

Cone, J. (1970). *A Black theology of liberation.* Philadelphia: Lippincott.

Crenshaw, K.W. (1988). Race, reform, retrenchment: Transformation and legitimation in anti-discrimination law. *Harvard Law Review, 101,* 1331–1387.

Crenshaw, K.W. (1993). Beyond racism and misogyny: Black feminism and 2 Live Crew. In M.J. Matsuda, C.R. Lawrence, R. Delgado, & K.W. Crenshaw (Eds.), *Words that wound: Critical race theory, assaultive speech, and the First Amendment* (pp. 111–132). Boulder, CO: Westview Press.

Crenshaw, K., Gotanda, N., Peller, G., & Thomas, K. (1995). Introduction. In K. Crenshaw, N. Gotanda, G. Peller, & K. Thomas (Eds.), *Critical race theory: The key writings that formed the movement* (pp. xii–xxxii). New York: New Press.

Cruse, H. (1984). *The crisis of the Negro intellectual: A historical analysis of the failure of Black leadership.* New York: Quill Books.

Culp, J.M. (1991). Toward a Black legal scholarship: Race and original understandings. *Duke Law Journal, 1,* 39–105.

Damarin, S.K. (1995). Gender and mathematics from a feminist standpoint. In W.G. Secada, E. Fennema, & L. Byrd Adajian (Eds.), *New directions for equity in mathematics education* (pp. 242–257). New York: Cambridge University Press.

Davis, M.D., & Clark, H.R. (1992). *Thurgood Marshall: Warrior at the bar, rebel on the bench.* New York: Birch Lane.

DeBouvoir, S. (1961). *The second sex.* New York: Bantam Books.

Delgado, R. (1984). The imperial scholar: Reflections on a review of civil rights literature. *University of Pennsylvania Law Review, 132,* 561–578.

Delgado, R. (1987). The ethereal scholar: Does critical legal studies have what minorities want? *Harvard Civil Rights-Civil Liberties Law Review, 22,* 301–322.

Delgado, R. (1988a). Critical legal studies and the realities of race—Does the fundamental contradiction have a corollary? *Harvard Civil Rights-Civil Liberties Law Review, 23,* 407–413.

Delgado, R. (1988b). Derrick Bell and the ideology of racial reform: Will we ever be saved? *Yale Law Journal, 97,* 923–947.

Delgado, R. (1989). Storytelling for oppositionists and others: A plea for narrative. *Michigan Law Review, 87,* 2411–2441.

Delgado, R. (1990). When a story is just a story: Does voice really matter? *Virginia Law Review, 76,* 95–111.

Delgado, R. (1991). Brewer's plea: Critical thoughts on common cause. *Vanderbilt Law Review, 44,* 1–14.

Delgado, R. (1992). Rodrigo's chronicle. *Yale Law Journal, 101,* 1357–1383.

Delgado, R. (1993). Rodrigo's sixth chronicle: Intersections, essences, and the dilemma of social reform. *New York University Law Review, 68,* 639–674.

Delgado, R. (1995a). The imperial scholar revisited: How to marginalize outsider writing, ten years later. In R. Delgado (Ed.), *Critical race theory: The cutting edge* (pp. 401–408). Philadelphia: Temple University Press.

Delgado, R. (1995b). Affirmative action as a majoritarian device: Or, do you really want to be a role model? In R. Delgado (Ed.), *Critical race theory: The cutting edge* (pp. 355–361). Philadelphia: Temple University Press.

Delgado, R., & Stefancic, J. (1989). Why do we tell the same stories? Law reform, critical librarianship, and the ripple helix dilemma. *Stanford Law Review, 42,* 207–225.

Delgado, R., & Stefancic, J. (1992). Images of the outsider in American law and culture: Can free expression remedy systemic ills? *Cornell Law Review, 77,* 1258–1297.

della Cava, M.R. (1996, May 17). Life's been brutal, but teen turns it around. *USA Today,* p. 8E.

Dewey, J. (1933). *How we think.* Boston: D.C. Heath.

Deyhle, D. (1995). Navajo youth and Anglo racism: Cultural integrity and resistance. *Harvard Educational Review, 65,* 403–444.

Dred Scott v. Sanford, 60 U.S. 393 (1857).

DuBois, W.E.B. (1990). *The souls of Black folks.* New York: Vintage Books. (Original work published 1906)

Dudziak, M.L. (1988). Desegregation as a cold war imperative. *Stanford Law Review, 41,* 61–120.

Durkheim, E. (1965). *The elementary forms of the religious life* (J.W. Swain, Trans.). New York: Free Press.

Elliot, R. (1987). *Litigating intelligence: IQ tests, special education, and social science in the courtroom.* Dover, MA: Auburn House.

Ewert, G.D. (1991). Habermas and education: A comprehensive overview of the influence of Habermas in educational literature. *Review of Educational Research, 61,* 345–378.

Fields, B.J. (1990). Slavery, race and ideology in the United States of America. *New Left Review, 181,* 93–118.

Ford, D.Y., & Webb, K.S. (1994). Desegregation of gifted educational programs: The impact of *Brown* on underachieving children of color. *Journal of Negro Education, 63,* 358–375.

Frankenstein, M. (1987). Critical mathematics education: An application of Paulo Friere's epistemology. In I. Shor (Ed.), *Friere for the classroom* (pp. 180–210). Portsmouth, NH: Boynton/Cook.

Fraser, S. (Ed.). (1995). *The bell curve wars: Race, intelligence, and the future of America.* New York: Basic Books.

Frierson, H.T. (1990). The situation of Black educational researchers: Continuation of a crisis. *Educational Researcher, 19*, 12–17.

Gage, N.L. (1989). The paradigm wars and their aftermath. *Educational Researcher, 18* (7), 4–10.

Gordon, B.M. (1992). The marginalized discourse of minority intellectual thought. In C.A. Grant (Ed.), *Research and multicultural education: From the margins to the mainstreams* (pp. 19–31). Washington, DC: Falmer.

Gordon, B.M. (1995). Knowledge construction, competing critical theories, and education. In J.A. Banks & C.A. McGee Banks (Eds.), *Handbook of research on multicultural education* (pp. 184–202). New York: Macmillan.

Gordon, R.W. (1984). Critical legal histories. *Stanford Law Review, 36*, 57–125.

Gould, S.J. (1981). *The mismeasure of man*. New York: Norton.

Gould, S.J. (1994, November 28). Curveball. *New Yorker*, pp. 139–149.

Gramsci, A. (1971). *Selections from the prison notebooks* (Q. Hoare and G. N. Smith, Eds. and Trans.). New York: International Publishers.

Grant, C.A., & Sleeter, C.E. (1986). Race, class, and gender in education research: An argument for integrative analysis. *Review of Educational Research, 56*, 195–211.

Grant, C.A., & Tate, W.F. (1995). Multicultural education through the lens of the multicultural education research literature. In J.A. Banks & C.A. McGee Banks (Eds.), *Handbook of research on multicultural education* (pp. 145–166). New York: Macmillan.

Greene, L. (1995). Race in the twenty-first century: Equality through the law? In K. Crenshaw, N. Gotanda, G. Peller, & K. Thomas (Eds.), *Critical race theory: The key writings that formed the movement* (pp. 292–302). New York: New Press.

Guinier, L. (1989). Keeping the faith: Black voters in the post Reagan era. *Harvard Civil Rights-Civil Liberties Law Review, 24*, 393–435.

Guinier, L. (1991a). No two seats: The elusive quest for political equality. *Virginia Law Review, 77*, 1413–1514.

Guinier, L. (1991b). The triumph of tokenism: The Voting Rights Act and the theory of Black electoral success. *Michigan Law Review, 89*, 1077–1154.

Guinier, L. (1994). *The tyranny of the majority: Fundamental fairness in representative democracy*. New York: Free Press.

Haney Lopez, I.F. (1996). *White by law: The legal construction of race*. New York: New York University Press.

Harding, S. (1986). *The science question in feminism*. Ithaca, NY: Cornell University Press.

Harp, L. (1996, March 6). Equity debates in states shift to standards and technology. *Education Week*, pp. 1, 25.

Harris, A.P. (1990). Race and essentialism in feminist legal theory. *Stanford Law Review, 42*, 581–616.

Harris, C.I. (1993). Whiteness as property. *Harvard Law Review, 106*, 1707–1791.

Herrnstein, R.J., & Murray, C. (1994). *The bell curve: Intelligence and class structure in American life*. New York: Free Press.

Hilliard, A.G. (1979). Standardization and cultural bias as impediments to the scientific study and validation of "intelligence." *Journal of Research and Development in Education, 12*, 47–58.

Hilliard, A.G. (1984). IQ testing as the emperor's new clothes: A critique of Jensen's "Bias in Mental Testing." In C. R. Reynolds & R.T. Brown (Eds.), *Perspectives on "Bias in Mental Testing"* (pp. 139–169). New York: Plenum.

Hirsch, J. (1975). The bankruptcy of "science" without scholarship. *Educational Theory, 25*, 3–28.

hooks, b. (1991). *Yearning: Race, gender, and cultural politics.* Boston: South End Press.

hooks, b., & West, C. (1991). *Breaking bread: Insurgent Black intellectual life.* Boston: South End Press.

Hutchinson, A., & Monahan, P. (1984). The "rights" stuff: Roberto Unger and beyond. *Texas Law Review, 62,* 1477–1539.

Jackson, S.A. (1993). Opportunity to learn: The health connection. *Journal of Negro Education, 62,* 377–393.

Jacob, E. (1987). Qualitative research traditions: A review. *Review of Educational Research, 57,* 1–50.

Jefferson, T. (1954). *Notes on the state of Virginia.* New York: Norton. (Original work published 1784).

Jensen, A.R. (1969). How much can we boost IQ and scholastic achievement? *Harvard Educational Review, 39,* 1–123.

Johnson, A.M. (1993). Bid whist, tonk, and *United States v. O.K. Fordice* : Why integrationism fails African-Americans again. *California Law Review, 81,* 1401–1470.

Jones, N.R. (1993). Civil rights after *Brown* : "The stormy road we trod." In H. Hill & J. E. Jones (Eds.), *Race in America: The struggle for equality* (pp. 97–111). Madison: University of Wisconsin.

Kamin, L. (1974). *The science and politics of IQ.* New York: Wiley.

Kennedy, R. (1989). Racial critiques of legal academia. *Harvard Law Review, 102,* 1745–1819.

King, J.E. (1995). Culture-centered knowledge: Black studies, curriculum transformation, and social action. In J.A. Banks & C.A. McGee Banks (Eds.), *Handbook of research on multicultural education* (pp. 265–292). New York: Macmillan.

Kozol, J. (1991). *Savage inequalities: Children in America's schools.* New York: Crown.

Ladner, J. (1973). *The death of White sociology.* New York: Vintage Books.

Ladson-Billings, G. (1994). *The dreamkeepers: Successful teachers of African American children.* San Francisco: Jossey-Bass.

Ladson-Billings, G. (1995). Toward a theory of culturally relevant pedagogy. *American Educational Research Journal, 32,* 465–491.

Ladson-Billings, G., & Tate, W.F. (1995). Toward a critical theory of education. *Teachers College Record, 97,* 47–68.

Lasswell, H.D., & McDougal, M.S. (1943). Legal education and public policy: Professional training in the public interest. *Yale Law Review, 52,* 203.

Lawrence, C.R. (1987). The id, the ego, and equal protection: Reckoning with unconscious racism. *Stanford Law Review, 39,* 317–388.

Lawrence, C.R. (1993). If he hollers let him go: Regulating racist speech on campus. In M.J. Matsuda, C.R. Lawrence, R. Delgado, & K.W. Crenshaw (Eds.), *Words that wound: Critical race theory, assaultive speech, and the First Amendment* (pp. 53–88). Boulder, CO: Westview Press.

Lawrence-Lightfoot, S. (1994). *I've known rivers: Lives of loss and liberation.* Reading, MA: Addison-Wesley.

Lee, C.D., Lomotey, K., & Shujaa, M. (1990). How shall we sing our sacred song in a strange land? The dilemma of double consciousness and the complexities of an African-centered pedagogy. *Journal of Education, 172* (2), 45–61.

Lightfoot, S.L. (1980). Families as educators: The forgotten people of *Brown.* In D.A. Bell (Ed.), *Shades of brown: New perspectives on school desegregation* (pp. 2–19). New York: Teachers College Press.

Livingston, D. (1982). 'Round and 'round the bramble bush: From legal realism to critical legal scholarship. *Harvard Law Review, 95,* 1669–1690.

Llwellyn, K. (1931). Some realism about realism: Responding to Dean Pound. *Harvard Law Review, 44,* 1222–1264.

Lomawaima, K.T. (1995). Educating Native Americans. In J.A. Banks & C.A. McGee Banks (Eds.), *Handbook of research on multicultural education* (pp. 331–347). New York: Macmillan.

Madaus, G.E. (1994). A technological and historical consideration of equity issues associated with proposals to change the nation's testing policy. *Harvard Educational Review*, *64*, 76–95.

Marable, M. (1983). *How capitalism underdeveloped Black America*. Boston: South End Press.

Margo, R.A. (1990). *Race and schooling in the South, 1880–1950: An economic history.* Chicago: University of Chicago Press.

Matsuda, M.J. (1989). Public response to racist speech: Considering the victim's story. *Michigan Law Review*, *87*, 2320–2381.

Matsuda, M.J., Lawrence, C.R., Delgado, R., & Crenshaw, K.W. (Eds.). (1993). *Words that wound: Critical race theory, assaultive speech, and the First Amendment.* Boulder CO: Westview Press.

McCarthy, C., & Crichlow, W. (Eds.). (1993). *Race identity and representation in education.* New York: Routledge.

McLaurin v. Oklahoma State Regents for Higher Education, 339 U.S. 637 (1950).

McNeil, G. R. (1983). *Groundwork: Charles Hamilton Houston and the struggle for civil rights.* Philadelphia: University of Pennsylvania Press.

Ming, W. (1948). Racial restrictions and the Fourteenth Amendment: The Restrictive Covenant Cases. *University of Chicago Law Review*, *16*, 203–238.

Missouri ex rel. Gaines v. Canada, 305 U.S. 337 (1938).

Moran, C.E., & Hakuta, K. (1995). Bilingual education: Broadening research perspectives. In J.A. Banks & C.A. McGee Banks (Eds.), *Handbook of research on multicultural education* (pp. 445–464). New York: Macmillan.

Morrison, T. (1992). *Playing in the dark: Whiteness and the literary imagination.* Cambridge, MA: Harvard University Press.

Morrow, R.A., & Torres, C.A. (1995). *Social theory and education.* Albany, NY: State University of New York Press.

Moskowitz, J., Stullich, S., & Deng, B. (1993). *Targeting, formula, and resource allocation issues: Focusing federal funds where the needs are greatest.* Washington, DC: U.S. Department of Education.

Narayan, K. (1993). How native is a "native" anthropologist? *American Anthropologist*, *95*, 671–686.

National Governors Association. (1993). *The debate on opportunity-to-learn standards.* Washington, DC: Author.

Nieto, S. (1992). *Affirming diversity: The sociopolitical context of multicultural education.* White Plains, NY: Longman.

Noddings, N. (1990). Feminist critiques in the professions. In C.B. Cazden (Ed.), *Review of research in education* (Vol. 16, pp. 393–424). Washington, DC: American Educational Research Association.

O'Day, J.A., & Smith, M.S. (1993). Systemic reform and educational opportunity. In S.H. Fuhrman (Ed.), *Designing coherent education policy: Improving the system* (pp. 250–312). San Francisco: Jossey-Bass.

Odden, A.R. (1992). School finance and education reform: An overview. In A.R. Odden (Ed.), *Rethinking school finance: An agenda for the 1990's* (pp. 1–40). San Francisco: Jossey-Bass.

Oh, R., & Wu, F. (1996). The evolution of race in law: The Supreme Court moves for approving internment of Japanese Americans to disapproving affirmative action for African Americans. *Michigan Journal of Race & Law*, *1*, 165–184.

Omi, M., & Winant, H. (1994). *Racial formation in the United States: From the 1960s to the 1990s* (2nd ed.). New York: Routledge.

Padilla, A.M., & Lindholm, K.J. (1995). Quantitative educational research with ethnic minorities. In J.A. Banks & C.A. McGee Banks (Eds.), *Handbook of research on multicultural education* (pp. 97–113). New York: Macmillan.

Pang, V.O. (1995). Asian Pacific American students: A diverse and complex population. In J.A. Banks & C.A. McGee Banks (Eds.), *Handbook of research on multicultural education* (pp. 412–424). New York: Macmillan.

Perry, T. (1993). *Toward a theory of African American achievement* (Report No. 16). Boston: Center on Families, Communities, Schools, and Children.

Peters, E. (1982). Stereotyping: Moving against consciousness. In *Ethnic notions: Black images in the white mind* (exhibition catalogue). Berkeley, CA: Berkeley Art Center.

Pitts, L. (1995, June 25). Racist status quo onerous on Blacks... *Wisconsin State Journal*, p. 3B.

Plessy v. Ferguson, 163 U.S. 537 (1896).

Regents of the University of California v. Bakke, 438 U.S. 265 (1978).

Reich, R.B. (Ed.). (1988). *The power of public ideas.* Cambridge, MA: Ballinger.

Reid, E. (1995). Waiting to excel: Biraciality in the classroom. In C.A. Grant (Ed.), *Educating for diversity* (pp. 263–274). Boston: Allyn & Bacon.

Roberts v. City of Boston, 59 Mass. (5 Cush) 198 (1850).

Rodríguez, C.A. (1995). Puerto Ricans in historical and social science research. In J.A. Banks & C.A. McGee Banks (Eds.), *Handbook of research on multicultural education* (pp. 223–244). New York: Macmillan.

Roediger, D. (1991). *The wages of Whiteness.* New York: Verso.

Ross, T. (1989). The Richmond narratives. *Texas Law Review, 68,* 381–413.

Russell, M.M. (1995). Race and the dominant gaze: Narratives of law and inequality in popular film. In R. Delgado (Ed.), *Critical race theory: The cutting edge* (pp. 56–63). Philadelphia: Temple University Press.

Scheppele, K.L. (1989). Forward: Telling stories. *Michigan Law Review, 87,* 2073–2098.

Schmitz, B., Butler, J.E., Rosenfelt, D., & Guy-Sheftall, B. (1995). Women's studies and curriculum transformation. In J.A. Banks & C.A. McGee Banks (Eds.), *Handbook of research on multicultural education* (pp. 708–728). New York: Macmillan.

Schrag, F. (1992). In defense of positivist research paradigms. *Educational Researcher, 21,* 5–8.

Secada, W.G. (1989). *Equity in education.* London: Falmer.

Secada, W.G. (1995). Social and critical dimensions for equity in mathematics education. In W.G. Secada, E. Fennema, & L.B. Adajian (Eds.), *New directions for equity in mathematics education* (pp. 146–164). New York: Cambridge University Press.

Selden, S. (1994). Early twentieth-century biological determinism and the classification of exceptional students. *Evaluation and Research in Education, 8* (1), 21–39.

Shujaa, M.J. (1993). Education and schooling: You can have one without the other. *Urban Education, 27,* 328–351.

Shulman, L.S. (1986). Paradigms and research programs in the study of teaching: A contemporary perspective. In M.C. Wittrock (Ed.), *Handbook of research on teaching* (pp. 3–36). New York: Macmillan.

Sipuel v. Board of Regents of the University of Oklahoma, 322 U.S. 631 (1948).

Sowell, T. (1984). *Civil rights, rhetoric or reality?* New York: Morrow.

Stick, J. (1986). Can nihilism be pragmatic? *Harvard Law Review, 100,* 332–401.

Takaki, R. (1993). *A different mirror: A history of multicultural America.* Boston: Little, Brown.

Tate, W.F. (1994). From inner city to ivory tower: Does my voice matter in the academy? *Urban Education, 29,* 245–269.

Tate, W.F. (1995a). School mathematics and African American students: Thinking seriously about opportunity-to-learn standards. *Educational Administration Quarterly, 31,* 424–448.

Tate, W. F. (1995b). Economics, equity, and the national mathematics assessment: Are we creating a national toll road? In W. G. Secada, E. Fennema, & L. B. Adajian (Eds.), *New directions for equity in mathematics education* (pp. 191–204). New York: Cambridge University Press.

Tate, W. F., Ladson-Billings, G., & Grant, C. A. (1993). The *Brown* decision revisited: Mathematizing social problems. *Educational Policy, 7*, 255–275.

Tatum, B. D. (1992). Talking about race, learning about racism: The application of racial identity development theory in the classroom. *Harvard Educational Review, 62*, 1–24.

Torres, G., & Milun, K. (1990). Translating *Yonnonidio* by precedent and evidence: The Mashpee Indian case. *Duke Law Journal*, 625–659.

Unger, R. M. (1983). The critical legal studies movement. *Harvard Law Review, 96*, 561–675.

Walker, C. (1991). *Deromanticizing Black history: Critical essays and reappraisals.* Knoxville: University of Tennessee Press.

Weinburg, M. (1977). *Minority students: A research appraisal.* Washington, DC: U.S. Government Printing Office.

White, G. (1972). From sociological jurisprudence to realism: Jurisprudence and social change in early twentieth-century America. *Virginia Law Review, 58*, 999–1028.

Wiecek, W. (1977). *The sources of antislavery constitutionalism in America: 1760–1848.* Ithaca, NY: Cornell University Press.

Wilkins, R. (1995, March 27). Racism has its privileges. *The Nation*, pp. 409–416.

Williams, P. J. (1987). Alchemical notes: Reconstructing ideals from deconstructed rights. *Harvard Civil Rights-Civil Liberties Law Review, 22*, 401–433.

Williams, P. J. (1991). *The alchemy of race and rights: Diary of a law professor.* Cambridge, MA: Harvard University Press.

Williams, R. A. (1989). Documents of barbarism: The contemporary legacy of European racism and colonialism in the narrative traditions of federal Indian law. *Arizona Law Review, 31*, 237–278.

Winter, S. L. (1989). The cognitive dimension of the *agon* between legal power and narrative meaning. *Michigan Law Review, 87*, 2225–2279.

Woodson, C. G. (1990). *The mis-education of the Negro.* Trenton, NJ: Africa World Press. (Original work published 1933).

Wynter, S. (1995, October). *Historical construction or cultural code? "Race," the "local culture" of the West and the origins of the modern world.* Paper presented at the University of Wisconsin Lecture Series on the Construction of Race, Madison.

Manuscript Received June 24, 1996
Accepted August 28, 1996

III.
TEACHING AND RESEARCH

Chapter 5

Professional Development Schools and Equity: A Critical Analysis of Rhetoric and Research

LINDA VALLI, DAVID COOPER, AND LISA FRANKES
University of Maryland at College Park

Tomorrow's Schools (1990) is the second report in the Holmes Group's trilogy on the reform of education in the United States. Centrally focused on the improved preparation of teachers, the three reports offer a vision of a new institution, the professional development school (PDS). Although the other two volumes, *Tomorrow's Teachers* (1986) and *Tomorrow's Schools of Education* (1995), discuss this new institution, the second volume elaborates on principles for its design. Given the growing popularity of the concept, the growing numbers of PDSs and PDS networks, and the work of the National Council for the Accreditation of Teacher Education in developing PDS standards, a close examination of the design principles and related research seems warranted.

While other reviews of the research have been conducted, this one differs in three fundamental ways.[1] First, it attempts to match the goals set out by PDS proponents with changes documented through research. Second, it seeks to determine whether those changes are what Cuban (1988) calls first- or second-order change. Finally, it specifically relates these PDS goals and changes to equity goals. Equity has long been a cherished, albeit controversial, goal of American education. It is also a driving force behind the vision for PDSs as articulated in *Tomorrow's Schools*. Therefore, a question worth asking is, What, if anything, would enable PDSs to accomplish a goal that has thus far eluded most of our nation's schools?

To answer that question, we begin with a definition of PDSs, an explanation of first-and second-order changes, and an overview of equity as a concept in educational literature. We then review both the advocacy and research literature on PDSs under six themes we have identified and extract equity implications. The specific questions guiding our research were as follows:

1. What does the literature say about aspirations for PDSs? What do proponents hope and claim these new organizational structures can accomplish? Are these first- or second-order change aspirations?

2. What do actual research studies of PDSs say has been accomplished? Under what category of reform do these accomplishments fall? Are they first or second order?

3. What are the equity implications of change efforts? Does the new organizational structure of the PDS promote equity?

Our comprehensive review of the research indicates that PDS achievements still fall short of expectations. In many instances, instrumental recommendations about linking theory to practice, strengthening school-university collaboration, and providing time for professional development seem to have become ends in themselves. Or they are linked to commonly accepted notions of higher achievement for students and teacher candidates. While there is some commitment to establishing PDSs in inner cities, broad issues of equity and social justice are often absent in both PDS research and practice. Part of the explanation might be that PDSs are still in initial stages of development. But our review also causes us to wonder whether the vision expressed in the Holmes Report (1990) is concrete enough to be realized, whether educators widely share (or even know about) the commitment to equity articulated in the report, and whether the conditions of teaching and teacher education enable such radical transformation.

DEFINITIONS

Professional Development Schools

We adopted the Holmes Group's (1990) definition of a PDS as "a school for the development of novice professionals, for continuing development of experienced professionals and *for the research and development of the teaching profession*" (p. 1). This definition guides the work of most PDS practitioners and researchers (Darling-Hammond, 1994; Koffman & Green, 1994; Winitzky, Stoddart, & O'Keefe, 1992). In our judgment, a school would not be a PDS unless it systematically and simultaneously engaged in teacher preparation, professional development, and research on a school-wide basis. Unlike Stallings and Kowalski (1990), we would not consider collaborations focusing only on in-service teachers to be PDSs. Nor would we include schools in which research, professional development, and teacher education are private arrangements among small groups of teachers and teacher educators. A PDS is an institutional commitment to a particular vision of change.

With this definition in mind, we developed a matrix to analyze the research. Using *Tomorrow's Schools* (Holmes, 1990) as the primary source, we found seven basic reform themes for PDSs: teacher education, teaching and learning, school organization, equity goals, professional development, inquiry, and collaborative alliances. An eighth category—curriculum and instruction—was collapsed into the teaching and learning category early in the analysis when distinctions were difficult to make. The other seven categories remained robust throughout the review of the literature, although some were clearly more salient than others. When we found no separate studies that focused primarily on equity issues, we decided to examine the implications for equity within each of the other six categories.

First- and Second-Order Change

In addition to the categories of change attributed to PDSs, we were also interested in the quality or degree of change. Therefore, we used Cuban's (1988) notion of first-and second-order change. First-order changes are those intended to make existing organizational goals and structures more efficient and effective. They are solutions to quality-control problems. Second-order changes restructure the organization itself. As solutions to design problems, they "introduce new goals, structures, and roles that transform familiar ways of doing things into new ways of solving persistent problems. . . . [They are] attempts to fundamentally alter existing authority, roles, and uses of time and space" (Cuban, 1988, p. 342). Because schools as organizations differ, a first-order change for one school might be a second-order change for another. Nonetheless, most schools have similar organizational and curricular characteristics. By using this categorical framework, we were able to plot out (proposed) changes in the research studies we analyzed.

Equity

"Everyone's Children: Diversity, Equity, and Social Justice" is a chapter title in *Tomorrow's Schools*. But what exactly is meant by equity? We found no explicit definition in the document itself, although the surrounding concepts—everybody's children, diversity, and social justice—offer a strong interpretive context, as do numerous sections of the report. The history of equity as a concept in American education also provides an important frame of reference.

In a paper presented at the Conference on Democracy and Education, Patricia Graham (1991) examines America's expectations for schools over the past century. Following Cremin, she argues that "the role of schools is powerfully shaped by the context in which they exist" and that expectations change over time (p. 2). In the first half of the century, laws and policies were devised for the purpose of increasing school attendance. Keeping more children in school for longer periods of time was a way to strengthen democracy. The second half of the century brought a shift in social policy to the goal of increased access. Merely keeping students in school longer was not enough. With the civil rights movement, the question of *who* had access to *what kinds* of educational opportunities became a central concern. Increased access provided

opportunities for students to enroll in institutions previously unavailable to them either because they could not afford them, they were the wrong race, ethnicity, religion or gender for them, or they were too old or too physically impaired for them. (Graham, 1991, p. 8)

More strikingly, the concept of equal educational opportunity started to be used in federal educational policy to argue that "children from poor families needed more from the schools than did the children of the rich" (p. 6).

While increased attendance and access are still widely discussed in policy arenas, current expectations for American schools include increased academic achievement for all students. Although once content to let most children slide through an academically weak vocational or general curriculum, "Americans are coming to recognize that our future depends on educating everybody well" (Graham, 1991, p. 23). The problem, she says, is that there are few models of how to achieve this goal in a heterogeneous society. One model, the one developed by the Holmes Group, is the PDS.

In Graham's broad historical analysis, the concept of equal educational opportunity shifts from merely receiving everyone's children to providing high-quality educational experiences for all students and additional resources to those with most need. This shift helps explain why the term *equity* has replaced the older concept of equal educational opportunity. Both are related to "egalitarian concepts of liberty, democracy and freedom from bias" (Grant, 1989, p. 89). But equity places more emphasis on notions of fairness and justice, even if that requires an unequal distribution of goods and services. While, historically, equality has been interpreted as *sameness* or *parity* between groups "along some agreed upon index," equity is seen as "a check on the justice of specific actions that are carried out within the educational arena and the arrangements that result from those actions" (Secada, 1989, p. 69). Equity becomes an issue when some social groups are perceived as privileged or as benefiting more than other groups; equity policies compensate for the negative consequences of stereotyping and discrimination (Harvey & Klein, 1989).

As Graham (1991) suggests, equity is not a static or unidimensional construct. Three changing dimensions are discussed in the literature: access, process or participation, and outcomes. *Equity of access* refers to opportunities to gain entry to what is viewed as desirable. Harvey and Klein (1989) describe "the need to provide appropriate routes of access that allow everyone to avail themselves of existing educational treatments and benefits" (p. 57). Equity advocates claim that this requires more than just opening doors. Different routes or supports (e.g., individualized educational plans, wheelchair ramps, Headstart, differentiated curriculum or materials) can be justified on the basis of need, merit, or past discrimination. Graham (1991) makes clear the difference between equal and equitable access by using the metaphor of a swim meet in which swimmers and nonswimmers alike are thrown into a pool without life support and told to make their way to the other end.

Equity of participation (treatment) refers to those things that go on in a school to educate students. This would include the structures and processes that define everyday life in schools (sometimes referred to as the hidden curriculum), as well as the overt or formal curriculum. Schools concerned about structural equity would make every effort "to eliminate tracking, biased testing, and other arrangements that so often deny such access on grounds of race, gender and socioeconomic class" (Beane & Apple, 1995, p. 11). Within the formal curriculum of the school, equity would require attention to student differences, teacher-student interactions, and instructional materials. It would mean "establishing a classroom environment that is not colorblind and teaching in a manner that affirms learning style differences, based on culture and gender socialization" (Grant, 1989, p. 9). Curriculum content would be interrogated for what and whose knowledge is legitimated and whose interests are served; it would help students understand and address social arrangements that produce inequality. In this respect, the concept of equity is more inclusive than the older notion of equal educational opportunities, which focused primarily on quantitative differences among groups (Secada, 1989). By implication, the concept also applies to the various ways in which educators' roles and relationships are defined.

Equity of outcomes refers to the result of educational processes: the equitable distribution of the benefits of schooling. Equitable outcomes of schooling would decrease, if not eliminate, group differences in school achievement, attitudes, dropout rates, college attendance, and employment. Since one of the functions of schooling is to prepare students for later life employment, it seems "patently unjust for equal levels of schooling and of school knowledge to result in unequal job opportunities in later life" (Secada, 1989, p. 76). Achieving more equitable social and economic outcomes might require unequal schooling outcomes.

As this analysis suggests, the history, definition, and use of educational equality and equity are complex and contested. Apple (1993) has argued that the liberal consensus around these concepts is breaking down as a result of upheavals in the U.S. economy, the scarcity of fiscal resources, the perception that gains made by social groups from affirmative action policies are unfair, and the ascendancy of New Right and conservative movements. An inclusive interpretation of equity that has taken decades to achieve is being redefined and narrowed.

No longer is it seen as linked to past group oppression and disadvantagement. It is now simply a case of guaranteeing individual choice under the conditions of a "free market." Thus, the current emphasis on "excellence" (a word with multiple meanings and social uses) has shifted educational discourse so that underachievement once again increasingly is seen as largely the fault of the student. (Apple, 1993, p. 19)

Educational interventions such as school choice, informed by a market rather than a democratic ideology, are offered as solutions to the economic and educational neglect of urban environments.

As described later in this chapter, the issue of school choice is raised in *Tomorrow's Schools*. By and large, however, the Holmes Group situates itself squarely within the tradition of social democratic principles, explicitly linking itself to "the concerns that brought the revolution for racial equality to American education" (1990, p. 2). Statements such as the following, which convey commitment to equitable access, processes, and outcomes, are found throughout the document; these statements address issues of equity for both children and those who work in these sites.

A major commitment of the Professional Development School will be overcoming the educational and social barriers raised by an unequal society. (p. 7)

We believe that PDSs, many of which will purposely be sited in poor areas, will engage in social and political action to acquire additional resources and to press the claims for justice in the larger society. (p. 33)

We should bring into both university and public school teaching more faculty from America's rainbow of nations and peoples. . . . The current situation calls for radical action by universities, colleges of education, and school systems—by professional development schools. (p. 40)

The purpose of this review is to determine the extent to which PDSs, as described in the research, embody this rhetoric.[2]

DATA SOURCES AND METHODOLOGY

A primary data source for this research review was Abdal-Haqq's (1993) annotated bibliography of resources on PDSs.[3] The resources include concept papers, handbooks, bibliographies, course outlines, policy statements, and historical perspectives. Of the 119 listings, 33 are identified as research reports, some of which were directories and syntheses of existing studies. Others were more general research studies of professional development or teacher education, such as Goodlad's (1990) *Teachers for Our Nation's Schools*, that did not report original research on PDSs. Still others focused on collaboration in general. Since some of these sources did not fit our specific research requirements, they were eliminated from the sample, leaving 23 from the original list.

These sources were supplemented by others found through an ERIC search of "professional development schools" and "research" from January 1992 through January 1996. Thirty-six sources were identified from this search, a number of which overlapped with the Abdal-Haqq list. Others were added from an ERIC search of technical reports and a hand search of 11 academic journals from January 1994 through January 1996.[4] By restricting ourselves to original research on actual PDSs and their participants, we arrived at the sources listed in Table 1. Of these, 20 focused primarily on key participants in a variety of roles and sites, 14 focused on elementary schools, and 6 focused on middle schools. Five studies examined high schools, and 5 examined urban settings.[5] Solitary studies were conducted on a rural setting, a state department of education, and Holmes Group members. Six other studies examined PDSs in general (see Table 1).

GOALS AND RESEARCH FINDINGS

What types of reform do advocates claim are possible through PDSs? As mentioned earlier, we found seven distinct areas of reform. Many of these goals are primarily second order, those which the research on organizational change has found to be most difficult to accomplish (Cuban, 1988; Fullan, 1991). We found it impossible, however, to always make a clear distinction between first-and second-order change. Change in one aspect of an organization always affects another. Take, for example, the practice of classroom teachers teaming with uni-

TABLE 1
Focus of PDS Research Articles

Focus	Number	Primary Sources
Key participants	20	Boyd, 1994; Driscoll et al., 1994; Francis, 1992; Lemlech et al., 1994; McGowan & Power, 1993; Moore et al., 1991; Morris & Nunnery, 1993; Navarro, 1992; Nihlen, 1992; Putnam, 1992; Romerdahl, 1991; Ruscoe & Whitford, 1991; Ruscoe et al., 1989; Sandholtz & Merseth, 1992; Shen, 1994; Stanulis, 1995; Teitel, 1992; Wiseman & Nason, 1995; Woloszyk & Hill, 1994; Yopp et al., 1993–94
Elementary schools	14	Barksdale-Ladd, 1994; Berry & Catoe, 1994; Boles & Troen, 1994; Fear et al., 1991; Francis, 1992; Gross, 1993; Harris & Harris, 1992–1993; Jett-Simpson et al., 1992; Karr et al., 1994; Lemlech & Hertzog-Foliart, 1993; McGowan & Powell, 1993; Nihlen, 1992; Rosaen & Lindquist, 1992; Rushcamp & Roehler, 1992
Middle schools	6	Francis, 1992; Grossman, 1994; Miller & Silvernail, 1994; Sagmiller & Gerhke, 1992; Schack & Overturf, 1994; Snyder, 1994
High schools	5	Francis, 1992; Lythcott & Schwartz, 1994; Sandholtz & Merseth, 1992; Whitford, 1994; Woloszyk, 1992
Urban settings	5	Jett-Simpson et al., 1992; Lewis, 1992; Pasch & Pugach, 1990; Stallings, 1991; Yopp et al., 1993–1994
Rural settings	1	Francis, 1992
State department	1	Teitel, 1993
Holmes Group members	1	Yinger & Hendricks, 1990
General	6	Brainard, 1989; Moore & Hopkins, 1993; Putnam, 1992; Theobald, 1991; Winitzky et al., 1992; Wolfe et al., 1994

versity professors as instructors in methods courses. According to Cuban, this would be a second-order change. It fundamentally alters the classroom teachers' role since they do not normally function as teacher educators and do not normally teach in teams. However, if this methods course did not reconceptualize "how" and "for what" to prepare new teachers, the change in teacher education would be first order. Similarly, building ongoing professional development opportunities into the school schedule would be a second-order change. But unless the vision of teaching and learning informing that professional development is fundamentally different than normal practice, the change in classroom teaching would be first order. Current practice would simply become more effective.

Studies of the various sites suggest that more time and resources are spent on implementing certain categories of reform than others. Although the advocacy lit-

TABLE 2
Number of Studies in Change Categories

Types of changes	Number	Primary sources
Teaching and Learning	4	Gross, 1993; Jett Simpson et al., 1992; Rosaen & Lindquist, 1992; Stallings, 1991
Teacher education	7	Driscoll et al, 1994; Lemlech & Hertzog-Foliart, 1993; Shen, 1994; Stanulis, 1995; Teitel, 1992; Woloszyk & Hill, 1994; Yopp et al., 1993–1994
Professional development	14	Barksdale-Ladd, 1994; Boles & Troen, 1994; Boyd, 1994; Gehrke & Sagmiller, 1991; Jett-Simpson et al., 1992; Morris & Nunnery, 1993; Navarro, 1992; Neufeld & Freeman, 1993; Nihlen, 1992; Putnam, 1992; Romerdahl, 1991; Ruscamp & Roehler, 1992; Shack & Overturf, 1994; Stallings, 1991
Organization and structure	6	Lewis, 1992; Ruscoe et al., 1989; Ruscoe & Whitford, 1991; Theobald, 1991; Wolfe et al., 1994; Woloszyk, 1992
Inquiry and research	3	Boles & Troen, 1994; Rushcamp & Roehler, 1992; Schack & Overturf, 1994
Collaborative alliances	23	Berry & Catoe, 1994; Fear et al., 1991; Francis, 1992; Grossman, 1994; Lemlech & Hertzog-Foliart, 1993; Lemlech et al., 1994; Lythcott & Schwartz, 1994; McGowan & Powell, 1993; Miller & Silvernail, 1994; Moore & Hopkins, 1993; Pasch & Pugach, 1990; Putman, 1992; Romerdahl, 1991; Ruscoe & Whitford, 1991; Sagmiller & Gehrke, 1992; Sandholtz & Merseth, 1992; Snyder, 1994; Teitel, 1993; Teitel, 1991; Wiseman, 1993; Wiseman & Nason, 1995; Whitford, 1994; Woloszyk, 1992

erature primarily emphasizes change in teaching and teacher education, by far the greatest focus of research (23 studies) has been on the development of collaborative relations (see Table 2). A secondary focus has been on professional development (14 studies). Less systematic attention has been paid to teacher education (7 studies), the organization and structure of schools (6 studies), the nature of teaching and learning (4 studies), and the process of inquiry (3 studies).

There can be several explanations for this unevenness: (a) Some goals, such as creating collaborative alliances, are viewed as prerequisites to other goals; (b) some are viewed as more important than others; (c) some are inherently part of others (e.g., equity in teaching and learning or inquiry in professional development); or (d) the research does not reflect what is actually occurring at various sites. Each of these explanations is plausible, but the literature offers few clues about which might be correct. We suspect that each is part of the explanation. Many of the PDSs were in initial stages of development, so collaboration was a natural focus for inquiry. A documentation study of six PDSs using group development stage theory suggests the plausibility of this conclusion (Putnam, 1992). Although we categorized each study by its dominant research focus, many did address multiple themes. The cases described in Darling-Hammond (1994), for instance, touch on almost all of the themes, although they are mainly about the collaborations themselves.

Teaching and Learning
Goals

Schools fail students if they deny them a passport to the mainstream; they also fail if students graduate with a sense that their own culture is worthless. (Holmes Group, 1990, p. 22)

This change category, which focuses on prekindergarten through Grade 12 schools, has received the most attention in the advocacy literature. In one listing of 11 features of PDSs, 5 are related to this category: understanding as the goal of the school, important knowledge, dialectical instruction, active pupils, and valid assessment (Murray, 1993). This comes as no surprise since (a) the primary goal of schools is to help children and adolescents learn and (b) schools have been repeatedly criticized for their inadequacy in this regard since *A Nation at Risk* was published (National Commission on Excellence in Education, 1983). In fact, all of the other categories of change are designed to bring about improvements in children's learning. The nature of classroom teaching is increasingly viewed as the most immediate and critical factor in that regard. As Murray, a founding member and current president of the Holmes Group, claims: "The gap between current schooling practices and sites in which ambitious and modern teaching can be practiced is the fundamental problem that the PDS is designed to solve" (1993, p. 62).

Some of the language in *Tomorrow's Schools* would represent only first-order changes for some schools. As recommended by the report, many teachers currently try to help students understand scientific analysis, use reading and writing across the curriculum, create cooperative classrooms, teach students to take responsibility for their own learning, and deepen understanding of their own practice by mentoring new teachers. Most of the language, however, evokes images of teaching and learning that differ radically from dominant practice. Although many teachers attempt "teaching for understanding," the regularities of classroom life do not often encourage the voice, conversation, and criticism this goal entails. Contrary to the advice in the report, many teachers still separate the teaching of basic facts and skill "from more complex and ambitious learning" (p. 14). Nor do many teachers generally use narratives as intellectual and moral frameworks across disciplines, create learning communities where heterogeneously grouped students co-construct more adequate understandings, or see curriculum as "a way of living and acting to make sense of experience" (p. 10).

For most schools, these changes would be second order, as would the emphasis on equity goals such as democratizing elite forms of schooling and helping all children use their minds well by collaboratively "making knowledge and taking part in culture" (p. 24). *Tomorrow's Schools* cautions against pitting excellence and equity goals against one another by adhering to one mode of teaching that is unresponsive to the multiple needs of culturally and linguistically diverse students. While acknowledging that PDSs, in and of themselves, cannot solve social problems, *Tomorrow's Schools* sets forth the goal of "disentangling social and class inequities from learning opportunities" and warns against evading social problems "under the pretext that they are beyond its grasp" (p. 34).

Research Studies

Although the mandate for PDSs stresses both changes in classroom teaching and improvements in student learning, research focuses almost exclusively on the former. Grossman's statement about one PDS could apply to most: "As yet, there are few data on whether or not students are learning better under the new approach to curriculum & instruction" (1994, p. 66). This is not surprising since changes in classroom teaching are easier to study and document than improvements in student learning. We also suspect that researchers and teachers in PDSs are so engaged in collaborative efforts to develop innovative practices that documentation of differences in student learning is premature. Nonetheless, this review of the research suggests important terrain left relatively unexplored. The one study that most systematically examined student outcomes found positive results in both learning and on-task behavior (Stallings, 1991). Student teachers ($N = 44$) in an inner-city PDS reduced off-task behavior by 9.5%. On average, off-task rates dropped in these schools from 21.9% to 12.4%. On a state-required test of comprehension skills, "PDS students performed better than most other schools in the district and were above average for the state" (p. 15). Minimal skills scores for the middle school students were higher than they had ever been, and mathematics scores for third and fifth graders, for whom tutors had been assigned, also improved. Ironically, the instructional model used in this PDS was more traditionally teacher directed than the Holmes Group envisioned. Other studies offered only generalized impressions of student change based on classroom observations and teacher reports (e.g., Gross, 1993; Jett-Simpson, Pugach, & Whipp, 1992).

Most studies describing instructional change point in the direction of more constructivist, child-centered, and cooperative approaches. The most detailed studies were from the federally funded Center for the Learning and Teaching of Elementary Subjects at Michigan State University. One study focused on changes in one classroom teacher's approach to mathematics instruction (Gross, 1993). Over a 3-year period, this teacher learned to change classroom discourse patterns and authority relations. Instead of checking students' answers from an authority position, she began to help students collectively determine the "reasonableness of solutions" (p. 72). She was involved in an intensive mathematics study group that met weekly or biweekly. For much of the time, she worked closely with a university collaborator to examine the nature of her beliefs about mathematics. The collaborator cotaught with her for a period of time.

Similarly, the second study discussed teaching changes in one classroom when two teacher-researchers (one from the university) formed a yearlong collaboration (Rosaen & Lindquist, 1992). Through coplanning, coteaching, and coresearching a writers' workshop in a fifth-grade classroom, the authors learned how to shift the classroom climate from a "workplace," where completion of work was highly valued and subject matter was neatly packaged and delivered, to a "learning" place, where knowledge is socially constructed and evidence, not authority, is the basis of judgment. As part of a well-funded center, these projects had research goals and resources beyond the reach of most PDSs. For that reason, they might not be a realistic model for widespread instructional change.

Other studies described more generally how university and school partners established interdisciplinary and "thinking" curricula, promoted active learning, gave students choices through activities clubs, and created developmentally appropriate learning environments (Jett-Simpson et al., 1992; Lemlech, Hertzog-Foliart, & Hackl, 1994; Lythcott & Schwartz, 1994; Miller & Silvernail, 1994). Two schools developed "no-fail" policies for students as a way of promoting mastery learning and student responsibility, although concern was raised at one school about unintended consequences of instilling poor work habits (Grossman, 1994; Whitford, 1994). Some of these schools were members of national networks such as the Goodlad Collaborative, the Coalition of Essential Schools, or the National Education Association Mastery in Learning Project that supported school restructuring and reconceptualized teaching. Although many positive changes were documented, some problems arose.

The most common problem was the clash between new instructional practices and traditional modes of assessment. Lemlech et al. (1994) noted project teachers' initial hesitance "to consider different means to evaluate students" and their "willingness to rely on district use of standardized testing for assessment and evaluation of student learning" (p. 164). Berry and Catoe (1994) discussed the push toward a more structured (and potentially incompatible) phonics approach to reading when test scores attributed to a constructivist approach were not as high as expected. And Grossman (1994) reported a teacher's concern that a mastery approach to learning "resulted in more multiple-choice, true-false tests and less emphasis on the assessment of higher-order thinking skills" (p. 65). These examples suggest that few PDSs made steady progress in transforming teaching and learning. Rather, it seems that various pressures and traditional modes of teaching and assessment often made change tentative and ambiguous.

In addition to this "nonlinear" transformation, some PDSs attempted changes that involved special projects and were thus somewhat peripheral to the core curriculum. One exciting, interdisciplinary project, for example, was an optional "January experience" for student teachers (Lythcott & Schwartz, 1994). It was not a required part of their program, and few classroom teachers agreed to participate. The authors claim that the experience "had the effect of moving teachers' consciousness from their self to the youngsters, and enabled student teachers to remake themselves into learner-centered professionals" (p. 144). We wondered, however, about the lasting impact of projects that are added to the regular curriculum rather than transforming that curriculum. Another type of partial change occurs with the "school-within-a-school" model. This model was attempted in a Los Angeles elementary school, but, as a result of workload and burnout, the PDS was having difficulty retaining the 12 teachers needed to keep the model viable (Lemlech et al., 1994). There were instances, however, in which permanent changes were attempted across the entire school. In an urban PDS described by Jett-Simpson et al. (1992), professional development efforts focused on changing the school's approach to literacy instruction from a teacher-directed basic skills approach to an integrated approach in which "instruction was embedded in reading authentic materials, such as children's literature, and writing in the context of authentic tasks" (p. 6). At other sites, progress was being made toward including the entire school (Grossman, 1994; Miller & Silvernail, 1994; Whitford, 1994).

Some changes in teaching and learning were less child centered than others. The Stallings (1991) study, for example, used direct instruction and observational feedback on teacher behavior as the model for change. Both student teachers and cooperating teachers were trained to use the Stallings observation instrument, which has nationally normed goals for variables such as off-task behavior, academic statements, organizing statements, direct questions, clarifying questions, higher order questions, praise and support, and guided correction. Whitford (1994) discussed a pull toward more traditional, teacher-directed instruction from the state department of education and the local teacher's union, and Pasch and Pugach (1990) discussed PDS teachers having a strong orientation toward basic skills and teacher-directed instruction. None of these cases—all involving inner-city schools—strongly support the instructional goals articulated in *Tomorrow's Schools*, although they encourage cooperative learning and higher order questioning. This finding raises important issues about school change. PDSs are part of larger systems, and beliefs about desirable directions for change diverge throughout those systems (Cohen, 1995). State departments of education continue with modes of assessment unaligned with recommendations for instructional change. Inner-city teachers want orderly classrooms where they have assurance that students are at least acquiring basic skills. This often takes them in a teacher-centered direction.

Moreover, there is continued controversy about the extent of our knowledge about "good instruction." According to Corcoran and Goertz (1995), "the extent and depth of our knowledge about what works under varying conditions is often exaggerated; our knowledge about instruction is in fact quite limited" (p. 29). This contention makes all the more important a PDS focus on research and inquiry. Rather than merely endorse generalized directions for instructional change, PDS participants need to implement research-based models of instruction that document student learning. Little is learned by claims that teaching has become more child centered in PDSs. Schram, Ricks, and Sands caution that reform consists of more than "adopting a new classroom organization, putting materials in children's hands, and allowing them to talk, without examining or questioning the nature of the [subject] being taught, or assumptions about learning and teaching" (as cited in Gross, 1993, p. 46). What is happening in settings that claim to be child centered? In which "teaching for understanding" is a goal? Are students learning more? Is that learning more meaningful and useful? These are important questions yet to be substantively answered by the PDS research.

Equity Implications

The quotation that began this section of the chapter embodies the pedagogical tension found in this set of studies. On one hand, PDSs are designed to provide students with the knowledge and skills they need to "make it" in mainstream culture. To do otherwise would be unfair and inequitable. It would leave students without the educational resources essential for economic survival and independence. This first part of the quotation is in keeping with traditional notions of schooling that emphasize teacher-directed whole-group instruction, on-task behavior, mastery approaches to learning, and standardized testing. On the other hand (and at the same time), PDSs are urged to help students retain and value their own culture. This part of the quotation is more in line with progressive notions of teaching and learning that encourage a whole-language approach to literacy, authentic assessment, dialectical instruction, interdisciplinary curricula, and co-constructed meaning. Many equity advocates would argue that accomplishing the first goal at the expense of the second is unfair and unnecessary and constitutes a "subtractive" approach to education in which individual and group identity are sacrificed to cultural assimilation.

The Holmes Group and others (Delpit, 1995; Ladson-Billings, 1994) have argued that schooling can simultaneously embrace both objectives, but a comparative reading of the studies we reviewed suggests that the two goals are often treated as contradictory rather than complementary. Integrating the teaching of basic facts and skills with complex and authentic learning seems to be an unrealized goal in most PDSs. What equitable teaching and learning processes look like has not been advanced very much by the PDS agenda. Which approaches, if any, equalize opportunities to learn for all children? The one study that offers evidence of equalizing student achievement outcomes (Stallings, 1991) was the most traditional in its pedagogical approach. Interestingly, this study also had the most explicit commitment to poor children of color. It involved 11 schools in the Houston Independent School District, some of which became shelters for neighborhood children, providing dinner, cots, and night courses to parents who wished to receive GEDs. This community-based approach to improving student learning might, in fact, be far more effective than isolated instructional changes, but evidence is not provided by the studies. We are still a long way from knowing whether PDSs can do better than other schools in terms of "disentangling social and class inequalities from learning opportunities" (Holmes Group, 1990, p. 34).

Teacher Education

Goals

A Professional Development School selected because of its staff's commitment to bridging cultural divides can provide novices with systematic occasions to study equity within diversity. (Holmes Group, 1990, p. 37)

The Holmes Group's goals for teacher education are a combination of first- and second-order changes. The variations in programs at different universities make our division problematic. However, drawing on our knowledge of teacher education and studies of teacher education programs (Goodlad, 1990; Howey & Zimpher, 1989; Valli, 1992), we believe the division is a sound reading of the general state of teacher education.

As first-order changes, we include recommendations for exemplary, authentic clinical settings; collaboration between school and university faculties; instilling habits of reflection; and making teacher preparation more intellectually sound by grounding theory in practice. This would include making arts and sciences knowledge more "pedagogically available" to novice teachers. More radical (i.e., second-order) transformation in the initial preparation of teachers would occur through the Holmes Group's recommendations about cultural diversity and social justice. While stopping short of calling for multicultural teacher education programs, *Tomorrow's Schools* does go further than most reform proposals in addressing the importance of a sequence of courses that emphasize various types of diversities (race, culture, language, gender, ability) from a range of disciplinary perspectives. It also emphasizes "commitment to the learning of the poor and the marginal" (p. 49) and teaching preservice candidates how to draw on student diversity in designing dynamic and interesting instruction. These second-order goals have a strong equity orientation.

Research Studies

The studies of teacher education in the PDS literature reflect the generally held belief that student teachers and classroom teacher/mentors are the key participants and thus the subject of change initiatives within the PDS. Appearing only in minor roles as participants in these studies are university faculty and school and university administrators (Stevenson, 1993). The studies, taken as a group, speak to the PDS reform goals of collaboration, reflective practice, simultaneous renewal of schools and colleges, and reconciliation of theory-practice discontinuities in teacher education.

We identified seven studies of teacher education, all published since 1992, that met our criteria for inclusion in the review. Lemlech and Hertzog-Foliart (1993) investigated the stages of development of collaborative, problem-focused reflection as a method of teacher education. The elementary school setting had been established as one of the American Federation of Teachers' (AFT) professional practice schools and served a diverse, inner-city population. A change in the organizational structure of teacher education was implemented in the form of a series of school-based, problem-solving clinics. These clinic sessions were codesigned by school and university faculty and featured case studies to which students, working in teams, were to apply data-based decision-making and evaluation techniques. Qualitative methods (participant observation, interviews, videotapes, journal analysis) were used to evaluate the program's effects on both student and practicing teachers. The findings were supportive of the model and suggested that the process of collegial, reflective practice evolves over time if the necessary conditions are met (i.e., structured, collaborative inquiry; time for purposeful interactions; and acknowledgment of shared expertise between professionals from the school and university).

Stanulis (1995) conducted a series of case studies of elementary teachers who served as mentors for undergraduate novice teachers in a 2-year, PDS-based program. At issue were the mentoring role and its effects on both mentors and novices. The cooperating teachers' role was expanded to include the additional roles of "cognitive coach," mentor, and guide to reflective practice. A unique feature of this program was the 2-year duration of each mentor-novice relationship. Videotapes of mentoring sessions stimulated recall of mentors' beliefs, goals, and evaluative statements to novice teachers. Using constant comparative methods, researchers identified a number of themes that characterized four of the five teachers studied. Sustained interactions between university and school-based personnel, based on shared responsibility and mutual respect, were successful in achieving congruence between both groups' understanding of teaching and learning, theory and practice. These "common understandings" were then communicated by mentors to the novice teachers. A noteworthy exception was a teacher who elected to abstain from full participation in the PDS effort as a result of apprehension about turning her classroom over to another teacher. The researcher used this finding to raise questions for future inquiry regarding the appropriate criteria for selection of mentors as well as the necessity to integrate teacher education with ongoing professional development of mentor teachers.

Yopp, Guillaume, and Savage (1993–1994) studied fifth-year undergraduate teacher candidates who were placed by cohort groups in one of four elementary PDSs. First-order changes were implemented in regard to school-wide mentoring of the students, frequent demonstration lessons by master teachers with time for reflection by teachers and interns, and extensive role expansion for teachers, administrators, and university faculty. Questionnaires were used to assess participants' perceptions of the PDS program's effects on student teachers' preparation and level of reflection on their training. The authors found general support for the program and its goals; however, the methodology and the specific outcomes were not reported in detail. Consistent with other studies, Yopp et al. concluded that time, trust, and incentives are key ingredients in establishment of a PDS. They added "grass roots" initiation of effort to the list of facilitating factors.

At semester's end, Woloszyk and Hill (1994) questioned small groups of PDS and non-PDS student teachers regarding their beliefs insofar as they were consistent with Holmes Group PDS principles. The results were inconclusive, revealing that only 4 of 42 questionnaire items reliably differentiated the groups. For 2 of those 4 items, the beliefs of the non-PDS-trained students were more consistent with Holmes Group principles than those of PDS-trained students.

Teitel (1992) conducted one of the few studies of simultaneous renewal (actually the lack thereof) as a result of PDS efforts. Using case study methods designed to be sensitive to second-order change in college programs, Teitel's analysis employed the approaches derived from the literature on interorganizational relations. In each case, the PDS program was responsible for the preparation of half or fewer of the teachers prepared in each college. Even though a number of individuals were serving well in the role of "boundary spanners" (cross-institutional change agents), the overall results were not supportive of lasting, institutional change. PDS efforts were isolated within their colleges, receiving marginal support in terms of resources and personal involvement. Faculty dynamics were proposed to explain such discouraging findings. For example, the effort of individual faculty members in achieving reform was perceived by others as "ownership" of the program and thus served to dissuade wider involvement. Similarly, faculty members not involved viewed with suspicion PDS efforts that received special attention and support from top-level administrators.

Driscoll, Benson, and Livneh (1994) examined the often-cited discrepancy between theory and practice that exists when university-based teacher education is disconnected from schools. In particular, these authors observed the effects on teacher education when schools' changing demographics are ignored by teacher educators. The goal of the collaboration was largely to achieve first-order changes in instructional practices. Using qualitative methods, Driscoll et al. analyzed the content of collaborative planning and inquiry in a PDS in an effort to identify and explain discrepancies among the perspectives of the participants, especially between university and school-based faculty. Results pointed to a number of logistical arrangements and programmatic limitations as inhibitors of collaboration: scheduling and time allocations, inadequacies in teacher preparation, and schools' needs to emphasize maintenance of order. It appears that the theory-practice gap is recursive; it both results in and is maintained by inadequate collaboration between school and university partners in teacher education.

In one of the few methodologically rigorous studies of teacher education in the PDS, Shen (1994) conducted intensive case studies to give voice to practicing teachers' views on the preparation of new teachers. Similar to the Driscoll et al. (1994) study of the theory-to-practice gap, Shen's analysis identified differences between PDS teachers' focus on the practicalities of teacher preparation (first-order change) and the visions of fundamental restructuring typically found in the literature (second-order change). Teachers' visions of student teaching focused on such first-order change issues as students' level of classroom responsibility, selection criteria for mentors and supervisors, and improved coordination between school and university personnel. As in other studies, time was identified as the major obstacle to change in the teachers' view.

Teachers' assumptions about teacher education differed from the reform literature in two specific ways. First, while the literature assumes that a PDS will be an exemplary setting for teacher education, teachers' visions do not include the concept of "exemplary site"; teachers do not see excellence as resulting from the same types of changes specified in the advocacy literature. Second, while the PDS literature strongly advocates for inquiry as both a basis and result of PDS-based reforms, teachers who served as Shen's informants omitted inquiry from their expectations for reform in teacher education.

Taken as a group, the studies of teacher education address mostly first-order change. Among the changes investigated, the expansion and redirection of the mentoring role of teachers appears to have the most empirical support as a change in practice (Lemlech & Hertzog-Foliart, 1993; Stanulis, 1995; Yopp et al., 1993–1994). Evidence of structural change in college programs appears to lag behind (Teitel, 1992). While there is some evidence of successful change, studies identified obstacles and only limited success in PDS sites reaching consensus on such fundamental matters as instructional approaches (Driscoll et al., 1994), use of reflective practice (Woloszyk & Hill, 1994), and organization of the student teaching experience (Shen, 1994). The results illustrate the challenges of addressing the second-order changes envisioned in the advocacy literature.

Equity Implications

None of the teacher education studies primarily focused on equity; nevertheless, each study managed to address one or more of the equity issues raised in the advocacy literature. All, however, were confined to equitable processes in teaching and teacher preparation; none reported the ultimate effects of equitable teacher preparation on the education of children. The overriding concern in school reform is the state of schools in poor and/or inner-city communities. The location of PDS sites in such communities is one example of more equitable allocation of limited school-reform resources. Two of these studies (Lemlech & Hertzog-Foliart, 1993; Yopp et al., 1993–1994) were conducted in PDS sites specifically identified as inner-city schools, or schools with a high proportion of families characterized as at risk as a result of factors such as limited English proficiency, poverty, unemployment, transience, or substance abuse. The conscious decision to designate these schools as PDSs represents a major commitment to more equitable school reform.

None of the studies addressed access to, admission into, and retention in high-quality teacher education programs as an issue of equity, yet therein lies a dilemma for teacher educators who advocate the extensive PDS internship following a strong liberal arts/academic foundation. The question of how to recruit and then financially support poor and culturally diverse college students during such extensive programs is unresolved.

Inclusion of children with disabilities is one of the most contentious issues in education and represents a significant challenge to the attainment of equity of access. The implication for teacher education, as addressed by Yopp et al. (1993–1994), is one of preparing teachers in PDSs where inclusion is practiced. The counterintuitive finding by Woloszyk and Hill (1994) that PDS-trained interns were *less* supportive of inclusion than the standard program control group is, therefore, especially troubling.

Tomorrow's Schools advocates "instilling a commitment to the learning of the poor and the marginal" (p. 49). Promising approaches to achieving such commitments through teacher education processes are (a) eliminating teacher isolation, a practice that perpetuates inequity in and across classrooms; (b) using constructivist approaches to adults' and children's learning that raise the level of importance of the learner's unique knowledge and experiences; and (c) engaging novices in systematic occasions to study equity within diversity.

The studies of collaboration, professional role exchange and release, shared reflective practice, and collegial activities address the concern regarding teacher isolation from a number of perspectives. For example, Teitel (1992) found that failure of college faculty to achieve collegiality in PDS initiatives inhibited the institutionalization of such efforts. Lemlech and Hertzog-Foliart (1993) examined the stages in development of collegiality of paired student teachers in the belief that starting early was the way to build a sense of equity, mutual respect, and shared expertise in teachers. Driscoll et al. (1994) extended the concept of collaboration to include families, thereby strengthening the equitable nature of the teacher education reform agenda by bringing greater reciprocity to the professional-parent relationship.

Stanulis (1995) is the only one in this group to address constructivist learning principles directly. From this perspective, the achievement of equitable processes in teacher education begins from the assumption that each teacher, teacher candidate, and child in the school brings highly relevant background knowledge and experience to the learning community and that curriculum and instruction should proceed from that knowledge and those experiences. The adoption of such assumptions was further shown to affect the attainment of "shared understandings" between college and school personnel regarding pedagogical and learning theories. No study indicated that the issue of equity within diversity was made a systematic part of any teacher education program.

The Holmes Group's (1990) principle most closely associated with equity states that PDSs "will make teaching and learning for understanding available for everybody's children" (p. 29). An equitable teacher education program would do the same for everybody's *teachers*. To date, the PDS research has not produced outcome studies that would support the attainment of this goal. We still know very little about efforts to recruit faculty of color in PDSs.

Professional Development

Goals

A [PDS] cannot be simply a technical invention for the promotion of more efficient forms of instruction; it must engage in the struggle to better its students' present and future lives. (Holmes Group, 1990, p. 33)

Reinforcing themes evident in previous categories, the Holmes Group calls for the continuous learning of all adults: teachers, teacher educators, administrators, and support staff. The professional development of teachers is addressed in the greatest detail, however, and the vision promoted in *Tomorrow's Schools* is of teaching as a political act of leadership (1990, p. 10). Through the exercise of greater authority, choice, and responsibility, empowered teachers develop their teaching practices as they seek to establish inclusive "democratic communities of learning" (p. 29) and "press the claims for justice on the larger society" (p. 33).

A broad commitment to equity and participation in social and political action informs the work of teachers as they engage in active inquiry, participate in the clinical supervision and development of novice teachers, collaborate with other professionals, and join in school goal setting and decision making. This transformational vision of the teaching role clearly supports the need for new, democratizing institutional contexts and structures that rest on a more equitable distribution of authority and responsibility among educators.

While many teachers currently work collaboratively to develop curriculum, explore alternative pedagogies, and reflect on practice—all actions that support more effective instruction—four primary roles for teachers are advanced by the Holmes Group that, if comprehensively implemented, would represent second-order change. In their role as "practical intellectuals," teachers would engage in political activism to further the goals of social justice and greater equality. Extending beyond the classroom, their responsibilities include taking action to bridge the family's culture and the academic culture of the school. In addition, teachers, through instruction, help diverse learners "take part in reasoned discourse and the making of cultural meanings" (1990, p. 27). In a separate role, teachers-as-researchers would collaborate with university colleagues to explore new curricula and methods of teaching, and together they would develop new standards of practice. According to the Holmes Group, research within PDSs must include studies of those structural aspects of schooling that may produce school failure. Research on teaching practices that may better support students' cultural, linguistic, and gender diversity is another priority.

The Holmes Group also advocates the transformation of the traditional support role of teachers in the preparation of new teachers. As teacher educators, classroom teachers would help to bridge the "enormous disjunction" between university instruction and the actual problems of schools serving children, particularly those children living in poor communities (p. 34). Greater continuity of purposes and methods is accomplished through teachers and university faculty who work collaboratively to develop preservice curriculum, teach courses at the university, and supervise and evaluate preservice teachers. Finally, while the Holmes Group cautions that many administrators perceive certain expanded roles for teachers as threatening (p. 83), new forms of leadership are tentatively advanced that portray teachers as empowered decision makers who create school goals and policies, promote new standards of practice, and further the creation of an inclusive and just school community.

Research Studies

Researchers who have examined professional development initiatives within PDSs have primarily documented the professional development of teachers. There are a number of plausible explanations for the paucity of research pertaining to the professional development of school administrators and university faculty: (a) Professional development for teachers is deemed most critical because teachers directly influence student learning; (b) university faculty usually act as both participants and researchers in PDSs and therefore would be required to study themselves; and, (c) historically, those groups with the least power in the educational hierarchy have been the primary subjects of research.

Although much of the research evidence documented is anecdotal and lacking in detail, a few studies do address important growth opportunities for university faculty who participate in PDS initiatives. For example, as first author, researcher, and consultant, Schack (Schack & Overturf, 1994), a professor at the University of Louisville, collaborated with four middle school teachers and a small group of preservice students on a professional development team. The professor stated that her "personal and professional growth was enhanced by the reality check of being in the classroom on a regular basis, participating in the intersection of theory and practice" (p. 11). Moreover, she was able to provide a "real-world connection" for her university students. The ability of professors to effectively integrate theory and practice in the context of instruction may serve to close the gap preservice students traditionally experience between the worlds of school and university.

In another study, University of Washington faculty involved in a PDS reported changing their curriculum to make subjects more integrated and coordinated as a result of their experiences in the school (Grossman, 1994). Within this PDS, new roles for university faculty were also created. Spending up to 1 day each week in the school, a "professor in residence" served as a resource for teachers through observing in classrooms, developing action research projects, and providing guidance and support. New roles for faculty were also reported by education faculty at the University of South Carolina. Of the 15 teacher education faculty members who were most involved with the PDS, 82% felt they had taken on new roles and responsibilities in teacher education (Berry & Catoe, 1994).

While the research cited here regarding the experiences of university faculty engaged in PDS initiatives provides insight, more studies are required that identify the nature of professional development within the PDS for both school administrators and university faculty. At present, we are not able to determine whether the mandate issued by the Holmes Group for the continuous learning of all adults is being met.

Another subject that requires further investigation pertains to those teachers in PDSs who are not engaged in professional development initiatives. Involvement thus far has primarily been voluntary and has focused on teachers who are active participants (Boles & Troen, 1994; Boyd, 1994; Lemlech et al., 1994; Neufeld & Freeman, 1993; Nihlen, 1992; Putnam, 1992; Rushcamp & Roehler, 1992; Stallings, 1991). In the case of whole school involvement, for example, initial selection processes often permitted uninterested teachers to transfer to other schools. In some schools, only a core of interested teachers participated. In still others, teachers determined their level of involvement or chose to withdraw after a period of time. Consequently, we question whether professional development opportunities within PDSs are reaching those teachers who would most benefit from participation.

In addition to wide variation among the types of participation structures adopted, there is also little uniformity between PDSs regarding the processes used to support professional development for teachers. Staff collaboratively developed reforms in one PDS established between the Milwaukee Public Schools and the University of Wisconsin (Jett-Simpson et al., 1992); in other instances, however, university personnel and school administration, at least initially, guide and direct professional development initiatives (Berry & Catoe, 1994; Boyd, 1994; Lemlech et al., 1994; Morris & Nunnery, 1993; Nihlen, 1992; Rushcamp & Roehler, 1992; Schack & Overturf, 1994; Stallings, 1991). Whether they present an agenda or strive to guide school staff to develop their own, university professors easily become identified as organizers and directors rather than as colearners themselves (Navarro, 1992, p. 11). We question whether second-order change is likely to occur when initiatives do not place teachers centrally in the process as decision makers and active participants in their own professional development.

For example, Morris and Nunnery (1993) developed an initiative to empower teachers primarily through their involvement in preservice education as mentors. But professional development looked quite similar to traditional in-service programs. Experts were brought in and provided teachers with 50 hours of "training" over the course of the year. Teachers felt their participation in the program most enhanced their sensitivity to the problems and stresses experienced by preservice teachers, their willingness to share and work with peers, and their confidence as professional role models; however, 56% did not feel empowered as decision makers. Similarly, in Barksdale-Ladd's study (1994), university involvement in the PDS was not a major contributor to teachers' feelings of empowerment or to their development of child-centered practices, in part because university personnel were perceived as "threatening" or as not attempting to work collaboratively (p. 110).

In another PDS established between Texas A&M University and an urban elementary school situated in the Houston School District (Stallings, 1991), teachers were trained to lead student intern seminars and evaluate interns through use of the Stallings observation instrument. University personnel observed and evaluated teachers and provided them with a profile of their own instructional behaviors. The researchers state that teachers who supervised student teachers and attended weekly seminars significantly improved their own teaching skills. While this study provides examples of new roles for teachers as teacher educators, initiatives were not constructed through collaborative processes. Moreover, knowledge was transmitted from university professors to teachers rather than constructed with them, and university faculty, working from a position of higher authority, acted as teacher evaluators.

In contrast, some university personnel, even while they lead, are able to present themselves as colearners. In some cases, they gradually cede authority and responsibility for professional development to teachers. This transfer of authority may be critical to the promotion of changes that are truly second order in nature, changes that support teacher leadership in a variety of capacities. Rushcamp and Roehler (1992), for example, describe how university professors sought to nurture "role shifts" among participants. Three teachers on the central planning team gradually became meeting facilitators as the university facilitator relinquished control (p. 21). Boyd (1994), a university professor who guided a group of teachers in implementing teaching practices according to the National Council of Teachers of Mathematics (NCTM) math standards, perceived her role as one of facilitator and leader, stating that "the professor must set the stage for that involvement . . . must facilitate the merging of theory and practice and the idea of teacher as learner and researcher" (p. 138). However, teachers in her study group perceived Boyd as a colearner and saw themselves as responsible for change. It appears that when university faculty facilitate rather than direct, teachers are encouraged to assume greater responsibility for their own development.

Apart from the processes that define professional development initiatives within the PDS, the content of these initiatives varies widely. The majority of studies document new roles for teachers in the context of preservice education (Berry & Catoe, 1994; Boles & Troen, 1994; Grossman, 1994; Lemlech et al., 1994; Morris & Nunnery, 1993; Stallings, 1991). As teacher educators, classroom teachers refine their own practices through overseeing the development of student interns. In addition, collaboration among university faculty, teachers, and interns promotes reflection, deliberation, and development. A tighter coupling of university and school is accomplished through "blurring boundaries" that traditionally have separated the two institutions (Gehrke, Young, & Sagmiller, 1991). For example, university faculty teach courses at the school site, teachers teach courses at the university, and both collaboratively share roles and responsibilities for the education of interns.

One example of professional development integrated with preservice education is provided by Lemlech et al. (1994). In their study, teachers in one urban elementary school shared readings and deliberated with other professionals as they planned school curriculum and the preservice program for interns. In addition, university professors provided teachers with information about various models of teaching. Consequently, teachers were able to provide meaningful feedback to interns regarding their use of the models.

In decision-making roles, teachers screened prospective student interns. They also led seminars and collaborated with university faculty to write instructional cases regarding the dilemmas and misconceptions faced by interns in their classes. Teachers used these cases during problem-solving clinics for interns and cotaught the clinics with university faculty. Increased collaboration, teacher reflection, and knowledge all are indicative of first-order change, while second-order changes were evident in the increased leadership roles and responsibilities for teachers as teacher educators and the transformed relationship between university and school staff. The researchers observed that this transformation occurred only when teachers became convinced of their capacity to effect change and make important decisions.

In another study, teachers who developed the Learning/Teaching Collaborative in Brookline, Massachusetts, described new roles for teachers as university instructors and guest lecturers. College teaching prompted them to critically examine their own practices. Additional responsibilities for teachers included screening student intern applicants, overseeing their experience, and writing their evaluations. One teacher explained, "Being forced to discipline yourself, to express what it is you do and why you do it . . . informs your teaching, and I would argue leads to greater success in teaching" (Boles & Troen, 1994, p. 15).

Apart from preservice education, researchers have examined the creation of new roles for teachers as "teacher leaders." Romerdahl (1991) studied the position of teacher leader coordinator, a newly created role for middle school teachers participating in a partnership with the University of Washington. A list of coordinator responsibilities included attending planning meetings and meetings with the PDS director, leading site meetings, overseeing PDS site budgets, screening and interviewing prospective student teachers, and involving other teachers in PDS activities. Only one teacher, however, was provided release time from her regular duties (Gehrke et al., 1991). The authors describe the need to find mechanisms for distributing leadership tasks more evenly.

Too many additional responsibilities may ultimately lead to greater disempowerment and isolation for teachers. Working as members of site-based management teams, as student teacher supervisors, and as university-school liaisons may detract from teachers' ability to fully perform their most critical role as classroom teachers. Apple (1986, p. 42) cautions that one of the most significant effects of work intensification is a reduction in the quality of services provided. Increasing teachers' responsibilities may force them to limit the time and effort they devote to any given area. One teacher leader coordinator in Romerdahl's study, for example, was forced to prioritize her commitments. She explained, "The [PDS] is not and never will be a top priority. My family is at the top, my students next, the various hats I wear at school . . . are next, then comes the [PDS]" (p. 7). Not surprisingly, then, some PDS initiatives have struggled to sustain teacher participation (Gehrke et al., 1991; Grossman, 1994; Lemlech et al., 1994).

While the previous studies identify teachers as decision makers and teacher educators, only one study documents the development of teachers as practical intellectuals who seek to address social and political issues that affect schools and their families. Nihlen (1992), a professor at the University of New Mexico, has taught a group of elementary school teachers to conduct research in their school. Indicative of second-order change, the researcher claims that teachers "were able to challenge their culturally negotiated role and move into the sphere of intellectual researcher" (p. 12). On completion of individual research projects, teachers jointly decided to examine how subordinate groups of students are silenced in their school, although at the time of publication they had not implemented this research. We can only speculate that this kind of examination might lead to change that is both social and political in nature, engaging teachers in the struggle to support greater equity and opportunity for all children. Because a formal methodology section was not included in the report, however, it was difficult to determine how evidence was obtained. A few descriptive examples and quotes from teachers provided minimal support for the researcher's claims.

Equity Implications

Research on the professional development of teachers, teacher educators, and administrators within PDSs has provided few portraits of these groups' engagement in initiatives that further educational equity and social justice goals. While promising initiatives in related areas are clearly being explored, such as small group experiments with heterogeneous grouping (Schack & Overturf, 1994), mainstreaming of special needs children (Boles & Troen, 1994), and the preparation of educators committed to teaching in urban school systems (Jett-Simpson et al., 1992; Pasch & Pugach, 1990; Stallings, 1991), professional development in the majority of partnerships revolves around the instrumental and technical concerns of teaching. This emphasis is exemplified in the following sample of questions that have been used to organize professional development activities in PDSs: How can the school move from a skills-based approach to literacy to a more holistic and child-centered approach (Barksdale-Ladd, 1994; Jett-Simpson et al., 1992)? How can teachers be supported in their attempts to implement the NCTM standards (Boyd, 1994)? How can teachers be trained to become self-efficacious and empowered mentors of student teachers (Morris & Nunnery, 1993)?

At present, explicit connections between these types of instructional reforms and a social justice agenda have not been identified. The particular needs of culturally diverse children, or descriptions of children, families, and communities, are rarely mentioned beyond general statistics pertaining to the race and socioeconomic status of students. This trend is accompanied by an absence in the literature of adequate descriptions of the local social and historical context of PDSs. Contextual factors are rarely a source of examination and are peripherally related to the goals and activities that are developed and implemented.

In addition, while the advocacy literature stresses the importance of faculty discussions pertaining to racial, ethnic, and social-class diversity (Holmes Group, 1990, p. 36), there is little evidence provided in the research literature of educators engaging in self-reflection regarding their beliefs about teaching diverse students or dialogue among educators regarding the particular problems and challenges they encounter as they attempt to provide experiences for children with different needs and background experiences. Delpit (1995) describes the critical importance of this kind of dialogue and its relative absence in our schools and colleges of education:

> Nowhere do we foster inquiry into who our students really are or encourage teachers to develop links to the often rich home lives of students, yet teachers cannot hope to begin to understand who sits before them unless they can connect with the families and communities from which their students come. To do that, it is vital that teachers and teacher educators explore their own beliefs and attitudes about non-white and non-middle-class people. (p. 179)

The majority of professional development initiatives within PDSs presently include new roles, new instructional methods, and increased decision-making opportunities for teachers that support their self-development, personal autonomy, and increased professional status; however, these reforms are most often linked to the narrow academic and personal consequences of teaching. Reflection, dialogue, and action pertaining to a broader set of social and political commitments are required of administrators, teacher educators, and teachers if the goal of educating everybody's children is to be achieved. Consequently, future research on PDSs that connects professional development opportunities with the goals of greater educational equity and social justice may be of primary importance.

Organization and Structure
Goals

> The bureaucratic organization of schools creates classifications that stereotype and segregate children. . . . This top down organization of schools, combined with constraints imposed by lack of knowledge and experience, makes it difficult for school people to serve a varied student body. (Holmes Group, 1990, p. 42)

The direction of this category is second-order change, calling for new forms of school governance and the invention of new organizational structures "in line with the school's new purposes and principles about teaching and learning" (p. 67). Many of these changes address equity issues. For the school as a whole, emphasis is on the creation of small schools or units within schools, connections to the work sector that provide students with rewarding jobs and incentives to stay in school, the establishment of standards through local school deliberations, new forms of family and involvement, and strong links with community and social service agencies as long as "the school's central teaching and learning functions . . . provide the rationale for any involvement with other kinds of concerns" (p. 70).

Similar emphasis is placed on greater empowerment and inclusion of teachers in decision making by restructuring work roles and assignments, use of time, and staff development opportunities. In a section titled "Organizing for More Equity," the authors of *Tomorrow's Schools* criticize the top-down organization of schools that isolates teachers, compartmentalizes knowledge, and blocks creativity, rendering teachers "powerless and unable to do what they believe is best for children" (p. 42). For students, the report encourages the end of tracking, pull-out, and special education programs that deny access to knowledge and participation in learning communities. To those who believe in or want to experiment with school choice, *Tomorrow's Schools* says the following: "A Professional Development School offering choice will have the burden of demonstrating whether choice is compatible with equity—which will mean getting involved with setting district-wide policy" (p. 92).

Research Studies

Tomorrow's Schools focuses primarily on the necessity to change the organization of public schools. The authors do not elaborate on the organizational structure of schools of education. That critique is left to the Holmes Group's subsequent report, *Tomorrow's Schools of Education* (1995). Both reports characterize PDSs as "types of schools" with which universities collaborate rather than a new organizational structure that is a blend of the two. The only research on organizational change occurring in higher education as a result of the PDS movement centered on role and reward changes for university and clinical faculty. Most of the research we found about organizational change in schools likewise focused on changes in roles, incentives, and the use of time and space that were the direct outcome of collaborative alliances with universities. We report these changes in the collaborative alliance section of this chapter.

If organizational changes are promoting linkages between the school and social service agencies, the work sector, families, or local communities, as the literature advocates, these changes either are not being researched or are occurring outside PDSs. We found no research in these areas and only two examples of the creation of a school within a school (Karr, Green, & Koulogeorge, 1994; Lemlech et al., 1994). In fact, a number of school restructuring efforts preceded or coincided with the establishment of a PDS partnership (Snyder, 1994; Whitford, 1994). These organizational changes might be thought of as a precondition rather than an outcome of a PDS. A number of universities seemed to select schools that had already begun to restructure (Miller & Silvernail, 1994; Ruscoe & Whitford, 1991).

The goal of restructuring efforts in the literature we reviewed was generally to involve teachers in decision making about classroom practices (instruction, the curriculum, grouping, inclusion). Most efforts were guided by the discourse of teacher empowerment and leadership. "Every leader is a teacher and every teacher a leader" is one example (Whitford, 1994, p. 77). In certain cases, change efforts were guided by an encompassing vision. In others, individual projects were unconnected or even in conflict with each other (Berry & Catoe, 1994; Grossman, 1994; Lemlech et al., 1994; Whitford, 1994).

Studies provide evidence that reforms are more apt to take hold when all teachers in a school are involved. A teacher in Barksdale-Ladd's study (1994) explained, "You feel like you're not a lone wolf out there because everybody is trying things, too" (p. 106). With collaboration, teachers may come to realize that their individual problems are shared by others, and problem solving becomes a joint venture that encourages teachers to perceive themselves as decision makers. For example, teachers involved in a PDS established between the Milwaukee Public Schools and the University of Wisconsin Center for Teacher Education found it easier to change their literacy instruction from a skills-based approach to a child-centered, integrated approach when the whole school was engaged (Jett-Simpson et al., 1992). Of the 34 teachers interviewed, 22 changed their instructional paradigm; morale improved for both teachers and students; and it was noted that, after a while, the initiative created its own momentum. One teacher reported that "even the teachers who have not been real involved with the new efforts in reading and writing are doing more constructive silent reading" (p. 19).

Whole school involvement also provides a context for examining broader issues such as how the school addresses the needs of diverse learners and which structures further equity and the creation of a democratic learning community. In contrast, when PDS initiatives are initiated with small, voluntary groups of teachers who reflect on isolated aspects of their practice, there is the danger that needed schoolwide structural reform will be ignored. Zeichner (1992) elaborates on this concern:

[An] emphasis on focusing teachers' reflections inwardly at their own teaching and/or on their students, to the neglect of any consideration of the social conditions of schooling that influence teachers' work within the classroom . . . makes it less likely that teachers will be able to confront and transform those structural aspects of their work that hinder the accomplishment of their educational mission. (p. 8)

On the other hand, whole school involvement may support a broadening of this focus and make it more likely that teachers can develop a unified and powerful voice in pressing for needed structural changes. Engaging the entire faculty also enables a principal to dedicate staff meetings and professional development sessions to PDS initiatives, and within these sessions participants have the opportunity to collaborate and develop shared goals and a common language for talking about them (Jett-Simpson et al., 1992).

One set of studies (Ruscoe & Whitford, 1991; Ruscoe, Whitford, Egginton, & Esselman, 1989) looked at the impact of restructuring on the attitudes of teachers who were involved in 24 PDSs in one county. Several of these schools were also involved in participatory management activities. The focus of these studies was on efficacy, empowerment, teaming, and learning climate. Overall, teachers involved in these 24 schools had "positive attitudes toward issues of teachers' efficacy, teachers' influence and role in school decisionmaking, and school learning climate" (1991, p. 2). Those working in schools with well-functioning teams had the highest efficacy scores. Those involved for the longest period of time in both PDS and participatory management activities had the most positive attitudes on all factors. Elementary teachers who were not involved in participatory management activities were least positive on the teacher governance factors, while those not involved in PDS activities were least positive about the teacher practice factors. These findings seem to bode well for restructuring efforts. At least at the level of attitude, teachers benefit from involvement.

Unfortunately, we do not know how, or whether, these attitudes inform practice. In other words, we do not know what changes have occurred in the school's curriculum and classroom instruction. Baseline data were not collected on these teachers, all of whom were voluntary participants. It is possible that their attitudes were just as positive before their involvement in these projects, although the relationship between teaming and efficacy suggests the positive impact of restructuring. This impact may, however, be short lived. The analysis of third-year data suggests some decline in efficacy, especially among middle and high school teachers (1991). Moreover, there is no way of knowing how many teachers interviewed in the first year were also interviewed in the third year. All we know is that the groups' demographic profiles are similar. Although the 1991 study provides quantitative, longitudinal data, changes in individual scores are not reported. And, finally, the article gives little description of the nature of the restructuring projects. Therefore, it is unclear what kinds of activities might have influenced teachers' beliefs in their own personal efficacy or their teaching techniques.

Committees, interdisciplinary teams, study groups, and instructional councils were common participatory structures reported across the studies. While additional meetings were sometimes perceived as an obstacle to change efforts, some PDSs developed creative processes to alter rather than merely add to teachers' use of time. At one site, teachers "banked" time by starting early 4 days a week (Lemlech et al., 1994). At another, student teachers freed their classroom mentors to participate in school change activities (Berry & Catoe, 1994).

Another longitudinal survey study was conducted at a high school using dimensions related specifically to PDS goals (Woloszyk, 1992). This school had restructured so that all faculty members participated in staff development activities every Wednesday morning. Some of the groups that regularly met were the At Risk Team, the Community Service Group, the Cooperative Learning Circle, the Inquiry Group, the Restructuring Committee, and the Teacher Education Group. Forty-two of the same faculty (nearly the entire full-time faculty) responded to a questionnaire about school effectiveness, equity, and climate in 1986 and 1991. There were significant differences on 9 of the 37 measures, including teachers having high expectations of students, positive attitudes toward parents, and opportunities to observe one another and discuss instructional issues at faculty meetings. Interestingly, two of the significant changes were in a negative direction. Fewer faculty believed that problems were dealt with openly or that special education was integrated within the school's regular curriculum. These last two findings suggest that while restructuring efforts can create changes in school culture and teacher attitudes, the dynamic and complex nature of schools requires constant attention to change efforts.

Equity Implications

When combined with the studies in other categories, these studies give the impression of organizational change aimed at providing opportunities for professional development and team planning around whole-language instruction, interdisciplinary units, and child-centered instruction. Teachers seemed to have more decision-making power and involvement in these curricular areas. Issues of school size, meaningful connections to the world of work, parent/community involvement, tracking, and segregated special education appear to receive less attention than other second-order changes mentioned earlier. No PDSs in our sample were experimenting with or studying school choice. There was some indication that progress toward shared decision making and inclusion can be reversed.

One major equity issue that emerges in this section is that of teacher selection. There appear to be four selection strategies in starting a PDS. The first is to involve only those teachers who express interest and commitment. This appears to be the "fairest" mode of selection since it depends on volunteers and avoids coercion. However, there are serious limitations on efforts to "reculture" a school when only a small number volunteer and some of those drop out after a brief period of time. A second teacher selection strategy is to determine PDS sites by teacher vote. One example is requiring a two-thirds favorable vote for site adoption. Again, this appears to be a sensible and equitable selection process, but issues remain. What happens to those who voted against the innovation? Is it fair to make them participate? Are they somehow "punished"? If the negative voters are not forced to participate, is the total school workload equitably distributed among both participants and nonparticipants?

The third and fourth strategies are related: inviting teachers to transfer to another school and/or closing the school and reopening it as a PDS. In one prospective site, for example, "teachers who did not want to stay in the highly visible school [PDS] were given first chance at openings in other schools" (Stallings, 1991, p. 5). Permission had been obtained by the school board to close the building as a traditional school and reopen it as a PDS. Both of these strategies raise fairness questions. While giving teachers transfer preference appears to be a just solution, other transfer teachers within the system might not perceive the situation this way. If first choice is not offered, teachers should be ensured that the transfers are not punitive. We could find no explicit research on the issue of teacher selection and equity, but anecdotes from the studies we reviewed suggest that this is an important area for further investigation.

Inquiry and Research

Goals

Its faculty share a commitment to make issues of diversity a central part of the professional discourse about curriculum, texts, pedagogy, classroom and school organization, and hiring decisions. (Holmes Group, 1990, p. 37)

While individual teachers have been the objects of others' research, have conducted their own action research, and have collaborated with "outsiders" on school and classroom research, schools have seldom been organized as centers for teachers' own reflection and inquiry. Therefore, most of the recommendations in this section would require second-order change. *Tomorrow's Schools* explicitly rejects research that treats teachers "as passive implementors of prescribed programs" (p. 61) and oversimplifies teaching by focusing on a few discrete behaviors. In contrast, the report encourages research that grows out of the daily work of teachers, uses strategies of inquiry that match the complexity of schools and teaching for understanding, and values the intellectual activity of teachers. The document calls for the participation of both arts/sciences and education faculty.

In addition to the process of inquiry, *Tomorrow's Schools* has much to say about the focus of inquiry. It encourages research on teaching content and methods, children's conceptual understanding, technology, management, and school staffing. Special emphasis is placed on exploring explanations of the failure of poor children, examining one's own assumptions about culturally diverse students, and using "collegial observation as a way to improve and refine teachers' responsiveness to student differences" (p. 61). Murray (1993) argues that the goal for school-based inquiry is not so much the improvement of teaching but the improvement of educational research, research that, although "directed at local action and the particular child," shapes our theoretical understandings (p. 68).

Two strong equity themes run through the orientation to inquiry promoted in *Tomorrow's Schools*. One theme deals with the process of inquiry, which is described as a "mutual" task and "a way for teachers, administrators, and professors to come together on equal footing" (p. 60). The process would level hierarchical distinctions typically embedded in traditional research designs. All participants involved in the implementation of ideas would also be involved in their conception. The other equity theme deals with the focus of inquiry: exploring and attempting to overcome the problem of school failure, making diversity a central and ongoing part of professional discourse, better understanding the needs of *all* learners, studying the relationship between culture and cognition, and investigating grouping practices in the school.

Research Studies

While we found few studies that explicitly examined the type of research being conducted in PDSs, we were able to draw some tentative conclusions based on emerging patterns of collaboration and professional development. PDS partnerships seem to enable research to occur in these sites and encourage a greater degree of peer observation and feedback. Teachers took advantage of formal and informal research opportunities (Snyder, 1994), studied teaching as a means of school improvement (Lemlech et al., 1994), and participated in action research projects and courses (Berry & Catoe, 1994; Rosaen & Lindquist, 1992). Regularly scheduled meetings were sometimes held so that teachers could share their research progress (Jett-Simpson et al., 1992). However, the depth with which these activities are described in the research literature varies widely (Boles & Troen, 1994; Grossman, 1994; Jett-Simpson et al., 1992; Rushcamp & Roehler, 1992; Schack & Overturf, 1994).

For example, Rushcamp and Roehler (1992) examined a school that historically promoted teacher inquiry. With the advent of the university partnership, research was extended to 11 classrooms. Unfortunately, the researchers do not state whether these research projects were conducted systematically or whether the results were used to inform teaching beyond the teacher-researcher's classroom. In contrast, teachers involved in the Learning/Teaching Collaborative (Boles & Troen, 1994) have conducted formal research with the intent of disseminating results among a wider audience. One teacher stressed the importance of this work:

I would say my role as teacher researcher is definitely in the theater of leadership in the sense that I'm committed to developing a voice for the teacher researcher in the context of the larger research world, in making that a viable voice that's different, yet heard in that context. (p. 19)

The researchers describe teachers' role transformation from "deliverers" of knowledge to "creators" of knowledge who have a responsibility to share what they know, a process clearly indicative of teacher empowerment and second-order change. Similarly, Schack and Overturf (1994) worked with four middle school teachers and a group of preservice students to research their reform efforts as a professional development team. One of many projects they undertook involved the creation of a heterogeneous setting for gifted, learning disabled, "at-risk," and nonlabeled students. To determine the effectiveness of their effort, team members surveyed students and parents, and the professor also conducted interviews with six student teachers and the four teachers. Teachers were involved in presenting at conferences as well as publishing in collaboration with the researchers. Dissemination of teachers' research beyond the local school community may be a critical step in the transformation of the teaching profession.

Unfortunately, the nature of research and inquiry remains the least elaborated aspect of PDS work. We know far less about these activities than we do about teacher education, professional development, and collaboration. Although teacher inquiry is generally listed as one of the three or four goals of PDSs (along with teacher education, professional development, and exemplary practice), the lack of research in this area suggests it does not have the same salience as the other goals. A survey by Moore and Hopkins (1993) supports this conclusion. Of all the skills viewed as important for PDS classroom teachers, research was regarded as the least important.

When research did occur, it was often on an individual, small group, or limited scale. PDSs with grant money sometimes sponsored action research projects (Wolfe, Steel, & Phillips, 1994). By and large, however, research still remained the domain of university personnel, those from education far more than those from arts and sciences. PDSs as centers of inquiry, where teachers are partners in defining the research agenda, are still in an early stage of development. More often than not, inquiry has focused on teaching methods, technology, or management. Little research has been done in PDSs about diversity issues and school failure.

While not having the power to transform schools into centers of inquiry, small-scale, individually paired research projects might have the greatest potential of achieving Murray's goal of improving educational research by shaping our theoretical understandings. The studies by Gross (1993) and Rosaen and Lindquist (1992) reported earlier are two such examples. These studies closely examine the complexity of teaching for understanding in the areas of mathematics and literacy. Both studies are supported by external funding. The relationship between them and the PDS seems somewhat incidental. More central to their success is the relationship between the partners and (secondarily) with a larger network of similar pairs. Perhaps this type of research needs to inform the work of PDSs but need not be conducted in PDSs. Schools that are restructuring to become centers of inquiry, to involve all school personnel in inquiry and reflection, might not be most conducive to the intensive, long-term research relationship that truly shapes theoretical understandings.

Equity Implications

Research evidence from a small number of PDSs indicates greater mutuality of participation in research and inquiry. This has generally occurred through peer observation and action research. But relatively speaking, little work has been done in this area, and survey evidence suggests that it is not highly valued. As Labaree (1995) and others continue to point out, schools and universities are differently cultured.

Teachers' expectations and schedules do not reward research, which is still regarded as the university's domain and responsibility. Of the small amount of research done by and with teachers, little of it focused on the equity issues raised in *Tomorrow's Schools*. One small example, alluded to in an earlier section of this chapter, involved the study groups formed at a particular high school. Several of these groups focused on equity themes: at-risk, community service, cooperative learning. There was, however, no evidence that the formation of these groups had any bearing on school practices or outcomes. In fact, faculty expressed the belief that the segregation of special populations was increasing rather than decreasing in the school.

Collaborative Alliances

Goals

The PDSs will work only if there is true reciprocity between school and university educators. If one party dominates, these schools may be successful in other respects, but they will fail to marry inquiry and practice. (Holmes Group, 1990, p. 86)

Tomorrow's Schools proposes three areas for collaboration: with the university, with the local community, and with other schools in the district. Indicators of collaborative alliances between schools and universities are stable, consensual government arrangements; permanent budget allocations; new positions that span institutional boundaries; new reward and incentive structures; and recruitment of those committed to PDS goals (pp. 82–83). Because of its vision of teaching and learning as deep cultural understanding, the report also calls for arts and sciences faculty to join in change efforts.

In relation to the local community, PDSs are called upon to be cultural bridges and organizers of community effort. As cultural bridges, they provide students with "passports" to the dominant culture while valuing and enhancing local cultures and traditions. As centers for community organization, they need to find ways to work with health and social service agencies to respond to children's needs and to connect youth to the possibility of meaningful work. In both of these efforts, the PDS is expected to involve parents in significant ways.

In order to justify the extra infusion of funds needed to accomplish its goals, the Holmes Group submits the PDS not as an isolated model school but as one that is networked with other schools in the district. The PDS potentially becomes, then, a center for the professional development of teachers throughout the school district. Since alliances with universities, local communities, or district schools are not common features of school organization, these recommendations would be considered second order.

Equity implications in the nature of these collaborative alliances are clear: greater voice and participation for parents and community groups, benefits from investment in PDSs shared with other schools, and equitable rewards for participation. The purpose of collaborative efforts is also clear. PDSs are asked to "form alliances with the broader community to anticipate solutions to emerging social, economic and political concerns" and to be "places where educators and community leaders work at the outer edges of the educational and social problems facing children" (p. 4).

Research Studies

Although *Tomorrow's Schools* clearly articulates three types of collaboration, we found little in the research on linkages with the local community or other schools. The single community exception described local business ties that gave school leaders access to executive training programs and taught them participatory management strategies such as quality circles (Whitford, 1994). While no doubt beneficial for the professional development of school personnel, this activity does not address PDS goals of enhancing local cultures, being centers of community organization, providing students access to the dominant culture, or overcoming social problems.

Similarly, the PDS networks that have been established have a different function than those envisioned by the Holmes Group. Presuming that PDSs would be "model" schools, the vision was to network them with non-PDSs. The examples we found were networks of PDSs. They were networked through a school of education or a state department of education for goal-setting and communication purposes (Francis, 1992; Grossman, 1994; Teitel, 1991, 1993). However, partnerships with a school of education did not guarantee that schools would be networked. Individual partnerships could operate in isolation from one another (Berry & Catoe, 1994; Pasch & Pugach, 1990).

Two types of networks that have received some research attention are a university network (Gehrke et al., 1991) and a state department of education network (Teitel, 1991, 1993). The university network links four middle schools and a college of education. The research question was, "What can and is being done in this instance (the PSPDC [Puget Sound Professional Development Center]) toward creating a new culture that can be sustained over time?" (p. 1). Drawing on criteria identified by Sarason as critical for sustaining new groups, the authors studied three factors: task distribution and performance, conflict resolution, and cooperative activities. Over the course of the 3 years, the planning committee (a) broke up tasks into discrete parts and carefully distributed those tasks, (b) developed a procedure (not described) for handling conflicts, and (c) purposefully created bonding rituals. These activities were relatively successful. Although minor tensions persisted and increased participation added to the complexity, the network was still operating with its original partners several years later (Grossman, 1994).

Teitel (1991, 1993) points to the necessity of attending to collaborative issues. But "simultaneous renewal" seemed to be even more challenging when a third institution (in this case, a state department) was involved. Asking "What can a third party do to promote collaboration?" Teitel (1993) answers, quite a lot. It can be a facilitator, obtain commitments, plan tasks and activities, require outcomes, and intervene in conflicts. Depending on the success of the partnerships, these activities got mixed reviews. During 3 years of negotiating roles and relationships, what began as a centralized, high intervention, top-down change strategy became more flexible, consultative, and inclusive. The state department decided not to create forced partnerships, instituted a competitive application process requiring evidence of commitment, and provided more on-site assistance.

Apart from this state department of education study, the research focus for collaboration clearly has been on the relationship between schools and universities. We found little on school networks or school and community networks. There are two possible reasons for the lack of information in this area. One is that these types of collaborative alliances have not been studied. Those doing most of the research and writing about PDSs are university faculty who are participants in the reform effort. These authors would have a stronger interest in issues involving their own institutions, have easier access to data in those arenas, and/or view the school-university relation as a more powerful impetus for reform than other types of relations. A second reason is that less activity around school-school and school-community collaboration has actually occurred. We suspect that both of these factors contribute to the imbalance.

There is reason to believe that three other types of collaboration occur primarily outside the PDS reform agenda. In fact, the PDS agenda might militate against other collaborations because of the central role played by universities and the strong emphasis on transforming the initial preparation of teachers. One clear finding from the literature is that teachers are overwhelmed by multiple agendas (Darling-Hammond, 1994; Fullan, 1991). Unless alliances with the community, universities, and business are part of an integrated effort, schools will have difficulty attending to them all.

Most alliances between schools and universities had created some type of governance structure and new roles for school and university personnel. These were the areas in which the greatest progress had been made. Less progress occurred in restructuring rewards and incentives to support new roles, in establishing permanent budgets, and in recruiting others committed to PDS goals. Problems in all of these areas may well prevent PDSs from becoming widespread or institutionalized.

Alliances between schools and universities took many forms. We found examples of one university partnered with one school (Lemlech et al., 1994; McGowan & Powell, 1993; Snyder, 1994; Wiseman & Nason, 1995) and an example of several schools and universities partnered through a state department of education (Teitel, 1991). The most common form was a single university partnered with multiple schools (Berry & Catoe, 1994; Francis, 1992; Grossman, 1994; Miller & Silvernail, 1994; Pasch & Pugach, 1990; Whitford, 1994). These alliances had formal governing bodies that were site based (Berry & Catoe, 1994; Wiseman & Nason, 1995), centralized (Francis, 1992; Teitel, 1991), or both (Grossman, 1994; Whitford, 1994). They functioned as avenues for communication and decision making on such issues as the defining characteristics of a PDS, best practice, and the selection and roles of student teachers and mentor teachers.

Two authors described partnerships as "systemic ad-hocism" or an "ad-hocracy" (Grossman, 1994; Miller & Silvernail, 1994). These concepts capture the change process in many of the partnerships we reviewed. In contrast to a carefully preplanned model, systemic ad-hocism is characterized by experimentation, risk taking, and role ambiguity. Many of the partnerships also followed the process that Teitel (1991) discovered in the partnership he studied. They "bypassed steps inter-organizational theorists view as critical to relationship building" (p. 11). These steps include developing administrators' positive attitudes, determining organizational need, selecting and evaluating appropriate partners, and assessing one's own institutional capacity.

Perhaps as a result of these missed steps in relationship building, lines of communication, shared understanding, and trust were sometimes difficult to establish and maintain (McGowan & Powell, 1993). In one instance, there was a major breakdown of communication between a college of education and a school district regarding in-service and preservice training programs (Berry & Catoe, 1994). Another major miscommunication occurred across institutions over funding expectations (Wiseman & Nason, 1995). Communication was sometimes a problem even among participants within the same institution (Wiseman & Nason, 1995). Teachers had to balance new leadership roles while maintaining egalitarian relations (Romerdahl, 1991), and university faculty struggled over the place of PDS partnerships within their teacher education programs and administrative units (Grossman, 1994; Miller & Silvernail, 1994).

Some tension also existed about areas of responsibility, direction of change, and sequence of change. Teacher preparation could still be viewed as the university's responsibility (Whitford, 1994) or as a lesser priority in relation to school restructuring (Pasch & Pugach, 1990). Professional development could be used to maintain the status quo and comply with state regulations rather than to reform the practice of teaching (Whitford, 1994). In many of the alliances, a university faculty member functioned as a site-based liaison and was expected to spend a significant amount of time, from 1 to 3 days, on site (Berry & Catoe, 1994; Grossman, 1994; Pasch & Pugach, 1990). Teachers or principals often functioned as site-based coordinators, and release from part of their regular teaching loads was at times successfully negotiated (Romerdahl, 1991). Grant money facilitated these arrangements (Grossman, 1994). In at least one case, the salaries of half-time teacher-coordinators were paid by the university (Miller & Silvernail, 1994). Faculty from schools of education had a much greater—and, in most cases, exclusive—involvement in PDSs than did arts and science faculty.

These new "bridging" roles did not mean, however, that close relations were established between institutions. A site-based coordinator might function alone and might end up more closely identified with the school than the university culture (Berry & Catoe, 1994; Miller & Silvernail, 1994). If, on the other hand, the coordinator was based at the university, as a result of space or other reasons, communication with the school could be inhibited and the project perceived as the university's (Snyder, 1994). In either case, mutuality of interest and intent is difficult to sustain. Partnerships could easily be seen as experiments operating at the periphery of both institutions. This tended to happen when the partnership was seen as the "project" of one or two people (Grossman, 1994). Teachers could also resent or misunderstand the partnership. If it was a top-down decision, they often chose not to participate, felt pressure to participate, or asked to transfer out (Grossman, 1994; Lythcott & Schwartz, 1994; McGowan & Powell, 1993).

Nonetheless, the biggest change in collaborative alliances seems to be a redefinition of traditional roles. Some teacher educators spent considerably more time in schools and shared their teacher educator roles with classroom teachers. And some classroom teachers wrote vision statements, engaged in strategic planning, and participated in centralized steering committee meetings (Francis, 1992). Cooperating teachers assumed active roles in designing and delivering college courses, often as co-instructors with university professors (Lemlech et al., 1994; Miller & Silvernail, 1994; Sandholtz & Merseth, 1992; Snyder, 1994). When information about the PDS was not directly communicated, however, teachers had difficulty reconceptualizing roles and relied on existing perceptions of their teaching roles (McGowan & Powell, 1993).

More progress has been made in providing rewards and incentives for teachers than for teacher educators, although this continues to be a complex issue (Sandholtz & Merseth, 1992). Time is an important incentive for teachers. Alliances have found ways to provide school time for planning periods, study groups, or in-service workshops. In one instance, teachers proposed banking time "by beginning school 15 minutes earlier, 5 days per week, in order to dismiss the students 75 minutes early 1 day per week" (Lemlech et al., 1994, p. 166). At this particular site, six positions (50%) were vacant. The time and energy required for participation were seen as major deterrents.

Reallocating teacher time for deliberation and group planning is, nonetheless, seen as helpful in breaking down the perception that teachers are not working unless they are with students (Putnam, 1992). Additional incentives were providing teachers with professional development opportunities (Pasch & Pugach, 1990) and giving them more control over their environment and professional growth (McGowan & Powell, 1993). Not surprisingly, one survey found that teacher educators supported release time for teachers more than principals did (Moore & Hopkins, 1993).

It is clear that the work of principals is critical to the establishment of a successfully functioning partnership. Lewis (1992) states that three school factors centrally related to the principal's role—the nature of school leadership and vision, school-wide decision-making processes, and staff development—play a critical role in the success of a PDS initiative. In her evaluation of seven schools seeking to become PDSs, four were deemed unready for participation, and the principal's role was a decisive factor in this evaluation. At one of the sites, the principal did not allow teachers to make decisions about their development and maintained tight control over their work. In another school, the principal assigned a teacher to coordinate the "project," thereby signaling an abdication of leadership and commitment that ultimately prevented the development of the partnership (p. 21). In a separate 3-year participant-observation study of individual and group development within a PDS, Putnam (1992, p. 8) described principals as either furthering or constraining reform. According to Putnam, leadership that supports traditional public school norms and the belief that power resides with the administrator of the school contributes to the status quo. In contrast, those principals who perceive teachers as initiators of action and professionals who can lead and make decisions may be more inclined to create contexts marked by incentives and rewards for personal initiative, innovation, and growth.

We could find little evidence of changed rewards and incentive structures for teacher educators. The emphasis on publication productivity was seen as a strong deterrent for faculty at research universities, especially nontenured faculty (Berry & Catoe, 1994). The lack of change in this area also makes it more difficult to recruit others who are committed to PDS goals. When coupled with the perception that PDSs are peripheral or the special projects of the grant writers or initial collaborators (Grossman, 1994), this lack of change could keep PDSs a marginal and perhaps fleeting undertaking.

The absence of permanent budget allocations might be a further stumbling block to institutionalizing or expanding PDSs. Most PDSs were supported by state and/or foundation grants. We could not find a single partnership that had a separate and permanent budget. Grant support ranged from a few thousand dollars per site (Teitel, 1991) to a multimillion dollar restructuring project across sites (Francis, 1992). Although participants sometimes claimed that partnerships were helped by, but not dependent on, grants and that the partnership would continue even if funding was revoked, few began without that incentive. When the university was seen as the "source" of funding, expectations were sometimes unrealistic, and misunderstandings about what would be funded occurred (Wiseman & Nason, 1995).

Two articles attempted to estimate the cost of PDSs. One constructed two hypothetical schools based on actual experience (Wolfe et al., 1994). The other developed a theoretical model (Theobald, 1991). Both make assumptions about essential or preferred design features. In these models, the cost of a PDS ranges from $48,000 to $105,000 a year. In the hypothetical model, the $48,000 was primarily used for a half-time coordinator, summer stipends, and classroom substitutes so that teachers could participate in restructuring efforts. Several cohorts of students are simultaneously placed in these schools. Private foundation funds supported these efforts, with additional small grants available to fund research.

Basing his estimates on the assumption that a PDS will be viable only if the partnership is mutually beneficial, Theobald (1991) arrives at the higher estimate of $105,000 per site, or 5% to 10% above normal operating costs. This higher allocation results even after building in efficiency mechanisms such as placing 6–15 interns at each school and clustering 25–30 interns within a geographical area. In this model, the average teacher teaches 3 hours less a week in order to work with preservice teachers. More staff, including a full-time PDS coordinator, are hired.

At this point, there is not enough research evidence to determine whether one type of governance structure is better than another or even whether site-based coordinators are essential. One certain thing from the organizational change literature (Fullan, 1991) is that if these alliances are to last, they must be institutionalized. Some start out on the periphery of both the school and the university as an interest of a small group. But remaining there will jeopardize their existence or severely limit their impact. Whether or not even the most highly reformed PDS can affect school reform at other sites remains to be seen, although some evidence points to the affirmative.

Equity Implications

It appears that little progress has been made by PDSs in creating local community networks. Without these networks in place, the overall goal of forming alliances to deal with social and economic concerns will remain beyond the grasp of the PDS. Furthermore, unless PDSs find ways of networking with non-PDSs, the additional resources invested in them run the danger of creating an "elite" stratum of schools that siphon off research, professional development, and restructuring opportunities from other schools. This problem may be exacerbated if some schools lack readiness to be selected as a PDS partner because of limited resources (Lewis, 1992), leaving mostly affluent or more resourceful schools to be selected (Sagmiller & Gehrke, 1992).

In terms of school-university alliances, more progress has been made, but several equity issues remain. These equity issues are particularly acute for untenured university faculty when reward and incentive systems fail to account for the labor-intensive nature of this work. As Winitzky et al. (1992) have pointed out, if workloads were more equitably distributed, PDSs would have a better chance of accomplishing their mission. If a small group of teacher education faculty are doing all of the PDS work, the question of fairness needs to be raised.

Rewards and incentives also remain a question for school faculty. Alliances seem to work best when faculty are given more control over the school environment and their professional development. Faculty, however, have difficulty fulfilling their new roles if these roles represent an additional set of responsibilities. The problem of work "intensification" needs to be carefully monitored. Teachers also have difficulty assuming leadership positions and maintaining egalitarian relations with colleagues. This issue warrants further investigation as well. Roles and tasks need to be carefully distributed in ways that promote trust, fairness, and open communication.

These shifting roles also create some tension and ambiguity around issues of equality and expertise between the school and the university. The basic dilemma involves the role of the university. Are university personnel equal partners in PDSs? Or are they outside experts who bring solutions to problems? At one site, there was concern about perceptions of "elitism" on the part of university faculty (Whitford, 1994). At another, teachers felt that the university coordinator talked "at them" during in-service meetings (Berry & Catoe, 1994). Yet, at other sites, teachers asked for effective teaching seminars and demonstrations (Pasch & Pugach, 1990) or were frustrated when university experts would not give them answers (Fear, Edwards, & Roehler, 1991). Collaborative alliances have made participants rethink traditional notions of expertise, authoritative knowledge, and power (Miller & Silvernail, 1994), but there is not yet agreement on this issue.

One example of a power imbalance that became more equitable is found in Teitel (1991, 1993). These studies of a state department's role in creating PDS partnerships indicate that the top-down approach of creating "arranged marriages" was less successful than allowing universities and schools to choose each other by using institutional commitment criteria.

DISCUSSION: IDENTIFYING FUTURE COMMITMENTS

A comparison between the equity goals outlined in the Holmes Report (1990) and the actual achievements of PDSs to date indicates a large gap between realities and expectations yet to be fulfilled. The Holmes Group has presented a vision of schools as instruments of social and political reform; however, the majority of research studies on professional development, teaching and learning, collaborative alliances, teacher education, and school restructuring within PDSs have provided a portrait of reform disconnected from a broader set of social and political commitments. Has the vision of those engaged in PDS development been too narrow? What equity issues are most critical to attend to as PDS initiatives mature? An assessment of research on equity access, participation, and outcomes for teachers, parents, children, and university faculty highlights issues for future consideration.

Access

There is little documentation at the present time regarding the drawbacks and benefits that accompany various participation structures within the PDS. Explicit information pertaining to which populations are served, who participates, and the types of opportunities provided necessarily incorporates a consideration of equity and social justice. The structure and availability of opportunities for various groups raises questions such as the following: Do certain participation structures within the PDS benefit certain groups more than others? and Are certain groups being ignored or denied participation opportunities? These are fundamentally matters of access. Surprisingly, there is little uniformity across studies regarding these issues.

In the area of site selection, for instance, the guiding criteria used to determine PDS sites are rarely elaborated in the research literature. While some collaborations occur in middle-class and upper-middle-class schools as a result of their status as promising models of excellence, a few PDSs have also been developed in urban centers with the explicit intent of exposing interns to "schools in transition": schools with difficult problems (high student attrition, little community involvement, high teacher turnover, minimal resources) that may require years of committed efforts to produce results (Jett-Simpson et al., 1992; Lemlech & Hertzog-Foliart, 1993; Pasch & Pugach, 1990; Stallings, 1991; Yopp et al., 1993–1994). The multiple challenges that attend these schools and make them appear as "poor risks" to some universities and school systems are the same challenges that are perceived as opportunities by others. For example, these sites offer educators the opportunity to examine and challenge teacher stereotypes regarding children's learning and to examine issues of equity and diversity.

Aside from the question of "Whom shall the site serve?" there is the additional matter of "Who shall participate in developing and implementing reform initiatives?" Recruiting teachers of color in order to diversify the teaching force remains a stated priority for school systems and colleges of education, but much work remains to be done in this area. In addition, within PDS sites, participant selection processes vary widely. While participation is most often voluntary, both at the university level and within the schools, there is evidence to suggest that school restructuring may be least equitable and effective under these circumstances. Partnerships that involve small groups of volunteer participants run a great risk of becoming marginalized, peripheral to the central concerns of both school and university. University faculty, for example, are not provided with rewards or incentives for PDS involvement. They risk fewer publications, heavier workloads, and lower status within the university. Not surprisingly, most initiatives rely on a few committed faculty who feel overwhelmed by the demands placed on their energy and time. Similar inequities obtain for teachers. Additional roles and responsibilities may intensify work demands and have a negative impact on their effectiveness in the classroom.

Within the classroom, access as opportunity for involvement pertains to students as well. Children require opportunities for decision making, collaborating, exchanging ideas, and constructing knowledge. The effects on children's learning of curricular and instructional reforms remains one of the least studied aspects of PDSs, however. Research on parent and community involvement is also limited (see Driscoll et al., 1994). Have these groups been provided with opportunities for active engagement in school affairs and a voice in decision making? Little is known about programs operative in PDSs that address family and community needs.

At present, policies that explicitly address issues of access and opportunity may be important as a means of clarifying university-school commitments and ensuring equity. Inconsistent or contradictory practices suggest the need for a coherent philosophy and set of shared goals that guide decision making and actions (Darling-Hammond, 1992). A lack of consensus regarding purposes and goals may otherwise threaten the future of the current reform effort.

Processes

Perhaps most documented in the PDS research literature is the link between equity and the relationships established between university and school faculty. Unequal power arrangements have been perceived as a primary obstacle to reform and teacher empowerment an important facilitator. A primary theme across studies is the blurring of status and boundaries and the nurturing of trust and role shifts in order to create a new collaborative culture. Participatory governance structures and collaborative teams are common structures used to build mutual, democratic relationships. Teachers and university professors codesign workshops and seminars and collaboratively instruct teaching interns. Time is provided for dialogue and research, and top-down approaches to decision making are being replaced with more democratic approaches.

The initiation of reforms that foster more equitable relationships between university and school has characterized the formational stages of school-university partnerships. Putnam (1992) suggests that the establishment of a working community built upon norms of inclusion, equality, trust, and collaboration is a priority for PDS participants and must precede any consideration of larger goals. According to Putnam, five cycles of sequential development characterize PDS growth and transformation. In a 3-year participant-observation study of six PDS sites, she observed that, initially, individuals grappled with self-focused survival concerns such as "What will be expected of me, and how will I be treated?" Fears of losing autonomy were common to teachers, administrators, and university professors. In the early stages of the partnership, teachers began to work in small groups on various instructional projects as they simultaneously built trust and rapport through collaboration. The norm of working in isolation was gradually replaced by one of collaboration. Ultimately, a cohesive learning community matured to the point where, together, the entire staff examined larger issues regarding the structure of the school, the relationship of the school to the broader community, and the roles and structures that could best support relationships among university, school, and community. Similarly, Boles and Troen (1994) described the metamorphosis of the Teacher's Collaborative as a process that entailed first creating a new culture conducive to supporting reform:

The PDS has established a new sub-culture in the schools that supports risk-taking, values leadership and simultaneously maintains the norms of equality and inclusion among teachers. The PDS enables teachers to circumvent the more traditional school culture that does not reward, and often obstructs, risk-taking and collaboration. (p. 26)

Perhaps issues focused on inclusion and diversity for students, families, and local community have yet to gain currency because PDSs are still in the early stages of development. The "readiness" of a school culture may be an important factor in establishing the ground from which broader goals are cultivated. However, Zeichner (1992) contends that a myopic focus on immediate issues of personal and intellectual concern must not be severed from broader commitments to equity and social justice for children and their families:

What concerns me is that the teacher empowerment and school restructuring movement, while attending very carefully to the intellectual and personal consequences of classroom and school events, often gives very little attention to how these events are joined to issues of social continuity and change, to issues of equity and social justice. How teachers' everyday actions challenge or support various oppressions and injustices related to social class, race, gender, sexual preference, religion, and numerous other factors needs to be a central part of teachers' reflections, teacher research, and collaborative decision-making schemes. (p. 12)

Against the grain of an unjust society, teaching "everybody's children" becomes a moral and political enterprise (Holmes Group, 1990, p. 7). However, at the present time, there are few indications that schools and universities engaged in establishing partnerships have adopted this mandate as their own.

Outcomes

In *Tomorrow's Schools*, the Holmes Group proposes that PDSs should engage in continuous renewal through self-evaluation and innovation, which ultimately benefit "everybody's children." The authors state that participants in PDS initiatives must question whether school structures and processes produce school failure and attempt to develop new strategies that will support the learning of diverse students, particularly those living in economically disadvantaged communities. However, these equity concerns are matched by concerns for school accountability that may place severe limits on the risks school systems are willing to take to implement innovations and reforms. Standardized testing as a means of teacher inspection and quality control encourages teaching practices that most efficiently produce student achievement scores. Influenced by the pressures to produce higher test scores, PDS participants have initiated reforms that are not necessarily supported by research. Tracking, for example, a mandated policy in many districts, is maintained in many PDSs, while others experiment with various forms of mainstreaming and heterogeneous grouping (Brainard, 1989).

The lack of a coherent curricular reform agenda may be due to the varying responses among school districts to pressures that originate outside the university-school partnership. Professional accountability systems that value practices that are client oriented and research based may more effectively support reform efforts (Darling-Hammond, 1989). Professional accountability, premised on the understanding that teaching is too complex to be controlled through prescriptive mandates and test scores, may be ensured through the careful and rigorous preparation of teachers in environments where professional judgments are valued, professional performance is assessed with validity and equity, and risk taking and experimentation inform practice. Research is needed that examines closely the problems of accountability and how schools can demonstrate student accomplishment through alternative measures consistent with PDS goals.

Although still in the initial phases of development, it may not be too early to conclude that the vision that has been established in many PDSs is quite narrow in scope (see Table 3). Initiatives focus on teacher development and empowerment, modifications to teacher education, the exploration of new instructional methods, or a combination of these. Yet few operate with the acknowledgment of any overarching commitments to equity and social justice. While the PDS cannot serve as a panacea for the severe inequalities that characterize life for many in this society, a more deliberate link between the mission of the PDS as an instrument of political and social reform and the daily work of educators may support the invention of a truly new organization.

TABLE 3
Goal/Results Comparison

First-order changes	Second-order changes
Teaching and learning	
1. Help students use scientific analysis	1. *Teach for understanding*
2. *Create cooperative classrooms*	2. Use narrative forms across all
3. Teach students to take responsibility for	disciplines
their own learning	3. Promote voice, conversation, and
	criticism
	4. Create learning communities where
	heterogeneously grouped students
	co-construct understanding and
	make sense of experience
	5. Combine basic facts/skills with
	complex learning
	6. Democratize elite forms of schooling
	7. Build on meanings and values
	students bring to school
Teacher education	
1. Use exemplary, authentic clinical settings	1. Stress service, an ethic of care and
2. *Instill habits of reflection*	social justice
3. Make teacher education more intellectually	2. Emphasize diversity in recruitment
sound	and curriculum
4. *Interweave and ground theory in practice*	3. Provide novice teachers systematic
5. Make arts and science knowledge more	occasions to study equity in diversity
pedagogically accessible	
Professional development	
1. *Provide for continuous learning about*	1. Emphasize respect for and use of
teaching (time for collaboration, reflection,	students' cultural knowledge
and exploration of alternative pedagogies)	2. Engage in political activism to further
	goals of educational equity and
	justice
	3. Develop new standards of practice
	through research
	4. *Adopt new roles as teacher*
	educators (co-teach university
	courses, supervise and evaluate
	student interns, lead seminars)
	5. *Participate in school reform through*
	the creation of school goals and
	policies
	6. Make diversity central to professional
	discourse
Organization and structure	
1. Establish new forms of governance	1. Create organization for new learning
2. Make connections to the work sector	goals
3. Create small schools or units	2. Create new forms of family/
	community involvement
	3. Promote links to social service
	agencies

(cont. on p. 295)

TABLE 3 (*Continued*)

First-order changes	Second-order changes
Inquiry and research	
1. *Focus on teaching* content/*methods*, conceptual understanding, *technology, management,* and staffing with arts and sciences and *education faculty*	1. Organize school as center of inquiry
	2. Promote research that values teachers' intellectual activity and the complexity of teaching for understanding
	3. Explore explanations of school failure and diversity to promote culturally responsive teaching
Collaborative alliances	
	1. *Create* stable, consensual government *arrangements between school and universities,* including arts and sciences faculty
	2. Have permanent budget allocations
	3. *Develop interinstitutional positions*
	4. Create new rewards and incentives
	5. Recruit others committed to PDS goals
	6. Create collaboration with local community
	7. Network with other schools
Equity	
	1. Overcome barriers raised by an equal society
	2. Engage in social/political action for greater justice/resources
	3. Engage in struggle to better students' lives
	4. Purposefully situate PDSs in poor areas

Note: Italicized phrases indicate goals where progress has been documented by research.

METHODOLOGICAL CRITIQUE

Research on PDSs, like the PDS efforts themselves, is presently in an early stage in its development. In addition to reviewing the extant studies for their content and findings, it is important to assess the strength of the methodologies used. That puts us in a better position to judge the validity of the findings and to set a worthwhile course for inquiry. As small errors in aim result in widely missed destinations when the trajectory is long, so may the research enterprise on PDSs miss the mark if the early studies fail to adhere to principles of sound inquiry. Unfortunately, this appears to be the case.

For purposes of this critique, we conducted a rather coarse-grained analysis to determine what proportion of the studies (a) were based on an explicitly stated theory, (b) reported having used methodological elements of rigor to ensure validity of the results, and/or (c) were conceptually linked to other studies either as extensions or replications of prior work.

Theory-Based Research

Inquiry that rests on theory has been described by Kaplan (1964) as informative in at least two ways. First, the findings of such studies have at least some chance of being explained in terms of fundamental principles or lawful relationships. Second, a reciprocal transaction is possible, meaning that theory guides the choice of questions and methods, while the results of such questions and methods can provide feedback to the further refinement or nullification of theory. Approximately half of the studies explicitly stated a theoretical basis for their initial questions and designs. Examples included interorganizational relationship theory (Teitel, 1992), Sarason's theory of change in school culture (Gehrke et al., 1991), and developmental phases of groups (Putnam, 1992). In each instance of these and similarly theory-based studies, the findings set the stage for further research and practice in PDSs.

For example, Teitel's (1992) finding that simultaneous renewal of schools and colleges is still more a goal than a reality reflects the difficult nature of interorganizational relationships. Future PDS work, both in research and practice, can benefit from Teitel's findings because they are explicable, although disappointing, in terms of interorganizational relationships. In contrast, atheoretical studies reported results that were both counterintuitive from a PDS perspective and constitute blind alleys for subsequent inquiry. Woloszyk and Hill (1994) reported that PDS interns were *less* likely to support inclusion of children with special needs than were non-PDS ("standard") interns. The fact that this finding conflicts with the generally held PDS commitment to diversity is not explained and therefore contributes little to the overall effort to evaluate the effects of the PDS on teacher education.

Methodological Rigor

Overall, there appeared to be a wide range of attention to the type of disciplined methods of inquiry that distinguish research from other forms of professional narratives. Fewer than half of the studies reported any procedures designed to support, or presented evidence in support of, the validity of their findings. Our analysis was not overly stringent. For qualitative studies (including case studies and ethnographies), any mention of such design elements as triangulation of sources (e.g., Driscoll et al., 1994), member checks (McGowan & Powell, 1993), or tests of intercoder agreement (Shen, 1994) was considered to be sufficient. For quantitative studies, numbering only six, statistical analysis of the data (e.g., Morris & Nunnery, 1993) or use of a control group (e.g., Stallings, 1991) was considered sufficient. Given our relatively liberal assessment of methodological rigor, the fact that only half of the studies met these criteria is cause for concern. It appears that, at this early stage of PDS research, there has been a primary emphasis in the literature and at professional conferences on descriptions of programs rather than systematic inquiry.

Extension or Replication

Knowledge in any area of inquiry is constructed incrementally and reflects the shared understandings of the community of scholars. Therefore, the research that serves to generate such knowledge is, in an ideal community of scholarship, linked conceptually to the other studies in that focused area of inquiry. In practice, this is evidenced by studies linked programmatically within one investigator's line of research or studies that both acknowledge prior efforts and build on them either as extension or replication.

Taken as a group, the PDS studies we reviewed failed in this regard. Only nine studies could be liberally categorized as extensions or replications of cited precedents. Again, our standards were not terribly demanding. Literature review and discussion sections of these papers were scanned for citation of prior studies that could have served as either logical or actual precedent studies. For example, Boles and Troen (1994) summarize the results of four previous studies of teacher leadership to set the stage for their current study:

> The research we have conducted since the inception of the Learning/Teaching Collaborative (Boles, 1990, 1991, 1994; Troen and Boles, 1993) has indicated that many teachers are assuming leadership roles through this PDS. . . . It is clear that teachers are assuming a variety of roles without any formal designation as leaders. *This finding led us to our current study.* (p. 8; italics added)

The Boles and Troen study is typical of the extension studies included in this review in that the authors' own work, rather than the work of other colleagues, serves as the precedent. This is likely to change over time as more authors look to the literature for examples of precedent studies. Currently, however, the literature reflects isolation of efforts. There does not appear to be a research agenda that would encourage investigators to replicate others' work or to conduct collaborative programs of research that could benefit from the combined power of studies designed with common elements.

In providing this methodological critique of the extant PDS research, our intent is neither to dismiss the findings of such studies, which have contributed much to our knowledge, nor to insist on tightly controlled experimentation. Rather, it is to urge caution in the interpretation of such reports and to suggest that an approach that is both disciplined and more communal may have value in the evolution and evaluation of PDS efforts.

CONCLUSION

Having carefully reviewed the text of *Tomorrow's Schools* and the research methodology and findings on PDSs, we can now return to our central question: Is there anything about this new institution that will enable it to create a more just and equitable society? Mixed answers come from an analysis of past educational reform efforts in the United States, a rhetorical reading of the text, and our review of the research.

The prospects for current reform proposals can be informed by the manner in which past reform efforts have been proposed and treated. By analyzing the success and failure of such diverse efforts as the Common School Movement, child-centered education, and the organization of teaching through behavioral objectives, Kliebard (1992) offers two broad historical lessons: (a) that successful reforms are not just slogan systems and (b) that local conditions must support their implementation. These lessons are supported by the school improvement literature (Fullan, 1991) and suggest what advocates of PDSs need to consider if their vision of equity is to be realized.

First, successful reforms must be more than good ideas or slogan systems. While good ideas are a necessary condition for change, they are insufficient. They must have a concrete agenda "supported by or at least consistent with broad social and political forces" (Kliebard, 1992, p. 102). Like *A Nation at Risk* and the *Paideia Proposal* (Adler, 1982), *Tomorrow's Schools* can be viewed as a slogan system. Successful slogan systems employ three rhetorical devices. They must be vague enough to allow diverse groups to agree, specific enough to offer a practical guide, and charming enough to motivate action (Apple, 1986). The power of slogan systems depends on their ability to create such a clear vision for change that broad coalitions believe the task is both desirable and achievable. This is what Apple (1986) and others call the language of possibility. It breaks the hegemony of dominant discourse, offering alternative visions of present institutional arrangements. *Tomorrow's Schools* is very compelling in this regard. Numerous PDS partnerships have been created from its vision.

The report has, however, been criticized for its lack of specificity. It has been called too diffuse, too inclusive, and too mystical to lead to any substantive reform (Labaree, 1992, 1995). Zeichner (1991), for instance, complains of its lack of attention to community empowerment:

It asserts that a greater sense of professionalism on the part of teachers should never distance them from parents and others in the community surrounding the school but then spends little space discussing how the legitimate interests of parents and communities on the one hand, and teachers and principals on the other, can be balanced to give everyone a meaningful role in school decision making. (p. 369)

The research evidence we have amassed adds significant weight to these complaints. *Tomorrow's Schools* offers an ambitious and compelling vision of reform. Partners are, however, having great difficulty in carrying out that vision. In many instances, the vision has become so narrowed as to be almost unrecognizable.

The second characteristic of successful reforms is that, in the local context, there must be congruence between their purposes and standards and the conditions of teaching. District policies, as well as school structures, processes, schedules, and resources, must support the reforms; teachers must share, and have the power to enact, the vision. If the conditions of teaching do not support the vision of reform, frustration and failure will occur: The desire to work hard and do good will quickly vanish. Reform efforts can inadvertently place unrealistic pressures and expectations on those with little power to achieve significant social change. Reform rhetoric can make the task sound too easy. The report has been criticized in this regard:

> *Tomorrow's Schools* provides no sociological or historical evidence to show that professional development schools would in fact serve the kind of democratic and egalitarian goals it proposes for them. Instead of looking for such evidence, the reader is supposed to respond to the report's stirring political appeal. We are swayed by the possibilities of professional development schools because we want to accomplish the kinds of generous and politically attractive goals to which this reform effort is dedicated. (Labaree, 1992, p. 635)

Tomorrow's Schools seeks nothing less than to invent new institutions committed to "overcoming the educational and social barriers raised by an unequal society" (p. 7). Given the alarming numbers of children living in poverty (Reed & Sautter, 1990) and the rising incidents of racial violence and other hate crimes, this is a tremendous responsibility for PDSs. While educational reform must be "evaluated for its contribution to the building of this more just and humane society," it cannot do the work alone (Zeichner, 1991, p. 375). School reform must be closely linked to social and economic reform, to solving problems of poverty, underemployment, racism, social isolation, and family instability (Wilson, 1994). To its credit, the Holmes Group has recognized the need to strengthen the relationship between schools and the broader political, social, and economic communities. But our review of the research indicates that most PDS partners have either not attempted or are floundering in this undertaking.

NOTES

[1] The first two studies, by Brainard (1989) and Stallings and Kowalski (1990), predate most research on and implementation of current PDSs. The Brainard study analyzes Ford Foundation and Holmes Group schools in initial stages of development. The Stallings and Kowalski chapter provides a historical account of related school reform initiatives such as laboratory schools and portal schools. Many examples listed under contemporary PDSs are really approximations and precursors such as teacher education centers and induction programs. Two, more recent studies, Book (1996) and Teitel (1996), are the first for which sufficient research permits comprehensive reviews. Our study differs from Book's in two respects. First, we found approximately 25 additional research articles. Second, we took a different analytic approach. As is customary, Book derived her categories from the research studies themselves. We derived ours from the advocacy literature. Because we were interested in the match between "aspirations" and "realities," we first laid out advocates' goals for PDSs and then compared those goals with what had actually been documented through research. Teitel's review covers a full range of literature, not merely research.

[2] The image of PDSs we get from the research might, of course, be quite different from the reality. Many sites now call themselves PDSs, and from the large number we are acquainted with through national and regional networks, most have not found their way

into research studies. Participants are often too busy to do research, or research is not part of the institutional culture. Therefore, it is impossible to know for certain whether the research sample is representative of the national scene. However, through our formal and informal contacts, our overall impression is that the picture that emerges from the research closely mirrors what is occurring in PDSs in general.

[3] Three graduate assistants, Christie Corbin, Chris Terry, and Beverly Whitest, contributed invaluable hours in locating and organizing sources, constructing tables, reading and reviewing studies, and sharing their insights. We thank them for doing the tedious work so graciously and the conceptual work so thoughtfully.

[4] The journals searched were *Action in Teacher Education, American Educational Research Journal, Contemporary Education, Curriculum Inquiry, Educational Policy, Journal of Teacher Education, Teacher Education Quarterly, Teachers College Record, Teaching Education, Teaching & Teacher Education,* and *Theory into Practice.* Most of the additional articles we found were in the teacher education journals.

[5] A few other PDSs were located in urban settings (e.g., Lemlech et al., 1994), but the implications of such settings were not addressed.

REFERENCES

Abdal-Haqq, I. (1993). *Resources on professional development schools: An annotated bibliography.* Washington, DC: ERIC Clearinghouse on Teacher Education and the American Association for Colleges of Teacher Education.

Adler, M. (1982). *The Paideia proposal.* New York: Macmillan.

Apple, M. (1986). *Teachers and texts: A political economy of class and gender relations in education.* New York: Routledge.

Apple, M. (1993). *Official knowledge: Democratic education in a conservative age.* New York: Routledge.

Barksdale-Ladd, M.A. (1994). Teacher empowerment and literacy instruction in three professional development schools. *Journal of Teacher Education, 45,* 104–111.

Beane, J., & Apple, M. (1995). The case for democratic schools. In M. Apple & J. Beane (Eds.), *Democratic schools* (pp. 1–25). Alexandria, VA: Association for Supervision and Curriculum Development.

Berry, B., & Catoe, S. (1994). Creating professional development schools: Policy and practice in South Carolina's PDS initiative. In L. Darling-Hammond (Ed.), *Professional development schools: Schools for developing a profession* (pp. 176–202). New York: Teachers College Press.

Boles, K., & Troen, V. (1994, April). *Teacher leadership in a professional development school.* Paper presented at the annual meeting of the American Educational Research Association, New Orleans, LA.

Book, C. (1996). Professional development schools. In J. Sikula (Ed.), *Handbook of research on teacher education* (2nd ed., pp. 194–210). New York: Macmillan.

Boyd, P.C. (1994). Professional school reform and public school renewal: Portrait of a partnership. *Journal of Teacher Education, 45,* 132–139.

Brainard, F. (1989). *Professional development schools: Status as of 1989* (Occasional paper 9). Seattle: Institute for the Study of Educational Policy, University of Washington.

Cohen, D. (1995). What is the system in systemic reform? *Educational Researcher, 24* (9), 11–17, 31.

Corcoran, T., & Goertz, M. (1995). Instructional capacity and high-performance standards. *Educational Researcher, 24* (9), 27–31.

Cuban, L. (1988). A fundamental puzzle of school reform. *Phi Delta Kappan, 70,* 341–344.

Darling-Hammond, L. (1989). Accountability for professional practice. *Teachers College Record, 91,* 59–80.

Darling-Hammond, L. (1992). Reframing the school reform agenda. *The School Administrator, 19,* 22–27.

Darling-Hammond, L. (Ed.). (1994). *Professional development schools: Schools for developing a profession.* New York: Teachers College Press.

Delpit, L. (1995). *Other people's children.* New York: New Press.

Driscoll, A., Benson, N., & Livneh, C. (1994). University school district collaboration in teacher education: Outcomes and insights. *Teacher Education Quarterly, 21* (3), 59–68.

Fear, K., Edwards, P., & Roehler, L. (1991). *A critical analysis of collaboration within professional development schools.* (ERIC Document Reproduction Service No. ED 343 083)

Francis, R. W. (1992, October). *Issues in establishing rural professional development schools.* Paper presented at the Annual Rural and Small Schools Conference.

Fullan, M. (1991). *The new meaning of educational change* (2nd ed.). New York: Teachers College Press.

Gehrke, N., Young, D., & Sagmiller, K. (1991, April). *Critical analysis of the creation of a new culture: A professional development center for teachers.* Paper presented at the annual meeting of the American Educational Research Association, Chicago, IL.

Goodlad, J. (1990). *Teachers for our nation's schools.* San Francisco: Jossey-Bass.

Graham, P. (1991, November). *What America has expected of its schools over the past century.* Paper presented at the Conference on Democracy and Education, Chicago, IL.

Grant, C. (1989). Equity, equality, teachers and classroom life. In W. Secada (Ed.), *Equity in education* (pp. 89–102). Philadelphia: Falmer.

Gross, S. (Ed.). (1993). *Constructing teaching and research practice in elementary school mathematics.* East Lansing: Michigan State University, Center for the Learning and Teaching of Elementary Subjects, Institute for Research on Teaching. (ERIC Document Reproduction Service No. ED 364 405)

Grossman, P. L. (1994). In pursuit of a dual agenda: Creating a middle level professional development school. In L. Darling-Hammond (Ed.), *Professional development schools: Schools for developing a profession* (pp. 50–73). New York: Teachers College Press.

Harris, R. C., & Harris, M. (1992–93). Partner schools: Places to solve teacher education problems. *Action in Teacher Education, 14* (4), 1–8.

Harvey, G., & Klein, S. (1989). Understanding and measuring equity in education: A conceptual framework. In W. Secada (Ed.), *Equity in education* (pp. 43–67). Philadelphia: Falmer.

Holmes Group. (1986). *Tomorrow's teachers.* East Lansing, MI: Author.

Holmes Group. (1990). *Tomorrow's schools.* East Lansing, MI: Author.

Holmes Group. (1995). *Tomorrow's schools of education.* East Lansing, MI: Author.

Howey, K., & Zimpher, N. (1989). *Profiles of preservice teacher education: Inquiry into the nature of programs.* Albany: State University of New York Press.

Jett-Simpson, M., Pugach, M. C., & Whipp, J. (1992, April). *Portrait of an urban professional development school.* Paper presented at the annual meeting of the American Educational Research Association, San Francisco, CA.

Kaplan, A. (1964). *The conduct of inquiry: Methodology for social science.* New York: Chandler.

Karr, J., Green, N., & Koulogeorge, M. (1994). *New school reform and a school/university partnership contributed to curriculum change.* (ERIC Document Reproduction Service No. ED 378 262)

Kliebard, H. (1992). *Forging the American curriculum. Essays in curriculum history and theory.* New York: Routledge.

Koffman, E., & Green, N. (1994). Appropriate research in professional development schools. *Critical Issues in Teacher Education, 4*, 9–21.

Labaree, D. (1992). Doing good, doing science: The Holmes Group reports and the rhetorics of educational reform. *Teachers College Record, 93*, 628–640.

Labaree, D. (1995). A disabling vision: Rhetoric and reality in *Tomorrow's Schools of Education. Teachers College Record, 97*, 166–205.

Ladson-Billings, G. (1994). *The dreamkeepers: Successful teachers of African American children.* San Francisco: Jossey-Bass.

Lemlech, J.K., & Hertzog-Foliart, H. (1993). Linking school and university through collegial student teaching. *Teacher Education Quarterly, 20* (4), 19–27.

Lemlech, J.K., Hertzog-Foliart, H., & Hackl, A. (1994). The Los Angeles professional practice school: A study of mutual impact. In L. Darling-Hammond (Ed.), *Professional development schools: Schools for developing a profession* (pp. 156–175). New York: Teachers College Press.

Lewis, M.D. (1992, April). *Professional development schools: Conditions for readiness.* Paper presented at the annual meeting of the American Educational Research Association, San Francisco, CA.

Lythcott, J., & Schwartz, F. (1994). Professional development in action: An idea with visiting rites. In L. Darling-Hammond (Ed.), *Professional development schools: Schools for developing a profession* (pp. 126–155). New York: Teachers College Press.

McGowan, T.M., & Powell, J.H. (1993, April). *In search of autonomy: Teachers' aspirations and expectations from a school-university collaborative.* Paper presented at the annual meeting of the American Educational Research Association, Atlanta, GA.

Miller, L., & Silvernail, D. (1994). Wells Junior High School: Evolution of a professional development school. In L. Darling-Hammond (Ed.), *Professional development schools: Schools for developing a profession* (pp. 28–49). New York: Teachers College Press.

Moore, K., & Hopkins, S. (1993). Professional development schools: Partnerships in teacher preparation. *Contemporary Education, 64*, 219–222.

Morris, V.G., & Nunnery, J. (1993). *Teacher empowerment in a professional development school collaborative: Pilot assessment.* (ERIC Document Reproduction Service No. ED 368 6478)

Murray, F.B. (1993). "All or none" criteria for professional development schools. *Educational Policy, 7*, 61–73.

National Commission on Excellence in Education. (1983). A nation at risk. Washington, DC: U.S. Government Printing Office.

Navarro, J. (1992). *Will teachers say what we want to hear? Dilemmas of teacher voice* (Report No. 92–5). East Lansing: National Center for Research on Teaching and Learning, Michigan State University. (ERIC Document Reproduction Service No. ED 351 283)

Neufeld, J., & Freeman, D. (1993, February). *Teachers as teacher educators within a professional development school context.* Paper presented at the annual meeting of the American Association of Colleges for Teacher Education, San Diego, CA.

Nihlen, A. (1992, April). *Schools as centers for reflection and inquiry: Research for teacher empowerment.* Paper presented at the annual meeting of the American Educational Research Association, San Francisco, CA.

Pasch, S.H., & Pugach, M.C. (1990). Collaborative planning for urban professional development schools. *Contemporary Education, 61*, 135–143.

Putnam, J. (1992). *Professional development schools: Emerging changes in educators and the professional community.* (ERIC Document Reproduction Service No. ED 370 890)

Reed, S., & Sautter, R.C. (1990, June). Children of poverty: The status of 12 million young Americans. *Kappan Special Report.*

Romerdahl, N. (1991, April). *Shared leadership in a professional development center.* Paper presented at the annual meeting of the American Educational Research Association, Chicago, IL.

Rosaen, C.L., & Lindquist, B. (1992). *Collaborative teaching and research: Asking "what does it mean?"* (Series No. 73). East Lansing: Center for the Learning and Teaching of Elementary Subjects, Institute for Research on Teaching, Michigan State University.

Ruscoe, G., & Whitford, B. (1991). *Quantitative and qualitative perspectives on teacher attitudes: The third year.* (ERIC Document Reproduction Service No. ED 336 351)

Ruscoe, G., Whitford, B., Egginton, W., & Esselman, M. (1989). *Quantitative and qualitative perspectives on teacher attitudes in professional development schools.* (ERIC Document Reproduction Service No. ED 310 068).

Rushcamp, S., & Roehler, L.R. (1992). Characteristics supporting change in a professional development school. *Journal of Teacher Education, 43* (1), 19–27.

Sagmiller, K., & Gehrke, N. (1992, April). *An historical-ethnographic study of an emerging professional development school.* Paper presented at the annual meeting of the American Educational Research Association, San Francisco, CA.

Sandholtz, J., & Merseth, K. (1992). Collaborating teachers in a professional development school: Inducements and contributions. *Journal of Teacher Education, 43* (4), 308–317.

Schack, G., & Overturf, B. (1994, April). *Professional development teams: Stepping stone to professional development schools.* Paper presented at the annual meeting of the American Educational Research Association, New Orleans, LA.

Secada, W. (1989). Educational equity versus equality of education: An alternative conception. In W. Secada (Ed.), *Equity in education* (pp. 68–88). Philadelphia: Falmer.

Shen, J. (1994, February). *A study in contrast: Visions of preservice teacher education in the context of a professional development school.* Paper presented at the annual meeting of the American Association of Colleges for Teacher Education, Chicago, IL.

Snyder, J. (1994). Perils and potentials: A tale of two professional development schools. In L. Darling-Hammond (Ed.), *Professional development schools: Schools for developing a profession* (pp. 98–125). New York: Teachers College Press.

Stallings, J. (1991, April). *Connecting preservice teacher education and inservice professional development: A professional development school.* Paper presented at the annual meeting of the American Educational Research Association, Chicago, IL.

Stallings, J., & Kowalski, T. (1990). Professional development schools. In W.R. Houston (Ed.), *Handbook of research on teacher education* (pp. 251–263). New York: Macmillan.

Stanulis, R.N. (1995). Classroom teachers as mentors: Possibilities for participation in a professional development school context. *Teaching and Teacher Education, 11,* 331–344.

Stevenson, R. (1993). Critically reflective inquiry and administrator preparation: Problems and possibilities. *Educational Policy, 7* (1), 96–113.

Teitel, L. (1991). *Getting started: Issues in initiating new models for school and university collaborations.* Paper presented at the Fifteenth Annual Eastern Educational Research Association Conference, Boston, MA.

Teitel, L. (1992). The impact of professional development school partnerships on the preparation of teachers. *Teaching Education, 4* (2), 77–86.

Teitel, L. (1993). The state role in jump-starting school/university collaboration: A case study. *Educational Policy, 7* (1), 74–95.

Teitel, L. (1996). *Professional development schools: A literature review.* Paper prepared for the Professional Development School Standards Project, National Council for the Accreditation of Teacher Education.

Theobald, N. (1991). Staffing, financing, and governing professional development schools. *Educational Evaluation and Policy Analysis, 13,* 87–101.

Valli, L. (Ed.). (1992). *Reflective teacher education: Cases and critiques.* New York: State University of New York Press.

Whitford, B. L. (1994). Permission, persistence, and resistance: Linking high school restructuring with teacher education reform. In L. Darling-Hammond (Ed.), *Professional development schools: Schools for developing a profession* (pp. 74–97). New York: Teachers College Press.

Wilson, W.J. (1994). Crisis and challenge: Race and the new urban poverty. *University of Chicago Record, 29* (2), 2–7.

Winitzky, N., Stoddart, T., & O'Keefe, P. (1992). Great expectations: Emergent professional development schools. *Journal of Teacher Education, 43* (1), 3–18.

Wiseman, D.L., & Nason, P.L. (1995). The nature of interactions in a field-based teacher education experience. *Action in Teacher Education, 17* (3), 1–12.

Wolfe, J., Steel, S., & Phillips, P. (1994, April). *Calculating the costs of restructuring: A tale of two professional development schools.* Paper presented at the annual meeting of the American Educational Research Association, New Orleans, LA.

Woloszyk, C. (1992, February). *A study of school climate in a secondary professional development school.* Paper presented at the annual meeting of the American Association of Colleges for Teacher Education, San Antonio, TX.

Woloszyk, C., & Hill, R. (1994). *Restructuring teacher preparation: Seminar and related activities within a secondary professional development school.* (ERIC Document Reproduction Service No. ED 374 076)

Yinger, R.J., & Hendricks, M.S. (1990). An overview of reforms in Holmes Group institutions. *Journal of Teacher Education, 41* (2), 3–20.

Yopp, H., Guillaume, A., & Savage, T. (1993–1994). Collaboration at the grass roots: Implementing the professional development school concept. *Action in Teacher Education, 15* (4), 29–35.

Zeichner, K. (1991). Contradictions and tensions in the professionalization of teaching and the democratization of schools. *Teachers College Record, 92,* 363–379.

Zeichner, K. (1992). *Connecting genuine teacher development to the struggle for social justice* (Issue paper 92–1). East Lansing: National Center for Research on Teacher Learning, Michigan State University.

Manuscript Received June 28, 1996
Accepted August 29, 1996

Chapter 6

Professional, Personal, and Political Dimensions of Action Research

SUSAN E. NOFFKE
University of Illinois at Urbana-Champaign

One of the earliest entries in the Educational Resources Information Center (ERIC) system under the descriptor action research is a reference to a talk given by Martin Luther King. In his address to the Conference on Social Change and the Role of Behavioral Scientists, King highlighted changes in the more than 350-year struggle for freedom and human dignity in the United States, calling for the involvement of social scientists in social issues:

> We do not ask you to march by our side, although, as citizens, you are free and welcome to do so. Rather, we ask you to focus on the fresh social issues of our day; to move from observing operant learning, the psychology of risk . . . to the test tubes of Watts, Harlem, Selma, and Bogalusa. We ask you to make society's problems your laboratory. We ask you to translate your data into direction— direction for action. (1966, p. 47)

In the long-standing tradition of research by activist-scholars within African American communities, King's invocation is by no means a surprise.[1] In the United States, education—literacy in particular—has been, by virtue of the "peculiar institution" of slavery and its descendants, an inherently political activity. Teaching enslaved people to read and write, the work of Ida B. Wells documenting the breadth and injustice of incidences of lynching (Duster, 1970), the works of Carter Woodson (1933/1993) and W.E.B. DuBois (1973), all of these point toward a version of scholarship that seeks interconnections between science and social change. Resonance is also to be found in the work of the Highlander Center in the United States (Adams, 1972; Horton, 1990) and in numerous projects in the 1960s and 1970s seeking to create social change toward greater social justice through the use of research (Barrera & Vialpando, 1974; Burges, 1976; Palmer & Jacobson, 1971). Some proponents of action research see the linkages between action research and social change invoked in the King quotation as a central core

I wish to thank the students, colleagues, and friends who have responded to this work. Lillie Albert, Marie Brennan, Edward Buendia, Georgia Garcia, Violet Harris, and David Hursh each provided insightful suggestions, as well as support and encouragement.

to its purposes as well as its procedures. Politics is seen as a constitutive element in action research, as well as all other forms of educational practice.

In contrast, other current proponents of action research might find the indexing of King's article under action research very disturbing. For these advocates, action research, as all other forms of research, is separated from the political sphere as a professional, neutral process of knowledge accumulation. While social goals may play a role, the methods of science are seen as transcending the political process. Action research, in this interpretation, bridges the traditional theory-practice, knowledge-action gap; it does not transform the constitutive elements. It recognizes the potential knowledge of practitioners within social situations and creates a means for communication between research and practice communities, but it does not intend to alter fundamental relationships between them.

Between these two focuses on political and professional dimensions lies a third purpose that, for many action research practitioners, is central: the personal. This emphasis denies neither the importance of political activity nor the generation of professional knowledge, but it views the main benefits of engaging in action research as lying in areas such as greater self-knowledge and fulfillment in one's work, a deeper understanding of one's own practice, and the development of personal relationships through researching together.

These three areas—the professional, the personal, and the political—form the frames for this review of the literature on action research. They may seem to be distinct emphases; within the context of action research, however, all clearly deal with issues of power and control. In that sense, the public sphere of professionalism and the domain of the personal are also particular manifestations of the political. However, as will be argued here, it is important to differentiate these dimensions, so that they can be more fully understood. The various ways in which they manifest themselves, both historically and in current efforts, represent the substantive focus of the review.

Rather than a particular research methodology, action research is best thought of as a large family, one in which beliefs and relationships vary greatly. More than a set of discrete practices, it is a group of ideas emergent in various contexts. It takes only a brief perusal of the action research literature to recognize that the growth and salience of work in this area in recent years have been marked by not only an increase in volume of references to it but also a proliferation of varied usages of the term. Yet, however action research (and the host of other terms with intersecting meanings) is defined, as a social movement it is fundamentally about emergent meanings of both action and research, as well as the relationships between them (see Winter, 1987). Whether seen as "contested terrain" (R. Edwards, 1979), with struggle over meanings linked to competing interests in society, or merely as particular voices striving to "make good with what they have"—a form of bricolage (Hatton, 1989),[2]—action research is an important area not only in education and educational research but in a wide range of social endeavors.

Action research is increasingly included in programs of preservice and in-service teacher education, in school reform initiatives, and in requests for proposals from foundations and from major educational research organizations, including federal agencies such as the National Science Foundation and the Office of Educational Research and Improvement. Its growth in highly localized centers of university-based or even "grass-roots" organizations is also evident. In many of these varied efforts, the multiple meanings of its approach to educational study and change are all too often minimally highlighted.

For some (e.g., Borg, Gall, & Gall, 1993), action research is focused on problem solving at a local level and follows the usual steps of traditional research, albeit "writ small" enough for practitioners to use. For others, it is seen as a new paradigm, a challenge to existing epistemologies, and, thereby, a competing (or complementary) entry into the political economy of knowledge production (e.g., Fals-Borda & Rahman, 1991). Still others focus on its role in professional development, highlighting its embodiment of principles of adult learning (e.g., Zuber-Skerritt, 1992). Finally, some see it more as an overall perspective, a series of commitments to problematizing social practices (including that of action research itself) in the interests of individual and social transformation (e.g., McTaggart, 1994).

This list of varying interpretations is by no means exhaustive. Some of the differences in definitions seem to be minor responses to particular contexts and are generally quite complementary. Yet others are reflective of fundamentally different assumptions about the processes and purposes of action research. At the very least, this situation signals a need for a better understanding of its history and growth in order to begin to evaluate its potential contributions to educational work.

In an attempt to address this need, this chapter builds on earlier comparative works (Grundy, 1988; Hult & Lennung, 1980; Kemmis & McTaggart, 1988b; King & Lonnquist, 1992; McKernan, 1988; Noffke, 1990, 1994; Peters & Robinson, 1984), focusing attention on historical as well as contemporary manifestations of professional, personal, and political dimensions, representing the varied goals that have been promoted through action research. The concern is less with questioning how the term ought to be used and more with understanding that family of work that is called action research. While there are by no means inconsequential differences between various versions, such differences are here seen as integrally connected to the goals each seeks to advance. The intention is to provide an interconnected series of guideposts as to what is at stake when the term action research is used. To this end, the review will take on the characteristics both of a traditional review of the literature and of a historical roadmap of where action research has been and to where it might lead.

After an overview of the scope and limitations of the review, the professional, personal, and political dimensions of action research are examined first historically and then in terms of more recent efforts. The final section raises questions directed at assessing the future of action research as a form of educational research. As will be evident in this chapter, some works in action research have articulated positions close to the political dimensions so evident in Martin Luther King's talk, while others emphasize professional and/or personal dimensions. While these dimensions are particularly salient in the action research literature and emerge quite clearly as areas of debate, they are nonetheless present in all forms of research, manifesting themselves in particular and taken-for-granted notions of what it means to be an educational professional, of the role of personal concerns in such a profession, and of what issues of power and authority have to do with the process of education.

The articulation of knowledge for the profession of education with knowledge for personal or social change is only one of a myriad of differing aspects to interpretations of action research that have emerged over the more than 50 years of its recognition in educational work. In some works on action research (e.g., Carr & Kemmis, 1988; Gitlin & Thompson, 1995; Grundy, 1982; McCutcheon & Jung, 1990; McKernan, 1988; McNiff, 1988), the tendency has been to create typologies or to mark its contested definition within academic circles. One could see the professional, personal, and political dimensions explored here as discrete categories by which to classify (and thereby dismiss) certain versions of action research. Yet the dimensions themselves have had multiple interpretations and emphases in differing contexts and in response to differing ideological underpinnings of action research efforts in education and in many other fields. While typologies are useful, they also tend to obscure the inconsistencies within, and relationships between, various forms of action research. The professional, personal, and political in this review are seen as interconnected circles offering bridges to understanding and evaluating the significance and potentials of the multiple interpretations and practices of action research in education.

If the assumption is that all research efforts, indeed all educational works, are inherently political (and that is an assumption underlying this review), then this chapter is no exception. Decisions about what to include and what to omit, about the overall organizational framework, and about the particular emphases are, of course, reflective of my professional, personal, and political commitments. It is hoped, nonetheless, that the breadth of the review will lead the debate over action research away from concerns with identifying "correct" definitions of the term and more toward clarity of purpose among those who would use the term.

SCOPE AND LIMITATIONS OF THE REVIEW

Despite its seemingly "newcomer" status on the scene of mainstream educational research, action research has a long history in education, and the body of literature on it is quite large. For a term whose meaning is highly contested, the review process partly involves identifying the various factors under contention. Several comparative works have identified significant areas of divergence (Hult & Lennung, 1980; King & Lonnquist, 1992; Peters & Robinson, 1984). These include the cyclical nature of action research or the nature of the spiraling of action and research, whether and to what extent action research must be collaborative and with whom, the sources for research topics (especially whether focuses must emanate from grass-roots concerns), and the purposes for engaging in action research, including its relationship to social issues. While there are points of similarity across several interpretations—for example, the common assumption that action research involves teachers inquiring in order to develop a richer understanding and an improved practice (McCutcheon & Jung, 1990)—these hold only if one narrows the literature considerably.

Defining action research for the purposes of this review involved, then, addressing some complexities. Many review efforts can presuppose a form of research that is linked to traditional means of dissemination. For the most part, such reviews rely almost exclusively on "official sources," namely academic publications, and do not address the issue of who is defining the field in relation to who is doing action research. Common sources for the review of research on a given topic are indexes and catalogues. For example, the ERIC system defines action research in its thesaurus quite broadly as "research designed to yield practical results that are immediately applicable to a specific situation or problem" and has abstracted around 1000 entries since 1966 under that descriptor. Given its long history in education, an important body of literature that predates ERIC is accessible through *Education Index*. There is also a considerable body of work referenced in other indexes and in *Dissertation Abstracts International*, covering a wide variety of fields with similar, broad definitions.

Clearly, one could do an extensive review based on such materials. For a field such as action research, however, there are multiple voices that require special attention: social activist voices, voices from outside the United States, works appearing under multiple labels, works outside education, and grass-roots voices outside academic institutions. First, in some forms of action research, the emphasis is on the action, the process of change in a particular situation. This is an area in which there is much work done internationally, often in highly localized efforts not always visible through "official sources." While there are some examples noted here, these cannot be seen as necessarily representative. There is a strong need for greater attention to such studies and to the kinds of relationships between research and action they embody. Second, given the international nature of action research efforts, a search of Canadian, Australian, and British educational indexes and catalogues of libraries, as well as in U.S. universities, was important. While a large body of work is available from other contexts and in other languages, this review is limited to those areas. Further work in other languages (there is a large body of Spanish and German literature, for example) and from other contexts is sorely needed in order to fully examine the implications of, for example, post-colonial (including Eastern European) work in action research.

Third, there have been a number of different efforts affiliated with action research, some of which have used the action research label and some of which have not, claiming alternative histories and assumptions. For example, the terms *action science* (Argyris & Schoen, 1989) and *action learning* (Bruce & Russell, 1992), while much more salient in the literature on management, are used in educational research as well (e.g., Clift, Johnson, Holland, & Veal, 1992). Some action research occurs under the labels of "interactive" or "collaborative" research. In several cases, the principal investigators for these projects were clearly building on an earlier educational action research tradition in the United States (e.g., Lieberman & Miller, 1984a; Ward & Tikunoff, 1982) and are therefore included in this review. Teacher-researcher efforts, particularly in the United States, share some common characteristics and historical roots with action research but have embraced a broader range of research forms (Cochran-Smith & Lytle, 1993). Some of these efforts, which Cochran-Smith and Lytle call "classroom and school studies," closely resemble action research. The teacher research literature, while much in need of its own review, has obvious implications for any consideration of the action research literature. In action research, it is frequently the teacher who plays a central, if not exclusive, role in the enactment and study of educational change.

Fourth, a growing influence on some forms of action research in education has been the participatory action research (PAR) movement. There are two forms of PAR, one of which is primarily focused on management issues (W.F. Whyte, 1991). Although also not directly focused on formal schooling, another form of PAR (e.g., Fals-Borda & Rahman, 1991; Park, Brydon-Miller, Hall, & Jackson, 1993) is increasingly influential and crucial to understanding some of the current efforts in educational action research. Finally, and perhaps most important, much of action research is occurring in increasing amounts outside of the usual academic circles of publication and indexing. Reports of action research projects by educational practitioners, for example, are still, for the most part, shared at conferences or through local publications (Madison Metropolitan School District, 1995; Nocerino & Harrison, n.d.). In this area, specific examples of reports from a few groups are noted as indicators of a need for broader access to such growing networks.

This review, then, includes works limited to English language literature that refer to themselves as action research, share some common history and goals, or clearly are influencing current action research practice in education. While the review pushes at the boundaries of "official definitions," it still relies heavily on them. The uneasy tension between social change and social research exemplified in the very term *action research* (see Winter, 1987) remains problematic, as does the role of the social issues invoked in the opening quote of this chapter. What part action research may play in the resolution of these problematics remains to be seen.

NEW WINE OR VINTAGE GRAPES: EXPLORING ACTION RESEARCH HISTORICALLY

One example of the starkly contrasting meanings of action research prevalent in contemporary educational research can be easily found by comparing the descriptions given in two widely used textbooks on research methodology. Borg et al. (1993), for example, identify the origins of action research with the work of social psychologist Kurt Lewin (1946) in "promoting positive social change" (p. 390). While they note various models that emphasize the role of planning and acting, their primary emphasis is on action research as a form of professional problem solving, and their description of the process reduces it to traditional notions of research involving defining the problem; selecting the design, sample, and measures; analyzing and interpreting; and reporting the findings. Action research, thereby, seems to be traditional research "writ small" enough for practitioners.

In direct contrast to this interpretation, Bogdan & Biklin describe action researchers "as citizens attempting to influence the political process through collecting information" (1992, p. 201). Social change and advocacy play major roles in a process deeply rooted in the history of qualitative research in general. In action research, this is perhaps best exemplified in contemporary efforts by the work of Lois Gibbs and others who worked to bring the dangers of toxic waste at Love Canal to light and to provide compensation for its victims (Gibbs, 1982; Levine, 1980). In this form of research, data are collected and used to expose injustices, direct policy development, and promote change. Contribution to knowledge production is not the primary goal; making people's lives better is the central focus of the work (Bogdan & Biklin, 1992, p. 231).

One way to understand the emergence of such contrasting views of action research is historically. There have been several studies focusing directly on the history of action research (Adelman, 1993; Altrichter & Gstettner, 1993; Foshay, 1994; Kemmis, 1982; King & Lonnquist, 1992; McKernan, 1988; McTaggart, 1991a; Noffke, 1989, 1994; Peters & Robinson, 1984; Schubert & Lopez-Schubert, 1984; Smulyan, 1983; Wallace, 1987), and a collection of primary source materials has been developed (Kemmis & McTaggart, 1988b). In addition, overviews of the history of action research are frequently included as preludes to works advocating a particular orientation to action research (e.g., Anderson, Herr & Nihlen, 1994; Elliott, 1991; Holly, 1991; McKernan, 1991). Such works, often done by scholars who have themselves worked at developing the field of action research, have contributed greatly to understanding its origins and growth, with particular attention to work in education. For the most part chronological in narrative and based solely in the academic literature (McTaggart, 1991a), the story of action research is traced out almost as a family tree, with clearly identifiable descendants and some debate over who is the patriarch.

Yet, as in all histories, ambiguities surround the telling of the stories. Differing emphases reflect the interests of those constructing and reading history. Each, too, is an indication of the importance of history not only in locating one's work but in grounding contrasting views while legitimizing one's own. After more than 50 years, action research is still seeking legitimacy in the academy and also in political arenas. History as an accepted field of knowledge is, of course, one source of legitimation, as well as an avenue to search for ways of making sense of current trends. As such, the search for the history of action research is itself part of the struggle in and around action research.

Understanding the context and the complex content and processes of the work of the various members, as well as the orientation they took, is central to understanding the particular constructions of the professional, personal, and political dimensions of action research in current works. What follows here is an attempt to trace out the pieces of the historical/genealogical work thus far addressed, as well as to identify those aspects in need of further attention. It is presented not as a history of action research but as histories with different centers, each revealing both struggles and pitfalls, subverting, it is hoped, the notion that any historical phenomenon can be understood as unified and unambiguous in its voice and narrative.

A Science of Education From a Science of Change

Most historical works emphasize the origins of action research in education in the fields of social services, social philosophy, and social psychology with the works of John Collier, a U.S. commissioner of Indian affairs, and/or Kurt Lewin, a social psychologist, during the 1930s in the United States (Adelman, 1993; Elliott, 1991; Holly, 1991; Kemmis, 1988; McKernan, 1988; McTaggart, 1991a; Noffke, 1989; Peters & Robinson, 1984; Wallace, 1987). Collier's work seems at first to be quite separated from education, but there were important connections. He and his wife established a school not unlike many "progressive" schools of the early part of the century, and he also worked with a school for community workers with which both John Dewey and William Heard Kilpatrick were involved (Collier, 1963). In addition, his concerns with both education and community were key elements to his work with the Bureau of Indian Affairs, and there were clear and substantive links between the development and administration of Indian education and the substance and leadership of the Progressive Education Association (Iverson, 1978).

Within the overall context of a growing trend toward documenting everyday practices and lives during the 1930s, as well as the incipient development of the methodology for fieldwork in anthropology, Collier's work is not often noted. Yet, in several areas it is important to the history of action research. First, Collier's policies as head of the bureau sponsored education based in local culture and language, with goals of self-sufficiency (Iverson, 1978). One manifestation of those policies was a form of "action-research, research-action" that was carried out in communities, particularly in the areas of soil conservation. In this work, he focused attention on the needs that the community felt were important and highlighted a nondirective role for consultants (Collier, 1945). The focus on grassroots interests, on collaboration within communities and across disciplines, and on the need for direct links to social action for improvement was a key element of this early form of action research (see Noffke, 1989).

For Lewin, too, connections to education and community are clear, albeit in slightly different ways. As a Jewish refugee from Nazi Germany, Lewin shared the faith in democratic forms of social organization, the interest in the "dynamics" of group, and the concern with "ethnic relations" salient in Collier's works. The efforts of the Commission on Community Interrelations of the American Jewish Congress and of the Research Center for Group Dynamics, with whom Lewin worked, resulted in many projects that addressed problems of assimilation, segregation, and discrimination, as well as class stratification, at a local level. For example, a form of action research was used to help resolve issues of prejudice, both by initiating change and by studying its impact (see Lewin, 1948; Lippitt & Radke, 1946).

Lewin's interest in and impact on education can be seen in several ways. Some of the work he and his colleagues conducted at the Iowa Child Welfare Station addressed the impact of patterns of leadership and social organization on children's groups and had clear relevance to educational settings. This work was published in educational journals (G. Lewin & Lewin, 1942; Lewin, 1938, 1944) and the ideas are salient in the writings of prominent educators of the time (e.g., Goodson, 1946). Yet also important to later work on teaching and teacher education, much of Lewin's work addressed the function of the group in changing individual attitudes as well as behavior, effecting a "reeducation" (Lewin & Grabbe, 1945).

Lewin's, as well as Collier's, version of action research emphasized the process as collaborative: a group of people addressing a social issue. It was cyclical, with each cycle of research affecting subsequent versions of planning, acting, observation, and reflecting (see Kemmis, 1988; McTaggart, 1991a). Research was not static and linear but, rather, dynamic and changing in response to the reflections of each phase. Actions for change were interventions in a social situation, planned with "outside" as well as "inside" participants and interests. Such research could inform policy and action, but it could also generate theory about the change process itself.

Both Collier and Lewin were concerned with social issues and with the process of studying theoretical and practical problems together, and they were interested in the process as well as the substance of orderly social change. Both, too, emphasized the need to work in the "field," with all of its complexities and the important role that the concerns and needs of the participants within social situations play in the process of change. Whether in agricultural development, in the management of industrial or military production, or in the effort to address attitudes and practices of prejudice and discrimination, the science of action research was at once about reform and about the development of theories of change.

In such social planning, the role of those scientists external to the situation was both to facilitate studies to enhance the goals of the participants and to understand the process by which change could be engineered. Participation, for example, was not only to be valued as a worthwhile philosophical and political aim, it also functioned to ensure a greater amount of change. Both Collier and Lewin were concerned about the potential for manipulation and sought ways to

address it. For Collier, a faith in democracy, in making sure that the local population involved in studies had the final word in decisions, played a role in his resolution of this dilemma, as it had in his educational work. Yet he also seemingly
felt that the evolving work in "group dynamics" might provide an alternative
framework (Collier, 1963). Lewin's resolution was less ambivalent. He noted a
need for management, seeing planning and democracy as interdependent
(Lewin, 1947, p. 153). Considering Lewin's life experiences both in the Weimar
Republic and as a Jewish refugee, a concern that democracy not be equated with
populism seems logical.

Although Lewin died in 1947, before his ideas could be further explored, his
work and those with whom he worked have been influential in several areas. The
work on group behavior continued, with many connections to industry and community work. The early studies of worker productivity at the Harwood
Manufacturing Corporation (see Adelman, 1993) and the work at the Research
Center for Group Dynamics, as well as projects for the National Research Council
and Office of Strategic Services during the Second World War, influenced a large
portion of a generation of social psychologists. Current efforts toward developing
"quality circles" in industry and education, using "action learning" (Bruce &
Russell, 1992), and articulating an "action science" (Argyris, Putnam, & Smith,
1985), as well as a host of projects in the areas of community and organizational
development (Bargal, Gold, & Lewin, 1992; J. Cunningham, 1993; Rapoport,
1985) share roots in the work of Kurt Lewin.

As will be recounted in the following section, action research appears to have
had a very short "heyday" in educational work in the late 1940s and 1950s, diminishing rapidly in prominence. Yet it continued to be salient in areas of social planning, in agriculture, and in applied anthropology. The question of the origins of
action research is complex and needs to be more clearly situated in the overall
context of social research developments. These linkages have not, thus far, been
sufficiently explored. In addition, looking closely at the interconnections with
changes in orientations to management, for example, that have had a direct impact
on schools (e.g., site-based management and quality circles) could do much to
enhance our understanding of the persistent tensions and struggles involved in the
field. Action research could, thereby, be seen to be as much about the process of
change as about the science of education.

SCIENCE, TEACHING, AND CHANGE: THE STRUGGLE
OVER THE PROFESSION

The efforts of Collier and Lewin did influence the shape of particular forms of
action research in education. Yet they were not the only influence. Another
"source" (Schubert & Lopez-Schubert, 1984) lies in developments within the
field of education itself, particularly as part of educational thought and work during the "progressive" era in the United States (Foshay, 1994). In the years surrounding the turn of the century, education and the preparation of teachers moved

closer to the universities. As such, the role of science in the legitimation and promulgation of teaching as a profession gained increasing visibility. Not surprisingly, the debates of the time were over both the technology of teaching (the emergence of pedagogy as a field of study) and the aims toward which such a pedagogy was to be directed.

Within this context, efforts to develop the profession of education, both in research and in practice, can be seen as intersecting with action research in two broadly defined streams. The first has to do with developing what would now be called the "knowledge base" of educational research, as well as the means for its use, and the second outlines an attempt to create a form of social inquiry responsive to the process of education. As direct as the connections may be between Collier and Lewin and educational efforts of the time, their influence in the formation of educational action research must be seen against these overall developments, which in turn reflect the multiple meanings of "progressive" education (Kliebard, 1986).

Several works on the history of action research pay particular attention to the role of teachers in the development of the knowledge base of teaching (McKernan, 1988; McTaggart, 1991a; Noffke, 1990). Part of the "scientific movement" in education—field-based projects such as the Eight-Year Study (Aiken, 1942) and the Virginia Curriculum Program (Kliebard, 1986), included "experiments" at the school level carried out by teachers and administrators with outside consultants. These early-20th-century works noted not only the ability of teachers to augment the growing field of educational research (Buckingham, 1926) but also the idea that participation in curriculum study facilitated a wider acceptance of reform efforts.

Alongside this must be seen the work of Dewey and others at developing a science of education unique to the field, one that unites the search for useful theory with a form of inquiry grounded in practice (Schubert & Lopez-Schubert, 1984). While several histories (e.g., Kemmis, 1982; McTaggart, 1991a; Wallace, 1987) do not directly explore Dewey's potential influence on the development of action research, they nonetheless acknowledge its importance. Others (Noffke, 1990; Schubert & Lopez-Schubert, 1984) highlight his focus on the need for the active participation of teachers in research as well as his focus on hypothesis formulation and testing, which were prominent characteristics of action research as it appeared in the educational context of the late 1940s and early 1950s. The later focus was not part of Lewin's orientation, which, as noted earlier, emphasized change for the participants and theory for the outside consultants.

The figure most often associated with early action research in education is Stephen M. Corey, whose work, *Action Research to Improve School Practices* (1953), is still frequently cited. Yet Corey was part of a larger group working with the Horace Mann-Lincoln Institute for School Experimentation at Teachers College. This group, which included interests in both social and developmental aspects of curriculum, moved outside the then prevalent experiments in "lab" schools to seek collaborations with schools that were not only undergoing tremendous growth but included various communities and organizational settings (R. Cunningham & Miel, 1947). Corey's work is most known for its attempt to defend action research as a legitimate form of educational research and for its careful outline of the process of action research. In the latter, the cyclical emphasis of Lewin has an ambivalent status, and the influence of Dewey appears to some (Schubert & Lopez-Schubert, 1984) more salient. Corey saw the distinction between action research and Dewey's notion of reflective thinking in three areas: "the greater emphasis upon evidence, upon the *action* hypothesis, and upon the importance of *cooperative* research" (1953, p. 40).

Corey's work, as well as that of others at the institute (e.g., R. Cunningham & Miel, 1947; Foshay,Wann, & Associates, 1954), highlights the knowledge, vitality, and dignity of teachers. The curriculum projects undertaken with teachers are reflective of the struggle over the curriculum at the time, with a change visible from the early developmental and social meliorist agendas to one more "life adjustment" in nature (Kliebard, 1986). Yet also visible is the continuing emphasis on group dynamics; on teachers, parents, children, and others as participants rather than "subjects"; and on the role of the outside researcher in identifying the barriers to change as well as the means for the enhancement of change (Mackenzie, 1946).

Seen in this light, action research efforts are not only projects directed at developing a new process for educational research; they are also examples of the many substantive arenas in which attempts to reform both curriculum and teaching were enacted. Corey's efforts to highlight the "scientific merit" of action research appear to be tied to a desire to promote the interests of the profession, to get beyond "hoping" and move into "beginning to know" (Corey, 1954). He was supportive of classroom teachers' knowledge and skeptical of the then increasing role of the federal government in the funding of educational research (Corey, 1957). Yet his position may also have led to a view of action research that highlighted the struggle over its legitimacy as a means of professional knowledge generation, instead of as a struggle over the formation of new theory-practice linkages.

With both the impetus for including teachers in research and the search for a new form of inquiry, a particular view of the teacher emerges (Noffke, 1992). Despite a context of increasing disillusionment with schools and those who work in them, Dewey's and Corey's works show a vision of the profession that has, at its core, a valuing of teachers' knowledge and work. That the work is by nature in need of constant renewal and rethinking is a central element of this early form of action research.

Rather than a deficit to be corrected by external advisors, action research is treated as an ongoing process, an inherent part of teaching. Research that is deeply connected to teaching is connected to action. Corey's definition of action research seems here very relevant. Although ambivalent about the use of the term, for him, action research was "research that is undertaken by educational practitioners because they believe that by so doing they can make better decisions and engage in better action" (1953, p. viii). The focus was on learning, which is central to knowledge production, but this was coupled with a strong emphasis on *doing*. The profession of teaching involved understanding one's work, but in order to *act* on that knowledge.

Toward the end of the 1950s, debates over the "rigor" of action research were evident (Hodgkinson, 1957; Kemmis, 1988; McTaggart, 1991a). While it is not clear what impact such critiques had, the emphasis in action research work was changing (Good, 1963). Perhaps with the growing teacher shortage (Noffke, 1990), action research became viewed as increasingly linear in orientation and also more as a version of problem solving or in-service teacher education (Taba & Noel, 1957; Wiles, 1953). As will be apparent in the next section, the concern with the profession remained but less frequently focused on the potential contribution of action research to curriculum knowledge, or even knowledge about change, and more frequently focused on its functions for personal and professional learning. The collaborative process remained, salient but with an increasing focus on the individual teacher, often in collaboration with an outside "expert."

From the School Group to the Individual: The Emergence of the Personal

In the early work of Lewin and Collier, as well as that of the Horace Mann Institute, the intellectual context was one of concern with broad social issues. Collaborative efforts for social change through action research focused on areas such as agricultural reform, decreasing prejudice, and promoting more democratic education. Yet the 1950s, when much of the work in education was developed, can also be seen as an era of increasing introspection, both sociological and psychological. Books such as Riesman's *The Lonely Crowd* (1950/1969) set off lively debates on the changing character of the "new middle class" in the United States. In education, works such as L. T. Hopkins's *The Emerging Self in School and Home* (1954) and Jersild's *When Teachers Face Themselves* (1955) reflect changes in dominant psychological perspectives in education: "The teacher's understanding and acceptance of himself is the most important requirement in any effort he makes to help the students to know themselves and to gain healthy attitudes of self-acceptance" (Jersild, 1955, p. 3). While the importance of this intellectual context has not yet been explored extensively in the action research literature, there is at least some indication that it did exert some influence (see McTaggart, 1991a). Tracing out developments in action research does reveal a change in the focus of some work from collaborative efforts with a professional focus to ones in which the individual struggles with issues of personal meaning alongside professional significance (see Kemmis, 1988; Noffke, 1990). While the teaching conditions of the era, especially the teaching shortage, may have influenced that change, it is unclear what other factors may have been involved.

Lewin and Collier had focused attention on the personal impact of the process on both the participants and the outside "experts," but their interest was primarily in terms of its function toward group change. The group was felt to be the source for both status and security, and perhaps thereby the most powerful influence toward individual change (J. Cunningham, 1993). In Corey's work, as well as that of others connected with the Horace Mann Institute, there are discussions of the development of confidence in one's work (e.g., Corey, 1954), but the primary focus was on collaborative efforts toward change (Corey, 1953; Foshay et al., 1954). While the actual topics of research often included the beliefs and attitudes of children, the individual teacher's self-knowledge was not a primary focus.

Perhaps because of their contexts, respectively, in supervision and in graduate seminars in educational research, it is in the work of Hilda Taba and Abraham Shumsky in the late 1950s that action research appears to gradually move away from the concept of teacher-researcher toward that of teacher-learner. Instead of the strong faith in teachers shown in Corey's work, a strong sense was emerging that action research could function not only to collaboratively address educational problems but also to make individual teachers more productive as professionals (Taba & Noel, 1957) or to explore areas of "inner conflict" in transitions in teaching practices (Shumsky, 1958).

Some works do address this transition (Noffke, 1989, 1992). McTaggart (1991a) analyzes Shumsky's work, emphasizing the possible influence of Fromm and Durkheim on Shumsky's conception of action research. While Shumsky argued for action research as a way to restore community in the modern world, it was the aspect of self-development, of research as having "personal significance", that was most salient. Taken together, the works of Taba and Shumsky, as well as those of Wiles (1953), represent a conceptualization of action research as a form of in-service teacher education, one in the supervision of relatively inexperienced teachers in the field and the other in graduate study by teachers. Increasingly, action research was finding a role not necessarily in the production of educational knowledge but in the process of staff development.

An interesting facet of this transition was that the role of university personnel also shifted from that of collaborator to that of external expert, facilitating the process. While this parallels many of the successors of Lewin in the United States and the Tavistock Institute in the United Kingdom (Wallace, 1987), it is a distinct change from the prior educational work. Instead of identifying a role for teachers in knowledge production or linkages to social change, action research came to be seen as a process for change in teachers. While thus far historical works in education do not deal extensively with this issue, a closer examination of other descendants of the action research family such as T-groups, action learning, or the more psychoanalytic orientations to some of the Tavistock work (J. Cunningham, 1993), which emphasized individual training to alter attitudes and practices, may prove useful in understanding the personal dimension as well as external consultants' role in it. Instead of collaborative action research highlighting the personal knowledge of practitioners as within a social profession, this model may have acted to establish more firmly the dominant role of the expert and his (or her, although rarely in this era) knowledge.

Is There a "Democratic Impulse" to Action Research?

Both Collier's and Lewin's works had clear social agendas, embodying their concern with social issues, especially with the development of democratic methods of work and living and with the need to address aspects of prejudice (Adelman, 1993; Kemmis, 1982; McTaggart, 1991a; Noffke, 1989, 1994). Yet, despite their apparent social critique (Collier, 1963; Marrow, 1969) and perhaps because of their anthropological or psychological orientations, it is also clear that the action research they developed did not take on issues of structural change toward greater social and economic justice. The industrial projects noted earlier, as well as their descendants in organizational development (J. Cunningham, 1993) and Collier's efforts to change the conditions of life for Native Americans, while arguably improving people's work lives, may actually have acted to reform and thereby sustain existing political and economic forms.

In the action research efforts in education, as well, the initial concern was with the development of more democratic forms of education (e.g., Goodson, 1946; Hopkins, 1948; Watson, 1940). Whether due to teacher shortages, demographic changes in the school population, or the effects of the Cold War and McCarthyism, this impetus seems to have given way to a concern for the development of teachers (Kemmis, 1988; McTaggart, 1991a; Noffke, 1994). The educational context became one in which decisions about curriculum and policy were increasingly seen as lying within the domain of "experts," with the designation of important research areas (and the funding for them) gradually becoming the arena of the state (Apple, 1986).

Corey (1957) was well aware of this change in the orientation of curriculum and research and warned of its potential impact on the setting of research agendas. The "professionalization" of educational work, ironically under the presumed "neutral" role of science, seems to have participated in the placement of educational research far closer to the center of the public political arena. Instead of a role for teachers in the collective production of knowledge leading to more democratic schools, the separation of the practitioner from the expert and the reduction of action research to individual development can be seen to remove teachers (and parents and children) from the potential political contestation over the profession that was possible through action research.

In what senses, then, can a "democratic impulse" be said to be part of action research? Focusing on the sources noted thus far, concerns with more balanced social relations, locally developed curriculum, and collaborative process among students, parents, teachers, administrators, and academics (Horace Mann-Lincoln Study Group, 1948) seem to have been salient features of the underlying conception of democracy in education and society. Altrichter and Gstettner (1993) offer an alternative "source" for the development of action research, one that takes its impulse from community development (McTaggart, 1994).

In the field of social philosophy, starting with the work of J. L. Moreno, another version of action research emerged. In his work during the early years of the 20th century, for example, with prostitutes in a Vienna suburb, he regarded participants as "co-researchers" and developed a social activist form of action research. This form of research advocated fieldwork, participation, and "improvement of social situations as an aim of research" (Altrichter & Gstettner, 1993, p. 332). The "democratic" impulse, then, was linked not to the generation of knowledge or of educational practices alone but to action in the larger social sphere.

In many of the historical works cited, and indeed in the previous sections of this chapter, there is a sense that the search for the history of action research has been a search for the originator of the term. Given the structures of race, class, and gender within those historical contexts (as well as those of contemporary society) and the resultant access to academic publishing, it should not be surprising that the effort has been largely a search for the "father," one who is also of European and middle class origins.

In contrast to these histories, Reinharz (1992) identifies Marion Talbot's work at the University of Chicago on gender and mathematical ability and Crystal Eastman's work on industrial accidents as early (turn-of-the-century) practices of feminist action research. In both efforts, the research was designed to influence the social conditions under study, not to be set apart for later implementation. Looked at this way, action research has a history beyond the origins of that particular term. It is a particular idea, a stream of thought developed over time in various contexts, and is integrally connected to political agendas. If we are to really understand the history of action research, there is a need to see it as part of the larger struggle in the 20th century over the relationship between research and action. Reinharz's work, especially in introducing research addressing developments in the social sciences (e.g., the differentiation between knowledge and action within the Chicago School of Sociology) is indicative of the kind of work that needs to be done.

In Reinharz's work, action research was feminist, centering on changes in the conditions of women's lives. Even regarding feminist political agendas in relation to research, though, is just a beginning point toward understanding research (action research in particular) as an embodiment of the search for linkages between knowledge and social and educational change. Great gaps lie in linking works dealing with race, class, and gender to those that explore the close connection between research and social and educational action embodied in action research. In this area, there are few hints in the literature, for example, to the work of Ida B. Wells (see Munro, 1995), W. E. B. DuBois, and Carter G. Woodson, toward connections between scholarship and action yet to be explored. These scholars saw research as integrally related to efforts for social and educational change. The work of Myles Horton and the Highlander Center (Adams, 1972;

Adelman, 1993; Watt & Watt, 1993) represents yet another area in which issues of economic justice and social class were integral aspects of the politics of some versions of action research. Here, too, the gathering and sharing of information in order to address social issues played a key role (Horton, 1990). From George S. Counts's endorsement of its establishment to its subsequent work with many historical and contemporary progressive educators (e.g., Clark, 1990), Highlander presents significant material for understanding action research work, especially that conducted outside of the academic grant world.

These few examples only begin to acknowledge how much we do not know about the history of action research and how much those silences can affect understandings of its professional, personal, and political dimensions. Pursuing the streams of purpose, rather than the particular academic label, may prove more beneficial, as well as using oral history and archival methods to capture the experiences of those involved who have not been part of academic publishing.

BRIDGING HISTORICAL STREAMS WITH CONTEMPORARY QUESTIONS

In many accounts of action research history, work in the 1950s is viewed as a brief "heyday," followed by a period of relative absence in the research literature (Kemmis, 1988; McTaggart, 1991a). Yet the question of "What ever happened to action research?" (Sanford, 1970) is complex, with only partial answers emergent historically, especially in relation to educational work. But reports of its "demise" are not only "greatly exaggerated," they may actually obscure an understanding of how current efforts are not rediscoveries but reemergences of residual forms shaped in part by a new context. The struggle over the professional, the emergence of the personal, and the salience of the political may have found other forms in the new context: one of federally funded projects with expert researchers doing the evaluation, of the development of "humanistic" and cognitive psychologies in sites other than in schools and with teachers, and of a politics at first deeply shrouded in McCarthyism and other social movements of the 1950s and 1960s, all of which expanded understandings of the nature and limits of democracy. Action research has remained a presence, both in education and elsewhere.

Multiple stories, especially ones with a predominantly U.S. base, cannot be viewed, of course, as an explanation for the emergence of various forms of action research within a global context. Yet the various manifestations of the professional, personal, and political in U.S. action research can provide a useful framework from which to view emergent patterns in contemporary places. While local histories have contextual effects not present in the United States (this is, after all, the most advanced capitalist state, "the heart of the beast"), the universalizing tendency can be seen in relation to the effects of a globalized dominant culture.

The predominance in the contemporary United States, for example, of a version of action research framed as a neutral and valid way to promote particular professional practices, to generate knowledge, or to bridge the knowledge-practice gap may or may not be a salient feature in efforts elsewhere. The personal dimension—developing teachers as individual staff members or highlighting feelings of self-awareness or the political—in terms of democratic agendas for school and society, likewise might not also be present or in the same form in other places. Yet professionalization, whatever the context and form, is always a political platform; personal development always takes place in relation to a particular ideology and embodies issues of power; and politics are always struggles between competing interests and agendas. While it is important to remember how the political is embedded in all dimensions, it is equally vital not to reduce everything to a universalized concept devoid of disparate meanings.

Looking carefully at some of the various manifestations of each dimension may provide greater clarity in understanding similarities and differences in the purposes for action research works. This process, it is hoped, will reveal the interconnections between the dimensions and the varied agendas being promoted. Without such attention to interconnected purposes and assumptions, the range of possibilities for action research may be clouded by seemingly rigid ideological boundaries. Each of the following sections, then, will attempt to analyze some of the professional, personal, and political dimensions of contemporary action research efforts in order to see not only what themes are recurrent but also what new interpretations are emerging. In these, as in the prior sections, it is important to note that what is presented is not a typology for neatly characterizing particular efforts, nor is it an exhaustive survey. All versions of action research have professional, personal, and political dimensions, but in the various efforts some aspects are more fully articulated, emphasizing different things in different ways. The intention here is for these examples to illuminate those aspects most in need of elaboration. As such, the object is not to thoroughly critique any one action research effort but to show various points of divergence and convergence.

On the "Professional": Knowledge Production, Staff Development, and Status

From historical studies, it is clear that a very salient aspect to action research in education is a concern with enhancing both the science of education and the status of the profession of teaching. There has been an ambivalence, though, on the issue of action research as a means of producing knowledge about teaching and curriculum. In the United States, beginning with Corey's (1953) work, there was an attempt to create alternative ways to think about issues such as generalizability, in some ways similar to more recent discussions of ethnography and case study. Yet, overall, the trend was toward seeing action research as a method for staff development, especially during the postwar era, when the United States was experiencing a period of shortages of teachers (Noffke, 1990). That same ambivalence is clear in the contemporary literature and has direct implications for attempts at reconceptualizing education as a field that employs action research as a means to professionalization.

This section begins with approaches to action research that highlight its potential contribution to the "knowledge base" for teaching, affirming in most cases teachers' ways of knowing *in* experience. Action research, though, is often employed primarily as a form of in-service education or staff development. In these approaches, efforts to redefine professional roles in education, particularly that of the teacher, are evident. The second part of this section highlights current efforts to improve the status of the education profession through action research.

The Knowledge Base, or "Shifting the Base"?

As McTaggart (1991a) and McKernan (1988) point out in their descriptions of the works of Buckingham (1926) and the Eight Year Study (Aiken, 1942), there has been a continuous stream of works highlighting the potential importance of teachers in building a knowledge base for teaching. Works such as those of Stenhouse (1975) highlight the crucial role of teachers in curriculum development. His emphasis on the process of making public the systematic inquiries of teachers in order to affect other teachers, but also the larger educational community (Stenhouse, 1983), represents the beginnings of contemporary attempts to place the work of teachers within a larger sphere of questions of knowledge claims, or epistemology, in educational research.

It is important to note, too, that the collaborations with teachers in the Humanities Curriculum Project and the Ford Teaching Project (Elliott, 1991; Elliott & Adelman, 1973) were not only about a knowledge base for teaching in a technical sense (i.e., the skills of a "delivery system"), but about fundamental questions of the nature of curriculum as a process rather than a product and of the role of teachers in its development. In that sense, the knowledge base for teaching was a very large arena. As Elliott (1991) points out, this conception of curriculum was built from teachers' experiences in theorizing from their own practice, in the process of transforming secondary education in response to demographic changes in the school population. This work offered not only a fundamentally different construction of the theory-practice relationship but also distinct forms of data, namely, the students' views of their own learning and teachers' reflections.

Teachers contributed to the knowledge base for teaching, in the mode of action research represented in the Ford Teaching Project (e.g., Ford Project Teachers, 1975; Iredale, 1975); not only through the production of descriptions of the "findings"—the effective teaching techniques discovered—but also in two other important ways. First, they contributed to curriculum theorizing, questioning not only the means to education but also the ends. Second, they provided the raw material, through transcripts of their classes and interviews with children, not for others to apply directly to their own teaching but to use for further reflection, theorizing, and subsequent actions.

These works have been followed by successive individual and collaborative efforts to enhance practitioners' opportunities to carry out research, either as part of funded projects or as part of degree-bearing programs of further education. In these efforts, the Centre for Applied Research in Education and the Cambridge Institute of Education seem to have played major roles in developing projects and providing opportunities for sharing the outcomes and processes of the studies. A central source for materials, as well as an organizing vehicle for the spread of action research ideas, is the Classroom Action Research Network, whose bulletins (e.g., Edwards & Rideout, 1991; Holly & Whitehead, 1986; Ryan & Somekh, 1991) present a mixture of reports of projects and papers developing the conceptual base for action research. Most recently, the group was instrumental in beginning the journal *Educational Action Research*, which seeks to provide a forum for a wide range of approaches to action research and is international in scope.

Work in Australia beginning in the 1970s shared the emphasis on practitioners examining their own practice as the basis for action research. Yet it also shared similar conceptions of curriculum and of the teacher's role. Works in literacy and other areas were interdisciplinary and involved teachers' careful study not only of their work but also that of the students. Another important element was that the actual projects, similar both to Stenhouse's work and to some of the early U.S. work, emphasized school-based efforts, participatory frameworks for decisions (Boomer, 1982), and attention to the needs of "disadvantaged" groups (Grundy & Kemmis, 1988).

While influenced by Stenhouse in some ways, what emerged was also shaped by study of Lewin's work and structured, through the then emergent critical social theory (e.g., Habermas, 1972; 1974), into a claim for action research as a distinct form of educational research (Carr & Kemmis, 1988). This form of research embodies a critical stance toward the interests represented in all research forms. It seeks not additions to a knowledge base for teaching but a transformation of educational theory and practice toward emancipatory ends. In this form of action research, it matters what kind of curriculum is being researched, but also what kind of analysis is employed. Trends toward seeing action research as cyclical in nature are clear, as are an insistence on collaboration and on historical and cultural analysis of forms of language and discourse, activities and practices, and organization and social relationships in education. In this form of analysis, the processes of institutionalization and contestation are seen as important ways of identifying the constant changes in education in order to collectively direct them toward democratic ends (Kemmis & Di Chiro, 1987/1989; Kemmis & McTaggart, 1988a).

In contrast to both the British and Australian efforts are those of the Interactive Research and Development in Teaching projects that emerged in the United States during the same period. In these, the attempt is not one of creating a new form of educational research but one of trying to create stronger connections between university researchers and educational practitioners so as to bridge the "theory-practice gap" (Jacullo-Noto, 1984; Tikunoff & Ward, 1983). Traditional methods of research were taught to teachers, who engaged in collaborative projects, presented their findings at conferences, and wrote for scholarly journals (e.g., Behnke et al., 1981). Such efforts highlighted the effort to "validate" via traditional means but also, in the process, emphasized the worth of teachers' findings and their understanding of their own practice.

While these works had a relatively narrow focus on techniques of teaching rather than broad curricular and social issues (see Noffke, 1992) and employed empirical-analytical rather than interpretive assumptions and methods, more recent works carrying either the teacher research or action research label have stretched educational understandings as well as pushed at the boundaries of legitimated research forms. These works, such as Goswami and Stillman's *Reclaiming the Classroom* (1987) and Atwell's *In the Middle* (1987), contrast strongly with the "research on teaching" tradition (Cochran-Smith & Lytle, 1993) and trace out a strong sense in which teachers, primarily those involved in literacy efforts, institute changes in their teaching, study those changes, and thereby add much to the knowledge of teaching (see also Branscombe, Goswani, & Schwartz, 1992). The amount of publication evident particularly in teacher research arenas (e.g., Goodman, 1994; Power & Hubbard, 1995), indicates an understanding of action research as knowledge production. Along with this has also been a strong movement toward methodologies that are interpretive in character and research topics that push toward issues of social justice (see Allen, Michalove, & Schockley, 1993; Krater, Zeni, & Cason, 1994; Noffke & Stevenson, 1995; Shockley, Michalove, & Allen, 1995).

The U.S. teacher research work, well exemplified in the writing of Cochran-Smith and Lytle (1993), expands the conversation about teaching and education to include the voices of teachers. Cochran-Smith and Lytle claim that

research by teachers represents a distinctive way of knowing about teaching and learning that will alter—not just add to—what we know in the field. Furthermore, we have argued that as it accumulates and is more widely disseminated, research by teachers will represent a radical challenge to our current assumptions about the relationship of theory and practice, schools and universities, and inquiry and reform. (1993, p. 85)

While this quote still implies a version of knowledge as something that can be amassed and distributed, there is clearly also a strong assertion that, in teacher research (and they include action research in that category), an epistemology of practice is emerging.

Epistemological questions within action research, whether seen as ways educational practitioners can add to the knowledge base or ways to shift the base, have recently acquired more salience in the literature. One way this can be seen is through the many handbooks created for use by practitioners. While some (Brause & Mayher, 1991; D. Hopkins, 1993; Hubbard & Power, 1993; McKernan, 1991; Mohr & Maclean, 1987; Sagor, 1992) seem to outline methods of data collection and analysis familiar in either empirical-analytical or interpretive traditions, there has also been a strong sense that, in some cases, something new is emerging. Many of the works in this area share an increasing emphasis on qualitative data collection methods. Some (Altrichter, Posch, & Somekh, 1993; Anderson et al.,

1994; Elliott, 1991; McNiff, 1988; Nixon, 1981; Winter, 1989) offer extensive summaries of data appropriate to practitioner investigation. However, they also share a commitment to the development of techniques that provide an evidential basis for action in classrooms rather than a centering on traditional notions of validity. Others (Kemmis & McTaggart, 1988a; Kincheloe, 1991) present a version of analysis that has less to do with the handling of data in the formal sense and more to do with how the data help in collectively raising and illuminating broad social questions, which, in turn, are to inform subsequent action.

One way to gauge the degree to which action research is seen as knowledge generation is through the sharing of findings. Despite the increasing publication of reports of research by practitioners noted earlier, the influence of action research on the official knowledge base for teaching or on teacher education is unclear (Somekh, 1995; Zeichner, 1993). While reports of the use, within teacher education programs, of teachers' knowledge produced through action research do exist (Ross, 1987/1989; Somekh, 1989), they are by no means common. Yet there are other means by which action research efforts are shared (Bassey, 1992). The impact of the growing number of regional and national conferences (e.g., the Teacher Research Day at the annual Ethnography in Urban Educational Research Forum) and the sharing of questions and projects via the Internet is as yet unclear.

An important way in which action research efforts are manifested as knowledge production is in the means of legitimation of knowledge claims. While extensive examinations of epistemological issues are rare (Carr & Kemmis, 1988; Cochran-Smith & Lytle, 1993; Coulter, 1994; Noffke, 1990; Winter, 1987), these works share a sense in which action research advocates are seriously examining issues of quality in their work (Adelman, 1989). Whether focused on methods of data analysis (Winter, 1982), described in ways similar to case knowledge in the legal profession (Elliott, 1987; Stenhouse, 1975), drawn from theories of action and knowledge (Altrichter, 1993), linked to recent developments in feminist theory (Feldman, 1994; Noffke, 1991), or justified in terms of the experiences of educators and their students (Gillespie, 1994), this body of works offer significant challenges to existing norms of educational knowledge production.

Changing Practices: Staff Development and the Status of Teaching

In many ways, the story of action research in the contemporary era is one of efforts to enhance the status of the profession. Contestations over the meaning of action research as a form of educational science have been important to issues of its legitimation, especially within the academy. However, it is the shifting context of teaching that is, for many, the primary focus. Within these contexts, action research as a form of staff development centered on areas for improvement is an increasingly visible aspect of school reform initiatives (Hollingsworth & Sockett, 1994).

On first glance, teaching seems an unlikely occupation in which to foster visions of professionals, individually and collaboratively, having the time, support, and circumstances necessary for systematic inquiry directed at changing conditions, understandings, and processes of their work. The literature on teachers' work often has included descriptions of isolation, norms of silence, and bureaucratic control as characteristics (Apple, 1986; Connell, 1985; Lieberman & Miller, 1984b; McTaggart, 1989). Yet it is just these and similar factors that action research efforts seem, in part, designed to address (Lawn, 1989).

Yet changing the nature of teachers' work and the conditions of the workplace through action research can proceed with very different assumptions and with contrasting purposes (Connelly & Ben-Peretz, 1980; Noffke, 1992). The Interactive Research and Development projects in the United States were strongly geared toward familiarizing teachers with the methods of traditional research while building linkages between teachers' own interests and the need for additions to the body of knowledge on teaching, thereby bridging the theory-practice gap (Ward & Tikunoff, 1982). The creation of partnerships between academic researchers and teachers was often seen in relation to a view of teaching as a craft (Jacullo-Noto, 1984).

Within more contemporary works, the context of school reform and the related questioning of teachers' and teacher educators' performances have produced a somewhat different emphasis. While still assuming a craft version of teaching practice (Adelman, 1989), there is a recognition, in some cases, of the value of accumulated academic knowledge about teaching, along with the highlighting of the teacher's voice, as an important part of educational research (Llorens, 1994b). Sagor (1992), for example, in his introduction to a handbook for action research, situates his version of action research within an era of reform in which teachers are seen to play major roles. Similar to the work of Schoen (1983), Sagor contrasts teaching with other professions (medicine, law, engineering, architecture) that he characterizes as having familiarity and respect for the "foundations of their practice" (p. 3) but also as less likely to be isolated from other professionals, more capable of contributing to professional knowledge, and more involved in the monitoring of practice.

Other works underscore that same faith in the need for a review of the capabilities of teachers, as well as a release from traditions of top-down reform. Sometimes couched in the language of industry, reflecting the descendants of Lewin in the Japanese auto industry, for example (McLean, 1995), and other times more directly articulated with the need for school-wide action for educational improvement (Calhoun, 1994), these works summon a positive note for the profession of teaching in the addressing of long-standing workplace issues. Yet they also carry with them the same dangers associated with the professional model they embrace. Without careful attention to the gendered nature of teachers' work (Apple, 1986), concerns with professional status can minimize attention to the social nurturing aspects of the labor and to the exclusive relationship between public and private spheres (Fraser, 1989) on which traditional conceptions of profession knowledge and work have been constructed. Efforts to promote professionalism as a means for educational improvement may actually hamper the very issues they seek to address. The potential isolation from communities that the enhancement of the authority of the teacher can entail (Labaree, 1992) has many implications. While adequately focusing on issues of excellence, for example, educators may not be able to hold on to images of equity. Consideration of the interests and assumptions of various communities of historically oppressed peoples may require the suspension of authority, especially that based in dominant knowledge forms (McTaggart, 1991c).

Along the same lines, Lawn (1989) criticizes the action research movement in general for its appeal to an "authentic professionalism" (p. 152) and for its inattention to workplace conditions and policy issues as sources for research efforts. The ideas of Lawrence Stenhouse, for example, in his use of the notion of an "extended professional" (1975), are characterized as part of a liberal humanism tradition in which the conditions for enlightenment and emancipation lie in teachers' "broadening their cultural and social horizons and allowing a creative classroom practice to be developed and shared" (Lawn, 1989, p. 150). Yet it should also be recognized that this tradition, while positing such ideas as reflection as something practitioners either have or do not have—a tradition reaching back to Dewey—also operated to reintroduce questions of ends, along with those of means, into action research efforts.

For Stenhouse, as well as others, the process of action research was one of recapturing the moral basis of teaching, as well as asserting the needed involvement of teachers in the transformation of the school curriculum and the society it embodied. Along those same lines, the kind of professionalism Carr and Kemmis (1988) advocate is one that articulates with human emancipation but also works against the bureaucratic forms of labor that have characterized teachers' work. In many of the current action research efforts, such ideals are salient. Yet it is also clear that issues of workplace transformation, let alone issues of social and economic justice, are not as salient in the existing literature as are the claims to professional knowledge, although there are exceptions. Whether over gender issues (Weiner, 1989), over issues of racial justice (Grudgeon & Woods, 1990), or over connections to parents and communities (Burch & Palanki, 1993), much work is clearly needed in articulating a practice of action research that would strive toward a profession of teaching that reaches beyond itself into broader social issues (Walker, 1993). In school reform and the staff development offered toward that end, whether including orientations such as action research or not, questions of form, of purpose, and of interests in professionalism need to continue to be addressed. Without serious questions of the quality of professional work, efforts may improve the status of educators but make no real changes in the status quo.

Who Is the "Self"? Personal and Interpersonal Aspects of Action Research

In much of the action research literature, there is significant attention paid to the impact of the process on the participants (Noffke & Zeichner, 1987). Some of this work highlights, as noted in the previous section, a growing familiarity with academic researchers and their methods on the part of educational practitioners. For a large portion of action research efforts, however, the major focus is on the personal knowledge or theorizing of teachers. As noted earlier, this can be seen as within the realm of knowledge production, as an issue of epistemology. But it can also be looked at as a concern with the personal development of teachers, along a given continuum of adult development (Oja & Smulyan, 1989), or in terms of self-awareness and growth in theorizing and learning about their practice (Elliott, 1990).

Each of these aspects of the personal echoes themes that were prevalent in the early literature, particularly in Lewin's attention to action research as a way to change attitudes and in Shumsky's emphasis on the personal significance of the process over the actual research product. Since the earliest contemporary work (e.g., the Ford Teaching Project in the United Kingdom), there has been a consistent concern among action research advocates with the matching of teachers' theories with their practices and with the role of outsiders in producing a closer linkage between them as well as in challenging underlying principles (Elliott, 1976–1977).

The idea of practitioners questioning the basis of their work is an essential element to action research efforts across a wide variety of contexts (e.g., Carr & Kemmis, 1988; Elliott, 1991; Whitehead, 1993; Zeichner, 1993). Some (e.g., Dadds, 1995) highlight subjectivity and practitioner reflection and are rich explorations of the layers of the self in action research. Others, while also including the subjective, lived experiences of practitioners, center on the personal and professional growth of the individual teacher as a "means for the principled modification of professional practice" (Wells, 1994, p. 25). There is some evidence, too, that concepts such as freedom, rationality, justice, democracy, and so forth, play a role in the examination of both personal theories and practices (e.g., McNiff, 1993). These, in turn, are seen as acting to encourage and support efforts to challenge trends within the educational system seen as obstructing the realization of the "living educational theory" (Whitehead, 1993).

As vital as such a process of self-awareness is to identifying the contradictions between one's espoused theories and one's practices, perhaps because of its focus on individual learning, it only begins to address the social basis of personal belief systems. While such efforts can further a kind of collective agency (McNiff, 1988), it is a sense of agency built on ideas of society as a collection of autonomous individuals. As such, it seems incapable of addressing social issues in terms of the interconnections between personal identity and the claim of experiential knowledge, as well as power and privilege in society (Dolby, 1995; Noffke, 1991). The process of personal transformation through the examination of practice and self-reflection may be a necessary part of social change, especially in education; it is, however, not sufficient.

One critique of action research, particularly that in the teacher researcher model, has drawn attention to the limited ways in which issues of social justice have been addressed (Weiner, 1989). Despite the concern with social issues and even social transformation on the part of academics writing about action research, there have been few examples of practitioners engaged in efforts to link their practices with efforts focused on gender and racial inequality, for example (Donald et al., 1995; Krater et al., 1994; Wood, 1988). Those that have been advanced have for the most part come out of a Lewinian, community development tradition of action research (Chisholm, 1984) that focuses attention primarily on the process of investigating a social phenomenon while changing it and to a lesser degree on the total involvement of all participants in the selection of the research topic and the actual research process (Chisholm & Holland, 1986; Kelly, 1984; J. Whyte, 1986).

The tension between claims and practices, often noted in writings on action research (Gore, 1991; Gore & Zeichner, 1991; Zeichner, 1993), often involves issues of facilitation, particularly in the form of funded projects led by academic researchers working with groups of teachers or occurring within degree-bearing courses that include action research. As Johnston and Proudford (1994) note, there is a tendency in funded projects to move toward a "top-down model of change," in part as a result of funding accountability and expectations for end products, particularly reports (p. 4). While academics may operate within circumstances that place great emphasis on the production of new knowledge, particularly of an abstract, generalizable nature, the value of the project for the teachers involved priorities of their own and the children's growing understanding of social issues. This difference highlights an important discrepancy between facilitators and participants that is also relevant to teacher education: "Rather than an expectation that each teacher would move a significant distance along her own learning continuum, all teachers were expected to produce outcomes which would move the general field forward" (Johnston & Proudford, 1994, p. 11). This is a reflection not only of differing forms of knowledge but of differing constructions of the teacher: one highly unitary, the other deeply grounded in individual identity.

Another aspect to the discrepancy between claims and practices, particularly over social justice issues, focuses on the critique of action research as too narrowly focused, not only on personal growth but also on the classroom (Lawn, 1989; Weiner, 1989). For many teachers, the growth and learning they most value is linked to their conception of purpose in teaching. Rather than looking toward a version of politics that emphasizes the public sphere, their focus is on their responsibility to children (Griffiths & Davies, 1993). While this tension is underexamined in the literature (Zeichner, 1993), it embodies a common feminist critique of the political (Fraser, 1989). The valuing of (gendered) practice in the classroom thus appears to be in tension with the way in which social justice issues have been framed.

Taken together, the aspects of the personal considered here highlight the need for consideration of issues of identity in teaching, because these issues frame both the questioning of educational practice and the "growth" resultant from it. One learns and develops in relation to historically and contextually shaped understandings, rather than along a "natural" continuum. Social justice issues thus are always part of the personal. But as with tensions over the form of professionalism, action research works within competing versions of the personal.

Where Is and What Is the "Political" in Action Research?

As it is hoped has been evident in the previous sections of this chapter, the professional as well as the personal dimensions of action research are distinct from the political only if they are constructed that way. Struggles over the meaning and status of the education profession, as well as the forms of legitimated and "produced" knowledge, occur within political contexts, with each version embodying particular interests, socially and economically. Even in those versions of action research often dubbed as "scientific" (Gitlin & Thompson, 1995) or as "technical" (Grundy, 1982), there is often a recognition that action research by teachers can lead to greater power over their own work (Patterson, Santa, Short, & Smith, 1993).

The personal dimension, as well, measures meaning and growth in terms of frameworks of ideology grounded in identity and experience within an unjust and unequal society. Growth and learning are thus also constructed, either to maintain privilege or to seek to transform it. The differing purposes within an action research project affect the personal value of the outcomes. The very nature of teaching as a gendered profession may mean that differing conceptions of the boundaries and intersections among the professional, the personal, and the political may need to be explored (Strachan, 1993).

In the previous sections, the political has also been evident through the fact that some versions of action research work from a theoretical framework that is explicitly political, whether in a transformative or meliorative form (Gitlin & Thompson, 1995). Issues of social justice, especially over racial and gender inequality, have played a role in the selection of research topics (Weiner, 1989). Teachers have been enjoined to consider "the social and political implications of their practices and act on them" (Zeichner, 1993, p. 213), within their classrooms, with and for the children they care for. What, then, has a particular section on the political in action research to add?

To deny the political aspect of action research is merely to support a tacit agenda. Much action research is explicitly connected to critiques of power and interest and has been thus far only minimally addressed. This section will address literature that overtly advances social agendas, focusing on two areas: the nature of community and the role of theory.

First, in addition to studies mentioned earlier focusing explicitly on issues of gender and schooling (Chisholm & Holland, 1986; Kelly, 1984; Weiner, 1989; Whyte, 1986), there are two other, intersecting aspects of action research that are linked to its social activism aspect, noted in the historical section. The first of these could be characterized as focusing in some ways on communities, using research for social action. In works associated with the Action Research Issues Center (Wadsworth, 1984) or with women who have been abused (Maguire, 1987; Mies, 1983), for example, research techniques are demystified so that they can be used by various groups, or the skills of the researcher are employed to support group efforts. These community groups are often disenfranchised by usual methods of political organization and the research that supports them; action research is used to gain greater control over their social and economic lives. Along the same lines, much of the participatory action research literature (Brown & Tandon, 1983; Gaventa, 1988; Hinsdale, Lewis, & Waller, 1995; Park et al., 1993) is rich with examples of people working together to alter their circumstances. While some of this work is more directly akin to the industrial consulting noted in an earlier section (W. F. Whyte, 1991), much of it involves critiquing traditional understandings of economics, for example, and at the same time seeking their transformation. Some work in participatory research (Maguire, 1987) takes on not only the task of developing projects of social welfare but also that of critiquing the research process through feminist frameworks.

In all of these cases, it is important to note that the communities involved in the research come together to address common concerns and work at developing the means to understand each other, to articulate their social position, and to effect change. Knowledge and power are interconnected through action and research (Fals Borda & Rahman, 1991). As a concrete instance of such work in education, one can look at the work of Aboriginal communities seeking greater control over the form and content of their schooling (Bunbury, Hastings, Henry, & McTaggart, 1991; Marika, Ngurruwutthun, & White, 1992). These efforts not only involved critiques of colonial education, they sought to reformulate action research in ways consonant with the culture rather than relying on Western critical social theory.

This form of participatory action research has its roots not in Lewin, but in contexts and cultures apart from the dominant. While drawing on social theorists such as Gramsci (Brown & Tandon, 1983), the work is more affiliated with popular struggles within the public political sphere (Torres, 1992). The communities and the social theorists (Fals-Borda, 1994; Freire, 1970) are connected, with a shared commitment to developing understandings and agendas for change.

The work presented in this chapter has been greatly influenced by social theory. As Walker (1995) notes, theoretical resources provide ways for people to see outside their taken-for-granted frames. Yet as basic as the transformation of the theory-practice relationship is to the action research process, it remains in some ways one of the least addressed aspects of action research, especially within the political. Black feminist theory (hooks, 1990; Collins, 1990) and postcolonial theory (Spivak, 1990) are only two examples of the rich theoretical resources not yet examined that could help in understanding important areas such as individual and social identity (Brennan, 1993), the subject and subjectivity (Kosmidou & Usher, 1991), and the nature of experiential knowledge claims (Dolby, 1995). Yet, as Fals-Borda notes (1994), they cannot be seen apart from their own construction within the dominant society. The development of social theory has been often the task of those in relatively privileged positions. Theory can make visible the processes historically marginalized peoples use to name and alter their world but must not appropriate them.

Because educational action research is in many ways both a practice whose community needs identification and "a practice in search of a theory" (Beattie, 1989, p. 110), there is much to consider in looking toward the future of the field. Central to this is the examination of the nature of the communities and agendas with which teachers and others choose to affiliate.

TOWARD UNDERSTANDING THE POTENTIALS OF ACTION RESEARCH

Over the past few years, various special sections or issues of academic journals have been entirely devoted to action research (Kyle & Hovda, 1987/1989; Llorens, 1994a; Manning & McLaughlin, 1995; McTaggart, 1991b; Oberg & McCutcheon, 1990; O'Hanlon, 1995). In addition, three new journals, *Teaching and Change, Teacher Research*, and *Educational Action Research*, have contributed greatly to both the visibility and richness of the literature. Furthermore, the dozens of books and hundreds of journal articles devoted to its exploration have done much to expand awareness and acceptance of action research. Yet they also can serve to underscore a seeming eclecticism in the use of the term, at times making it seem as if any research that takes place in classrooms and involves teachers somehow in the process is called action research.

What this situation emphasizes is not the need for a clear answer to the oft-revisited question "What is action research?" although that is important. Instead, what is vital is to see the action research family as a representation of a series of contestations within the interconnected spheres of the professional, personal, and political. Defining action research in terms of a particular process or series of steps may help to identify it as a research technique, but in so doing one also clouds the issues of the purposes to which it is advanced: the political agendas, both overt and embedded in the constructions of the professional and personal.

Understanding the potentials of action research requires looking carefully at the tensions revealed in each of these areas. First, in the professional dimension, there is a need to carefully address the relationship between action research as knowledge production and action research as a form of staff development. On the one hand, this requires greater attention to epistemological questions, especially those related to the nature of experiential knowledge. Such analysis needs to take into account issues related to the political economy of knowledge production, however. The growth in publications, both local and commercial, of teachers' writings about their work must not presuppose entry into a competitive market dominated by norms of academic publishing. Other forms of sharing thoughts and actions must be explored.

On the other hand, seeing action research as a means for professional development raises a complex set of questions related to issues of power: Who and what is being "developed" and by whom, and, most important, in whose interests? The literature on educational action research frames issues related not only to the quality and status of the profession but also to the meaning of quality in education in general. While some action research embodies technocratic models of teaching and learning, the majority of works push at the boundaries of curriculum, offering at least the possibility of changes that address not the legitimation of practices structured by existing conditions of schooling but the transformation of education through continuing thought and action.

Second, in the personal dimension, works addressing action research as enhancing self-knowledge, fulfillment in one's work, and understanding of one's own practice have also highlighted the importance of relationships to those ends. A point of tension in these works revolves around the construction of action research as an individual activity rather than as a search for personal knowledge within a social world. This manifests itself in a contradiction between the both supportive and coercive nature of educational (including action research) communities. Recent action research works that begin to address issues of identity may prove useful in articulating the historical roots of both individual and collective belief systems that form a base from which personal awareness emerges. Such awarenesses are crucial if action research efforts are to be transformative rather than legitimating.

Finally, in the political dimension, it is important to remember that those action research efforts that highlight issues of democracy and social justice are no more political (or more holy) than those that claim a neutral base in either technical rationality or in hermeneutic/interpretive thought. Whether constructed in terms of creating teaching that acknowledges the voice and power of children; of addressing particular issues such as class, race, and gender; or of articulation with larger movements for social justice, the largest tensions in action research may exist in terms of living out democratic values. The development of elegant theoretical frameworks for action research can contribute much to its coherence. Yet the core of action research lies in the term itself. Whether addressed in terms of the action-research relationship, in terms of theory and practice, or in terms of blurred lines between research and advocacy, the dual agenda of interrogating the meanings of democracy and social justice at the same time as we act to alter the social situation shapes the potential of action research.

This review has not been about definitional battles; it does not establish whose version of action research is correct. Instead, it has been an attempt to explore the purposes toward which such research is directed, the benefits it might offer. The identification of some of the multiple interpretations of the professional, personal, and political dimensions and some of the tensions they embody is but a beginning point for an area much in need of clarification. While it is hoped that this work will provide a useful base for such efforts, it is also recognized that, given the topic, words and thoughts alone will not provide such clarifications; they must be linked with action.

NOTES

[1] I am particularly indebted to Violet Harris for the suggestion to pursue this point.
[2] The usefulness of the work on "bricolage" in understanding action research was suggested by Henry St. Maurice.

REFERENCES

Adams, F. (1972). Highlander Folk School: Getting information, going back and teaching it. *Harvard Educational Review, 42*, 497–520.

Adelman, C. (1989). The practical ethic takes priority over methodology. In W. Carr (Ed.), *Quality in teaching: Arguments for a reflective profession* (pp. 173–182). London: Falmer Press.

Adelman, Clem. (1993). Kurt Lewin and the origins of action research. *Educational Action Research, 1*, 7–24.

Aiken, W.M. (1942). *The story of the Eight-Year Study.* New York: Harper & Brothers.

Allen, J., Michalove, B., & Shockley, B. (1993). *Engaging children: Community and chaos in the lives of young literacy learners.* Portsmouth, NH: Heinemann.

Altrichter, H. (1993). The concept of quality in action research: Giving practitioners a voice in educational research. In M. Schratz (Ed.), *Qualitative voices in educational research* (pp. 40–55). London: Falmer Press.

Altrichter, H., & Gstettner, P. (1993). Action research: A closed chapter in the history of German social science? *Educational Action Research, 1*, 329–360.

Altrichter, H., Posch, P., & Somekh, B. (1993). *Teachers investigate their work: An introduction to the methods of action research.* London: Routledge.

Anderson, G.L., Herr, K., & Nihlen, A.S. (1994). *Studying your own school: An educator's guide to qualitative practitioner research.* Thousand Oaks, CA: Corwin Press.

Apple, M.W. (1986). *Teachers and texts: A political economy of class and gender relations in education.* New York: Routledge & Kegan Paul.

Argyris, C., Putnam, R., & Smith, S.M. (1985). *Action science.* San Francisco: Jossey-Bass.

Argyris, C., & Schoen, D. (1989, May/June). Participatory action research and action science compared. *American Behavioral Scientist, 32*, 612–623.

Atwell, N. (1987). *In the middle: Writing, reading, and learning with adolescents.* Portsmouth, NH: Boynton/Cook-Heinemann.

Bargal, D., Gold, M., & Lewin, M. (1992). Introduction: The heritage of Kurt Lewin. *Journal of Social Issues, 48* (2), 3–13.

Barrera, M., & Vialpando, G. (Eds.). (1974). *Action research in defense of the barrio.* Los Angeles: Aztlan.

Bassey, M. (1992). Creating education through research. *British Educational Research Journal, 18*, 3–16.

Beattie, C. (1989). Action research: A practice in need of a theory? In G. Milburn, I. Goodson, & R. Clark (Eds.), *Reinterpreting curriculum research* (pp. 110–120). East Sussex, England: Falmer Press.

Behnke, G., Labovitz, E.M., Bennett, J., Chase, C., Day, J., Lazar, C., & Mittleholtz, D. (1981). Coping with classroom distractions. *Elementary School Journal, 81*, 135–155.

Bogdan, R.C., & Biklin, S.K. (1992). *Qualitative research for education: An introduction to theory and methods* (2nd ed.). Boston: Allyn & Bacon.

Boomer, G. (1982). *Negotiating the curriculum.* Sydney: Ashton Scholastic.

Borg, W.R., Gall, J.P., & Gall, M.D. (1993). *Applying educational research: A practical guide* (3rd ed.). New York: Longman.

Branscombe, N.A., Goswami, D., & Schwartz, J. (Eds.). (1992). *Students teaching, teachers learning.* Portsmouth, NH: Boynton/Cook-Heinemann.

Brause, R.S., & Mayher, J.S. (1991). *Search and re-search: What the inquiring teacher needs to know.* London: Falmer Press.

Brennan, M.T. (1993). *Living the individual-society dualism in educational action.* Unpublished doctoral thesis, University of Wisconsin, Madison.

Brown, L.D., & Tandon, R. (1983). Ideology and political economy in inquiry: Action research and participatory research. *Journal of Applied Behavioral Science, 19,* 277–294.

Bruce, C., & Russell, A.L. (Eds.). (1992). *Proceedings of the Second World Congress on Action Learning.* Nathan, Queensland, Australia: Action Learning, Action Research and Process Management Association.

Buckingham, B.R. (1926). *Research for teachers.* New York: Silver Burdett & Co.

Bunbury, R., Hastings, W., Henry, J., & McTaggart, R. (1991). *Aboriginal pedagogy: Aboriginal teachers speak out.* Geelong, Victoria, Australia: Deakin University Press.

Burch, P., & Palanki, A. (Eds.). (1993). Circles of change: Parent-teacher action research [Special issue]. *Equity and Choice, 10*(1).

Burges, B. (1976). *Facts for a change: Citizen action research for better schools.* Boston: Institute for Responsive Education.

Calhoun, E. (1994). *How to use action research in the self-renewing school.* Alexandria, VA: Association for Supervision and Curriculum Development.

Carr, W., & Kemmis, S. (1988). *Becoming critical: Education, knowledge and action research.* London: Falmer Press.

Chisholm, L. (1984). *Comments and reflections on action research in education* (Working Paper No. 2, Girls and Occupational Choice Project). London: Sociological Research Unit, Institute of Education, University of London.

Chisholm, L., & Holland, J. (1986). Girls and occupational choice: Anti-sexism in action in a curriculum development project. *British Journal of Sociology of Education, 7,* 353–365.

Clark, S. (1990). *Ready from within: A first person narrative.* Trenton, NJ: Africa World Press.

Clift, R., Johnson, M., Holland, P., & Veal, M.L. (1992). Developing the potential for collaborative school leadership. *American Educational Research Journal, 29,* 877–908.

Cochran-Smith, M., & Lytle, S.L. (1993). *Inside/outside: Teacher research and knowledge.* New York: Teachers College Press.

Collier, J. (1945). United States Indian administration as a laboratory of ethnic relations. *Social Research, 12,* 265–303.

Collier, J. (1963). *From every zenith.* Denver: Sage Books.

Collins, P. Hl. (1990). *Black feminist thought: Knowledge, consciousness, and the politics of empowerment.* Boston: Unwin Hyman.

Connell, R.W. (1985). *Teachers' work.* Sydney: Allen & Unwin.

Connelly, F.M., & Ben-Peretz, M. (1980). Teachers' roles in the using and doing of research and curriculum development. *Journal of Curriculum Studies, 12*(2), 95–107.

Corey, S.M. (1953). *Action research to improve school practices.* New York: Teachers College Press.

Corey, S.M. (1954). Hoping? Or beginning to know! *Childhood Education, 30,* 208–211.

Corey, S.M. (1957). The support of research in education. *Teachers College Record, 59,* 129–136.

Coulter, D.L. (1994). *Dialogism and teacher research.* Unpublished doctoral thesis. Simon Fraser University, Burnaby, British Columbia, Canada.

Cunningham, J. B. (1993). *Action research and organizational development.* Westport, CT: Praeger.

Cunningham, R., & Miel, A. (1947). Frontiers of educational research in elementary school curriculum development. *Journal of Educational Research, 40,* 365–372.

Dadds, M. (1995). *Paasionate enquiry and school development.* London: Falmer Press.

Dolby, N. (1995). *Relocating experience: Implications for epistemic privilege.* Unpublished manuscript, University of Illinois at Urbana-Champaign.

Donald, P., Gosling, S., Hamilton, J., Hawkes, N., McKenzie, D., & Stronach, I. (1995). "No problem here": Action research against racism in a mainly White area. *British Educational Research Journal, 21,* 263–275.

DuBois, W. E. B. (1973). *The education of Black people: Ten critiques.* Amherst: University of Massachusetts Press.

Duster, A. M. (1970). *Crusade for justice: The autobiography of Ida B. Wells.* Chicago: University of Chicago Press.

Edwards, G., & Rideout, P. (1991). *Extending the horizons of action research.* Norwich, England: University of East Anglia.

Edwards, R. (1979). *Contested terrain: The transformation of the workplace in the twentieth century.* New York: Basic Books.

Elliott, J. (1976–1977). Developing hypotheses about classrooms from teachers' practical constructs: An account of the work of the Ford Teaching Project. *Interchange, 7*(2), 2–22.

Elliott, J. (1987). Educational theory, practical philosophy, and action research. *British Journal of Educational Studies, 35,* 149–169.

Elliott, J. (1990). Teachers as researchers: Implications for supervision and for teacher education. *Teaching and Teacher Education, 6*(1), 1–26.

Elliott, J. (1991). *Action research for educational change.* Philadelphia: Open University Press.

Elliott, J., & Adelman, C. (1973). Reflecting where the action is: The design of the Ford Teaching Project. *Education for Teaching, 92,* 8–20.

Fals-Borda, O. (1994, July). *Postmodernity and social responsibility: A view from the Third World.* Paper presented at the 3rd World Congress on Action Learning, Action Research and Process Management. Bath, England.

Fals-Borda, O., & Rahman, M. A. (Eds.) (1991). *Action and knowledge: Breaking the monopoly with participatory action-research.* New York: Apex Press.

Feldman, A. (1994). Erzberger's dilemma: Validity in action research and science teachers' need to know. *Science Education, 78,* 83–101.

Ford Project Teachers. (1975). *Ways of doing research in one's own classroom.* Cambridge, England: Cambridge Institute of Education.

Foshay, A. W. (1994). Action research: An early history in the United States. *Journal of Curriculum and Supervision, 9,* 317–325.

Foshay, A. W., Wann, K. D., & Associates. (1954). *Children's social values: An action research study.* New York: Teachers College Press.

Fraser, N. (1989). *Unruly practices: Power, discourse and gender in contemporary social theory.* Minneapolis: University of Minnesota Press.

Freire, P. (1970). *A pedagogy of the oppressed.* New York: Seabury Press.

Gaventa, J. (1988). Participatory research in North America. *Convergence, 21*(2 & 3), 19–28.

Gibbs, L. (1982). *Love Canal: My story.* Albany: State University of New York Press.

Gillespie, T. (1994). Interview with Dixie Goswami. *Teacher Research, 1,* 89–103.

Gitlin, A., & Thompson, A. (1995). Foregrounding politics in action research. *McGill Journal of Education, 30,* 131–147.

Good, C. V. (1963). *Introduction to educational research.* New York: Appleton-Century-Crofts.

Goodman, M. R. (Ed.) (1994). Spring issue. *Visions and Revisions: Research for Writing Teachers, 4,* 3–69.

Goodson, M. R. (1946). Charting a course for educational progress. *Teachers College Record, 48,* 35–60.

Gore, Jennifer M. (1991, Oct.). On silent regulation: Emancipatory action research in pre-service teacher education. *Curriculum Perspectives, 11*(4), 47–51.

Gore, J.M., & Zeichner, K.M. (1991). Action research and reflective teaching in preservice teacher education: A case study from the United States. *Teaching and Teacher Education, 7,* 119–136.

Goswami, D., & Stillman, P. R. (Eds.). (1987). *Reclaiming the classroom: Teacher research as an agency for change.* Portsmouth, NH: Boynton/Cook-Heinemann.

Griffiths, M., & Davies, C. (1993). Learning to learn: Action research from an equal opportunities perspective in a junior school. *British Educational Research Journal, 19,* 43–58.

Grudgeon, E., & Woods, P. (1990). *Educating all: Multicultural perspectives in the primary school.* London: Routledge.

Grundy, S. (1982). Three modes of action research. *Curriculum Perspectives, 2*(3), 23–34.

Grundy, S., & Kemmis, S. (1981/1988). Educational action research in Australia: The state of the art (an overview). In S. Kemmis & R. McTaggart (Eds.), *The action research reader* (3rd ed., pp. 321–335). Geelong, Victoria, Australia: Deakin University Press.

Habermas, J. (1972). *Knowledge and human interests,* (J.J. Shapiro, Trans.). London: Heinemann.

Habermas, J. (1974). *Theory and practice* (J. Viertel. Trans.). London: Heinemann.

Hatton, E. (1989). Levi-Strauss's "bricolage" and theorizing teachers' work. *Anthropology and Education Quarterly, 20,* 74–96.

Hinsdale, M. A., Lewis, H. M., & Waller, S. M. (1995). *It comes from the people.* Philadelphia: Temple University Press.

Hodgkinson, H. L. (1957). Action research—A critique. *Journal of Educational Sociology, 31,* 137–153.

Hollingsworth, S., & Sockett, H. (1994). *Teacher research and educational reform.* (93rd yearbook of the National Society for the Study of Education, Part I). Chicago: National Society for the Study of Education.

Holly, P. (1991). Action research: The missing link in the creation of schools as centers of inquiry. In A. Lieberman & L. Miller (Eds.), *Staff development for education in the '90s* (pp. 133–157). New York: Teachers College Press.

Holly, P., & Whitehead, D. (Eds.). (1986). *Collaborative action research* (CARN Bulletin No. 7). Cambridge, England: Classroom Action Research Network, Cambridge Institute of Education.

hooks, b. (1990). *Yearning: Race, gender, and cultural politics.* Boston: South End Press.

Hopkins, D. (1993). *A teacher's guide to classroom research* (2nd Ed.). Philadelphia: Open University Press.

Hopkins, L. Thomas. (1948, May). Democratic education: The hope of the world. *Teachers College Record, 49*(8), 501—509.

Hopkins, L. T. (1954). *The emerging self in school and home.* New York: Harper & Brothers.

Horace Mann-Lincoln Study Group. (1948). Recommended: Group research for teachers. *Teachers College Record, 50,* 108–113.

Horton, M. (1990). *The long haul: An autobiography.* New York: Doubleday.

Hubbard, R. S., & Power, B. M. (1993). *The art of classroom inquiry: A handbook for teacher-researchers.* Portsmouth, NH: Heinemann.

Hult, M., & Lennung, S. (1980, May). Toward a definition of action research: A note and bibliography. *Journal of Management Studies, 17*, 241–250.

Iredale, B. (1975). *A third-year form tries to enter a freer world: Research into ways towards inquiry/discovery working.* Cambridge, England: Cambridge Institute of Education.

Iverson, K. (1978). Progressive education for Native Americans: Washington ideology and Navajo reservation implementation. *Review Journal of Philosophy and Social Science, 3*, 231–255.

Jacullo-Noto, J. (1984). Interactive research and development—Partners in craft. *Teachers College Record, 86*, 208–222.

Jersild, A.T. (1955). *When teachers face themselves.* New York: Teachers College Press.

Johnston, S., & Proudford, C. (1994). Action research—Who owns the process? *Educational Review, 46*, 3–14.

Kelly, A. (1984). Action research: What is it and what can it do? In R.G. Burgess (Ed.), *Issues in educational research* (pp. 129–151). Philadelphia: Falmer Press.

Kemmis, S. (1988). Action research in retrospect and prospect. In S. Kemmis & R. McTaggart (Eds.), *The action research reader* (2nd ed., pp. 11–31), Geelong, Victoria, Australia: Deakin University Press.

Kemmis, S., & Di Chiro, G. (Spring, 1987/1989). Emerging and evolving issues in action research praxis: An Australian perspective. *Peabody Journal of Education, 64*, 101–130.

Kemmis, S., & McTaggart, R. (1988a). *The action research planner* (3rd ed.). Geelong, Victoria, Australia: Deakin University Press.

Kemmis, S., & McTaggart, R. (Eds.). (1988b). *The action research reader* (3rd ed.). Geelong, Victoria, Australia: Deakin University Press.

Kincheloe, J.L. (1991). *Teachers as researchers: Qualitative inquiry as a path to empowerment.* London: Falmer.

King, J.A., & Lonnquist, M.P. (1992). *A review of writing on action research.* Minneapolis: Center for Applied Research and Educational Improvement, University of Minnesota.

King, M.L. (1966, May). *The social activist and social change.* Paper presented at the Conference on Social Change and the Role of Behavioral Scientists, Atlanta, GA.

Kliebard, H.M. (1986). *The struggle for the American curriculum, 1893–1958.* Boston: Routledge.

Kosmidou, C., & Usher, R. (1991). Facilitation in action research. *Interchange, 22*(4), 24–40.

Krater, J., Zeni, J., & Cason, N.D. (1994). *Mirror images: Teaching writing in black and white.* Portsmouth, NH: Heinemann.

Kyle, D.W., & Hovda, R.A. (1987/1989). The potential and practice of action research, Parts I & II. *Peabody Journal of Education 64* (2 & 3), 1–127, 1–175.

Labaree, D.F. (1992). Power, knowledge, and the rationalization of teaching: A genealogy of the movement to professionalize teaching. *Harvard Educational Review, 62*, 123–154.

Lawn, M. (1989). Being caught in schoolwork: The possibilities of research in teachers' work. In W. Carr (Ed.), *Quality in teaching: Arguments for a reflective profession* (pp. 147–161). London: Falmer Press.

Levine, A.G. (1980). *Love Canal: Science, politics, and people.* Lexington, MA: Heath.

Lewin, G., & Lewin, K. (1942). Democracy and the school. *Understanding the Child, 10*, 7–11.

Lewin, K. (1938). Experiments on autocratic and democratic principles. *Social Frontier, 4*, 316–319.

Lewin, K. (1944). The dynamics of group action. *Educational Leadership, 1*, 195–200.

Lewin, K. (1946). Action research and minority problems. *Journal of Social Issues, 2*(4), 34–46.

Lewin, K. (1947). Frontiers in group dynamics: II. Channels of group life; social planning and action research. *Human Relations, 1,* 143–153.

Lewin, K. (1948). *Resolving social conflicts.* New York: Harper.

Lewin, K., & Grabbe, P. (1945). Conduct, knowledge, and acceptance of new values. *Journal of Social Issues, 1*(3), 53–64.

Lieberman, A., & Miller, L. (1984a). School improvement: Themes and variations. *Teachers College Record, 86,* 4–19.

Lieberman, A., & Miller, L. (1984b). *Teachers, their world, and their work.* Alexandria, VA: Association for Supervision & Curriculum Development.

Lippitt, R., & Radke, M. (1946). New trends in the investigation of prejudice. *Annals of the American Academy of Political and Social Science, 244,* 167–176.

Llorens, M.B.. (Ed.). (1994a). Action research. [Special issue]. *Elementary School Journal, 95*(1).

Llorens, M.B. (1994b). Action research: Are teachers finding their voice? *Elementary School Journal, 95,* 3–10.

Mackenzie, G.N. (1946). The Horace Mann-Lincoln Institute of School Experimentation. *Teachers College Record, 47,* 438–445.

Madison Metropolitan School District. (1995). *Elementary Classroom Action Research.* Madison, WI: Author.

Maguire, P. (1987), *Doing participatory research: A feminist approach.* Amherst: Center for International Education, University of Massachusetts.

Manning, B.H., & McLaughlin, H.J. (Eds.). (1995). Action research and teacher education [Special issue]. *Action in Teacher Education, 16*(4).

Marika, R., Ngurruwutthun, D., and White, L. (1992). Always together, Yaka Gana: Participatory research at Yirrkala as part of the development of a Yolngu education. *Convergence, 25*(1), 23–39.

Marrow, A.J. (1969). *The practical theorist: The life and work of Kurt Lewin.* New York: Basic Books.

McCutcheon, G., & Jung, B. (1990). Alternative perspectives on action research. *Theory into Practice, 29,* 144–151.

McKernan, J. (1988). The countenance of curriculum action research: Traditional, collaborative, and emancipatory-critical conceptions. *Journal of Curriculum and Supervision, 3,* 173–200.

McKernan, J. (1991). *Curriculum action research: A handbook of methods and resources for the reflective practitioner.* London: Kogan Page.

McLean, J.E. (1995). *Improving education through action research: A guide for administrators and teachers.* Thousand Oaks, CA: Corwin Press.

McNiff, J. (1988). *Action research: Principles and practices.* London: Routledge.

McNiff, J. (1993). *Teaching as learning: An action research approach.* London: Routledge.

McTaggart, R. (1989). Bureaucratic rationality and the self-educating profession: The problem of teacher privatism. *Journal of Curriculum Studies, 21,* 345–361.

McTaggart, R. (1991a). *Action research: A short modern history.* Geelong, Victoria, Australia: Deakin University Press.

McTaggart, R. (Ed.). (1991b). Action research: Issues for the next decade. *Curriculum Perspectives, 11*(4), 44–65.

McTaggart, R. (1991c). Action research for Aboriginal pedagogy: Beyond "both-ways" education?. In O. Zuber-Skerrit (Ed.)., *Action research for change and development* (pp. 157–178). Aldershot, England: Avebury.

McTaggart, R. (1994). Participatory action research: Issues in theory and practice. *Educational Action Research, 2,* 313–337.

Mies, M. (1983). Towards a methodology for feminist research. In G. Bowles & R.D. Klein (Eds.), *Theories of women's studies* (pp. 117–139). London: Routledge & Kegan Paul.

Mohr, M.M., & Maclean, M.S. (1987). *Working together: A guide for teacher-researchers.* Urbana, IL: National Council of Teachers of English.

Munro, P. (1995). Educators as activists: Five women from Chicago. *Social Education, 59,* 274–278.

Nixon, J. (Ed.). (1981). *A teacher's guide to action research: Evaluation, enquiry and development in the classroom.* London: Grant McIntyre.

Nocerino, M.A., & Harrison, M. (n.d.). *Invitations to action: A variety of ways in which teachers report their research.* Fairfax, VA: Fairfax County Public Schools.

Noffke, S.E. (1989, March). *The social context of action research: A comparative and historical analysis.* Paper presented at the annual meeting of the American Educational Research Association, San Francisco, CA.

Noffke, S.E. (1990). *Action research: A multidimensional analysis.* Unpublished doctoral thesis, University of Wisconsin, Madison.

Noffke, S.E. (1991). Hearing the teacher's voice: Now what? *Curriculum Perspectives, 11*(4), 55–59.

Noffke, S.E. (1992). The work and workplace of teachers in action research. *Teaching and Teacher Education, 8,* 15–29.

Noffke, S.E. (1994). Action research: Towards the next generation. *Educational Action Research, 2,* 9–21.

Noffke, S.E., & Stevenson, R.B. (Eds.). (1995). *Educational action research: Becoming practically critical.* New York: Teachers College Press.

Noffke, S.E., & Zeichner, K.M. (1987, April). *Action research and teacher thinking: The first phase of the action research on action research project at the University of Wisconsin-Madison.* Paper presented at the annual meeting of the American Educational Research Association, Washington, DC.

Oberg, A.A., & McCutcheon, G. (Eds.). (1990). Teacher as researcher [Special issue]. *Theory into Practice, 29*(3).

O'Hanlon, C. (Ed.). (1995). Teacher research [Special issue]. *British Educational Research Journal, 21*(3).

Oja, S.N., & Smulyan, L. (1989). *Collaborative action research: A developmental approach.* London: Falmer Press.

Palmer, P.J., & Jacobson, E. (1971). *Action-research: A new style of politics, education and ministry.* New York: National Council of Churches.

Park, P., Brydon-Miller, M., Hall, ., & Jackson, T. (Eds.) (1993). *Voices of change: Participatory research in the United States and Canada.* Westport, CT: Bergin & Garvey.

Patterson, L., Santa, C.M., Short, K.G., & Smith, K. (Eds.). (1993). *Teachers are researchers: Reflection and action.* Newark, DE: International Reading Association.

Peters, M., & Robinson, V. (1984). The origins and status of action research. *Journal of Applied Behavioral Science, 20,* 113–124.

Power, B., & Hubbard, R. (Eds.). (1995). Tensions. *Teacher Research: The Journal of Classroom Inquiry, 3*(1), iii–143.

Rapoport, R.N. (Ed.). (1985). *Children, youth, and families: The action-research relationship.* Cambridge, England: Cambridge University Press.

Reinharz, S. (1992). *Feminist methods in social research.* New York: Oxford University Press.

Riesman, D. (1969). *The lonely crowd.* New Haven, CT: Yale University Press. (Original work published 1950)

Ross, D.D. (1987/1989). Action research for preservice teachers: A description of why and how. *Peabody Journal of Education, 64,* 131–150.

Ryan, C., & Somekh, B. (Eds.). (1991). *Processes of reflection and action* (CARN Publication 10B). Norwich, England: Classroom Action Research Network, University of East Anglia.

Sagor, R. (1992). *How to conduct action research.* Alexandria, VA: Association for Supervision and Curriculum Development.

Sanford, N. (1970). Whatever happened to action research? *Journal of Social Issues, 26*(4), 3–23.

Schoen, D. (1983). *The reflective practitioner.* New York: Basic Books.

Schubert, W., & Lopez-Schubert, A. (1984, April). *Sources of a theory of action research in progressive education.* Paper presented at the annual meeting of the American Educational Research Association. New Orleans, LA.

Shockley, B., Michalove, B., & Allen, J. (1995). *Engaging families: Connecting home and school literacy communities.* Portsmouth, NH: Heinemann.

Shumsky, A. (1958). *The action research way of learning: An approach to in-service education.* New York: Teachers College.

Smulyan, L. (1983). *Action research on change in schools: A collaborative project.* Durham, NH. (ERIC Document Reproduction Service No. ED 235 192)

Somekh, B. (1989). The role of action research in collaborative enquiry. In B. Somekh, J. Powney, & C. Burge (Eds.), *Collaborative enquiry and school improvement* (CARN Bulletin 9A, pp. 3–11). Norwich, England: Classroom Action Research Network, University of East Anglia.

Somekh, B. (1995). The contribution of action research to development in social endeavours: A position paper on action research methodology. *British Educational Research Journal, 21,* 339–355.

Spivak, G.C. (1990). *The post-colonial critic: Interviews, strategies, dialogues.* New York: Routledge.

Stenhouse, L. (1975). *An introduction to curriculum research and development.* London: Heinemann Educational Books.

Stenhouse, L. (1983). *Authority, education and emancipation.* London: Heinemann Educational Books.

Strachan, J. (1993). *Including the personal and the professional: Researching women in educational leadership. Gender and Education, 5*(1), 71–80.

Taba, H., & Noel, E. (1957). *Action research: A case study.* Washington, DC: Association for Curriculum & Supervision.

Tikunoff, W.J., & Ward, B.A. (1983). Collaborative research on teaching. *Elementary School Journal, 83,* 453–468.

Torres, C.A. (1992). Participatory action research and popular education in Latin America. *Qualitative Studies in Education, 5,* 51–62.

Wadsworth, Y. (1984). *Do it yourself social research.* North Sydney, Australia: Allen & Unwin.

Walker, M. (1993). Developing the theory and practice of action research: A South African case. *Educational Action Research, 1*(1), 95—109.

Walker, M. (1995). Context, critique, and change: Doing action research in South Africa. *Educational Action Research, 3,* 9–27.

Wallace, M. (1987). A historical review of action research: Some implications for the education of teachers in their managerial role. *Journal of Education for Teaching, 13,* 97–115.

Ward, B.A. & Tikunoff, W.J. (1982, February). *Collaborative research.* Paper presented at the Research on Teaching: Implications for Practice National Invitational Conference, Warrenton, VA.

Watson, G. (1940). What are the effects of a democratic atmosphere on children? *Progressive Education, 17,* 336–342.

Watt, M.L., & Watt, D.L. (1993). Teacher research, action research: The Logo Action Research Collaborative. *Educational Action Research, 1,* 35–63.

Weiner, G. (1989). Professional self-knowledge versus social justice: A critical analysis of the teacher-researcher movement. *British Educational Research Journal, 15,* 41–51.

Wells, G. (Ed.). (1994). *Changing schools from within: Creating communities of inquiry.* Portsmouth, NH: Heinemann.

Whitehead, J. (1993). *The growth of educational knowledge: Creating your own living theories.* Bournemouth, England: Hyde Publications.

Whyte, J. (1986). *Girls into science and technology.* London: Routledge & Kegan Paul.

Whyte, W.F. (Ed). (1991). *Participatory action research.* Newbury Park, CA: Sage.

Wiles, K. (1953). Can we sharpen the concept of action research? *Educational Leadership, 9,* 408–419, 432.

Winter, R. (1982). "Dilemma analysis": A contribution to methodology for action research. *Cambridge Journal of Education, 12,* 161–174.

Winter, R. (1987). *Action research and the nature of social inquiry.* Aldershot, England: Avebury.

Winter, R. (1989). *Learning from experience: Principles and practice in action-research.* London: Falmer Press.

Wood, P. (1988). Action research: A field perspective. *Journal of Education for Teaching, 14,* 135–150.

Woodson, C.G. (1993) *The miseducation of the Negro.* Trenton, NJ: Africa World Press. (Original work published 1933)

Zeichner, K.M. (1993). Action research: personal renewal and social reconstruction. *Educational Action Research, 1,* 199–219.

Zuber-Skerritt, O. (1992). *Action research in higher education: Examples and reflections.* London: Kogan Page.

Manuscript received March 1, 1996
Accepted May 20, 1996